Inhuman Conditions

On Cosmopolitanism and Human Rights

Pheng Cheah

HARVARD UNIVERSITY PRESS

Cambridge, Massachusetts

London, England

2006

Library of Congress Cataloging-in-Publication Data

Cheah, Pheng.
  Inhuman conditions : on cosmopolitanism and human rights / Pheng Cheah.
    p.   cm.
  Includes bibliographical references and index.
  ISBN-13: 978-0-674-02295-9 (cloth: alk. paper)
  ISBN-10: 0-674-02295-5 (cloth: alk. paper)
  ISBN-13: 978-0-674-02394-9 (paper: alk. paper)
  ISBN-10: 0-674-02394-3 (paper: alk. paper)
  1. Cosmopolitanism.   2. Human rights.   3. Globalization.
4. Social justice.   5. Capitalism—Social aspects.   I. Title.

  JZ1308.C47 2006
  303.48′2—dc22   2006043507

Acknowledgments

Books are always the products of collaborative intellectual conversation and learning, especially books that do not fit neatly within disciplinary boundaries. I began thinking and writing about cosmopolitanism and human rights within a postcolonial framework as a humanities doctoral student slightly more than a decade ago. But nationalism always remained in the background as a cautionary note in the form of my teacher Benedict Anderson's passionate defense of nationalism, and my classmate Caroline Hau's incisive questions about the conflictual relations between diasporic Chinese nationalism and Philippine nationalism. In my view, the interaction among these three movements and discourses constitutes one of the most important sites for the articulation of what it means to be human in the contemporary world.

Ben and Carol gave me the benefit of their expertise on the Philippines and Southeast Asia by carefully commenting on Chapters 6 and 7. Carol also helped me find materials from the Philippines. I thank Elizabeth Povinelli as well for reading these chapters, my first attempt at "fieldwork," with the meticulous eye of an anthropologist. My colleagues at Berkeley, the political theorist Wendy Brown and the Frankfurt School scholar and intellectual historian Martin Jay, gave me invaluable feedback on my discussion of Habermas's writings on cosmopolitanism in Chapter 2, and Elizabeth Grosz provided incisive comments on the introductory chapter.

Earlier and partial versions of the book's chapters were delivered at Amherst College, Columbia University, Cornell University, Duke University, Harvard University, the National University of Singapore, SUNY-Buffalo, the University of Hawaii, the University of Melbourne, the University of Michigan, the University of Pittsburgh, the University of Sydney, the University of Western Australia, and the University of California at Berkeley, at Irvine, at Los Angeles, at Riverside, and at Santa Cruz. My thanks to the colleagues and friends who were part of those occasions for their support and questions, including Emily Apter, Jonathan Arac, Srinivas Aravamudan, Tani Barlow, Paul Bové, Judith Butler, Craig Calhoun, Chua Beng Huat, James Clifford, Drucilla Cornell, Mike Featherstone, Rodolphe Gasché, Deniz Göktürk, Judith Grbich, Janet Gyatso, Ulf Hannerz, Michael Hardt, Michael Herzfeld, David Hollinger, Tony Kaes, Ranjana Khanna, John Kim, Claire Kramsch, Françoise Lionnet, Lydia Liu, Henk Maier, Rosalind Morris, Andrew Parker, Vince Rafael, Lisa Rofel, Michael Salman, Austin Sarat, Gayatri Spivak, Anna Tsing, Prnina Werbner, Geoff White, Alison Young, Yue Ming-Bao, and Susan Zieger. My thanks to my editor, Lindsay Waters, for all his gentle reminders about my truant manuscript and for patiently seeing this project to its conclusion.

Financial support for field research in Southeast Asia came from the University of California at Berkeley in the form of a Junior Faculty Research Grant, 2001–2, and a University of California Pacific Rim Research Grant, 2001–2. Chua Beng Huat helped coordinate research as part of the Pacific Rim Grant endeavor. My thanks to my sister Cheah Su Yin, an exemplary corporate cosmopolitan, for providing me with a comfortable base in Singapore, even when she was always rushing around to set up call centers throughout Asia and shuttling between Asia, Britain, and Australia to maintain her personal life. A University of California Humanities Research Institute Fellowship in fall 2003 and a Humanities Research Fellowship from the University of California, Berkeley, in spring 2004 provided much-needed time to complete the bulk of the manuscript. My thanks to David Goldberg, director of the UCHRI, for his support and friendship, and Yoon Seo for her invaluable research assistance at Irvine.

Chapter 1 is a substantially revised version of "The Cosmopolitical—Today," in *Cosmopolitics: Thinking and Feeling Beyond the Nation,* ed. Pheng Cheah and Bruce Robbins (Minneapolis: University of Minnesota Press, 1998). An earlier version of Chapter 3 also appeared in *Cosmopolitics* as "Given Culture: Rethinking Cosmopolitical Freedom in Transnationalism." Chapter 4 was previously published as "Chinese Cosmopolitanism in Two Senses and Postcolonial National Memory," in *Cosmopolitan Geographies: New Locations of Literature and Culture,* ed. Vinay Dharwadker (New York: Routledge, 2000). An earlier version of Chapter 5 was published as "Posit(ion)ing Human Rights in the Current Global Conjuncture," *Public Culture* 9, no. 2 (Winter 1997): 233–266. Permission to include these materials here is appreciated.

Contents

Inhuman Conditions

Introduction

Globalization and the Inhuman

Whether *globalization* is defined in terms of a transnational market of production sites with an equally transnational labor market under the regime of flexible capitalist accumulation, the global spread of speculative finance capital and its plethora of sophisticated instruments, the rise of regional and supranational political formations, the accelerating mass migration of peoples, or the worldwide flows of culture, images, and data via the mass media and information technologies, the humanities appear to have very little to contribute to its study. The various component processes of globalization are empirical phenomena that are the proper objects of investigation for the social sciences. Even the study of images, data, and cultural flows and transfers, where humanistic modes of inquiry can be said to have some purchase, is arguably more efficiently conducted under the technical expertise of anthropology or mass communications and media studies.

In fact, however, the humanities are intimately connected to globalization in at least two ways. First, the intensive universality of the idea of humanity always already implies the extensiveness of globality as its concrete mode and sphere of actualization. Hence, Immanuel Kant, who distinguished humanity from animality in terms of the ability of the former to overcome the limitations of immediate existence and expand the circle of identification and belonging through sociability (*Geselligkeit*), attributed to the humanities (*humaniora*) the power of cultivating our humanity by instilling in us "*the universal feeling of sympathy,* and the ability to engage universally in very intimate *communication.*"[1] Second, whether they are explicitly normative or merely descriptive, discourses about globalization almost always pre-comprehend a certain under-

1

standing of the human that is continuous with the canonical idea of humanity with which it shares cognate terms such as freedom and dignity. In arguments in praise of globalization as well as those about the need to regulate or curb its vicissitudes, human freedom (and whatever is inimical to it) is always at stake. In 1963, Frantz Fanon already pointed to the urgent need for humanity to reassert itself against the depredations of an unequal global capitalist system of accumulation in the postcolonial Cold War conjuncture:

> Now that the colonial countries have achieved their independence the world is faced with the bare facts that make the actual state of the liberated countries even more intolerable. The basic confrontation which seemed to be colonialism versus anticolonialism, indeed capitalism versus socialism, is already losing its importance. What matters today, the issue which blocks the horizon, is the need for a redistribution of wealth. Humanity will have to address this question, no matter how devastating the consequences may be.[2]

Identical sentiments have been expressed in the current post–Cold War conjuncture by Kofi Annan, who characterizes the inhumanity of globalization processes in terms of the alienation of humanity from itself:

> Workers may find their jobs made suddenly obsolete or uneconomic by imported technology or foreign competition. . . . Instead of widening our choices, globalization can seem to be forcing us all into the same shallow, consumerist culture—giving us all the same appetites but leaving us more unequal than ever before in our ability to satisfy them. That feeling accounts for much of the fear and anger we see in today's world. In many places, very destructive forces have been unleashed. We like to call them inhuman, but in reality they are all too human: They are one of the ways our human nature reacts when we feel ourselves threatened.[3]

This discourse of human self-alienation, which views globalization processes as human creations that require urgent sociopolitical collective regulation because they have escaped the grasp of their creators, is exemplary of most social-scientific accounts of globalization. The inhuman is here understood as a finite limit of man, a defective feature of human existence that is not *proper* to the true end of man but that we have thus far failed to control, for example, commodification, technology, totalitarian domination, and the like. We quite properly compare such phenomena to animals or ghosts, associate them with death, and characterize them as subhuman precisely because they are improper to us but also reducible to us and must be overcome or transcended if we are to actualize the freedom that is our due.

This book is concerned with the ways in which such discourses of the human, which derive from the humanities, influence, irrigate, and underwrite our understandings of globalization. But more significantly, to the extent that the humanities do not take the humanity of the human being as a given but set as their basic task the inquiry into how humanity is constituted, this book also broaches the unsettling issue of whether the vicissitudes of globalization force us to question these axiomatic discourses of humanity, to radically rethink what it means to be human. In other words, if social-scientific solutions to the problems of globalization have always already pre-comprehended an idea of humanity as the bearer of dignity, freedom, sociability, culture, or political life, and therefore as an ideal project that needs to be actualized, the task and challenge of the humanities today in relation to globalization may be to question this pre-comprehension of the human and, somewhat perversely, even to give it up.

In the chapters that follow, I take up this challenge through engagements with two theoretical debates in which there has been a concerted attempt to give a softer, normative face to globalization by figuring it as an indispensable material condition for achieving humanity. These are the debates concerning the possible rise of new cosmopolitanisms in a world of movement, flux, and flow, and the establishment of international human rights regimes in a world no longer cleft by Cold War ideological scissions. Simply put, cosmopolitanism and human rights are the two primary ways of figuring the global as the human. Both phenomena are generally viewed as placing actual and normative limits on the efficacy of national culture and the sovereignty of the nation-state, which is seen as particularistic, oppressive, and even totalitarian. Yet the abiding question that insinuates itself into both these debates is whether or not the infrastructural and constitutive character of the contemporary international division of labor, with its stratification and polarization of the world into a prosperous postindustrial North (the United States, the European Union, and Japan), hyperdeveloping but authoritarian capitalist East Asia, industrializing India and Latin America, and low-growth Africa and the Arab and Islamic world, as well as the historical legacies of colonialism and anti-imperialist struggle in the last three regions, indelibly compromises, circumscribes, and mars the face of global human solidarities and belongings staged by new cosmopolitanist and human rights discourses.[4]

The constitutive power of the international division of labor in these two fabrications of humanity ought to be understood through two related theoretical prisms: the problem of *technē* and the inhuman, and the power of transcendence that co-belongs with the human capacity for freedom. As a function and expression of global capitalism, the international division of labor can be understood as the composite product of technical, instrumental, or rational-purposive (*zweckrationale*) imperatives and actions. But although *technē* as a form of intentional or final causality requires human rational consciousness and therefore implies humanity's freedom from nature, it is also paradoxically inhuman. As the theorists of the Frankfurt School argued, *technē* can be inimical to the achievement of freedom because, taken to its extreme, a technical attitude toward other human beings reduces them to objects for instrumental use. Kant already described the "technical predisposition for manipulating things [*Handhabung der Sachen*]" as merely "a mechanical predisposition joined with consciousness," and characterized pragmatic action as "using other men skilfully for [one's] purposes."[5] Accordingly, the moral law categorically prohibits the instrumentalization or technologization of human beings—the use of another human as a means rather than as an end in itself—because all human beings are persons and not things by virtue of their ontological constitution as rational and free beings: "So act that you use humanity [*die Menschheit*], whether in your own person or in the person of any other, always at the same time as an end [*Zweck*], never merely as a means [*Mittel*]."[6]

This proscription of instrumentality informs the fundamental axiom of human rights discourse, namely, that the human being, who is capable of rationality, is free and possesses dignity, and therefore is the bearer of inviolable rights. Although it is impossible to avoid instrumentality altogether, since human interaction mostly consists of pragmatic actions in which we routinely treat others as useful means in our pursuit of self-interest, human rights instruments constitute a quasi-juridical framework for regulating human relations so that people can act according to their self-interests and freedom of choice as long as their actions do not deprive others of the same freedom that they ought to have because of their humanity. Hence, if the material aspects of concrete human life, for instance, the deployment of people as labor power, are viewed as a now globalized system of means and ends, then human rights regimes attempt to counteract and regulate this global field of instrumentality from a transcendent position. In a word, they seek to *humanize* the field of instrumentality.

The most glaring deficiency, however, in the protection and enforcement of human rights is their paradoxical link to the civil rights provisions of individual nation-states and, therefore, their natural dependence on citizenship within a sovereign state. As Hannah Arendt reminded us in *The Origins of Totalitarianism*, "civil rights—that is the varying rights of citizens in different countries—were supposed to embody and spell out in the form of tangible laws the eternal Rights of Man, which by themselves were supposed to be independent of citizenship and nationality."[7] For present purposes, we can gloss this dilemma as follows: although human rights are supposed to regulate and humanize the field of instrumentality, they are themselves dependent on the political *technē* of states for their enforcement and realization. This particular scene of the contamination of the human by *technē* has been historically understood in terms of the hampering and even vitiation of the universalistic vocation of Western democratic republicanism (with its internal link to human rights) by the particularism of membership in a people defined in terms of an artificially constructed homogeneous national culture that is mythically projected as natural. Under neoliberalism, the political culture of democratic republicanism is further undermined by another form of *technē:* the erosion of the social welfare state's powers of regulation by the purely economic imperatives and dictates of transnational capital. In this context, cosmopolitanism has an intrinsic affinity for human rights. As a form of collective consciousness that erodes national parochialism and facilitates the arduous process of establishing a platform for transnational political regulation, cosmopolitanism can help to release human rights from their historical bondage to the instrumentality of sovereign national states.

The normative ability of cosmopolitanism and human rights to regulate the global system of means and ends is moreover entwined with a normative concept of culture as the human power of transcendence. One needs only to note that the normative dimension of cosmpolitanism resides primarily in its being a form of will-formation (*Willensbildung*) to fully grasp this leitmotif of culture (*Kultur* or *Bildung*) as *the human condition,* that is to say, culture as the condition that humanizes our existence by raising it beyond inhumanizing *technē.* Strictly speaking, culture itself is a form of *technē* because it involves the purposive shaping of objects. But as the self-recursive purposive shaping of subjects, it is also a form of individual and collective self-instrumentalization that lifts us beyond mere instrumentality, either because it points us toward moral ideals or because it is work that inspirits reality with norms, thereby actualizing these norms even as facticity itself becomes normative in the same process.

I have already pointed to this idea of culture in Kant's celebration of the humanities. But this understanding of culture as the means by which humanity achieves itself through the overcoming of its finitude and, therefore, as the medium of expression and the performative self-actualization of the human spirit also informs the Hegelian idea of *Geist* and Marx's account of social intercourse (*Verkehr*) and socialized labor as the substrate for the epigenesis of humanity. The same power of transcending finite limitations underwrites Horkheimer and Adorno's sharp opposition between instrumental reason and critical reason. Instrumental or technical reason, which is the essence of scientific knowledge and material progress, is synonymous with power. "What human beings seek to learn from nature is how to use it to dominate wholly both it and human beings. Nothing else counts."[8] This lower form of reason needs to be overcome and transcended through a higher, self-recursive form of reason: "If enlightenment does not assimilate reflection on this regressive moment, it seals its own fate. By leaving consideration of the destructive side of progress to its enemies, thought in its headlong rush into pragmatism is forfeiting *its sublating [aufhebenden] character, and therefore its relation to truth.*"[9] Accordingly, "the critique of enlightenment. . . is intended to prepare a positive concept of enlightenment *which liberates it from its entanglement* in blind domination."[10] Jürgen Habermas's distinctions between technical and communicative action and between "lifeworld" and "system" are part of this genealogy.[11] What lies at the heart of this human capacity for overcoming or regulating finite or material limitations is essentially the power to remake the world and ourselves through meaningful, mediational forms such as symbols and images. In Ernst Cassirer's words: "Human culture taken as a whole may be described as the process of man's progressive self-liberation. Language, art, religion, science, are various phases of this process. In all of them man discovers and proves a new power—the power to build up a world of his own, an 'ideal' world."[12]

This understanding of culture tacitly informed discourses of economic progress and national-social development espoused by the social welfare states of OECD (Organization for Economic Cooperation and Development) countries, but especially by postcolonial states of the ci-devant Third World. In both cases, *Bildung* was recoded as the cultivation of the well-being of the national body conceived in analogy with an individual person striving to maximize its capacities, and the *Bildung* of the nation-state was regarded as the condition for the cultivational relation between the state and its individual citizens, whether this was understood as the protection of individual civil and political freedoms or the respect for socioeconomic rights. Of course, this sort of cultivation often modulated into social control through official bourgeois nationalist ideology. But with the inability of the postcolonial state to fulfill its promises of freedom in an unequal neocolonial global economy, and the gradual decline of the Northern social welfare state under neoliberalism, this concept of culture was increasingly refigured in the more extensive shapes of cosmopolitanism and human rights. This is the conjuncture where we currently find ourselves.

The constitutive power of the international division of labor over cosmopolitanism and human rights discourses, however, problematizes the human capacity for transcending instrumentality in at least two ways. First, the fact that these humanizing forms of solidarity are themselves enabled by and inextricably imbricated within instrumental relations points to the irreducible crafting of the human capacity for freedom by *technē*. Indeed, these technologies are not just economic. They are multifarious and operate at every level. They stretch from global political negotiations, diplomatic relations, and even military deployment in the name of global security to policies and technologies of global competition and economic development, as well as those techniques for the management and enhancement of populations and the disciplining of individual bodies as human capital which are indispensable to capitalist development—what Michel Foucault has called bio-power.[13] Second, the power of remaking the world into a higher spiritualized nature through normative ideals and images also opens up the possibility of the coagulation of purportedly mutable social norms and cultural forms into a second nature that is lived and incarnated in every pore of our corporeal lives and that stubbornly persists even after radical critique has exposed them as contingent nonnatural processes. Second natures of this kind can be either constraining and oppressive or enabling. I have called the postcolonial nationalisms induced by uneven globalization cases of "given culture." The crucial point is that this aporetic oscillation between culture *qua* human formation and nature, which does not always serve the ends of the human spirit, points to something profoundly inhuman in the constitution of the human being. Analyzing this oscillation in the Foucauldian terms of the tug-of-war between subjection and the ethical practice of freedom, the interplay between technologies of power and technologies of the self in the constitution of subjects in a given historical situation, is a valuable exercise.[14] But it does not exactly address the more difficult question of the radical susceptibility of human life, and perhaps even life itself, to the constitutive play of *technē*.

Moreover, the constitution of human freedom by *technē* also points to the need for an alternative account of change that does not issue in the first instance from the human power of transcendence. Rightful or legitimate political transformation has conventionally been regarded as a change in the *form* of the ordering of collective political life. Such alteration is understood as an effect of the freedom that stems from the human capacity for self-activity and the transcendence of finite limitations through our various rational faculties. The problem, however, is that neither human rights nor cosmopolitan solidarities can escape from being entangled within the field of instrumentality. They are pulled back into and find themselves mired within the imperatives and techniques of globalization at many different levels. And yet these phenomena also have a normative dimension that cannot simply be reduced to the ideological reflection of the global system. I have suggested that normative change should be thought in terms of the *inscription* of universal norms within a global field of forces, their repeated generation from an infinite textile back into which they are repeatedly woven.

We can understand the peculiar dynamism at work here by borrowing from Saussure's account of linguistic change. The perverse uniqueness of language as a social institution, Saussure argued, stems from the fact that it is not the product of a consensual contract by a limited number of individuals but the result of entirely arbitrary conventions that are constantly affirmed through time by the haphazard participation of every member of a language community. "Language—and this consideration surpasses all others—is at every moment everybody's concern; spread throughout society and manipulated by it, language is something used daily by all. . . . [I]n language . . . everyone participates at all times, and that is why it is constantly influenced by all. This capital fact suffices to show the impossibility of revolution. Of all social institutions, language is least amenable to initiative."[15] Language cannot undergo a revolution, a transformation based on rational principles of what is legitimate or right, because no rational will, either general or of a smaller collective, can be found behind it. But, conversely, language is also unlike other human institutions because, by virtue of its very arbitrariness, it is radically mutable for *no reason* at all. In Saussure's words, "As it is a product of both the social force and time, no one can change anything in it, and on the other hand, the arbitrariness of its signs theoretically entails the freedom of establishing just any relationship between phonetic substance and ideas."[16] The freedom at stake here is that of a paradoxical interplay between radical mutability and social inertia. It is a peculiar form of agency or act that is neither the blind necessity of nature nor the dynamism of rational human activity. This freedom is properly unnatural because it is social. But it is also inhuman because, since language is an unplanned system composed of units that are connected by neither natural motivation nor rational relation, it cannot be controlled or changed by rational decisions or calculations of the individual or collective human will. Instead, since we become subjects capable of thought and signification only through language, this inhuman freedom constitutes the human rational subject and all its capacities.

The early Derrida generalized the inhuman dynamism issuing from the sign's unmotivated and arbitrary character into a movement that exceeds language in the narrow sense and also all anthropologistic structures such as sociality or culture. He argued that this movement generates but also destabilizes presence in general because it inscribes any form of presence within "a structure of reference where difference appears *as such* and this permits a certain liberty of variations among the full terms."[17] The later Derrida characterized this appearance of pure difference or absolute alterity as an experience of the impossible, arguing that such an experience was nothing other than an infinite justice that enables the recasting and refounding of law and politics and demands an interminable responsibility from the self-present rational subject.[18] The later Foucault spoke of the engendering of unstable states of power by "the moving substrate of force relations" and argued that although the exercise of power involves calculations and tactics with intentional aims and objectives, power relations are nevertheless nonsubjective because the coherence of these local tactics into a comprehensive system is unplanned and cannot be attributed to and exhausted by the rationality or cunning design of a collective subject.[19] Power relations, Foucault stressed, are reversible precisely because their effects cannot be fully predicted or calculated in advance, and this instability means that resistance is always immanent to power.

Both Foucault and Derrida therefore suggest that the substrate of ethics and politics is an inhuman dynamism. But the inhuman is emphatically not antihuman. The denigration of this kind of thought as involving the liquidation of the human is mistaken because what is at issue here is precisely the crafting of the human, how humanity and all its capacities are not primary, original, and self-originating but product-effects generated by forces that precede and exceed the *anthropos*.[20] These forces are the inhuman conditions of humanity. But to say that humanity is a product-effect does not mean that humanity is a myth or a mere ideological abstraction. These humanity-effects are concretely real and efficacious, and can be progressive and enabling. It is therefore a matter of situating such humanity-effects in terms of their conditions of possibility and actuality, and also their limits. How do these effects constrain lives? What do they necessarily exclude in a given conjuncture? This should be the task of the humanities, whose contribution to the study of globalization would be the articulation of a framework that renders intelligible the inhuman ways of achieving humanity in the contemporary world. By suggesting that the rational principles that function as norms, maxims, or imperatives impelling action are responses to inhuman forces, by showing that the very capacity for progressive action is generated by technologies of power, this line of thought leads to an understanding of resistance and normativity that is no longer based on human transcendence. It is therefore immensely useful for analyzing the contaminated normativity of human rights in global capitalism and the interminable circumscription of any form of resistance or progressive movement by instrumentality in the current conjuncture.

This book is divided into two parts. The first part offers a critical assessment of several influential arguments from the humanities, cultural studies, and the social sciences about the rise of new cosmopolitanisms in contemporary globalization. Chapter 1 situates these new cosmopolitanisms within broader debates in modern intellectual and philosophical history about nationalism and cosmopolitanism as vehicles of freedom. It then examines arguments about the rise of postnational formations and the emergence of cosmopolitan consciousness from the new geography of transnational networks of global cities. Chapter 2 explores the explicit normative claims of the new cosmopolitanism through an examination of Jürgen Habermas's writings on cosmopolitan democracy, and Chapter 3 focuses on arguments from postcolonial cultural studies of a postmodernist complexion about the rise of hybrid cosmopolitanisms. In these chapters I examine the various limits of these different new cosmopolitanisms by situating them within the polarized world of actually existing global capitalism and its hierarchical international division of labor.

The plausibility and cogency of these examples of new cosmopolitanism—their claim to be the harbingers and bearers of freedom—is partly premised on the conflation of globalization with migratory flows to North Atlantic centers. This ruse equates the power of transcendence with travel, mobility, and migration and tacitly establishes the metropolitan scene of multicultural recognition as the model for cosmopolitan freedom as such. But in each of these cases, the freedom that is promised is not only inaccessible to the majority of the world's population, who inhabit the other side of the international division of labor and are unable to move to OECD countries and the top-tier global cities. It is also severely undermined by the fact that the efficacy of these new cosmopolitanisms is generated by, and structurally dependent on, the active exploitation and impoverishment of the peripheral majorities. The postnational solidarities generated by South-North migration and the cosmopolitan consciousness emerging in global cities is largely the consciousness of transnational upward class mobility, especially that of the new technocratic professional class that manages and benefits from the global production system of flexible capitalism. Even the cosmopolitan *Öffentlichkeit* Habermas celebrates as crucial to the cultivation of a cosmopolitan consciousness that can lead to the establishment of global democracy is not immune to instrumentality. This kind of publicness amounts to the projection of the national public sphere of the economically hegemonic North Atlantic, and it derives its strength from this hegemony. Hence, the inclusiveness of global democratic processes envisioned on this basis is necessarily compromised because the economic stratification of the world makes it impossible to institutionalize conditions for discursive debate that will include the participation of peoples across the globe. What the delimitation of new cosmopolitanisms puts into question is the understanding of freedom as the transcendence of the given.

Another common thematic thread that runs through these chapters is the argument that claims about the imminent decline of the nation-state and the obsolescence of popular nationalism as a normative force are precipitous and fail to attend to the ongoing global exploitation of the postcolonial South. More generally, the New World Order has generated an entire spectrum of popular and official postcolonial nationalisms and more extensive forms of cultural reassertion that stretch from progressive postcolonial nationalism as a normative source for defending the peoples in the South against the vicissitudes of capitalist globalization, to Islamic fundamentalism and the Confucian chauvinism sanctioned by East Asian capitalist regimes. This peculiar persistence of nationalism and culture in an era when globalization is supposed to have undermined cultural areas can also be understood in terms of the questioning of freedom as transcendence. I have characterized these forms of nationalism as cases of given culture, of cultural collectivity as a response/responsibility to and negotiation with the economic, political, and historical forces that give us ourselves as opposed to the canonical idea of culture as the transcendence of the given that underwrites the various new cosmopolitanisms. But if given culture in the case of popular postcolonial nationalism has a decidedly progressive dimension, this is not always so with every instance of given culture, since the very givenness of culture also refers to its contamination by economic and political forces. In Chapter 4 I explore the less salutary side of given culture, where the machinations of colonial regimes in Southeast Asia produced a cosmopolitan cultural identity of the Chinese diaspora that has become integral to the workings of contemporary global capitalism because it is the bearer of the culturalist understanding of East Asian capitalism as *Confucian*. This type of diasporic cosmopolitanism is also a cautionary antidote to the new cosmopolitanist celebration of diasporic cultures as harbingers of progressive change.

The second part of the book is concerned with human rights as the other way of figuring the global as the human. I focus, however, not on the violation and protection of human rights in exceptional situations of emergency or crisis, but on human rights abuses that are intimately tied to daily situations of economic exploitation outside the North Atlantic. I have chosen this focus because, although these mundane and quotidian settings are not generally viewed as situations in which humanity is in crisis, they are precisely where we are best able to glimpse how globalization processes are implicated in the repeated crafting of the human by *technē*. Chapter 5 is a critical analysis of the Asian values debate on human rights. Here I argue that the normativity of human rights is necessarily contaminated because they are repeatedly rewoven back into the workings of global capitalism, and I offer an alternative account of normativity that breaks with the motif of transcendence. In Chapter 6 I consider the human rights abuses that arise from the transnational trade in female domestic workers in Southeast Asia. I show that the agency of the labor-exporting nation-state is crucial in efforts to humanize such migrant workers because existing human rights instruments are relatively ineffective. In Chapter 7 I make the case that such workers can only ever be partially humanized in the current conjuncture because of the imbrication of progressive humanizing endeavors at various levels in inhuman technologies that are continuous with those that sustain global capitalism.

It should be apparent that this book draws some of its material and examples from the postcolonial world and so falls within that niche of academic publishing called "postcolonial studies." But I have used this material to illuminate broader and, I hope, fundamental theoretical issues concerning the nature of humanity. In doing so, I have not respected the academic division of labor between area studies and the disciplines. I offer no modest apologies for this. Europeanists universalize European milieus and experiences all the time. Instead of provincializing Europe, I have attempted a necessarily provisional universalizing of one corner of postcolonial Asia.[21] Humanity (and theorizing about it) is, after all, an interminable work of collaboration and comparison.

I

Critique of Cosmopolitan Reason

The Cosmopolitical—Today

The entire world can now observe the actions of any person. And
people can observe the actions of the entire world.
                              Pramoedya Ananta Toer, *This Earth of Mankind*

We live in an era when nationalism seems to be out of favor in academia.
The catchwords of the moment are *globalization, transnationalism,* even
postnationalism. Many argue that the accelerated pace of economic globalization—the intensification of international trade, fiscal and technology transfers, and labor migration, and the consolidation of a genuinely
global mode of production through foreign direct investment and subcontracting—in advanced post-Fordist or late capitalism, the transnationalization of military command structures through NATO, and the
rise of global hybrid cultures from modern mass migration, consumerism, and mass communications since the 1980s have combined to create
an interdependent world in which the nation-state faces imminent obsolescence as a viable economic unit, a politically sovereign territory, and a
bounded cultural sphere. Even official U.S. nationalism feels the need to
put on nonnational costume now and then, either as the champion of
world trade liberalization or as the protector of international human
rights.

Indeed, the unprecedented growth of academic research on nationalism in recent years predominantly takes the tone of an officiation at a
wake foretold. Scholars of both liberal and leftist persuasions in the humanities and the social sciences have tried to hasten the demise of nationalism by pointing to its pathological nature. Nationalism has been
linked to the right-wing racist ideologies of the Axis powers of the Second World War, the rise of new right-wing movements and xenophobia

in Western Europe, and genocidal wars in Eastern Europe. Third World statist ideologies justifying the oppression of religious and ethnic minorities and, more recently, Islamic patriarchal fundamentalism and oppressive identity politics in the postcolonial South have also been described as nationalist. It is argued that these nationalist discourses give the lie to the promise of freedom made by national liberation movements during decolonization. The subfield of postcolonial studies emerges from this general disenchantment with nationalism, more specifically exemplified by the argument of the subaltern studies scholars of India that nationalism is an ideological humanism engendered from colonialist discourse.[1]

The New Cosmopolitanism

In this intellectual climate where nationalism is rejected as a particularistic mode of collective consciousness or a privative ethnic identity that disguises itself as a universalism and the political institution of the nation-state is viewed as undesirable and outmoded, cosmopolitanism has emerged as a political alternative. Of course, there were earlier articulations of cosmopolitanism in the history of philosophy which celebrated it as an ideal political project or a practical consciousness that could overcome nationalist particularism and offer a better embodiment of genuine universalism. What is distinctively new about the revival of cosmopolitanism that began in the 1990s is the attempt to ground the normative critique of nationalism in analyses of contemporary globalization and its effects. Hence, studies of various global phenomena such as transcultural encounters, mass migration and population transfers between East and West, First and Third Worlds, North and South, the rise of global cities as central sites for the management of global financial and business networks, the formation of transnational advocacy networks, and the proliferation of transnational human rights instruments have been used to corroborate the general argument that globalizing processes, both past and present, objectively embody different forms of normative, non-ethnocentric cosmopolitanism because they rearticulate, radically transform, and even explode the boundaries of regional and national consciousness and local ethnic identities.[2] In comparison with older philosophical approaches, cosmopolitanism is regarded no longer as merely an ideal project based on universal reason but as a variety of actually existing practical stances. It is suggested that whatever its shortcomings, contemporary transnationalism furnishes the material conditions for new radical cosmopolitanisms from below that can regulate the excesses of capitalist economic globalization. These new cosmopolitanisms are therefore the human face of globalization.

Although the remilitarization of Northern imperialism and the proliferation of "anti-globalization" movements exemplified by the protests against the World Trade Organization (WTO) in the early years of the twenty-first century have posed serious challenges to the new cosmopolitan visions of the 1990s, the issues raised by the new cosmopolitanism are not reducible to or exhausted by its origins in the post–Cold War pro-globalization discourse of the end of the twentieth century.[3] "Anti-globalization" movements are in fact not against globalization per se but against the neoliberal regime of globalization. Indeed, one possible response to the remilitarization of the world is a renewed project of cosmopolitan democracy that will lead to the establishment of an international criminal court and genuinely multilateral institutions for the enforcement of public international laws governing crimes against humanity, including the unjustified "war against terrorism" waged by the United States. It is therefore productive to assess some of the claims of the new cosmopolitanism.

New theories of cosmopolitanism can be reduced to three related propositions, two of which are empirical and one normative. First, it is suggested that cultural and political solidarity and political agency should not be automatically restricted to the sovereign nation-state as a unified spatiotemporal container because globalization has undermined many of the key functions from which the nation-state derives its legitimacy.[4] Second, a stronger positive link is posited between globalization and cosmopolitanism. It is argued that the various material networks of globalization have formed a world that is interconnected enough to generate political institutions and nongovernmental organizations (NGOs) that have a global reach in their regulatory functions as well as global forms of mass-based political consciousness or popular feelings of belonging to a shared world. Third, building on the conventional critique of nationalist particularism, it is argued that the new cosmopolitan consciousness is normatively superior to nationalism. Even if cosmopolitanism is no longer grounded in universal reason, it is a more expansive form of solidarity that is attuned to democratic principles and human interests without the restriction of territorial borders. In some cases it is also suggested that the new cosmopolitan consciousness is in a relation of mutual feedback with emerging global institutions, taking root and finding sustenance from these institutions and influencing their functioning in turn.

The emancipatory potential of these new cosmopolitanisms turns on the nature of their relation to capitalist globalization. In this chapter I address some of the new cosmopolitanist arguments from the softer social sciences that have been influential in the humanities. The next two chapters deal with theories of cosmopolitanism from philosophy and cultural studies.

Cosmopolitanism and Nationalism as Vehicles of Freedom in the History of Ideas

The normative critique of the nation-state as a particularistic straitjacket that limits the circle of political belonging and action is based on a restrictive understanding of the nation as a cultural formation that serves the modern territorial state's bureaucratic and administrative imperatives to stabilize the intense mobility and transformation that characterize modern societies. Hence, a static and primordialist self-understanding is imputed to the nation, which is invariably linked to the state instead of the people. It is then suggested that the primordial unity of the nation, which has become a fundamental methodological assumption of social-scientific research, is in fact an ideological mystification. The apparent solidity of the national container easily decomposes into a multiplicity of transnational processes that traverse national space and undermine its fabric, thereby pointing to the emergence of cosmopolitan forms of political solidarity and action. Essentially, the normative deficiency of the nation-form is seen to derive from its mystificatory character and its connection to the particularistic imperatives of the territorial state. In contradistinction, cosmopolitanism breaks down these particularistic barriers and envisions borderless modes of belonging.

But is nationalism in fact reducible to an ideological appendage of the territorial state? Is the space-time of the nation necessarily static and primordial, and is nationalism always a particularistic form of consciousness that is antithetical to cosmopolitanism? Benedict Anderson, for example, has argued that the nation originates in global pilgrimages from the Creole Americas to the European metropole, and that unlike ethnicity, nationalism operates according to the universalistic logic of an un-bounded seriality.[5] Indeed, from an intellectual-historical perspective, the understanding of cosmopolitanism as an erosion of the particu-laristic barriers of the national imagination, as something that comes af-ter and seeks to transcend an anterior mass-based nationalism, turns out to be an anachronistic projection. The relation between nationalism and cosmopolitanism is more supple and complex, and the putative the-matic opposition between these terms has always been unstable.

As a central concept of the eighteenth-century French *philosophes,* cosmopolitanism is derived from *kosmopolitēs,* a composite of the Greek words for "world" and "citizen," by way of the *esprit cosmopolite* of Re-naissance humanism.[6] It primarily designates an intellectual ethic, a uni-versal humanism that transcends regional particularism. It is important to note that contrary to conventional understandings, the cosmopolitan spirit is not one of rootlessness. What is imagined is a universal circle of belonging that embraces the whole of humanity, as a result of the tran-scendence of the particularistic and blindly given ties of kinship and country. Hence, the cosmopolitan embodies the universality of philo-sophical reason itself, namely, its power of transcending the particular and contingent. The regional particularism opposed by cosmopolitan-ism may be defined territorially, culturally, linguistically, or even racially, but it is not defined *nationally* as we now understand the term, because in a Europe made up of absolutist dynastic states, the popular national state did not yet exist. Nor, indeed, had the doctrine of nationalism been fully articulated. Cosmopolitanism thus precedes the popular nation-state in history and nationalism in the history of ideas.

French Enlightenment cosmopolitanism, however, is merely an intel-lectual ethos or perspective espoused by a select clerisy. Its philosophers could not envision feasible political structures for the regular and wide-spread institutionalization of mass-based cosmopolitan feeling. Rous-seau lamented that in relations between different societies, the Law of Nature, or natural pity, the original root of social virtues such as clem-ency and humanity, has lost "almost all the force it had in the relations between one man and another, [and] lives on only in the few great Cos-mopolitan Souls [*grandes âmes cosmopolites*] who cross the imaginary boundaries that separate Peoples and, following the example of the sov-ereign being that created them, embrace the whole of Mankind in their benevolence."[7] The true inaugurator of modern cosmopolitanism is Immanuel Kant, whose vision of institutional cosmopolitanism involves a shift from a merely voluntary ethical community of intellectuals to a world political community grounded in right. Kant articulated four different modalities of cosmopolitanism that have become the main topoi of contemporary discussions of the concept in normative international relations theory (including accounts of global civil society and the international public sphere), liberal political economy, and theories of globalization. These modalities, which are part of a systemic whole, are: a world federation as the legal-political institutional basis for cosmopolitanism as a form of right; the historical basis of cosmopolitanism in world trade; the idea of a global public sphere; and the importance of cosmopolitan culture in instilling a sense of belonging to humanity.

What Kant calls "a universal *cosmopolitan existence*" is nothing less than the regulative idea of "a perfect civil union of mankind."[8] This global federation of all existing states is also more ambitiously described as "a universal federal state [*allgemeiner Völkerstaat*]."[9] Its constitution is "one in accord with the *right of citizens of the world* [*Weltbürgerrecht*], insofar as individuals and states, standing in the relation of externally affecting one another, are to be regarded as citizens of a universal state of mankind [*eines allgemeinen Menschenstaats*] (*ius cosmopoliticum*)."[10] Although it would not possess the coercive means of enforcement available to a world state, it would nevertheless be a legitimately institutionalized world community, able to make rightful claims on its constituent states regarding their treatment of individuals and other states. Individual states would retain their sovereignty but would be held accountable by a universal citizenry—humanity—on issues such as disarmament and imperialist expansion. Kant's world federation would therefore fall somewhere between the political community of the state in its lawful relations with other states and a world state.[11]

In Kant's view, world trade provided the historical basis of cosmopolitan unity. As the spirit of commerce spreads throughout the world, states find that it is in their self-interest to enter into this world federation to prevent war and violence, which deplete their financial power (*Geldmacht*).[12] Moreover, the unity brought about by trade and other forms of encounter between countries creates something like a global public sphere that will safeguard cosmopolitan right by protesting any violations of it in the same manner that a critical national public sphere safeguards the rights of citizens vis-à-vis the territorial state: "Since the (narrower or wider) community of the peoples [*Völkern*] of the earth has now gone so far that a violation of right in *one* place of the earth is felt in *all*, the idea of a cosmopolitan right is no fantastic and exaggerated way of representing right; it is, instead, a supplement to the unwritten code of the right of a state and the right of nations necessary for the sake of any public rights of human beings [*öffentlichen Menschenrechte*]."[13] In addition, forms of culture also instill a deeper subjective sense of cosmopolitan solidarity or the feeling of belonging to humanity by encouraging universal social communication and sympathy. The fine arts and the sciences play a crucial role in developing our humanity (*Menschheit*) because they involve "a universally communicable pleasure."[14] The humanities (*humaniora*) cultivate our mental powers by instilling in us "the universal feeling of sympathy, and the ability to engage universally in very intimate communication [*das Vermögen, sich innigst und allgemein mitteilen, zu können*]. When these two qualities are combined, they constitute the sociability [*Geselligkeit*] that befits humanity and distinguishes it from the limitation of animals."[15]

Kant's cosmopolitanism signifies a turning point where moral politics or political morality needs to be formulated beyond the *polis* or stateform, the point at which "the political" becomes, by moral necessity, "cosmopolitical." For present purposes, what is striking is that Kant's cosmopolitanism is not identical to "internationalism," and its antonym is not "nationalism" but "statism." The historical timing of Kant's vision indicates that it is formulated prior to the spread of nationalism in Europe. Written in 1795, *Toward Perpetual Peace* clearly precedes what Lord Acton disparagingly names the age of "the modern theory of nationality"—the period between 1825 and 1831, when nationality, in search of statehood, emerges for the first time as the primary basis of revolution.[16] This era of the nationality principle saw the rise of Greek, Belgian, and Polish nationalist movements, first aroused by the Napoleonic invasion, and now rebelling against their Ottoman, Dutch, and Russian governments for the primary reason that these were foreign regimes. Kant's idea of the cosmopolitical is formulated too early to take into account the role of nationalism in the transition between the age of absolutism and the age of liberalism. It is more a philosophical republicanism and federalism designed to reform the absolutist dynastic state than a theory opposing the modern theory of nationality.[17] Indeed, because Kant writes at a time when the phenomenon and concept of "the nation" is still at an embryonic stage, he points out that the right of peoples or nations (*Völkerrecht*) is a misnomer since it actually refers to the lawful relation of states to one another, *ius publicum civitatum*.[18]

The original antagonist of Kant's cosmopolitanism is therefore absolutist statism. Its appropriate historical context is not the age of nationalism but the interstate system of anarchy established by the Treaty of Westphalia after the breakup of the vast religious political communities of the medieval period. This interstate system, which arguably prevails through the early twenty-first century, is anarchic in at least two senses.[19] First, because the states within the system are not subject to an overarching universal sovereign authority, they are sovereign actors who claim absolute authority over the territories they govern. Second, much like corporations in a market, these states relate to one another and to individuals according to utilitarian principles of self-help and self-interest, without any cohering normative principles or moral purposes to regulate their actions. Kant's vision of cosmopolitical right asserted in the name of a common humanity attempts to provide an ideal institutional framework for regulating the anarchic behavior of states. It is not anti- or postnationalist. A prenationalist attempt to reform absolutist statism, it is not in the least an ideal of detachment opposed to national attachment. It is instead a form of right based on existing attachments that bind us into a collectivity larger than the state. This collectivity also includes states because international commerce is a form of sociability that brings states and individuals into relation, connecting all of us into a larger whole.

Kant, however, could not possibly predict that capitalism, or more specifically print capitalism, to use Benedict Anderson's felicitous phrase, was also the material condition of possibility of a different type of collective glue with similar humanizing aims. I am, of course, speaking of nationalism, which, like cosmopolitanism, also sought to provide rightful regulation for the behavior of absolutist states toward their individual subjects. In the initial moment of its historical emergence, nationalism is a *popular* movement distinct from the state it seeks to transform in its own image. Thus, before the nation finds its state, before the tightening of the hyphen between nation and state that official nationalism consummates, the ideals of cosmopolitanism and European nationalism in its early stirrings are almost indistinguishable. As late as 1861, Giuseppe Mazzini would emphasize that the nation was the only historically effective threshold to humanity:

Your first Duties . . . are . . . to Humanity. You are *men* before you are *citizens* or *fathers*. . . . But what can *each* of you, with his isolated powers, *do* for the moral improvement, for the progress of Humanity? . . . The *individual* is too weak and Humanity is too vast. . . . But God gave you this means when he gave you a country, when, like a wise overseer of labour, who distributes the different parts of work according to the capacity of workmen, he divided Humanity into distinct groups upon the face of our globe, and thus planted the seeds of nations. . . . Without Country you have neither name, token, voice, nor rights, no admission as brothers into the fellowship of Peoples. You are the bastards of Humanity. . . . Do not beguile yourselves with the hope of emancipation from unjust social conditions if you do not first conquer a Country for yourselves. . . . Do not be led away by the idea of improving your material conditions without first solving the national question. . . . In labouring according to the true principles for our Country we are labouring for Humanity; our Country is the fulcrum of the lever which we have to wield for the common good. If we give up this fulcrum we run the risk of becoming useless to our Country and to Humanity. Before *associating* ourselves with the Nations which compose Humanity we must exist as a Nation.[20]

Indeed, even when cosmopolitanism is diluted in its usage to designate a universally normative concept of culture identified with the culture of a certain ethno-linguistic people such as in Fichte's *Addresses to the German Nation* (1808), it is still compatible with nationalism because the national culture in question is not yet bonded to the territorial state and can be accorded world-historical importance without being imperialistic. The crucial point here is that prior to its annexation of the territorial state, nationalism is not antithetical to cosmopolitanism. In his classic study *Cosmopolitanism and the National State,* the German social historian Friedrich Meinecke argued that in its initial phase, German spiritual or ethical national feeling was also cosmopolitan in nature and that cosmopolitanism was superseded by nationalism only with the birth of a genuinely national state.[21] This unbounded and cosmopolitical extensiveness of pre-statized nationalism may further indicate that nationalism is not reducible to ethnicity and that nationalist politics is not necessarily a form of particularistic identity politics.

In the history of ideas, the notorious tensions between nationalism and cosmopolitanism become more apparent from Marx onwards. Whereas cosmopolitanism in idealist philosophy had designated a normative horizon of world history, for Marx, cosmopolitanism is realized as exploitation on a world scale through international commerce and the establishment of a global mode of production:

> The bourgeoisie has through its exploitation of the world market given a *cosmopolitan* character to production and consumption in every country. To the great chagrin of reactionists, it has drawn from under the feet of industry the national ground on which it stood. All old-established national industries have been destroyed or are daily being destroyed. . . . In place of the old local and national seclusion and self-sufficiency, we have intercourse in every direction, universal interdependence of nations. And as in material, so also in spiritual [*geistigen*] production. The spiritual creations of individual nations become common property. National one-sidedness and narrow-mindedness [*Beschränktheit*] become more and more impossible, and from numerous national and local literatures, there arises a world literature.[22]

This passage documents the two crucial developments that occur between the cosmopolitanisms of Kant and Marx. For Marx, cosmopolitanism is no longer just a normative horizon or a matter of right growing out of international commerce. It is an existing and necessary condition resulting from the development of forces of production on a global scale. But more important, in the intervening years between *Toward Perpetual Peace* and the *Manifesto of the Communist Party* (1848), a significant sense of national belonging had obviously developed. Nationality was not even an issue in Kant's vision of the cosmopolitical. It is therefore a little startling to see Marx characterizing the nation and its appendages—national economy, industry, and culture—in naturalistic and primordial terms only fifty-three years later. Indeed, by then the nation is sufficiently annexed to the territorial state (which has in turn naturalized its boundaries through official nationalism) for it to be characterized as a particularity to be opposed and eroded by (capitalist and proletarian) cosmopolitanism. For Marx, nationality belonged to an initial phase of capitalist production, the natural or immediate stage of the appearance of the capitalist form of capital. Even though this natural/national phase of capitalism was antiquated and in the process of being sublated (*aufgehoben*) into the higher and truer phase of cosmopolitan capitalism, it still existed, and its passing had to be hastened by ideology critique. The nation may have a weak compensatory dimension insofar as it provides the appearance of a natural collective-psychological or affective barrier against the dehumanizing, atomizing effects of capital. But it is a false natural community, an ideological construction: the appeal to nationality in Listian exhortations to protect the national economy and industry mystifies the class interests of less developed bourgeois states.[23]

Marx's anti- and postnationalist cosmopolitanism is thus different from Kant's prenationalist cosmopolitanism. Kant missed the potential of popular nationalism as an emancipatory force against statism because he could not predict that the material interconnectedness brought about by capitalism would engender the bounded political community of the nation. Marx summarily dismissed nationalism although he witnessed its rise. Identifying the nation too hastily with the bourgeois state, Marx reduced the nation to an ideological instrument of the state and saw nationalism as a tendentious invocation of anachronistic quasi-feudal forms of belonging in modernity. The antagonistic relation between socialist cosmopolitanism and nationalism is premised on a collapsing of the nation into the state. Marx's cosmopolitanism presupposes a historical scenario in which the masses are able to recognize the nation as a tool of oppression because the hyphen between nation and bourgeois state has been rendered so tight that it has completely disappeared. The aphorism "the working men have no country" refers to the inevitable inability of bourgeois nations to command the loyalty of their proletariat in global exploitation and pauperization. Indeed, Marx was more concerned about abolishing the state apparatus than its epiphenomenon, the nation-form. Since he believed that nationality was already becoming obsolete, its dismantling would not require much effort, and the proletariat should direct their efforts at seizing state power instead: "The supremacy of the proletariat will cause [national differences] . . . to vanish still faster. . . . In proportion as the antagonism between classes within the nation vanishes, the hostility of one nation to another will come to an end."[24]

Marx's teleological argument about socialist cosmopolitanism is often dismissed for ignoring the continuing disparity between the working classes of different countries, a fact illustrated by the breakup of the Second International. But the more important reason why Marx missed the tenacity of nationalism so badly is that he deduced the ideological nature of nationality too hastily from the economic and cultural nationalism of European states and so foreclosed its popular dimension and its potential as an ally of Marxist cosmopolitanism. Furthermore, the fa-

ther of historical materialism works with an entirely ahistorical premise. He takes it for granted that the hyphen welding the nation to the
state is immutable. Capitalism is certainly the progenitor of the European territorial national state. But in different historical situations, the
global interconnectedness brought about by capitalism can also mutate
to loosen the bourgeois state's stranglehold over the nation so that the
state can undergo a popular renationalization. Marx seems to make a
similar point in his unelaborated concept of the proletarian nation that
occupies the interregnum between the bourgeois nation-state and the
proletarian world community: "Since the proletariat . . . must constitute
itself as the nation, it is, so far, itself national, though not in the bourgeois sense of the word."[25]

The most notable revaluation of the national question in socialism so
far has occurred in response to anticolonialist struggles.[26] Using national
liberation movements in Asia as his example, Lenin argued in 1914 for a
strategic alliance between the proletarian struggle and the right of nations to political self-determination based on the principle that the former would be served by supporting the bourgeoisie of an oppressed nation to the extent that it fights against imperialism:

> *If* the bourgeoisie of the oppressed nation fights against the oppressing
> one, we are always, in every case, and more resolutely than anyone
> else, *in favour.* . . . But if the bourgeoisie of the oppressed nation stands
> for *its own* bourgeois nationalism, we are opposed. We fight against the
> privileges and violence of the oppressing nation, but we do not con-
> done the strivings for privileges on the part of the oppressed nation. . . .
> The bourgeois nationalism of *every* oppressed nation has a general
> democratic content which is directed *against* oppression, and it is this
> content that we support *unconditionally,* while strictly distinguishing it
> from the tendency towards national exceptionalism.[27]

Lenin's argument widens the small foothold opened by Marx's tenta-
tive acknowledgment that as a form of collective solidarity that shelters
the worker against capital's atomizing effects, nationality has a compensatory dimension. Decolonizing nationalisms flourish in this opening,
seizing this precarious foothold and filling Lenin's abstract notion of nationality with positive cultural content.

In the colonial situation, global capitalism has enslaved African and
Asian territories either by establishing colonial administrative states (co-

lonial India, Africa, or Malaya) or by indirectly colonizing traditional dynastic states through extraterritorial demands (China, Siam, Ethiopia). At the same time, it leads to the birth of nations with interests that diverge from those of existing colonial or colonized states. No longer just an ideological tool of the state, the decolonizing nation can now serve as an agent of socialist cosmopolitanism to the extent that it attempts to save the state from the clutches of cosmopolitan capital. By bringing to the fore again the similar aims of cosmopolitanism and nationalism that Marx obscured, and by distinguishing these progressive goals from those of an imperializing cosmopolitanism, decolonizing nationalism destabilizes Marx's rigid antithesis between the two terms.[28] Thus, in words that seem to adapt Mazzini's position to decolonizing Asia, Sun Yat-sen, the father of modern China, argues that nationalism is the necessary basis of genuine cosmopolitanism:

> [Western colonial powers] are now advocating cosmopolitanism to inflame us, declaring that, as the civilization of the world advances and as mankind's vision enlarges, nationalism becomes too narrow, unsuited to the present age, and hence, that we should espouse cosmopolitanism. In recent years some of China's youths, devotees of the new culture, have been opposing nationalism, led astray by this doctrine. But it is not a doctrine which wronged races should talk about. We . . . must first recover our position of national freedom and equality before we are fit to discuss cosmopolitanism. . . . We must understand that cosmopolitanism grows out of nationalism; if we want to extend cosmopolitanism we must first establish strongly our own nationalism. If nationalism cannot become strong, cosmopolitanism certainly cannot prosper.[29]

But it is not only progressive nationalism that can ally itself with genuine cosmopolitanism. Reactionary (bourgeois) nationalism can also be the accomplice of capitalist cosmopolitanism. Thus, Frantz Fanon suggests that the retrograde national consciousness of underdeveloped countries is the result of "the apathy of the national bourgeoisie, its mediocrity, and its deeply cosmopolitan mentality."[30] Similarly, in the Second World War, Japanese imperial nationalism actively modulated into a violent military cosmopolitanism: the Greater East Asian Co-Prosperity Sphere that stretched from Southeast Asia through Korea and China to conquered Russian territory.

The Cosmopolitical in Contemporary Globalization

We have seen that the relationship between cosmopolitanism and nationalism has fluctuated historically between varying degrees of alliance and opposition and that both discourses have progressive as well as reactionary dimensions. This shifting relationship and the unpredictable content and consequences of both practical discourses have several implications. First, it is precipitous to consider nationalism an outmoded form of consciousness. An existing global condition should not be mistaken for an existing mass-based feeling of belonging to a world community (cosmopolitanism), because the globality of the everyday does not necessarily engender an existing popular global political consciousness. Second, neither cosmopolitanism nor nationalism can be seen as the teleologically necessary and desired normative outcome of past and present globalizing processes. Popular nationalist movements contain exclusionary aspects that can easily develop into oppressive official nationalist ideologies when these movements achieve statehood. Conversely, the staging of an international civil society of elite NGOs at UN World Conferences can become an alibi for economic transnationalism, which is often U.S. economic nationalism in global guise. Through strings-attached funding to elite NGOs that take over some social services from the public sector in developing states, international aid agencies can erode the ability of these already weakened states to implement genuine social redistribution. In the latter case, the point is to look at the consequences of cosmopolitanist claims in a given historical situation, just as in the first case the point is not to demonize the state as the corruptor of the nation-people but to account for the necessary link between decolonizing nation and state and the in-built dangers of official nationalism.

In other words, the ethico-political work that nationalism and cosmopolitanism can do at any given moment depends on how either formation emerges from or is inscribed within the shifting material linkages and interconnections created by global capitalism at a particular historical conjuncture. The corollary to this is that although capitalism is the condition of possibility of both nationalism and cosmopolitanism, neither discourse can be reduced to its simple reflection and ideological instrument. The tightness or laxity of the hyphen between nation and state is an important factor in evaluating the aims of nationalism and their compatibility with normative cosmopolitanism. Hence, instead of indulging in the complacent demystification of nationalism as "a derivative discourse" or moralistically condemning cosmopolitanism as uncommitted bourgeois detachment, we ought to turn our critical focus to the mutating global field of political, economic, and cultural forces in which nationalism and cosmopolitanism are invoked as practical discourses. I will call this global force field of the political "the cosmopolitical." The question is whether the cosmopolitical today is conducive to the rise of new normative cosmopolitanisms, mass-based emancipatory forms of global consciousness, or actually existing imagined political world communities.

Arguments in the affirmative point to the undermining of the nation-state's key functions by neoliberal economic globalization. For the Southern majority of the world's population, the Bandung model of national development for nonaligned countries, ideally directed by electoral democratic processes and based in the spirit of decolonization and resistance to neocolonialism, is the primary normative anchor of national consciousness. It is argued that this normative basis has been undermined because rapid economic globalization in the post–Cold War era has rendered untenable the center-periphery topography of theories of dependency and uneven development. The thesis of the spatial-geographical destriation or flattening out of the world economy is most clearly expressed in Saskia Sassen's work on global cities. Whereas the globalization of industrial production under post-Fordism created a hierarchical new international division of labor between center and periphery, Sassen argues that the outstripping of industrial capital by much more profitable nonindustrial forms of capital such as international finance (which has invented highly sophisticated financial instruments that can be traded on an international market) and the production of high-value specialized producer services (those that are crucial for the managing of global production networks, such as legal, accounting, and business management services) has led to the rise of new geographical formations, global networks of interlinked cities that no longer respect the center-periphery distinction.

As locations for the concentrated production of services and financial instruments, global cities are first and foremost members of a global economic order, integral sites for "the *practice* of global control: the work of producing and reproducing the organization and management of a global production system, and a global marketplace for finance."[31] Hence, New York, London, and Tokyo, the paradigmatic global cities, have become dislocated from their respective nation-states, functioning instead as "a surplus-extracting mechanism vis-à-vis a 'transnational hinterland,'" a "transterritorial marketplace" in which each plays a different complementary role.[32] These networks therefore constitute a complex border zone that facilitates the penetration of the nation-state by global forces. As states engage in the implementation of the global economic system by internalizing its legal, economic, and managerial rules, standards, and concepts, they become denationalized.[33] Furthermore, as extraterritorial outposts of the global in the national spaces of developed countries, as it were, the internal organization of global cities—the peripheralization within their labor markets and economic polarization within their urban geographies—replicates the unevenness of the global economy. Sassen argues that consequently "the geography of centrality and marginality, which in the past was seen in terms of the duality of highly developed and less developed countries, is now also evident within developed countries and especially within their major cities. . . . [P]eripheralization processes are occurring inside areas that were once conceived of as 'core' areas . . . and alongside the sharpening of peripheralization processes, centrality has also become sharper."[34]

Yet for the "partial unbundling" of the nation (Sassen's phrase) through global economic processes to have any normative significance, it has to be aligned with the rise of new supranational political formations that can replace the normative deficit caused by the weakening of the nation. Otherwise, the denationalization of state sovereignty and power by transnational production processes, market structures, and the transnational regimes of commercial law needed for their functioning merely serves the predatory rights of global capital. As Sassen herself puts it, "deregulation is a vehicle through which a growing number of states are furthering economic globalization and guaranteeing the rights of global capital, an essential ingredient of the former."[35] Here, Sassen's focus shifts, perhaps inevitably, to three rapidly expanding forms of transnationality, which she sees as interconnected: the proliferation of global political institutions radiating from the UN system and organizations and discourses centered on human rights, the virtual electronic space of the Internet as an increasingly powerful site for the critical confrontation between civil society and corporations, and the rise of a new cosmopolitan culture through transnational migration and global cultural and media flows. A combination of these three phenomena is seen as constituting the normative payoff of globalization, namely, a cosmopolitan political culture that exceeds the imperatives of merely economic globalization.

Thus, Sassen suggests that governments' use of international covenants to formulate national policy indicates a transnationalization of the legitimation process that creates new subjects able to make political claims: "This is a move away from statism—the absolute right of states to represent their people in international law and international relations—toward a conceptual and operational opening for the emergence of other subjects of, and actors in, international law. The international human rights regime has been a key mechanism for making subjects out of those hitherto invisible in international law—first nation people, immigrants, and refugees, women."[36] At the same time, Sassen argues that even as new information technologies have enabled the intensification of capital accumulation and the hyperconcentration of resources and infrastructure through the digital formation of transterritorial centers, the Internet is also a powerful transnational resource for civil society forces. As a result of the deregulation and privatization of telecommunications, the Internet exceeds the control of national governments. It is therefore a *forum* where public interests can engage with and confront transnational corporations, "a space for *de facto* (i.e., not necessarily self-conscious) democratic practices."[37]

Sassen wisely cautions us against celebrating this transnational digital form of democratic space as the space of unlimited freedom. The Internet can be used by civil society, "but this also means that the full range of the social forces will use it, from environmentalist to fundamentalists. . . . It becomes a democratic space for many opposing views and drives, and for a range of criminal uses—often referred to as the 'blacknet.'"[38] The issue that is raised here is precisely that of the formation of a popular collective consciousness that can evaluate, formulate, and express transnational norms such as those of human rights regimes through the (technical) use and deployment of new transnational forums such as the Internet so that they can become effective forces in regulating economic globalization. For if, as Sassen puts it, "the material conditions necessary for many global economic processes—from the infrastructure for telematics to the producer services production com-

plex—. . . signal the possibility of novel forms of regulation and conditions of accountability," the questions that remain to be answered are
"Accountable to whom?" "According to what normative interests and
criteria?" and most important "How is the collective subject to which
globalization is accountable formed?" and "Is such a subject limited by
the material conditions of its formation?"[39]

Sassen herself does not answer these questions. Given her focus on
sociological structures and geographical space rather than collective
subject-formation, the possible development of a cosmopolitan consciousness is merely implied in Sassen's brief suggestion that the global
city, with its cosmopolitan corporate work culture, the sophisticated
consumption patterns of this high income bracket, and the global culture of its growing immigrant population from the Third World (which
is needed to support the lifestyle of the former group), can be the crucible for the formation of a new cosmopolitan consciousness that can have
political implications.[40] As Sassen puts it: "National attachments and
identities are becoming weaker for these global players and their cus-
tomers. . . . Major international business centers produce what we could
think of as a new subculture. . . . [M]ajor cities contribute to denational-
ize the corporate elite. Whether this is good or bad is a separate issue;
but it is . . . one of the conditions for setting in place the systems and
subcultures necessary for a global economic system."[41]

The progressive implications of this kind of cosmopolitan consciousness are dubious since it is essentially the cosmopolitanism of a new
technocratic professional class whose primary aims in life are profit
making and conspicuous consumption. The only feelings of solidarity
manifest here are with the global firm as a terrain for professional self-
interest and advancement. This type of attachment is gradually dissemi-
nated throughout the world by the global outsourcing of white-collar
jobs, which in turn establishes more bridges for higher-end South-North
migration. The *New York Times* reports:

> At top Indian business schools, like the Indian Institute of Manage-
> ment, the prospect of a job with Wall Street firms has students ex-
> cited. Gayatri Srinivasan, 24, in the graduating class of the institute's
> Bangalore campus, says she dreams of a job with a top American in-
> vestment bank; she will be competing for her dream job with at least
> 50 of the 200 students on her campus. "Imagine working directly for a
> Wall Street firm while continuing to live in India," said Ms. Srinivasan,
> who interned this summer at Lehman's office in Tokyo.[42]

The questionable tendency to connect transnational migrancy and global cultural flows to the political culture of human rights activism in the service of a postnational spatialization of politics is even clearer in contemporary studies of culture that focus on postcoloniality. For instance, Arjun Appadurai suggests that contemporary transnational cultural flows create a zone in which emergent global forms of cosmopolitanism are brought into a conflictual relationship with nationalist forms of culture. Appadurai claims that the cosmopolitanization of cultural consumption—the widening of its horizons by increased frequency of travel and improved media communications—has political repercussions because national culture is the site where oppressive politics and culture are conjoined.[43] He suggests that insofar as the state attempts to tether the masses to it by deploying ideologies of "national belonging" and "national culture," subnational and local uses of transnational cultural messages and deterritorialized ideas of nationhood formed from population flows challenge the nation-state's cultural hegemony and contribute to its crisis.[44] For Appadurai, these are signs of the dawning of a postnational, post-statist age, which requires a theoretical vocabulary that can express "complex, non-territorial, postnational forms of allegiance" and "capture the collective interests of many groups in translocal solidarities, cross-border mobilizations and postnational identities." Otherwise, "the incapacity of many de-territorialized groups to think their way out of the nation-state is itself a cause of much global violence since many movements of emancipation and identity are forced, in their struggle against existing nation-states, to embrace the very imaginary they seek to escape."[45]

Appadurai usefully details the three fundamental presuppositions of the postnationalist position. First, like Marx, postnationalists presuppose a restrictive definition of the nation as an appendage of the state. In Appadurai's words, the nation is "the ideological alibi of the territorial state."[46] Consequently, popular nationalism involves masses duped by state ideology. Second, postnationalism subscribes to the teleological argument that flexible capitalist accumulation tends toward a postnational age. The argument that global networks inevitably give rise to mass-based global solidarities is rooted in an almost deterministic assumption of a perfect adequation or fit between the spatial extension of material conditions and the scope of forms of consciousness. Appadurai, for instance, suggests that a global economy constituted by disjunctive flows offers greater resources for undermining the oppressive nation state. Thus, whereas intellectuals participating in anticolonial liberation movements had considered the loose hyphen between emerging nation and state in colonialism an opportunity for a popular re-nationalization of the state, postnationalists take the distending of the hyphen in contemporary globalization as a sign of the disintegration of both nation and state.

Finally, postnationalism is at heart a discourse of transcendence. It suggests that there is a large variety of existing global social and political movements emanating from the grassroots level that exhibit autonomy from dominant global economic and political forces ("grassroots globalization" or "globalization from below") and that these movements can be the sustaining basis for transcending or overcoming the constraining discourse of nationalism/statism.[47] Grouping transnational NGOs and philanthropic movements, diasporic communities, refugees, and religious movements under the rubric of actually existing "postnational social formations," Appadurai suggests that these organizational forms are "both instances and incubators of a postnational global order" because they challenge the nation-state and provide nonviolent institutional grounding for larger-scale political loyalties, allegiances, and group identities.[48] The motif of transcendence is clearest in the importance accorded the power of the imagination *qua* the global circulation of mass media images to transform social life by generating new forms of solidarity. Hence, the imagination "allows people to consider migration, resist state violence, seek social redress, and design new forms of civic association and collaboration, often across national boundaries."[49] Indeed, Appadurai suggests that unless academic research is more imaginative, it will not be able to transcend the limits of a myopic nation-centered vision and grasp these new transnational social forms that are autonomous of both global capital and the nation-state.

There are, however, many cogent reasons to be more cautionary about the virtues of contemporary transnationalism and less dismissive of the future of the nation-state and nationalism. First, as Sassen notes, the deterritorialization of political formations by globalization is limited: "The global does not (yet) fully encompass the lived experience of actors or the domain of institutional orders and cultural formations; it persists as a partial condition."[50] Nor does the contemporary intensification of transnational capitalism undermine the utility of states. Michael Mann observes that "the increasing density of global society gives states new geopolitical roles," notably in negotiations over tariffs, communications, and environmental issues. "Though capitalism has reduced the social citizenship powers of the nation-state, and in association with military and geopolitical trends it has also reduced the military sovereignty of most states, it still depends on continuous negotiations between sovereign states in a variety of ad hoc agencies."[51] The important role of strong states for imposing the conditions required for economic growth through export-oriented industrialization is especially clear in the East Asian poster children for hyperdevelopment under flexible accumulation. One should also note that even something as immaterial as money is traded in national (or, in the case of the Eurodollar, regional) denominations, thereby indicating that the political and economic strength of nation-states or regions is an important factor of speculative value.

This suggests that while globalization has certainly complicated the nation-form and national belonging, they will not disappear. Transnational economic migrants certainly appreciate the benefits of a strong national passport and currency. They may also eventually develop feelings of national belonging and responsibility to their new countries. As I noted earlier, arguments about the decline of nationalism subscribe to the rather Gellnerian position that the nation is a cultural epiphenomenon of the territorial state's economic and political functions. This is why the deindustrialization of the world economy under finance capitalism is seen to lead to a destriation that undermines the nation's organizational and normative basis. If, however, we follow Benedict Anderson's account of the generation of the nation through print capitalism, where the nation is not reduced to an epiphenomenon of the state although it coincides with its territorial borders, then the contemporary transformation of the global economy does not necessarily render the nation obsolete. Indeed, its normative basis for peoples in the South remains intact notwithstanding the failed promises of national development, given that globalization has not removed the North-South divide. As Giovanni Arrighi points out:

> [Although] the signs of modernity associated with the wealth of the former First World . . . have proliferated in the former Third World; and it may also be the case that the signs of marginalization associated with the poverty of the former Third World are now more prominent in the former First World than they were twenty or thirty years ago[,] . . . it does not follow . . . that the distance between the poverty of the former Third World (or South) and the wealth of the former First World (or North) has decreased to any significant extent. Indeed, all

available evidence shows an extraordinary persistence of the North-South income gap as measured by GNP per capita. . . . [I]n 1999 the average per capita income of former "Third World" countries was only 4.6 per cent of the per capita income of former "First World" countries, that is almost exactly what it was in 1960 (4.5 per cent) and in 1980 (4.3 per cent).[52]

Indeed, other than the argument that globalization undermines the evils of nationalism, what is sorely missing among proponents of new cosmopolitanism in the softer social sciences and cultural studies is a thorough discussion of the normative implications of globalization or, more precisely, the relationship between universality or normative inclusivity and the global extensiveness of economic, political, and cultural processes. Why are global forms of political identification automatically accorded greater normative value than the nation?

The normative value of popular nationalism as an agent of ethico-political transformation becomes clearer once we observe that notwithstanding increased transnational labor migration in contemporary globalization, the deterritorialization of peoples remains limited for reasons that are structural to the global political economy. Samir Amin points out that the globalization of production—liberalization of trade and capital flows—involves the global integration of commodities and capital but stops short of an unlimited integration of labor, that is, the free movement of workers worldwide through the unrestricted opening of the North to labor migration from the South, where the bulk of capital's reserve army is located. Consequently, "the mobility of commodities and capital leaves national space to embrace the whole world while the labour force [largely] remains enclosed within the national framework."[53] Contrary to the neoliberal sermon that the global spread of free-market mechanisms will lead to generalized development and global democratization, the truncated globality of capital exacerbates economic polarization and in many cases leads to the formation of comprador states. More generally, resource-intensive and wasteful macro-policies of economic development and market economy–driven linear models espoused by international development agencies and financial institutions such as the World Bank and the International Monetary Fund (IMF) mortgage the state to transnational capital.

State adjustment to global restructuring loosens the hyphen between nation and state. Because the state cannot actively shape its own society and political morality, democratic national projects for social welfare in the South are either killed off or handicapped from the start. For social redistribution to occur, the state must resist structural adjustment. But resistance is possible only if the state is made to serve the people's interests. Thus, instead of producing large groups of deterritorialized migrant peoples who prefigure the nation-state's demise and point to a postnational global order, *uneven* globalization makes the formation of popular nationalist movements in the periphery the first step on the long road to social redistribution. In this spirit, Amin suggests that in an uneven capitalist world system that largely confines the most deprived masses of humanity to national-peripheral space, popular nationalism in the periphery is a necessary component of socialist cosmopolitanism.

The contrast between this argument for the sociopolitical necessity of democratic popular nationalism in the South and postnationalism in cultural studies is even more striking because of Amin's Marxist-internationalist bent. Amin rightly notes that the rise of an autonomous global economy through heightened forms of financial and technological transnationalization beginning in the 1970s is not matched by the emergence of supranational social and political mechanisms for regulating accumulation. Even as the historic role of the nation-state as a framework for economic management is eroded in the new phase of globalization, existing forms of social and political power remain based on national realities. Amin points out that "the US and Japan are not merely geographical areas of a world economy that is under construction. They are and will remain national economies, with a state that ensures the continuance of national structures while grabbing the lion's share of world trade. . . . These national options remain decisive at such levels as: spending on research, development, and labour force retraining; de facto protection of agriculture; mineral and oil resource development; and even manufacturing and financial management."[54] Consequently, the increasing interpenetration of national productive systems at the center "destroys the effectiveness of traditional national policies and delivers the overall system to the dictates and errors of the constraint of the world market, which cannot be regulated as there are no genuinely supranational political institutions, or even a political and social consciousness that really accepts this new demand of capitalism."[55]

In Amin's view, only an international political and social consciousness can equitably regulate the uneven global economy. But his internationalism is emphatically not postnationalist because it begins from and revolves around the success of popular nationalist movements in the periphery. In the initial instance, popular nationalisms, whatever their shortcomings, are needed to save the state from capitulating to the demands of transnationalization. They alone can renationalize the state and allow it to gain control over accumulation: "The system of real existing capitalism being first and foremost a system condemned to perpetuate, reproduce and deepen world polarization, the revolt of the peoples of the periphery against the fate that had been ordained for them constitutes the central axis of the recomposition of the internationalism of the peoples."[56] As was the case with decolonizing nationalisms, this proposed alliance between nationalism and cosmopolitanism also grows out of a situation in which the hyphen between nation and state needs to be strengthened because globalization has unmoored the state from its nation. Amin's example is the comprador state in Africa, but his general argument can be extended to describe people's diplomacy in the Philippines, the popular mobilization in support of Sukarnoputri in Indonesia, and other such instances.

These arguments about the structural necessity of the nation-state in the global political economy certainly show us the untenability of postnationalism. But they do not answer the question of whether the cosmopolitical today is conducive to the rise of new cosmopolitanisms of greater normative value than the popular nation-state. Proponents of new cosmopolitanisms suggest that existing transnational movements translate into actually existing popular cosmopolitanisms understood as pluralized forms of popular global political consciousness comparable to the national imagining of political community. But is this claim premature? One is never entirely certain whether the new forms of cosmopolitan consciousness from below celebrated by the academic critic are hopeful ideals of the imagination, since the exact relation between the critic's theoretical imagination and the political imagination or imagined community of transnational movements is never clearly investigated.

The necessity and even urgency of a cosmopolitical frame of analysis is not in question here. The problem is not whether there is material interconnection on a global scale, whether more women and men of discrepant class and cultural backgrounds are transnationally mobile and inhabit competing worlds. The world is undoubtedly interconnected, and transnational mobility is clearly on the rise. One should not, however, automatically take this to imply that popular forms of cosmopolitanism already exist. Whether this mobility and interconnectedness give rise to meaningful cosmopolitanisms in the robust sense of pluralized world political communities is an entirely separate issue. Anthony Smith, for instance, suggests that a mass-based global loyalty is anthropologically impossible:

> A timeless global culture answers to no living needs and conjures no memories. If memory is central to identity, we can discern no global identity-in-the-making, nor aspirations for one, nor any collective amnesia to replace existing "deep" cultures with a cosmopolitan "flat" culture. The latter remains a dream confined to some intellectuals. It strikes no chord among the vast masses of peoples divided into their habitual communities of class, gender, region, religion and culture. Images, identities, cultures, all express the plurality and particularism of histories and their remoteness from . . . any vision of a cosmopolitan global order.[57]

And if a popular global consciousness does exist, is it or can it be sufficiently institutionalized to become a feasible political alternative to the nation-state form? Or is it merely a cultural or social consciousness that needs to forge a strategic alliance with the nation-state to increase whatever limited political effectivity it has? Should we also not cast a more discriminating eye on the various emergent forms of cosmopolitanism and distinguish them in terms of how they are connected to the operations of neoliberal capital?

The uneven force field of the cosmopolitical has produced and will continue to produce inspiring examples of politically oriented cosmopolitanisms: Amnesty International, Médecins sans Frontières, or the Asian Pacific People's Environmental Network based in Penang, Malaysia, for example. Mainly articulated by intellectuals and activists in both North and South, these cosmopolitanisms deserve support and admiration. But the argument that existing transnational political networks and social movements constitute and are animated by mass-based cosmopolitan solidarities that can displace and replace all the functions of national solidarity despite the erosion and downsizing of the role of the nation-state is questionable. First, the issue of whether these cosmopolitanisms are mass-based even when they initiate or participate in grassroots activities needs to be addressed on a case-by-case basis in terms of the nature of their funding and their structures of participation. Even grassroots feminist NGOs do not represent "all women." Second, although transnational advocacy networks at the grassroots level may be animated by principles that are global in scope, and although they are unconnected to traditional political parties within the national system of electoral democracy or national unions and are able to voice their interests at global forums such as the World Social Forum, it is unclear that the members of these movements and the participants in such forums have transcended feelings of national solidarity or the desire to make their respective nation-states take better care of their peoples. The central concept of food sovereignty—the idea that "every people, no matter how small, has the right to produce their own food"—articulated by the Sem Terra Movement, a movement of landless agrarian workers based in Brazil, indicates that although the goals of the movement are global in scope, it begins from the principle of a people's national integrity.[58] Moreover, the activities of these social movements have to connect with the nation-state at some point because it is the primary site for the effective implementation of equitable objectives for redistribution on a large scale.

It is also vital to distinguish these cosmopolitan activities from transnational underclass migrant communities and their interests. For instance, over and above interventions on behalf of underprivileged migrant minority groups on an ad hoc basis, to what extent can activist cosmopolitanisms take root in such groups in a consistent manner to create a genuinely pluralized mass-based global political community within the Northern constitutional nation-state as distinguished from the defensive identity politics of ethnic, religious, or hybrid minority constituencies? Can these cosmopolitanisms be embedded in a global community in the South forged from transnational media networks? This question leads to the most difficult one of all: In an uneven world, how can struggles for multicultural recognition in constitutional-democratic states in the North be brought into a global alliance with postcolonial activism in the periphery? The possibility of realizing a global civil society or an international public sphere capable of representing or mediating the needs and desires of humanity's radically different constituencies through cross-identifications stands or falls here.

Transnational mobility notwithstanding, it is doubtful whether transnational migrant communities can be characterized as examples of cosmopolitanism in the robust normative sense even after we have acknowledged that this normative dimension is necessarily diluted or compromised by historical contextualization. It is unclear how many of these migrants feel that they belong to a world. Nor has it been ascertained whether this purported feeling of belonging to a world is analytically distinguishable from long-distance, absentee national feeling.[59] In addition, the argument that transnational print and media networks extend a world community beyond transnational migrancy to include peoples dwelling in the South has to reckon with the banal fact that many in the South are illiterate and/or do not have access to television or to hardware capable of receiving CNN and Rupert Murdoch's Asia-based Star TV. Finally, if we recall that the nation is a *mass-based* imagined *political* community, it is unclear whether in the current interstate system the so-called international public sphere or global civil society (names for mass-based global political communities) formed by transnational networks can achieve social redistribution on a global scale without going through the institutions and agencies of the nation-state at some point.[60]

Especially in the postcolonial South, relying on the state as an agent for social development involves changing its political morality, more often than not by counter-official popular nationalism and electoral education of the masses that proceeds from below. As long as the state is mortgaged to global capital and unmoored from its nation-people, talk of social democracy in the South is meaningless. If transnational networks need to work with and through popular nationalism to achieve maximum political effectivity, then one could also describe such activity as nationalisms operating in a cosmopolitical force field rather than mass-based cosmopolitanisms. This would also allow us to exercise due caution with regard to the World Bank's cosmopolitan rhetoric: its utilization of the concept of international civil society to bypass the beleaguered sovereignty of Southern states and dictate adjustment according to the imperatives of global restructuring. Gayatri Spivak calls the non-Eurocentric ecological movement and the women's movement against population control and reproductive engineering "globe-girdling movements" and emphatically distinguishes them from both the international civil society of elite NGOs and the postnationalism of "Northern radical chic."[61] All of the foregoing illustrates that in the cosmopolitical today, even activist cosmopolitanisms are in a conflictual embrace with the popular nationalisms that seem imperative in the postcolonial South. These popular nationalisms cannot afford to refuse the resources and gifts of aid offered by transnational networks. Yet, given their irreducible inscription within the material linkages of global capital, these giving cosmopolitanisms can also unintentionally undermine popular attempts to re-nationalize the state, whose structures and functions have been penetrated and transformed by neoliberal globalization. In other words, because both popular nationalisms and activist cosmopolitanisms alike are engendered from and circumscribed by the uneven and shifting force field of the cosmopolitical, neither is inherently progressive or reactionary. Their normative value derives from their provisional and strategic location within the global force field.

In this chapter I have discussed some arguments from proponents of the new cosmopolitanism from the culturally and societally oriented social sciences which maintain that the decomposition of nation-state functions as a result of global processes provides a basis for the generation of cosmopolitan consciousness. I have suggested that this claim is premature because the partial and uneven character of globalization hampers the formation of mass-based global solidarity. I have also suggested that we need to reflect more carefully on the normative basis of the new cosmopolitanism, especially its connection to economic globalization. The accounts of new cosmopolitanism which I have outlined point to forms of global solidarity such as transnational advocacy networks or human rights instruments and NGOs that exceed the limitations of nationalism while exhibiting a degree of autonomy from the predatory imperatives of economic globalization. Thus, despite their claims of newness for their objects of analysis, these accounts actually rely on the old humanist understanding of normativity as freedom or the ability to transcend or overcome contingent, finite limitations that co-belongs with human cognitive powers such as reason and imagination and their various collective forms. In their view, nationalist particularism and capitalist globalization are temporary historical obstacles to freedom that can be regulated by varieties of new cosmopolitanism from below. Ultimately, such an understanding of normativity cannot account for the constitutive contamination of rational human consciousness by the material conditions that craft it. Perhaps the most difficult and troubling theoretical implication of the persistence of national solidarity and the circumscription of emerging cosmopolitanisms by the uneven global force field in which they are constituted is that it requires us to rethink this humanist understanding of normativity. In the next chapter I take up this question by considering the more erudite account of normativity in Habermas's philosophical postnationalism.

2

Postnational Light

The German philosopher Jürgen Habermas has undertaken what is probably the most systematic exploration of the normative implications of globalization for the realization of a cosmopolitan political project. What is especially valuable about his efforts is that unlike those who argue for global justice in contemporary analytical philosophy, Habermas does not simply evaluate the normative shortcomings of nationalism and/or statism and make pronouncements about what reasonable actors ought to do from a merely abstract or scholastic standpoint.[1] Instead, he has focused on concrete systemic features of globalizing processes to examine whether their institutional forms contain normative elements or empirical consequences conducive to the achievement of a cosmopolitan form of political regulation. In so doing, Habermas has self-consciously assumed the role of heir to the legacy of Kant's moral and political thought. He has attempted to revive Kant's project of cosmopolitan right by removing its obsolete features and deficiencies and affirming its pertinence to the contemporary world.[2] Accordingly, cosmopolitanism for Habermas is not merely an intellectual ethos or "moral outlook," as it generally is in analytical philosophy.[3] It is the progressive extension of universalistic Enlightenment political principles, namely, those of democratic republicanism, into a cosmopolitan regime with a "world domestic policy." This goal can be brought to fruition with the formation of cosmopolitan *Öffentlichkeit,* a public consciousness of cosmopolitan solidarity that will exert pressure on already existing supranational political entities and global actors to regard themselves as members of a cosmopolitan community who should act in cooperation and respect one

45

another's interests.[4] In Habermas's view, globalizing processes contribute to this project. Notwithstanding their oppressive neoliberal orientations, they usher in a "postnational constellation" in which national sovereignty and its requisite particularistic tendencies are rapidly eroding.

Cosmopolitanism, then, is an attempt to give a human face to globalization. Habermas is exemplary in this regard as in his diagnosis of the historical transcendence of nationalism. In this chapter I focus on the uneven character of globalization in order to provide a critical assessment of his arguments that the postnational constellation is conducive to the formation of cosmopolitan solidarity, and that the decline of national sovereignty has positive consequences for the worldwide realization of the universalistic principles of democratic republicanism. A radical questioning of the ideal content of the principles of equality and freedom lies beyond the scope of this discussion. What is in question is the feasibility and efficacy of the institutional form Habermas prescribes for their realization. As he acknowledges, economic globalization creates an unequal world: "One must speak of a 'stratified' world society because the mechanism of the world market couples increasing productivity with growing impoverishment and, more generally, processes of economic development with processes of underdevelopment. Globalization splits the world in two and at the same time forces it to act cooperatively as a community of shared risks [*Risikogemeinschaft*]" (*IO,* 214/ 183). Furthermore, "in a stratified world society, unredeemable conflicts of interest seem to result from the asymmetrical interdependencies between developed nations, newly industrialized nations, and the less developed nations" (*PC,* 87/54). If national forms of solidarity remain important, especially for economically weak countries bearing the brunt of capitalist exploitation, does uneven development constitute a crippling impediment to the formation of cosmopolitan solidarity? Does it place such constraints on the efficacy of cosmopolitanism that we may regard it as a constitutive condition of contemporary arguments for the transcendence of nationalism, the limit beyond which theories of cosmopolitanism lose their coherence and become unworkable?

This chapter is divided into three sections. The first section outlines the key features of Habermas's project of a supranational political regime, paying special attention to its complex relationship with the nation-state form. I then examine how Habermas forecloses the uneven character of global capitalism, especially the contemporary international division of labor, by conflating struggles for multicultural recognition in the scene of North Atlantic migrancy with struggles for economic and political survival in the postcolonial South.[5] This elision of the postcolonial world enables the utopian projection of a model of global political regulation from a prototype derived from the republican welfare state in the economically hegemonic North. Despite the pragmatic postmetaphysical turn of discourse ethics, Habermas's cosmopolitanism contains residues of a philosophy of transcendence. I conclude by proposing an alternative understanding of normativity in a globalizing world that is not based on transcendence. I hope that my argument as a whole will be understood as somewhat different from the pious accusation that Habermas ignores questions of racial or cultural difference because he is European. What his cosmopolitan project ultimately puts at stake is the autonomy of the political itself, perhaps even the freedom we commonly regard as co-belonging with humanity.

Global Democratic Self-Steering and the *Aufhebung* of the Nation-State

The positive connection Habermas makes between globalization and cosmopolitan citizenship is premised on the relative autonomy of the political from the economic. This autonomy enables him to dissociate transnational will-formation from the economic dimension of globalization. Habermas characterizes the separation of the two spheres by means of a neat opposition between two forms of social regulation: the undemocratic logic of money and the market and the democratizable logic of power: "The regulatory power of collectively binding decisions operates according to a different logic than the regulatory mechanisms of the market. Power can be democratized; money cannot. Thus, the possibilities for a democratic self-steering of society slip away as the regulation of social spheres is transferred from one medium [political power] to another [money]" (*PC*, 119–120/78). The democratic character of modern power lies in the fact that in a modern democratic constitutional state, the actions of the administrative-bureaucratic state apparatus can be rationally regulated through collectively binding decisions. In contradistinction, the regulation of society in terms of maximizing market efficiency and profit making is undemocratic because it depends on and generates exploitation, competition, and inequality. Because economic globalization has undermined the territorialized political power of nation-states, human life can be protected from being completely taken over by the logic of money only by establishing new deterritorialized forms of political regulation. It is therefore a matter of reconsolidating the autonomy of the political from the economic. This has to occur at a supranational level in order to match and counteract the global reach of economic processes.

The autonomy of the political should be understood in at least two senses. It refers to a certain independence of the rational processes of political legitimation and participation from the capitalist economic system and the bureaucratic state. But, more important, this independence merely brings out the deeper truth that the democratic political process is the sphere of human freedom itself, understood in the Rousseauian and Kantian sense of self-determination through rational self-legislation. For Habermas, freedom is optimally institutionalized in the democratic process because the latter is the ongoing formation of the opinions and wills of citizens through rational deliberation. This process of *Bildung* generates a solidarity that reproduces itself through political participation. Hence, the democratic process is a form of political auto-causality in which the collective subject of politics repeatedly generates itself through discursive debate and communicative action. This auto-causality is derived from the spontaneous auto-causality of the Kantian moral will, which is always thought in analogy with the self-recursive causality of a self-generating organism in its adaptive interaction with its external environment.[6]

In Habermas's view, the collective political identity will be strong and stable only if the democratic process reconciles the public autonomy of citizens—the principle of (democratic) republicanism—with the prepolitical liberties of private individuals (the principle of liberalism), popular sovereignty, and human rights.[7] This necessary internal link between democratic legitimation and universal human rights, which is established with the post-conventional separation of morality from legality, clearly indicates the cosmopolitan vocation of democracy's normative content. Accordingly, Habermas's cosmopolitanism is organized by the same circular figure of spontaneous auto-causality. We glimpse this figure in the recurring key phrases that give schematic form to his project. For Habermas, "the transnational political project of drawing in and controlling global networks [*Entwurf einer transnationalen Politik des Einholens und Einhegens globaler Netze*]"—Habermas's metaphor is one of fishing nets—ought to be understood in terms of the interaction between a "lifeworld" (a community with a collective identity constituted through mutual understanding, intersubjectively shared norms, and collective values) and "networks" of exchange constituted through market imperatives (*PC*, 124–125/81–82, translation modified). Like an organism, a lifeworld's ability to survive hinges on its capacity to protect itself by controlling its opening and closing in relation to the external world. Hence, it is a matter of developing "new forms for the democratic self-steering of society" that will bring about a "renewed political closure [*Schließung*] of an economically unmastered world society [*Weltgesellschaft*]" (*PC*, 134/88; 167/111).

The autonomy of the political is an old Habermasian theme. It is already present in the early Habermas's celebration of the autonomous spontaneity of the critical public sphere and his critique of Marx for conflating communicative action/interaction with instrumental action/labor under the rubric of social praxis, as well as his arguments for the independence of political structures from capital and the importance of democratic socialism—that is, the progressive democratization of society—for developing a constitutional welfare state to check the excesses of late capitalism.[8] The later postmetaphysical Habermas modifies Kant's ontological understanding of freedom in two ways. First, he unmoors moral normativity from its transcendental anchor in the free will of the moral person by offering a discursive interpretation of the categorical imperative that emphasizes the intersubjective formation of moral agents by rational deliberation over the shared values and traditions of their concrete communities.[9] Second, in his discussion of political and legal freedom, he argues that in post-traditional pluralistic societies where comprehensive worldviews and binding ethics at the prepolitical level have disintegrated, the legitimacy of the legal order can only be grounded in the participatory processes of constitutional democracy that secure both private and public autonomy by protecting social and cultural rights in addition to private individual rights and the public rights of political participation.[10] The intricacies of Habermas's arguments need not detain us. What is important is that he displaces the circular and organismic figure of auto-causality that typifies Kantian freedom into a thick analogy of the moral actor as a self-legislating citizen and an even thicker conception of the autonomous legal subject (the citizen proper). The moral actor exercises "the legislative competence, in which he 'participates' . . . in accordance with the constitution of a political community whose citizens govern themselves" (*IO*, 46/31). The legal subject's quasi-epigenetic capacities include "the jointly exercised autonomy of citizens, and the capacities for rational choice and for ethical self-realization." The citizen's auto-causal character is heightened by the fact that even private individual rights are not prepolitical givens but are elaborated through legally institutionalized procedures of democratic public discussion.[11]

The extension of this reformulated understanding of political freedom to a supranational order requires several additional steps. As Habermas points out, despite its universalistic normative content, democratic republicanism has been realized historically only within the territorial borders of the nation-state. In a multicultural society, a constitutional democratic welfare state espousing a moral universalism sensitive to difference may show equal respect for all its members through "a *nonleveling* and *nonappropriating* inclusion of the other *in his otherness*" (*IO*, 58/40). But such solidarity would still be based on the common culture or collective identity of a particular nation-state, although this culture now takes democratic processes as its focal point, and collective identity is constituted through respect for the constitution. There is therefore a potential tension between republicanism and nationalism. Yet Habermas also disagrees with projects for cosmopolitan democracy that are based solely on the normative ties of human rights as enshrined in UN instruments. He argues that while universal moral norms may in themselves generate a reactive form of cosmopolitan cohesion through feelings of outrage over the violation and repression of human rights, this social cohesion is too weak for the formulation and enforcement of global policies (*PC*, 162/108). Hence, a supranational collective identity needs to be developed and cultivated. But because the *Bildung* of cosmopolitan identity can occur only in analogy with the earlier historical development of national solidarity, Habermas's cosmopolitanism has a complex relationship to the nation-state form that we can describe as one of dialectical sublation (*Aufhebung*): the annulment or annihilation of the national form of solidarity in which its deficiencies are removed and its salutary characteristics are preserved and raised up to a higher, cosmopolitan form of political existence. Let us now look more closely at Habermas's account of the nation-state.

Habermas has a rather Hegelian understanding of nationalism that is continuous with his critique of the abstract nature of (Kantian) moral universalism. Moral judgments are unconditional and context-independent because they demand equal respect for each and every person. Nevertheless, they can be actualized only when they are carried out or acted upon by individuals or groups within the concrete setting of a particular community with its own ethos/ethical life or evaluative self-understanding. By the same token, the universal principles of democratic republicanism can be actualized only in a particular political culture. Historically, it has taken root within the framework of the modern nation-state. The historical achievement of the modern democratic state is that it provides a new mode of legitimation (the popular sovereignty of citizens freely exercising their capacities of will-formation) in the wake of the undermining by secularization of political authority based on divine right. In Habermas's view, what the nation-form contributes is a new abstract form of social integration on which democratic participation can be securely based. National consciousness provides a more concrete (self-)delimitation of the *demos* or people in addition to legalistic citizenship. One can say that the nation is the sexy cultural dressing that makes the modern democratic state more sensuously appealing to its citizens. It gives them a prepolitical unity and instills the feeling of mutual responsibility such that they will be willing to make sacrifices, for example, in redistributive taxation or in military service. As Habermas puts it in a passage that reminds us of Fichte: "Only a national consciousness, crystallized around the notion of a common ancestry, language, and history, only the consciousness of belonging to 'the same' people, makes subjects into citizens of a single political community [*Gemeinwesens*]— into members who can feel responsible *for one another.* The nation or the *Volksgeist,* the unique spirit of the people—the first truly *modern* form of collective identity—provided the cultural basis for the constitutional state" (*IO,* 136–137/113).

The value of the nation, therefore, lies in its capacity for social and political integration, something that is indispensable for the institutionalization of democratic self-determination. This capacity is essentially the power of abstraction, the ability to project artificially a virtual, imagined, or symbolic solidarity between persons who would otherwise be strangers because they are not bound to one another by the daily and familiar face-to-face or immediate encounters that characterize local and kinship relations. But despite surface resemblances, Habermas's understanding of the nation is not the same as Benedict Anderson's much-cited account of the nation as an imagined community.[12] Because Anderson locates the origins of nationalism in the impact of print capitalism in the Spanish Americas, he attributes to nationalism a mass-based, popular spontaneity, draws a sharp distinction between nationalism and racism, and also differentiates national belonging from ethnic identity.[13] In contradistinction, because Habermas's frame of reference is European nationalism, especially the German concept of the *Volksnation,* he suggests that the democratic nation is not the product of popular spontaneity but the conception of intellectuals: "The democratic transformation of the *Adelsnation,* the nation of nobility, into a *Volksnation,* the nation of the people . . . presupposes a deep transformation in consciousness inspired by intellectuals, a transformation first accomplished by the urban, and above all formally educated, middle classes before it found a resonance in the wider population and gradually brought about a political mobilization of the masses" (*IO,* 134/110). I will later consider the Eurocentric consequences of Habermas's understanding of the nation, especially his failure to attend to the importance of radical-popular nationalism in the postcolonial South. For the moment, let us note that because he is anxious about the violent legacy of German nationalism, Habermas, unlike Anderson, suggests that the political concept of the popular nation cannot be completely dissociated from a prepolitical community of descent. It never quite manages to break away from the earlier concept of the nation "as an index of descent and origin" (*IO,* 134/111).[14] Hence, Habermas characterizes national consciousness as Janus-faced and deeply ambivalent. It vacillates between two poles that it contains within itself—the voluntary nation of citizens (*die gewollte Nation der Staatsbürger) qua* agent of democratic legitimation and "the inherited or ascribed nation [*die geborene Nation der Volksgenossen*] founded on ethnic membership that secures social integration" (*IO,* 139/115).

It is important to emphasize that it is not a matter of choosing between two mutually exclusive types of nation, as the conventional moralistic understanding of the "bad" cultural versus the "good" political nation dichotomy has it. These are two tendencies inhering in the modern nation-state, the two sides of an originary aporia sedimented at the moment of its historical constitution. It should be obvious which side of the aporia of nationalism should be preserved and which side should be overcome. From an internal or domestic standpoint, the voluntary nation of citizens leads to a civic patriotism that is compatible with the republican idea of a democratic constitutional state. It reaches its highest development in the social welfare state of OECD countries. The social welfare state, Habermas argues, is the felicitous product of a historically unprecedented positive confluence of capitalism and republican democracy in which capitalism makes it possible to fulfill the republican promise of the equality of all citizens before the law. The liberal principle that "all citizens are to have an equal opportunity to exercise their rights" has equitable-distributive implications that are brought to fruition when the economic wealth produced by capitalist growth enables the construction of the social welfare state.[15] Although the redistributive policies of the welfare state and its provision of benefits, services, and social security may be seen as the undermining of the economic independence of citizens by state planning, they make capitalism's social costs tolerable and enable social integration by offsetting the disruptive consequences of high economic productivity (exploitation, highly unequal distribution of wealth, and intensification of class differences).[16] Considered from an international perspective, constitutional patriotism is also conducive to cosmopolitan will-formation since it is not tied to a closed cultural identity. In contradistinction, a cultural nationalism founded on ethnic membership and based on descent leads to a xenophobic cultural chauvinism that can be used to justify the territorial state's belligerent self-assertion of sovereignty at the international level.

Habermas suggests that from an analytical standpoint, the aporia of nationalism can be resolved by decoupling political identity from cultural identity. In other words, the abstractive solidarity-generating capacity of nationalism must be purified of its cultural elements. This suggestion is misleading because the vacillation in national consciousness is in fact not between a prepolitical cultural identity and a political identity. The aporia is already found within culture (*Kultur*), in the oscillation between the normative and anthropological senses of the word. The abstraction from particularistic ties of kinship and locality crucial to constitutional patriotism requires the cultural-spiritual work of will-formation, that is, identification not through blood and descent but through literature, art, ethics, and other universalistic spiritual products and media that necessarily involve the constructive, artificial (*künstlich*)

powers of the imagination. Culture in this sense is clearly not particularistic or exclusionary. Since it enables identification with what is not
immediate, it puts an end to parochialism by broadening perspectives
and widening the circle of belonging. Even if culture's mediational forms
are rooted in a particular language, language barriers are porous because
languages can be learned and can change as the result of borrowings
from other languages. Culture, however, can also be understood in the
quasi-naturalistic and exclusionary terms of ethnicity, race, and descent.
This particularistic form of culture must be expunged.

Since the aporia is not merely a logical paradox but a consequence of
the historical connection between democratic citizenship and cultural
membership in the nation, it cannot be overcome by mere theoretical in-
genuity or philosophical wisdom. The sundering of political citizenship
from cultural identity depends on a structural transformation of the
conditions that engendered the aporia in the first place. This structural
change, which will lead to the explosion of the nation-form, is what
Habermas terms "the postnational constellation." Ideally, constitutional
patriotism will emerge fully preserved by being raised up to a higher
level where it is no longer a national consciousness but democratic republicanism with a global reach.

We ought to understand the overcoming of the aporia of nationalism
as a reaffirmation of the autonomy of the political in an even stronger
sense than either independence from external influences or Kantian self-
determination. It is nothing other than the liberation of the universalistic normative content of the democratic process in the same way that
Marx spoke of the gradual historical liberation of productive forces from
capital—their freeing through the removal of the external barriers or
contingent historical limitations that restrict them:

> The means of production and of exchange, on whose foundation the
> bourgeoisie built itself up, were generated in feudal society. At a certain
> stage in the development of these means . . . the feudal relations of
> property became no longer compatible with the already developed pro-
> ductive forces. They restricted production instead of advancing it [*Sie
> hemmten die Produktion statt sie zu fördern*]. They became so many fet-
> ters. They had to be exploded [*gesprengt*]; they were exploded.
>
> Into their place stepped free competition, accompanied by a social
> and political constitution adapted to it, and by the economical and po-
> litical sway of the bourgeois class.

A similar movement is going on before our own eyes. . . . The productive forces at the disposal of society no longer tend to further the development of the conditions of bourgeois property; on the contrary, they have become too powerful for these conditions, by which they are restricted [*gehemmt*], and so soon as they overcome these restrictions [*Hemmnis*], they bring disorder into the whole of bourgeois society, endanger the existence of bourgeois property.[17]

The operative logic in Marx's passage is Hegelian rather than Kantian, not the abstract self-determination of moral willing but the teleology of freedom's concrete self-actualization through the self-conscious negation of all finite limitations obstructing it. In Hegel's formulation, spirit's "freedom does not consist in static being, but in a constant negation of all that threatens to destroy freedom."[18] In other words, the liberation of the democratic process on a global scale requires that it be spliced to a dialectic of transcendence. Just as Marx had argued that the globalization of markets and production was a necessary condition of the worldwide proletarian revolution because it brought an end to national parochialism, so too for Habermas, the actualization of democracy's universalistic normative content in a supranational shape derives its efficacy from the energies of globalization. Its dialectic takes the form of a narrative of historical progress in which modernization involves increasing degrees of complexity, pluralization, and rationalization of human life. First, the nation-state as a higher, more abstract form of social integration and political solidarity replaces the legitimation of political authority through divine right and corporative social ties. But civic patriotism remains tied to the quasi-naturalistic entity of the cultural nation, which carries mystical residues from the feudal period because the *Volk* is "a prepolitical fact . . . , that is, something independent of and prior to the political opinion- and will-formation of the citizens themselves" (*IO*, 139/115). This limitation must now be removed.

The dialectic Habermas sketches is, however, considerably weaker than that of the proletarian revolution. The latter is the endpoint of the exponential development of productive forces. In contradistinction, the actualization of democratic processes with a global reach depends on the historical felicity of the postnational constellation. In Habermas's view, the curse of globalization turns out to be a potential blessing in disguise. For globalization is not reducible to global capitalism. It has relatively autonomous cultural and political aspects, and these create the conditions for an *Aufhebung* (sublation or transcendence) whereby the earlier national shell that imprisoned democratic republicanism will be destroyed and its kernel or truth-content, preserved in the form of deliberative democratic procedures, may rise up phoenix-like to a higher supranational state of existence.[19] First, the homogeneous national-cultural base of civil-political solidarity, which is already undermined by the global dissemination of mass culture, is further eroded by economically driven South-to-North and East-to-West migration, which changes the ethnic, religious, and cultural composition of European nations. While this cultural pluralization or multiculturalization of society can lead to populist ethnocentrism and xenophobic conflict, it is in fact a boon. Xenophobic conflicts and the tyranny of the hegemonic cultural majority can be controlled only by the construction of a multicultural civil society that respects the differences of minority cultures. Hence, transnational migration, Habermas argues, actually accelerates the decoupling of political culture from the prepolitical identity of the majority cultural group so that it can be completely coextensive with the public-discursive democratic process.[20] Second, following Ulrich Beck's thesis of the rise of a world risk society, Habermas suggests that political solidarity is also decoupled from its national base by the creation of globally shared risks such as ecological and environmental damage, or international organized crime such as the traffic in arms, drugs, and women. Because the political interests of the people affected by these global issues will no longer be coextensive with the territorially based decisions of nation-states, these actions will suffer from a legitimation deficit.[21] Third, the growing number of regulatory political institutions and forms of cooperation at various levels beyond the nation-state that attempt to compensate for its declining competencies suggest the blurring of the distinction between foreign and domestic policy, thereby indicating the irreversible development of a genuinely global politics (*PC*, 108–109/70–71). These bodies range from the United Nations and its agencies to international regimes, some more tightly organized than others, such as the North American Free Trade Association (NAFTA), the Association of Southeast Asian Nations (ASEAN), and the European Union, as well as informal networks of NGOs. Finally, the increasing proliferation of human rights instruments indicates the emergence of a weak form of cosmopolitan solidarity, that of a quasi-legal community of world citizens.

These phenomena are certainly necessary components of the external framework or "hardware" of democratic cosmopolitanism because they point to the imminent removal of the external limitations to the cosmopolitan reach of democracy. But by themselves they are not sufficient conditions for the creation of a truly democratic cosmopolitanism. On the one hand, the solidarity of world citizens grounded solely in the moral universalism of human rights is too weak to generate the cohesion required for the implementation of global policies. On the other hand, existing international and supranational institutions are neither cosmopolitan nor democratic. They are lacking in democratic legitimation because they constitute an international negotiation system whereby compromises are reached through power politics and instrumental reasoning as opposed to the deliberative procedures and common values and conceptions of justice, that is, the shared ethico-political self-understanding available in negotiations within the organizational framework of a state (PC, 163/109). The idea of cosmopolitan solidarity also does not inform the self-understanding of governments, which participate in these negotiations from the standpoint of furthering national interests.

We ought to understand Habermas's title "The Postnational Constellation and the Future of Democracy" in light of the original meaning Theodor Adorno gave to the term "constellation": a group of concepts or objects surrounding an object of investigation that can help us understand the historical process sedimented within it. Adorno writes: "The history locked in the object can only be delivered by a knowledge mindful of the historic positional value of the object in relation to other objects. . . . Cognition of the object in its constellation is cognition of the process stored in the object. As a constellation, theoretical thought circles the object it would like to unseal, hoping that it may fly open like the lock of a well-guarded safe-deposit: in response, not to a single key or a single number, but to a combination of numbers."[22] For Habermas, Öffentlichkeit is the agent for unlocking democracy's cosmopolitan vocation. It is the implicit truth of the postnational constellation's component phenomena. He argues that the twin deficits of democratic legitimation and cosmopolitan solidarity can be solved by a dynamic complex of interconnected public spheres at both the national and transnational level. Electoral and representative democratic structures for a world citizenry may not exist. But in addition to political participation and the expression of the political will, democratic will-formation (*Willensbildung*) also involves the public use of reason (*der öffentliche Vernunftsgebrauch*). Hence, "a functioning public sphere [*Öffentlichkeit*], the quality of discussion, accessibility, and the discursive structure of opinion- and will-formation" can confer democratic legitimacy on existing institutions beyond the nation-state (*PC*, 166/110–111). Similarly, the shift in perspective on the part of states so that they will self-identify as members of a cosmopolitan community and view international relations as world domestic policy instead of acting according to selfish national interests depends on the development of cosmopolitan consciousness on a mass scale within populations that will then pressure their governments to alter their self-understandings through their respective national public spheres (*PC*, 88/55; 167–168/111–112).

Habermas's focus on a global public sphere updates Kant's prescient argument about the rise of a global public sphere in his cosmopolitan project. In Kant's view, one can speak of the existence of cosmopolitan right (*Weltbürgerrecht*) "insofar as individuals and states, standing in the relation of externally affecting one another, are to be regarded as citizens of a universal state of mankind [*eines allgemeinen Menschenstaats*] (*ius cosmopoliticum*)."[23] As we saw in the previous chapter, Kant argued that the unity brought about by world trade and other forms of interaction between states creates something like a functioning global public sphere that will safeguard cosmopolitan right by protesting any violations of it in the same manner that a critical national public sphere safeguards the rights of citizens vis-à-vis the territorial state. Habermas suggests that such a global public sphere is now being formed through global communications. Examples of its emergence and development stretch from the polarized global public debates over the Vietnam War and the Persian Gulf war (and we may now add the U.S. invasion of Iraq) to the series of UN-organized conferences on important global issues such as poverty, population growth, and the status of women. "These 'global summits,'" he writes, "can be interpreted as so many attempts to bring at least some political pressure to bear on governments simply by thematizing problems important for human survival for the worldwide public, that is, by an appeal to world opinion" (*IO*, 205/176–177). Although the global public attention elicited here is channeled through national public sphere structures and is issue-specific and temporary, the ability of the international civil society of transnational NGOs to create and mobilize transnational public spheres through press and media coverage indicates the beginnings of more permanent communicative structures for genuine global debate (*IO*, 205–206/177). Such NGO participation gives greater legitimacy to the deliberations of international negotiating systems by making them transparent for national public spheres and reconnecting them to grassroots decision making (*PC*, 166–167/111).

In summary, Habermas regards the contemporary conjuncture as postnational in three related senses. First, it is culturally postnational because the homogeneous national culture that had historically sustained democratic citizenship has, in many cases, undergone pluralization. This has in turn led to the need for constitutional norms that enable the coexistence of different subcultures and forms of religious life, that is, for multicultural recognition that upholds social and cultural rights. Second, it is politically postnational in that many issues requiring political regulation and, hence, the political interests of citizens of every country now exceed the territorial borders of the nation-state. This indicates the need for alternative political institutions beyond the sovereign state as well as the need to supply existing international regimes and looser international arrangements and networks such as IGOs (intergovernmental organizations) and NGOs with a genuinely supranational procedure of legitimation. Finally, it is normatively postnational in that the supranational institutions that will ideally grow out of this conjuncture will propel relations between nation-states from an anarchic pursuit of self-interests analogous to a state of nature (Hobbes) or a prepolitical condition of private persons engaged in the atomistic pursuit of self-interest in the marketplace (Hegel's view of civil society) into a state of cooperative self-legislation. The model for the supranational institutionalization of the democratic process Habermas describes is not that of a world organization. Instead, it emphasizes the importance of democratizing the processes of international negotiation that lead to agreements between states through global *Öffentlichkeit*. Insofar as such processes connect internal nation-state politics to policies of world organization, global *Öffentlichkeit* exploits existing structures for the formation of solidarity in national public spheres to further develop cosmopolitan solidarity in individual citizens and foster a world domestic policy on the part of state actors.

Prototypical Eurocentrism and the New International Division of Labor

I have argued that in Habermas's cosmopolitan project, global democratic processes can be successfully institutionalized only if regulatory political structures with a global reach can be in an intimate relation of mutual feedback with a cosmopolitan political consciousness such that cosmopolitan consciousness can take root within and be sustained by supranational political institutions at the same time as it influences their functioning. Both are joined together through the mediation of various overlapping transnational public spheres. The self-reflexivity of this model is a relay of the self-recursive, auto-causal character of freedom.

The feasibility of Habermas's model is premised on the existence of globalizing processes that are autonomous from the logic of capitalist accumulation. But this premise is questionable. As we have seen, Habermas makes his case for the realization of democracy's cosmopolitan vocation through a series of transpositions that recast in supranational terms organizational forms and institutional mechanisms that have historically been tied to the nation-state, such as ethico-political solidarity, the welfare state, and the public sphere. Their efficacy for achieving the universal principles of constitutional democracy, however, is closely connected to their location in the economically hegemonic North. This is most obvious in the case of the welfare state of OECD countries. Its ability to provide social security and redistribution comes from the high economic productivity of these countries, a direct consequence of their powerful positions within the global economy. Hence, we must ask whether the key features of Habermas's cosmopolitan project, formulated as it is by abstracting from "prototypical" evidence from the sociohistorical situation of the North Atlantic and the European experience of globalization, can retain their efficacy in other scenes of globalization. Two related questions arise here. First, despite the postnational spirit of Habermas's arguments, have they in fact not left the borders of Europe because the prototypical institutions he prescribes are Eurocentric projections? Second, how effective are these projections considered within the context of the economic stratification of global society? Conversely, does his focus on the overcoming of national solidarity and the importance of transnational *Öffentlichkeit* in the procedures of international agreements have unfortunate consequences for countries in the postcolonial South, on the other side of the international division of labor?

I should stress from the outset that I am not dismissing Habermas's arguments by means of a genetic fallacy. His arguments are not contaminated and compromised by their point of origin. The fact that they are based on prototypical evidence from the North Atlantic and that Habermas writes from the perspective of Europe's experience of globalization does not necessarily mean that his ideas cannot have a general validity and applicability. My point is simply that unless we begin to examine some of their concrete implications within other scenarios, his arguments remain lofty predictions or grand statements that are untested. By analyzing them within the framework of the international division of labor, I am only reformulating Albrecht Wellmer's earlier observation about Habermas's theory of communicative action: "Every communalist, as long as he unmistakably wants to side with the Enlightenment tradition, has to come to terms with the fact that modern bourgeois society is the paradigmatic society of the Enlightenment in the modern world: the only society in which human rights, the rule of law, public freedom, and democratic institutions have to some extent become safely institutionalized."[24] Wellmer's astute remark points to the historical connection between bourgeois capitalism and communitarian theories based on Enlightenment ideals. What I am questioning is the historical connection between uneven globalization and theories of cosmopolitan democracy. In other words, is the international division of labor the unacknowledged condition and therefore also the non-transcendable limit of Habermas's cosmopolitan project and the efficacy of its institutional prototypes?

The Eurocentrism of Habermas's cosmopolitanism lies in his magnifying projection of two prototypes on a global scale: multicultural recognition in metropolitan migrancy and the First World constitutional welfare state. Struggles for multicultural recognition undoubtedly point to the erosion of the homogeneous national culture of the dominant majority in European nation-states as a result of transnational migration and the importance of decoupling political solidarity from this dominant culture. Focusing on multiculturalism, however, also enables one to be postnationalist while staying within the borders of Europe. It enables one to bid farewell to German cultural nationalism without leaving Germany, on the grounds that the German population itself has become culturally cosmopolitan. The cultural consequences of globalization are then examined only in the attenuated form of multicultural diversity, which is read under the sociological sign of the pluralization of North Atlantic societies as a result of global mass migration. As we have seen, this pluralization is now regarded as a blessing because it leads to the refinement of the constitutional democratic state so that it will recognize claims to cultural rights in addition to individual liberal rights. Indeed, Habermas seems to understand all social movements as equivalent struggles for cultural recognition or the affirmation of a collective identity:

> Feminism, multiculturalism, nationalism, and the struggle against the Eurocentric heritage of colonialism are related . . . in that women, ethnic and cultural minorities, and nations and cultures defend themselves against oppression, marginalization, and disrespect and thereby struggle for the recognition of collective identities, whether in the context of a majority culture or within the community of peoples. We are concerned here with emancipation movements *whose collective political goals are defined primarily in cultural terms,* even though social and economic inequalities as well as political dependencies are always also involved. (*IO*, 246/211, emphasis added)[25]

This culturalist understanding of decolonization is unfortunate because it glosses over the economic and political aspects of popular struggles for emancipation in the postcolonial South, namely, the struggle for freedom against repressive political regimes that are complicit with transnational capital and the broader struggle for economic justice in an uneven world. Moreover, the conflation of postcolonial struggles with multiculturalism allows Habermas to export European multiculturalism to the rest of the world by prescribing the cosmopolitan identities formed by South-North migration as a paradigm for forging genuinely cosmopolitan relations between countries on a global stage. The interminable "intercultural contacts and multiethnic connections" arising from global migration, he writes, "[strengthen] a trend toward individualization and the emergence of 'cosmopolitan identities,' already evident in postindustrial societies" (*PC*, 116/75–76). We can see the seamless connection between Northern multiculturalism and cosmopolitan democracy if we remember that for Habermas, the development of a world domestic policy depends on the cultivation of a cosmopolitan self-understanding on the part of individual states by their already cosmopolitan-minded citizens. It would, of course, be a good thing if global politics could be organized along the lines of a magnified multicultural constitutional democracy, provided this would also include respect for the economic rights of all peoples. The problem is that the new cosmopolitan subjects of Northern multiculturalism can already rely on an existing organizational framework for the regulation of social and political conflict and economic redistribution that is lacking for the world as a whole. Cultural hybridization alone will not establish this framework on a global scale.

This brings us to the second Eurocentric projection. Although Habermas's model for global democratic self-steering is that of a world domestic policy without a world state, its key features are extrapolated from the Northern constitutional welfare state and the European Union. Habermas justifies this extrapolation on the basis of the relative peace and stability of First World countries. They are not plagued by national, ethnic, or religious conflict and disintegration (as in Third World countries) or by social instabilities that are held together by authoritarian constitutions (as in Second World countries) (*IO*, 215/184). The many admirable characteristics of a First World state include "the increasing irrelevance of territorial disputes and the tolerance of internal pluralism; . . . the increasing fusion of domestic and foreign policy; the sensitivity to the influence of liberal public spheres; the renunciation of military force as a means of solving conflicts and the juridification of international relations; and finally, the preference for partnerships that base security on the transparency and reliability of expectations." Hence, in a stratified world, the model for cosmopolitan democracy can only come from the already cosmopolitan First World state. "Only the states of the First World can afford to harmonize their national interests to a certain extent with the norms that define the half-hearted cosmopolitan aspirations of the UN," writes Habermas. "The First World thus defines so to speak the meridian of a present by which the political simultaneity of economic and cultural nonsimultaneity is measured" (*IO*, 215/184). It is important to emphasize that Habermas does not minimize or brush aside the serious obstacles posed by social tensions, political inequality, and economic disparity at the global level. But in his view, these problems can be overcome through a consensus among the community of nations over the need for peaceful coexistence based on mutual cultural respect and a shared understanding of human rights. Such a consensus would lead to the development of global processes of democratization which would be implemented through strategies of "nonviolent intervention" that seek to "influence the internal affairs of formally sovereign states with the goal of promoting self-sustaining economies and tolerable social conditions, democratic participation, the rule of law, and cultural tolerance" (IO, 216/185). The two crucial conditions for implementing global democracy are therefore symbolic parity among all nation-states and the ability of the various national public spheres to pressure their states to adopt cosmopolitan policies.

Habermas's goodwill is not in question here. Nevertheless, his proposal for overcoming the divisions of world society is unfeasible for three reasons. First, it relies on a utopian overidealization of the cosmopolitan virtues of the First World state. In view of the U.S. war in Iraq, one could argue that the world's remaining superpower fails to meet any of the criteria that Habermas uses to define a First World country. Second, these criteria that make the First World welfare state the ideal model of political self-steering depend on a high degree of economic development that cannot be attained in the postcolonial South because its capacities have been actively deformed by the structures of the global economy. As Samir Amin has argued, "Accumulation on a world scale produces structures that are not conducive to struggles like those that occurred in the West."[26] In the center, the crystallization of hegemonic bourgeois power involves the generating of a broad social consensus by means of a Fordist organization of the mechanized labor process (ensuring mass production) and a social-democratic or Keynsian wages policy (ensuring an expanding outlet for this mass production). This consensus, which confines class struggle to the economic division of the fruits of capitalism, provides the very foundation that makes possible the operation of electoral democracy as we know it.[27] In contradistinction, because the periphery is constituted in a world system unfavorable to the enlargement of overall social integration, Fordism there is not accompanied by working-class social democracy. Instead, "the constraints of modern technology, essential for competitiveness, demand the massive importation of equipment, know-how and capital that is [offset] . . . by a willingness to pay industrial labour at much lower rates so as to be able to export. Unequal exchange finds a logical place here."[28] Postcolonial states forced to undergo structural adjustment, especially those in Africa and Latin America, are too impoverished to provide social welfare to their citizens. Worse still, states adopting the neoliberal path of export-oriented industrial development actively sacrifice the welfare of their people to provide conditions to attract transnational capital flows. This scenario is not exactly friendly to any of the three aspects of democratic will-formation (political participation, the expression of political will, or the public use of reason) which Habermas desires and celebrates.

Finally, while a degree of mass-based cosmopolitan solidarity has a-risen in the domestic domains of Northern countries in response to exceptionally violent events such as the Vietnam War, the Rwandan genocide, and the war in Iraq, it is unlikely that this solidarity will be directed in a concerted manner toward ending economic inequality between countries because Northern civil societies derive their prodigious strength from this inequality. Indeed, we can even say that global economic inequality is simultaneously the material condition of possibility of democratic legitimation in the North Atlantic and that which hampers its achievement in the postcolonial South. What I am broaching here is the connection between regulatory political structures and economic globalization. Habermas's cosmopolitan project is plausible only because he forecloses the irreducible imbrication of his normative prototypes in global capitalist relations through repeated assertions of the autonomy of the political. Let us now consider a key mechanism and expression of global inequality, the new international division of labor, so that we can resituate Habermas's account of cosmopolitan *Öffentlichkeit*.

A postnational understanding of Germany that does not just remain within its borders should also have focused on the transnationalization of German industrial production:

> The Federal German textile and garment industries represent one of the best-known examples of such relocations [of production]. Trousers for the Federal German market are no longer produced for example in Mönchengladback, but in the Tunisian subsidiary of the same Federal German company. The process of relocation is also gaining momentum in other branches of industry. Injection pumps which were formerly made for the Federal German market by a Federal German company in Stuttgart are now manufactured partly to the same end by the same company at a site in India. Television sets are produced on the same ba-

sis by another company in Taiwan; car radio equipment in Malaysia, car engines in Brazil, watches in Hong Kong, electronic components in Singapore and Malaysia all fall into the same category.

The Federal German worker rendered unemployed by the relocation of production has been replaced by a newly hired worker in a foreign subsidiary of "his" or "her" own company.[29]

This description of another kind of postnational Germany comes from *The New International Division of Labour* (1977), the classic study of a new dynamic of the global stratification of labor based on empirical research on the relocation of production outside the European Economic Community (EEC) by Federal German industrial companies in various economic sectors. Its key ideas are now axiomatic in the social sciences. Simply put, three developments in the character of the means and forces of production have caused a structural change in the system of capital accumulation: the availability of an inexhaustible reservoir of disposable cheap labor in developing countries; the decomposition and fragmentation of the production process into partial operations that can be undertaken with minimal skills which can be taught in a very short time; and the development of transportation and communications technologies that make it possible to produce goods anywhere in the world without organizational and cost disadvantages. Because of the high cost of labor in the traditional centers of industrial production, the greatest maximization of profits necessitates the relocation of industrial production to the developing peripheries. What is created is a truly global production process. Since industrial production can take place anywhere and is easily relocated overnight, labor and production sites are bought and sold in a competitive global market where labor prices and production costs have to be kept low to attract transnational capital (*NIDL*, 13–14). What is generated is a qualitatively new international division of labor (NIDL) in which Third World countries are no longer just the suppliers of agricultural and mineral raw materials. Through foreign direct investment and international subcontracting, developing countries are now also sites for the production of manufactured goods for export to a world market, especially goods requiring intensive labor, even as research and development and the technical and managerial control of production remain in the centers of the world economy.

This outsourcing of production is the underside of South-North labor migration and an important cause of its contemporary acceleration.

The earlier stage of outsourcing, when production was moved to countries with close geographic and commercial ties to the industrial centers (such as from the United States to Western Europe and Latin America or from Western Europe to Ireland, Greece, Portugal, and southern Italy), was also accompanied by "the appearance of *Gastarbeiter* [guest workers] in Western Europe, and Mexican and Puerto Rican immigrant workers in the USA" (*NIDL*, 14). The subsequent relocation of production to export-oriented production zones beyond European borders establishes even stronger channels for the entry of migrant workers seeking to escape the extreme poverty of the peripheries. As Saskia Sassen has observed, "The strong presence of foreign firms facilitates access to information and a sense of familiarity with the potential destination," thereby removing the deterrence of distance by giving the "promised land" a more imaginable, sensuous presence.[30] The NIDL is thus the catalyst for contemporary European multicultural migrancy. The pluralization of European national cultures is its symptom.

As Habermas correctly notes, the more recent neoliberal dispensation of the NIDL has led to a weakening of the welfare state in OECD countries. Increased capital mobility has reduced the state's access to profits and wealth through taxation. Financial and tax incentives offered to corporations to slow down capital flight have to be offset by a downsizing of the administrative state. What is obscured, however, is that the social recklessness of neoliberal globalization is borne unevenly across the globe. Despite the structural unemployment it has caused in OECD countries, the NIDL has also generated high levels of the economic wealth that had buttressed the social welfare state in the first place. For instance, the German state played an active role in promoting the NIDL and global inequality. In 1962 it established the Deutsche Entwicklungsgesellschaft, a financial institution that encouraged and assisted private corporations to invest in developing countries through direct participation and equity loans because the profitability of these corporations strengthened the German economy (*NIDL*, 167–168). As the Entwicklungsgesellschaft notes in one annual report: "The possibility of seizing such opportunities for investment and putting them at the disposal of the German economy can only be grasped by private oriented development aid. We regard the particular task of our agency as being this form of active, formative development policy."[31] This economic strength is something that the state can fall back on in leaner times to support its welfare functions. Moreover, existing structures of labor unionization maintain tolerable labor conditions in OECD countries despite the pressure of neoliberal globalization.

The NIDL has more devastating consequences for countries in the periphery. Although export-oriented industrialization is justified as a solution to underdevelopment on the grounds that it creates new jobs and eliminates unemployment, provides training for a skilled industrial workforce and gives access to modern technology, and increases foreign exchange reserves, it is in fact a form of superexploitation that largely benefits multinationals and deepens global economic divisions. Multinationals are given preferential treatment such as tariff-, tax-, and currency-related privileges that are unavailable to local industry outside the export production zone. Workers are paid extremely low wages and have no fringe benefits such as social security contributions or paid leave. But worse still, workers have no political and social rights in these zones. The training of skilled workers and the transfer of technology is limited because the techniques of production are elementary and new manufacturing processes are centrally controlled by the multinationals, which utilize expatriate staff when complex techniques are involved. The high profits generated do not benefit the local economy because capital can be easily repatriated or sent elsewhere, since restrictions on foreign investment and capital transfers are negligible. Consequently, Folker Fröbel and his colleagues argue that export-oriented industrialization only intensifies the dependent development of developing countries.[32]

This pessimistic diagnosis needs to be qualified in view of East Asian hyperdevelopment, whereby countries such as South Korea, Taiwan, and Singapore have managed to achieve high levels of growth by carving out a niche for themselves within the NIDL. Nevertheless, the question remains: Since the NIDL and any development within its framework is based on competition between different countries to supply the cheapest labor and production costs to attract foreign capital, how can the superexploitation of labor in the periphery and global economic inequality be overcome? The struggle for an economic edge necessarily generates regional divisions and inequality among developing countries and intensifies the more general inequality between capital-investing and capital-receiving countries. Habermas is aware of this problem. He stresses that a genuine postnational political project cannot be confined to the creation of a broadened regional economic base that will give one regime an edge over others in global competitiveness. It must aim at "the gradual elimination of the social divisions and stratification of world society without prejudice to cultural specificity."[33] Otherwise, "the creation of larger political units leads to defensive alliances opposed to the rest of the world, but does not change the *pattern* of competition between countries and continents as such. It does not *per se* bring about a change of mode, replacing adaptation to the transnational system of world economy by an effort to exert political influence over its overall frame."[34]

Habermas fails, however, to address the tenacity of global competition and the profound effects of the NIDL. Instead, he glosses over the economic dimension of globalization by asserting the autonomy of the political dimension of globalization, the existing tendencies toward the formation of a cosmopolitan consciousness, and the contributions made by multiculturalism to cosmopolitan *Bildung*. The weakness of his solution is twofold. First, a cosmopolitan consciousness formed in North Atlantic space that is attentive to struggles for multicultural recognition is not necessarily concerned with the problems of uneven development and the superexploitation of labor in the peripheries. The difficulties and injustices experienced in Northern multicultural migrant space—struggles over citizenship rights, problems of internal colonization, racism and discrimination within a constitutional framework where justice will be done in the best scenario—are not continuous with the struggles for subsistence of former compatriots left behind on the other side of the NIDL. At its best, multicultural recognition will regulate the conflict between "indigenous" or local labor and migrant labor by redefining national membership in an inclusive manner that is sensitive to the cultural differences of migrants. But for the formation of a global labor movement that is sensitive to the exploitation of labor in general regardless of its location, the apparent conflict between national and outsourced production must first be removed. As it is, a quasi-protectionist anxiety over outsourcing is a key issue in the relationship between the electorate and the state in OECD countries. It is moreover unclear whether cultural minorities who have achieved multicultural recognition will naturally be sensitive to the plight of their former compatriots in the peripheries. It is more likely that they will be driven by the desire for upward class mobility and will become the new bearers of the imperatives of national and regional economic competition. The example of Asian American entrepreneurship shows that Americans of South Asian, Chinese, or Vietnamese heritage are often in the vanguard of outsourcing initiatives in their countries of origin, justifying superexploitation in the name of transnational ethnic solidarity. The NRI (nonresident Indian) businessman or multinational executive professes diasporic patriotism as he sets up call centers in India, just as the diasporic Chinese investor who exploits cheap female labor in southern Chinese factories wishes to benefit people in his ancestral village. Second, Habermas's argument about the formation of a popular cosmopolitan consciousness within domestic civil society and public sphere structures that will exert internal pressure on states to adopt a global domestic policy ignores the formative power that the NIDL has in relation to those domestic civil society structures. The economic well-being of an OECD nation-state and its ability to provide social welfare, two important criteria in democratic legitimation, derive from its position within the hierarchy of the NIDL. This means that global competition has renationalizing effects at the level of civil society that are antithetical to the formation of popular cosmopolitan consciousness.

What does the productive power of uneven economic globalization in the formation of political solidarity and cultural consciousness imply for the efficacy of cosmopolitan *Öffentlichkeit,* the second component of Habermas's solution to global economic inequality? This component was supposed to overcome conflicts of interest between countries by working at the level of international negotiations to confer democratic legitimacy on existing supranational political institutions and agreements. In Habermas's words: "In a stratified world society, unredeemable conflicts of interest seem to result from the asymmetrical interdependencies between developed nations, newly industrialized nations, and the less developed nations. But this perception is only correct as long as there are no institutionalized procedures of transnational will-formation that could induce globally competent actors to broaden their individual preferences into a 'global governance'" (*PC,* 87/54). Here, emphasis was placed on the democratizability of existing supranational institutions based on two examples: UN summit conferences on issues of global survival and the weak but increasing legitimating power of an international civil society of NGOs that participate in the deliberations of international negotiating systems. The efficacy of cosmopolitan *Öffentlichkeit* for the achievement of global democracy, however, becomes more problematic and compromised in view of the infrastructural character of the NIDL. It is well known that instead of bringing about economic redistribution and promoting all-around economic growth, international economic bodies and the "cooperative" agreements they orchestrate, such as the WTO and GATT (General Agreement on Tariffs and Trade), make up a transnational capitalist superstructure that institutionalizes uneven economic relations between states and reproduces the conditions for global capitalist accumulation. As Fröbel and his colleagues put it:

> However much the transnational valorisation and accumulation of capital may take advantage of national disparities (in infrastructure, corporate taxation, wage levels, labour legislation etc.), the expansion and deepening of transnational reproduction nonetheless requires certain elements of an international superstructure. These elements include, for example, the rudiments of institutionalised multilateral or bilateral cooperation in monetary and trade policies (IMF, GATT); tax agreements to avoid double taxation; treaties for investment protection; increasing the compatibility of training and education; international military cooperation; [and] "neutral" international organisations which pave the way for transnational capital under the guise of supplying technical and managerial expertise for "development" (World Bank, UNIDO, FAO). (*NIDL*, 36–37)

UN summits are not organic components of this transnational superstructure. Nevertheless, participating government agencies represent the particularistic interests of their respective states in maintaining and improving their competitiveness for development purposes. The NGOs attending these forums are supposed to constitute an international civil society that represents cosmopolitan-popular interests which do not have to be tied to any particular nation. But the voices of more radical NGOs engaging in direct advocacy at the grassroots level are inevitably underrepresented in these summits. They are vetted and screened out by the authorization and funding structures that form the mise-en-scène of these meetings. The more acceptable, professionalized NGOs become Janus-faced organizations. They are at once surrogates or "sub-contractors" for the provision of welfare services that should have been the responsibility of the state and proxies for civil society.[35] In this situation, so-called international civil society can be co-opted as an ideological alibi. Its activities can be used to dress up Northern hegemony in the garb of cosmopolitan democracy, notwithstanding the benevolent intentions of NGOs. Hence, despite Habermas's stringent critique of neoliberalism, his faith in the cosmopolitan public sphere of international civil society can serve to mystify global market relations, giving neoliberalism a warmer face by cosmetically disguising it as socially responsible liberalism.[36] As David Hulme and Michael Edwards note:

> The dangers of imposing foreign models (economic or political) on other societies have been well documented. . . . With increased funding from Northern governments, NGOs are now in danger of being used in precisely this way, especially where large numbers of new organizations are being formed on the back of readily available donor funds, with weak social roots and no independent supporter base. . . . Is this really strengthening civil society, or merely an attempt to shape civil society in ways that external actors believe is desirable? Will it promote sustainable forms of democracy?[37]

The susceptibility of international civil society to co-optation by transnational capital is exacerbated if one accepts Habermas's argument about the need to transcend nationalism. To recapitulate, for Habermas, the decoupling of constitutional patriotism from national cultural identity is part of a larger dialectic of the self-actualization of the democratic process, its liberation from all the limitations that fetter its cosmopolitan vocation. His argument is fundamentally Eurocentric, however. Its implicit point of reference is the North Atlantic welfare state, and it glosses over the effects of the NIDL. Transcending the nationalism of the hegemonic nation-states of the North Atlantic may be desirable because their national self-interests are formed by and seek to maintain the inequality generated by the NIDL. But as I argued in the previous chapter, in postcolonial space, where the establishment of the welfare state is thwarted by corrupt bourgeois political regimes and structural adjustment policies, a popular nationalism that takes shape within the national public sphere and presses against the state to bend it toward popular interests is crucial for social development. Here, uneven development and the historical legacy of anti-imperialist struggles can lead to the formation of positive forms of national identity that are not inevitably fundamentalist or authoritarian in character. In other words, national culture and national self-determination need to be understood in terms other than that of the self-assertion of a chauvinistic prepolitical identity. Following the work of Frantz Fanon and Amilcar Cabral, national self-determination can be understood as a people's achievement of collective dignity so that it can participate as an equal member in democratic self-legislation on the global stage. To the extent that it obscures the strategic importance of popular postcolonial nationalism, Habermasian postnational light unwittingly replicates the economic stratification of the world by transnational capital at the symbolic level of theoretical production. Its utopian celebration of international civil society can be deployed by transnational capital to bypass and further undermine the struggles of beleaguered postcolonial peoples for economic and political self-determination.

The Technics of *Öffentlichkeit*

I have argued that the burden of Habermas's project of global democracy is borne by a cosmopolitan *Öffentlichkeit* made up of interconnected public spheres at the national and transnational levels. The autonomy of the political lies in the ability of communicative action to influence and regulate the global capitalist economy by imparting democratic legitimation and cosmopolitan values to existing supranational institutions and international political agreements. I have also suggested that Habermas's vision of global democratic politics is indelibly marked by a Eurocentric gaze that takes the North Atlantic welfare state as its reference point and forecloses both the constitutive connection between the welfare state and the NIDL as well as the devastating effects of the latter in the postcolonial peripheries. The NIDL's constitutive power undermines the autonomy of the political at various levels. At the supranational level, international civil society can always be co-opted by the transnational capitalist superstructure. At the national level, the democratic legitimation of welfare states in OECD countries is premised on their global economic hegemony. This interweaving of economic globalization and political processes has a broader theoretical significance. It exposes and puts into question the residual metaphysics of transcendence that underwrites almost every aspect of Habermas's cosmopolitan vision.

It is well known that the later, postmetaphysical Habermas attempts to free his account of *Öffentlichkeit* from its initial moorings in ideology critique and philosophies of history and praxis inherited from German idealism and Marxist materialism by diffusing its normativity into the constitutive presuppositions of everyday practices of communication.[38] First, whereas a philosophy of history conceives of norms as regulative ideals abstracted from their prototypical institutional manifestation in a specific historical instance, the later Habermas's quasi-transcendental understanding of normative validity sees it as "the rational potential intrinsic in everyday communicative practices" that operate across an entire spectrum of cultural and societal rationalization processes throughout history (FR, 442). The ideals of communicative freedom are universal pragmatic norms we presuppose in rational linguistic agency. Since the making of political decisions in a post-traditional world involves rational debate and argumentation, these decisions can be judged from a normative viewpoint in terms of whether they satisfy the preconditions for communication that define rational discourse. Second, in the proceduralist understanding of publicness, the focus shifts from the realization of an ideal prototype by transcending the capitalist economic system and a bureaucratic system of political domination to the development of institutional procedures that encourage the discursive processes of opinion- and will-formation and maximize their accessibility so as to best generate rational outcomes. The validity of norms is measured in terms of whether there is a rationally founded agreement among all affected parties who are also participants in a rational debate (FR, 447). Thus, a political decision possesses normative validity if it is the product of the democratic deliberation of all citizens. Third, the goals of communicative action are less ambitious. Instead of seeking to replace the bureaucratic state apparatus or transform the economy, it endeavors to maintain an appropriate separation and equilibrium between powers through the procurement and withdrawal of legitimation (FR, 452). The image Habermas uses to characterize this kind of influence is that of regulation through a sluice-and-dam structure:

> The goal is no longer to supersede an economic system having a capitalist life of its own and a system of domination having a bureaucratic life of its own but to erect a democratic dam against the colonializing *encroachment* of system imperatives on areas of the lifeworld. . . . A radical-democratic change in the process of legitimation aims at a new balance between the forces of societal integration so that the social-integrative power of solidarity—"the communicative force of production"—can prevail over the powers of the other two control resources,

i.e., money and administrative power, and therewith successfully assert the practically oriented demands of the lifeworld. (FR, 444)

Through this series of moves, the self-recursive causality of human freedom becomes detranscendentalized. It finds a concrete home in the democratic processes of the political public sphere, which Habermas describes as "the quintessential concept denoting all these conditions under which there can come into being a discursive formation of opinion and will on the part of a public composed of the citizens of a state" (FR, 446). His cosmopolitan project merely extends this nexus between freedom and the democratic process beyond the fetters of the nation-state. In fact, however, Habermas does not completely break with the rational-redemptive horizon of a philosophy of history. First, whether a universal norm is characterized as an empirical potentiality (that is, quasi-transcendental) or as a projected ideal, the norm is something that needs to be actualized or brought into the open by dealing with any impediments that prevent it from being realized or that restrict its full operation. This process necessarily contains the outline of a dialectic of transcendence, however weak it may be. We see this dialectic most clearly in Habermas's account of the gradual erosion of the unnecessary historical limitations restricting the cosmopolitan vocation of the democratic process. Second, Habermas regards the constitutional welfare state of OECD countries as a prototypical ideal. In his view, its processes and institutions most clearly and self-consciously expose and thematize the implicit democratic rationality of communicative action.

Third, the motif of transcendence has not disappeared. The transcendental turn of Kantian moral philosophy is more than just the argument that moral criteria are to be derived a priori or the identification of moral freedom with a pure intelligible world outside spatiotemporal coordinates (the noumenal kingdom of ends). It implies an entire line of thought that defines reason's fundamental trait as standing against that which is merely given, conditioned, or finite, and understands reason's constitutive activity as the striving against and surpassing of finitude. In the postmetaphysical Habermas, the motif of transcendence has been watered down and reinscribed as the regulation of the system by the lifeworld, which maintains its autonomy through the process of legitimation via the self-recursive structures of public rational deliberation. The normativity of this process is figured through a thematic opposition between spontaneity and manipulation derived from a Marxist theory of ideology, which Habermas reinscribes as an opposition between critical and deceptive publicity. The important point here is that social-political regulation by self-legislating citizens remains derived from freedom in the Kantian sense, namely, the power of reason to transcend the finitude of nature through self-determination. Indeed, the distinction between system and lifeworld is a version of the Frankfurt School distinction between instrumentality and critical reason. The latter replicates Kant's distinction between the heteronomy of nature and *technē* and the autonomy of moral reason. In Habermas's view, the vicissitudes of economic globalization are consequences of the instrumental dynamics of systems, from which the global public sphere must attempt to shield the lifeworld. In all this, there is an admirable belief that the universal validity of publicness constitutes a quasi-transcendent state of rational human existence that is somehow quarantined from the vicissitudes and contingencies of the world of self-interested, instrumental relations, notwithstanding the constant struggle between rational existence and instrumentality. Perry Anderson makes a similar point when he describes Habermas's philosophy as being tinged with a curious innocence and angelism and organized by a benign providentialism.[39]

Habermas's redemptive rationalism, however, hits its limits in a series of empirico-historical impasses that do not appear to be resolvable. First, economic growth is closely tied to opinion-and will-formation through discursive debate or effective participation in the public sphere. This is especially obvious when we situate *Öffentlichkeit* in a global frame. Strong structures for popular education are crucial to democratic will-formation, or the *Bildung* of subjects who can participate in informed debate. The protective guarantee of crucial socioeconomic rights and public liberties is needed to secure the framework for effective participation. All these factors are premised on the economic well-being of the nation-state or region in question. Because Habermas's model is always the welfare state of the economically hegemonic North Atlantic, he takes the social and economic conditions for optimal opinion- and will-formation for granted. When he projects the formative powers of the public sphere onto a transnational plane, however, they hit their limits in the NIDL, which hampers the establishment of both effective public spheres in the postcolonial South and a transnational public sphere. Hence, the (in principle) complete openness or inclusiveness of global democratic processes is always already compromised, not because of cultural differences, but because the economic division of the world makes it impossible to institutionalize conditions for discursive debate that will be accessible to all peoples across the entire globe.

Second, the validity of specific norms formulated through public discussion at the national level is similarly compromised by global competition. These norms are not inevitably ideologemes, mere components of ideational superstructures that serve the economic interests of the territorial public spheres from which they arise. But because these public spheres coincide with and depend on the economic positions of their nation-states or regions, the norms they generate can always be inflected to serve particularistic interests through linkages to the instrumental actions that surround the public sphere. Instead of regulating instrumentality, the norms generated by public deliberation can always be contaminated by it.

Third, the formation of a genuinely transnational public sphere requires the removal of the economic divisions of the world. At the national level, redistributive functions are performed by the welfare state. The absence of global consensus about the need for thoroughgoing global economic redistribution (as opposed to the occasional benevolence of debt forgiveness and strings-attached economic aid) means that redistribution can occur only through the competitive ascension of the hierarchy of the NIDL. In this scenario, no genuine global consensus can develop to regulate economic globalization because the development of the public sphere of each country to the point where it can participate in a global public sphere once again presupposes the advancement of less developed countries within the same competitive structures that the global consensus was supposed to check.

These empirico-historical impasses problematize Habermas's cosmopolitan project in two fundamental ways. First, the fact that the NIDL stalls the formation of a genuinely cosmopolitan world society points to the importance of a progressive popular nationalism in the postcolonial South that can influence the state to regulate economic development so that its benefits can be diverted from transnational capital and the indigenous elite and shared among the masses. Here, a national culture generated from an oppressed people's struggle for economic autonomy and equality is not a limitation that needs to be transcended for the actualization of the democratic process on a global scale but rather an important part of the process. It is the first step toward the formation of a postcolonial welfare state. This means that we cannot always assume, as Habermas does, that rational or humane outcomes can be generated only from cosmopolitan political formations. Neither the normativity of cosmopolitan public spheres nor that of national public spheres can be predicted in advance. Both forms of *Öffentlichkeit* are not and cannot be self-legitimating. Their effectivity for actualizing human freedom is radically dependent on their shifting alignments with the techniques and instrumental formations that sustain them.

Second, from a theoretical standpoint, this should lead to a rethinking of normativity that dissociates it from the principle of transcendence to which it has always been tied. The fact that the proper functioning of a political public sphere is always dependent on external formative conditions puts the autonomy of the political into question. Put another way, the spontaneity of *Öffentlichkeit* is not quite that of the self-recursive organism. Because the economic conditions for public deliberation are established by instrumental action or *technē*, its spontaneity is itself a product of *technē*. This means that the lifeworld cannot be clearly separated from the system. The lifeworld's very ability to maintain this boundary originates from its prior constitution and penetration by the system. I have described this constitutive interpenetration in the macrological terms of competitive economic development. But, following Michel Foucault's work on bio-power, it can also be located at the micrological level. The constitution of the democratic public sphere relies on the cultivation and/or subjectification of citizens through technologies of discipline, while governmental technologies enhance economic well-being through the development of the population as human capital. My emphasis on the formative power of *technē* over the political should not be confused with the economic determinism of Marxism's base-superstructure model. Both the economic system of capitalist accumulation and existing political institutions are sustained by the thorough penetration of society by *technē*, whether this is understood in terms of the instrumental imperatives of moneymaking or of technologies of bio-power. *Technē* in this sense can no longer be understood within the oppositions of manipulation versus spontaneity, deception versus critical self-knowledge, because it forms the collective social or political subject. This does not mean that the results of critical public deliberation—that is, its ideational *contents*—are necessarily ideological or distorted and distorting. It is just that the normativity of the public deliberative process is always vulnerable to manipulation because of the technical crafting of the material and subjective conditions for its operation. This constitutive heteronomy subjects public deliberation to a strict law of contamination whose consequences have to be analyzed on a case-by-case basis. For example, since the development of a democratic public sphere in a given country is dependent on that country's ability to develop itself economically within the hierarchies of the global economy, the normative validity of political decisions generated by any public sphere can be contaminated by particularistic interests. The same can be said about political deliberations on a global level such as those concerning international human rights.

Questioning the normativity of the public use of reason, or, what is the same thing, human reason's capacity for transcendence, does not inevitably lead to nihilism or moral relativism. We have always identified reason's capacity for transcending finite limitations with human freedom. But it might be more honest to acknowledge that although freedom is a universal value, something that we all rationally want, it also has a contaminated facticity because the rational desire for freedom and the capacity to achieve it are generated by forces outside us. Indeed, this contaminated existence is the only effective reality freedom has ever had. To admit this is not to oppose ideas (whether in the Platonic or Kantian sense) to reality and lament their profanation, but to examine how deliberative consensus and public reason, in their very material effectivity, are always already imbricated in and circumscribed by the techniques that craft the framework of consensus as well as the rational subjects of critical deliberation. This would require us to reconceptualize freedom in terms of an interminable negotiation with and responsibility to the forces that give us ourselves instead of the transcendence of the given. In the next chapter I elaborate on an alternative understanding of radical postcolonial nationalism as a responsibility to given culture.

3

Given Culture

Rethinking Cosmopolitical Freedom in Transnationalism

In the previous chapter we saw how the Eurocentric framework of Habermas's universalistic philosophical cosmopolitanism foreclosed the international division of labor and its devastating consequences for the realization of cosmopolitan democracy in the postcolonial South. I now turn to consider a strand of the new cosmopolitanism that claims affiliation to postmodernism and speaks in the name of the diversity of the postcolonial world, the hybrid cosmopolitanism of cultural studies.

The celebration of cultural differences and the anti-Eurocentrism that characterizes postcolonial cultural studies belong to a broader intellectual milieu. In the humanities and the narrative social sciences, the fact of decolonization has been turned into another occasion for the ongoing debate between relativists and universalists on the possibility of knowledge that transcends cultural boundaries. In this spirit, Jean-François Lyotard linked the *défaillance* of modernity to "resistance . . . on the part of the insurmountable diversity of cultures."[1] The shift from universal culture to cultures in the plural, from cosmopolitical freedom to local autonomy, is, however, accompanied by a turn toward a primitivist construction of cultural others along quasi-anthropological lines.[2] This tendency can be politically dangerous because freedom has not come with independence from territorial imperialism. A metropolitan cultural politics that espouses a hands-off approach to a "museumized" cultural other leaves the staging of that other by capitalist globalization—fundamentalism, ethnicism, patriarchal nationalism—untouched. Yet if we intervene in those spaces as the self-proclaimed didacts of freedom, we forget that we too are part of the crisis, for the problems of uneven development and the postindustrial feudalization of the periphery are fundamental structures of the global staging of *our* everyday.[3]

80

In the face of this impasse where neither post-Enlightenment universalism nor nationalist communitarianism is a viable ideologico-institutional vehicle for freedom, cosmopolitanism as a philosophical ideal is up for modest reinvention. A cosmopolitical frame of analysis is a necessary response to our continuing integration into a global system at various levels: economic, political, social, and cultural. Any contemporary revival of cosmopolitanism, however, must take a critical distance from the ancestor cosmopolitanism of philosophical modernity best represented by Kant's project for perpetual peace. As we saw in Chapter 1, Kant argued that international commerce was a form of sociability between states that paved the way for a world federation in which a cosmopolitan culture would flourish. Such a culture is cosmopolitan in two senses. It can attain its fullest development only in the state of peace that world federation brings, and its ideational and affective content transcends ethnic or racial boundaries because it fosters universally communicable values and pleasures which promote our sociability, the constitutive feature of our humanity. Mutually enhancing each other, the objective historical tendency of international commerce toward world federation and the humanizing processes of self-cultivation would bring about the empirical unity of humanity as a whole. Indeed, for Kant, cosmopolitan culture is a universally normative ideal because it is an asymptotic historical approximation of the universal moral community, the noumenal realm of human freedom that is no longer bound by deterministic laws of nature.

No revival of cosmopolitanism in contemporary globalization can in good faith return fully to this robust sense of cosmopolitan culture. Few are now convinced of its rational-universalist grounding. The history of colonialism has disproved Kant's benign view of the unifying power of international commerce and discredited the moral-civilizing claims of cosmopolitan culture. Furthermore, although contemporary globalization has complicated the nation-state form, it has not rendered it obsolete as a form of political organization. Given that globalization requires a cosmopolitical frame of analysis, however, the question is whether we can speak of the emergence of a new cosmopolitanism, that is to say, a critical or emancipatory project of a global consciousness, and if so, of what practical-logical forms it has taken or ought to take. In this chapter I address these broader questions about cosmopolitanism in the current conjuncture by focusing on how the peculiar revival of postcolonial nationalism in globalization—a phenomenon I call "given culture"—

requires us to question the dominant concept of culture in postcolonial studies today. This detour is instructive because postcolonial cultural studies grew out of a critique of cosmopolitan culture but is currently reclaiming cosmopolitanism. Broadly speaking, postcolonial studies has modulated from anti-universalist or anti-cosmopolitan discourses of cultural diversity to discourses of cultural hybridity that criticize the former's neo-Orientalist organicist presuppositions. James Clifford and Homi Bhabha are the most representative theorists of hybridity. Although their accounts of cultural hybridization were initially formulated on the basis of the colonial encounter, they also view hybridity as an inevitable consequence of contemporary globalization. More recently, as exemplified by Clifford's term "discrepant cosmopolitanisms," both have suggested that globalization leads to the formation of hybrid, radical cosmopolitanisms that attest to the ethico-political inefficacy of the nation-state. This makes hybridity theory a useful test case for assessing new articulations of cosmopolitanism in cultural studies.

In this chapter I argue that the accounts of radical cosmopolitan agency offered by hybridity theory obscure the material dynamics of nationalism in uneven globalization. This foreclosure occurs because hybridity theorists subscribe to the same concept of normative culture as the older philosophical cosmopolitanism they reject: the understanding of culture as the realm of humanity's freedom from the given. I further contend that the forms of transnational activity that we are witnessing today are not new cosmopolitanisms but instead aporetic cases of nationalism as given culture in a cosmopolitical force field. I suggest that these cases of given culture deform the philosopheme of normative culture that is at the heart of old and new cosmopolitanisms, including Marxist cosmopolitanism. They require us to reconceptualize the relation between culture and political-economic forces in terms of our responsibility to the given rather than our freedom from the given.

Hybridity as Cultural Agency and as New Cosmopolitanism

The concept of hybrid culture is formulated in polemical opposition to both the canonical concept of culture that grounds philosophical cosmopolitanism and the anthropological concept of culture that leads to multiculturalist relativism. Universal or cosmopolitan culture refers to a process of growth regulated by rational human self-cultivation and bound to the historical progress of entire societies. This is the canonical understanding of culture in philosophical modernity as *Bildung* (Hegel) or *Kultur* (Kant), a process and state of social existence that has universal normative validity. Homi Bhabha and James Clifford reject this canonical concept of culture for its colonialist implications and its historical link to neocolonial developmental narratives of political and economic modernization. Yet they are also suspicious of the anthropological concept of culture, which they regard as a spurious organicist and cultural-relativist attempt to manage the crisis of universalism. Hence, their theories of hybrid culture have both a negative and a positive aspect.

In its demystificatory aspect, hybridity theory exposes the violent implications of the canonical view of culture as an organic and coherent body, a process of ordering, and a bounded realm of human value determinable by and coextensive with human reason.[4] Clifford detects this concept of culture in the Eurocentric narrative of modernization but also in the relativist celebration of local cultures, which he sees as a displacement of the former.[5] Thus, in his discussion of ethnography and exhibitions of "primitive" art, Clifford makes the pertinent criticism that a relativist culturalism engaged in an essentialist search for authentic cultural alterity murders local cultural futures by "museumizing" cultural otherness. For present purposes, however, I will focus on the positive formulation of hybridity as a more enabling theory of cultural resistance in postcolonial globality.

Unlike culturalist relativism, which emphasizes the autonomy and uniqueness of different cultures, a theory of hybrid culture does not deny the fact that Eurocentric cosmopolitan culture has achieved a factual universality through the imperialist project. Bhabha and Clifford argue, however, that the implementation of cosmopolitan culture on other soil leads to its hybridization with native cultures, thereby subverting imperialism's cultural project. Indeed, they make the further claim that hybridization constitutes a site of resistance to the neotraditionalist, nativist cultural face of national liberation movements and postcolonial nation-states. Clifford describes the current era as syncretic and "postcultural": "The privilege given to . . . natural cultures is dissolving. . . . In a world where syncretism and parodic invention are becoming the rule, not the exception . . . it becomes increasingly difficult to attach human identity and meaning to a coherent 'culture.'"[6] He celebrates a dispersed polycentric globe where cultures are hybrid, inorganic, and indeterminate because they are relational and in persistent flux.[7] Similarly, Bhabha suggests that hybrid culture is "the strategic activity of 'authorizing' agency; not the interpellation of pre-given sites of celebration or struggle."[8]

Hybridity theorists thus break with the object theory of culture common to cosmopolitanism and traditional anthropology (culture as a self-identical and knowable entity, norm, or subject) and attempt to articulate a theory of culture as a process of production in language. They suggest that positivist accounts of culture as an empirical object that is merely given can have violent consequences because such accounts can be used to justify historical cases of social hegemony or oppression. If, however, we view culture as something constructed by discourse or signification, then the subject of culture becomes the site of permanent contestation. For example, Bhabha's anecdotal accounts of mimicry and ambivalence employ a vocabulary combining the enunciative split with the psychoanalytic thematic of disavowal. He suggests that the moral and civilizing aspects of colonial discourse are split from its unacknowledged racist enunciatory conditions.[9] The disavowal is, however, expressed in the desire of colonial discourse for a subject of cultural difference that is not-quite/not-white, different but almost the same. The colonial project implements this relationship of mimicry between colonizer and colonized metaleptically to authorize its own discourse.[10] Bhabha suggests that since colonial cultural authority is constituted through the production of hybrid objects, these objects can subvert the moral truths of colonial authority by reflecting the wound of its split self-presence and reversing colonial disavowal.[11]

Bhabha's description of anticolonial subversion as the moment when the quasi-naturalistic authority of the colonial symbolic reverts to its prior state as arbitrary sign depends on a reductive understanding of colonial rule as the establishment of *cultural* authority through the deployment of symbols (the Bible, the Law, and so on).[12] Without any argumentation, he subsequently inflates hybridity into a wellspring for the political contestation of all forms of cultural symbolization and the general articulation of all marginal political identities by extending this definition of cultural authority to cover all hegemonic forms of social and cultural organization. This simplistic analogy between the contingency of signification and the contingency of sociocultural formations repeats the axiom that reality is discursively constructed. But what exactly is the political purchase in postcolonial cultural studies of this commonplace assertion that discourse produces the real? What are the ontological presuppositions behind these political claims?

Edward Said's *Orientalism* was a pathbreaking study of the discursive construction of the Orient as an object of colonial knowledge. But in invoking the oppositional humanist intellectual as an antidote to the inequities of Orientalist discursive effects, Said assumed the possibility of a self-reflective critical consciousness capable of grasping the limits of its own situated perspective in order to transcend provisionally the discursive formation that this consciousness inhabits. These redemptive moments of transcendence are premised on the freedom of the rational human will from discourse in the final instance. Situating themselves within a linguistic understanding of antihumanism, Clifford and Bhabha criticize Said for maintaining the exteriority of critical consciousness and the freedom of the rational will from discourse in the final instance.[13]

For Clifford, cultural identity is not something to be grasped outside discourse because it is a matter not of what was or what is but of becoming. Cultural identity is "never given but must be negotiated," "made in new political-cultural conditions of global relationality" (*PC,* 273, 275). This emphasis on the hybrid invention of culture extends the rhetorical play of self-reflective ethnographic writing into an account of agency. In postmodern ethnographic critique, cultural identity *qua* organic totality is said to be "written" in the narrow sense: it is artificially produced by the rhetorical/stylistic fiction of ethnographic authority in field notes. An awareness of the constructed nature of cultural identity, Clifford argues, enables resistance to cosmopolitanism, because instead of basing political claims on a nostalgia for an impossible authenticity, it opens up possibilities for hybrid local futures. Hence he urges us to rethink cultures "not as organically unified or traditionally continuous but rather as negotiated, present processes" (*PC,* 273). In Clifford's account of Mashpee identity, hybrid resistance is a matter of reflexive symbolic self-invention, a strategic traffic with the processes of cultural meaning.[14] Indeed, he generalizes the hybrid inventiveness of Aimé Césaire's poetry into an alternative model for cultural-political agency. Césaire's anti-essentialist negritude is a reflexive model for rebellion, a "New World Poetics of continuous transgression and cooperative cultural activity" (*PC,* 181).

While Clifford's account of strategic agency does in fact presuppose an intentionalist notion of willed agency, the more important point is that despite his purported linguistic antihumanism—or, better yet, because of it—Clifford's anti-naturalist account of hybrid agency is an anthropologistic culturalism. This is because it articulates the distinctive ontological *predicament of culture,* the symbolic and fluid nature of human identity and existence, as opposed to the givenness of the natural or nonhuman. This residual anthropologistic culturalism is the fundamental ontological presupposition of theories of hybrid culture. It resurfaces as the notion of linguistic freedom in Bhabha's claim that hybrid resistance arises from the contingency of language as a sign system. For Bhabha, "the discourse of the language-metaphor suggests that in each achieved symbol of cultural/political identity or synchronicity, there is always a repetition of the sign that represents the place of psychic ambivalence and social contingency."[15] This claim is typical of cultural analyses from literary studies, which have unfailingly confined the dictum of the discursive production of reality within an anthropocentric horizon. These analyses operate on the unspoken assumption that because discourse consists of language, and language is the mark of the *anthropos,* the discursive construction of reality indicates the freedom of the human agent *qua* linguistic-social subject from the material constraints and bondage of being-in-nature. Thus, regardless of whether hybrid resistance is conceived as intentional strategic agency (Clifford) or as inhering in the enunciatory processes of symbolic forms and cultural authority (Bhabha), the imminence of subversion is perpetually present in the rifts between nature and culture, the Real and its representation/signification, matter and language/form, necessity and freedom.

For present purposes, my question is whether these theories of hybrid cultural agency, as they have developed into accounts of new radical cosmopolitanisms, are feasible accounts of political transformation in uneven globalization. This is indeed the claim made by Bhabha and Clifford, who invoke the terms "transnationalism" and "cosmopolitanism" to assert the importance of hybridity to an understanding of cultural contestation and political transformation in contemporary globalization. Like his account of hybridity, Clifford's revaluation of cosmopolitanism in his essay "Traveling Cultures" is also a polemic against dominant practices within cultural anthropology that privilege relations of dwelling.[16] For Clifford, such localizing moves elide "the wider global world of intercultural import-export in which the ethnographic encounter is always already enmeshed" (TC, 100). As an antidote, he suggests that we should focus on "hybrid, cosmopolitan experiences" (TC, 101), on how culture is produced through travel relations and local/global historical encounters. Within its polemical limits, this is a valuable critique of "the organic, naturalizing bias of the term culture" in anthropology (TC, 101). Nevertheless, just as Clifford's critical use of hybridity had modulated into a positive account of hybrid cultural agency, this critical deployment of cosmopolitanism as traveling culture also graduates into a positive account of practical agency.

In his use of the term, Clifford tries to dissociate cosmopolitanism from the mobility of the privileged by focusing on "the ways people leave home and return [as the] enacting [of] differently centered worlds, interconnected cosmopolitanisms" (TC, 103). He describes the non-European servants, helpers, companions, guides, and translators of European travelers as bearers of "cosmopolitan" viewpoints and characterizes working-class traveling culture as "a cosmopolitan, radical, political culture" (TC, 107). He champions a comparative study of cosmopolitanism which accounts for the fact that, in certain cases, "mobility is coerced, organized within regimes of dependent, highly disciplined labor" (TC, 107). It is, however, at this point that Clifford endows cosmopolitan mobility with a normative dimension, claiming for it an important role in cultural and political transformation. For even as he acknowledges that materially oppressed travelers move under strong cultural, political, and economic compulsions, he also insists that "even the harshest conditions of travel, the most exploitative regimes, do not entirely quell resistance or the emergence of diasporic and migrant cultures" (TC, 108). These cosmopolitan movements are presented as exemplary instances of active resistance to localism and cultural homogenization under global capitalism: "Such cultures of displacement and transplantation are inseparable from specific, often violent, histories of economic, political, and cultural interaction, histories that generate . . . *discrepant cosmopolitanisms*. In this emphasis we avoid, at least, the excessive localism of particularist cultural relativism, as well as the overly global vision of a capitalist or technocratic monoculture" (TC, 108).

We see from this that in Clifford's understanding, emancipatory cultural agency involves the outstripping of oppressive economic and political forces by cultural flux and activity. He implies that cultural stasis is a regressive product of oppressive forces, whereas physical mobility is the basis of emancipatory practice because it generates stasis-disrupting forms of cultural displacement. In Bhabha's hands, this physical mobility is raised to the higher level of linguistic freedom from naturalized culture. Bhabha suggests that since "the transnational dimension of cultural transformation—migration, diaspora, displacement, relocation" involves a translational sense of culture, the formation of the transnational postcolonial subject ought to be seen as one of "the historical traditions of cultural contingency and textual indeterminacy (as forces of social discourse)."[17] Consequently, it appears that analyses of postcolonial, postmodern transnationalism *ought* to deploy Bhabha's vocabulary of hybridity, now hyper-ambitiously characterized as the project of a postcolonial countermodernity.[18] He writes:

> The postcolonial prerogative seeks to affirm and extend a new collaborative dimension, both within the margins of the nation-space and across boundaries between nations and peoples. My use of poststructuralist theory emerges from this postcolonial contramodernity. . . . It is as if [concepts like] the arbitrariness of the sign, the indeterminacy of writing, the splitting of the subject of enunciation . . . produce the most useful descriptions of the formation of "postmodern" cultural subjects. (*LC*, 175–176)

The corollary to this translational understanding of transnationalism is a linguistic antinationalism. Bhabha suggests that it is politically reactionary and debilitating to view the nation as an empirical sociological category (for instance, in the modernist theories of Gellner and Anderson) or a holistic cultural entity (organic theories of the nation) because organic theories define national identity in totalizing ways, whereas sociological theories suppress possibilities of resistance to the nation.[19] He suggests that if we denaturalize the nation and understand national identity as "a form of social and textual affiliation" (*LC*, 140), an "ambivalent signifying system" (*LC*, 146), and a narrative process ridden with contestation, then we become more alert to the constitutive ambivalence within the nation that leads to its undermining.

The hybrid revival of cosmopolitanism therefore has two limbs: an antilocalist/antinationalist argument and an argument that new radical cosmopolitanisms already exist. The second argument reduces globalization to cultural hybridization in transnational mobility. Transnational migrant cultures are then characterized as existing radical cosmopolitanisms that subvert national culture (Bhabha) or localism (Clifford). These moves to recosmopolitanize postcolonial studies are not entirely surprising. First, insofar as hybridity theory was initially a critique of the cosmopolitan and anthropological concepts of culture deployed by the imperialist civilizing mission and colonialist disciplines such as ethnography, the original type case of hybridization is the colonial cross-cultural encounter. Since colonialism is a historical precondition of contemporary transnationalism, the topos of cultural hybridization is easily extended to describe alternative cosmopolitanisms from below. Second, both Clifford and Bhabha criticize organic theories of local culture for their continuity with nationalist ideology. Hence, especially in Bhabha's case, the suggestion that contemporary cultural hybridization gives rise to new cosmopolitanisms merely develops this implicit theoretical antinationalism into speculations about the nation-state's imminent ethico-political inefficacy.

There is, however, a more fundamental theoretical reason why hybridity theory develops into a new cosmopolitanism: its predication of culture as the human realm of flux and freedom from the bondage of being-in-nature, and its understanding of national culture as an ideological or naturalized constraint to be overcome. Indeed, it is not excessive to say that hybridity theorists are especially attracted to historical cases of migration and diasporic mobility because they see such cases as empirical instances of the flux they regard as the ontological essence of culture.

These attempts to erect actually existing radical cosmopolitanisms on the back of anthropologistic culturalism or linguistic freedom, however, rely on a cultural-reductionist argument. The suggestion that hybrid cultural practices constitute the birth of cosmopolitan consciousness and indicate the impending obsolescence of national identity and the nation-state makes sense only if we reduce the complexity of contemporary globalization to one of its strands: cultural hybridization. Many have pointed out ad nauseam that theories of hybrid agency are culturalisms that notoriously sidestep the constraints and tendencies of politico-economic processes by reducing them to cultural-significatory practices. I am making a similar but more specific point. Although they are subsequently generalized into accounts of historical agency, the ideas of linguistic freedom and cultural flux actually originate from two very limited areas of analysis: the undermining of colonial authority and the ethnographic gaze in academic critique. Their alleged pertinence is limited to their demystificatory power. Any extrapolation from this negative use of hybridity to articulate a general theory of transformative agency inevitably exaggerates the role of signification and cultural representation in the functioning of sociopolitical life and its institutions.[20]

It is not to deny the importance of cultural legitimation in the formation of sociopolitical institutions and collective identities if I suggest that social consensus is not secured by ideological means alone. The social is not coextensive with, or exhausted by, its symbolic dimensions. Over and above identification with a naturalized cultural unity or linguistic interpellation into a national ideal, the formation and deformation of group loyalty also involves political-organizational and economic factors such as law enforcement, the provision of welfare and other services by the state, and the establishment of a framework for the distribution and regulation of economic resources and capabilities to satisfy human needs. Social transformation is not achieved simply by "relocating alternative hybrid sites of cultural negotiation" (*LC*, 178). To be materially effective, emancipatory consciousness cannot subsist on linguistic dynamism or cultural-symbolic flux alone. The subversion that linguistic freedom makes possible, however, operates on a purely ideational level, where the capacity and potential for transformation is the freedom from the merely given inhering in the anthropologistic realm of culture. Thus, even as hybridity theorists evacuate the human agent *qua* intentional consciousness, its role is surreptitiously filled by language or culture, a nonnatural sign system or a process sans subject that is a relay of human freedom. This closet idealism is especially clear in Bhabha's anecdotes of historical resistance: Algerian liberation fighters are agents of interpretation who "destroy . . . the nationalist tradition" and are "free to negotiate and translate their cultural identities in a discontinuous intertextual temporality of cultural difference" (*LC*, 38). For Bhabha, the resistant subaltern is a reader who grasps modernity's discrepant moral truths and introduces an indeterminacy or "time lag" which short-circuits modernity's enunciative present.[21]

These linguistic culturalisms elide the point that even though culture is not reducible to empirical determinations such as politics and economics, it is not entirely autonomous or free from the taint of such determinations because it emerges from its relationships with these forces. These sociological and empirico-material constraints constitute and bind culture. They are part of the process by which culture is given, the material conditions of its effectivity as a historical force. To claim otherwise is to espouse the most absurd of idealisms: it is to deprive culture of any effectivity by dematerializing it. Hence, when Bhabha tries to referentialize or historicize the subject of hybrid culture, as indeed he must in order to claim that it has historical effectivity, "social experience" becomes a mere placeholder for linguistic indeterminacy, now abstractly renamed "the contingency of history—the indeterminacy that makes subversion and revision possible" (*LC,* 179).

The shortcomings of unmooring cultural agency from the field of empirico-material forces that overdetermine it are especially pronounced in hybrid revivals of cosmopolitanism. These new cosmopolitanisms cannot explain why globalization has paradoxically led to the intensification of nationalism in the postcolonial South without resorting to the knee-jerk dismissal of the national/local as an ideological form. As we have seen, for Bhabha, hybridity's denaturalizing power is also an antinationalism. He views the postcolonial nation as a naturalized ethno-national culture imposed from above and argues that its internal identification is plagued by the indeterminacies of signification. Because his focus on the internal destabilization of national cohesion extracts the nation from its geopolitical context, Bhabha ignores the fact that national consciousness can be formed through negative identification, induced by political-economic factors such as interstate relations within an uneven capitalist world economy. Although Clifford's position is not explicitly antinationalist, his chronotope of traveling culture does not give equal time to the tenacity of national dwelling. Neither can explain the persistence of the postcolonial nation-state in contemporary globalization, for their heady celebration of the subversive possibilities of global flows prevents them from grasping that in the absence of a world state capable of ensuring an equitable international political and economic order, *the unevenness of political and economic* globalization makes the nation-state an important political agent for defending the peoples of the South from the shortfalls of capitalist global restructuring. Contra Bhabha, it is the defense against *uneven* globalization that makes national formation through negative identification both historically unavoidable and ethically imperative.

But perhaps it is asking too much from these hybrid cosmopolitanisms to expect them to respond to the precarious necessity of postcolonial nationalism in uneven globalization. For is it not obvious from the start that the paradigm for these radical cosmopolitanisms is not really decolonized space but the metropolitan scenario of migrancy and mobility? Notwithstanding Bhabha's copious sermonizing about postcoloniality, the occluded model for hybridity turns out to be the migrant "minority" subject who subverts *metropolitan* national space: "colonials, postcolonials, migrants, minorities—wandering peoples who will not be contained within the *Heim* of the national culture . . . but *are themselves* the marks of the shifting boundary that alienates the frontiers of the modern nation" (*LC*, 164). I should not, of course, be understood as dismissing the pain and suffering of migrants, political refugees, and exiles. My point, however, is that they do not represent the whole picture of contemporary globalization. For even when Bhabha makes the rare reference to transnational capitalism, the focus is not on the exploitation of labor in free trade zones in the South but instead on migrant workers who move to wealthier territory: "Transnational capitalism and the impoverishment of the Third World certainly create the chains of circumstance that incarcerate the Salvadorean and the Filipino/a. In their cultural passage, hither and thither, as migrant workers, part of the massive economic and political diaspora of the modern world, they *embody* . . . that moment blasted out of the continuum of history" (*LC*, 8, emphasis added).

Indeed, we discover that in essence, hybrid cultural agency is concerned with physical freedom from being tied to the earth. Such freedom is the phenomenal analogue and material condition of possibility for endless hybrid self-creation and autonomy from the given: "There is a return to the performance of identity as reiteration, the re-creation of the self in the world of travel" (*LC*, 9). This is why Bhabha is not interested in those who do not migrate, or those who cannot migrate and for whom coerced economic migration would be a plus, or in the vicissitudes of uneven economic development in the postcolonial South. Indeed, he cannot even be said to be very interested in those who leave the South temporarily, in order to return, or in the repatriation of funds by migrant workers to feed their kin in the Third World. In Bhabha's world, postcoloniality *is* the hybridity of metropolitan migrancy. Everything happens as if there were no postcolonials left in decolonized space. With the onset of decolonization, all the former colonial hybrids have become postcolonials. And it seems that to keep their hybrid powers and status intact, they have had to depart for the metropolis, following on the heels of their former colonizers, to torment them and enact moral retribution by subverting their cultural identity.

It is, therefore, at least tendentious to personify linguistic freedom and hybrid cultural flux in the diasporic subject and to celebrate these forms of cosmopolitanism, at the expense of nationalism, as the most progressive type of postcolonial transformative agency in contemporary globalization. Hence, even though Bhabha allegedly considers sub-alternity, his "postcolonial perspective" is devoid of any analytical speci-ficity, because hybrid freedom is an abstract theory of marginality gen-eral enough to accommodate experiences as diverse as slavery, diaspora, the position of ethnic or racial minorities in constitutional democra-cies, and queer sexuality, as well as subaltern resistance. This general postcolonial perspective effaces the unbridgeable divide between the mi-grant literary critic in the metropolis and the subaltern in decolonized space. It elevates the time lag–diagnosing postcolonial critic into the paradigmatic resistant hybrid who is able to grasp the condition of the possibility of resistance before it is realized in experience. My point here is that Bhabha's picture of contemporary globalization is virulently postnational because he pays scant attention to those postcolonials for whom postnationalism through mobility is not an alternative.

Unlike Bhabha, Clifford cautions that he is not offering a nomad-ology: "I'm not saying there are no locales or homes, that everyone is— or should be—traveling, or cosmopolitan, or deterritorialized" (TC, 108). He tries to reconsider dwelling in its dialectical relationship with traveling and gestures toward a redefinition of mobility beyond literal travel to include different modalities of inside-outside connection so that "displacement can involve forces that pass powerfully *through*— television, radio, tourists, commodities, armies" (TC, 103). Yet the pri-mary emphasis of his analysis of discrepant cosmopolitanisms still re-mains on physical mobility. When generalized into an account of hy-brid resistance, it is inevitably confined to the scene of metropolitan migrancy, border transactions, and those subjects who have class access to globality. Limited to the viewpoints of translators, guides, suppliers of anthropologists and migrant labor, Clifford's "cosmopolitan radical po-litical culture" from below also leaves out the subaltern subjects in de-colonized space who have no access to globality and who view coerced economic migration as a plus. The subaltern lies outside the circuit of the international division of labor and must bear the impact of global-systemic inequality on food production, consumption, and superexploitation outside wage labor. Such actions of survival cannot easily be romanticized or recuperated as hybrid resistance.

My position on hybridity theory can be summed up as follows. First, as a paradigm of postcolonial agency in globalization, hybridity is a closet idealism. It is an anthropologistic culturalism, a theory of resistance that reduces the complex givenness of material reality to its symbolic dimensions and underplays the material institution of capitalist oppression at a global-systemic level. Second, as a new cosmopolitanism, it is feasible only to the extent that it remains confined to metropolitan migrancy and forecloses the necessity of the postcolonial nation-state as a precarious agent defending against the imperatives of global capitalist accumulation. Third, there is a fundamental link between this new cosmopolitanism and culturalism. Hybrid cosmopolitanisms can ignore the necessity of the nation-state precisely because they regard cultural agency as unmoored from, or relatively independent of, the field of material forces that engender culture. They privilege migrancy as the most radical form of transformative agency in contemporary globalization because for them, it is the phenomenal analogue of hybrid freedom from the given. As Bhabha puts it, "The great connective narratives of capitalism and class drive the engines of social reproduction but do not *in themselves,* provide a foundational frame for those modes of cultural identification and political affect that form around issues of. . . the lifeworld of refugees or migrants" (*LC,* 6).

As purported analyses of globalization, however, these accounts of transformative agency and cosmopolitanism sadly miss the mark. For although the meaning and symbols of neocolonial culture are unmotivated, their materialization via economic and political institutional structures in an unequal global order means that they cannot be translated, reinscribed, and read anew in the ways suggested by theories of hybridity. For thoroughgoing global transformation to occur, some recourse to the ambivalent agency of the postcolonial nation-state, and, therefore, to nationalism and national culture, seems crucial even as we acknowledge that this agency is not autarchical but is inscribed within a global force field. Clifford is not entirely unaware of this, since he notes that he has not gone far enough in reconceiving practices of dwelling in a transnational context (*TC,* 115). My point is that in the current conjuncture, such practices of dwelling, if they are to be mass-based, are more likely to engender a national consciousness than a cosmopolitanism, no matter how "discrepant." To comprehend the possibility of the national-in-the-cosmopolitical—and I use this awkward phrase to indicate a condition of globality that is still short of a mass-based cosmopolitan consciousness—we need to understand postcolonial national culture in terms other than as an immutable natural substrate or as an ideological form imposed from above, a constraint to be transcended by the formation of an emancipatory cosmopolitan consciousness.

The Culture Concept in Philosophical Modernity and Given Culture in Uneven Globalization

Despite their flaws, theories of hybridity can be valuable as ironic reminders of the tenacious lineaments of the canonical concept of culture they claim to subvert. The axiom of the autonomy of human existence found in hybrid cosmopolitanism is remarkably similar to Habermas's belief in the spontaneous and autonomous character of cosmopolitan *Öffentlichkeit*. Precisely because they see cultural resistance as a function of the freedom of human (discursive/linguistic) reality from the givenness of nature, theories of hybridity repeat the essential feature of the culture concept in philosophical modernity even though they are painfully oblivious to the ethical stakes involved. This concept of culture has very deep roots, and it has always governed discourses of nationalism and cosmopolitanism.

Broadly speaking, the culture concept articulates the formative power over nature that co-belongs with humanity. For the human being is not only an animal capable of rational contemplation but also a purposive being with the ability to shape its natural self in the image of rationally prescribed ideal forms. This practical aspect of culture involves a metaphorical extension of cultivation as agrarian activity *(cultura)* into the individual-pedagogic task of the ethical and intellectual cultivation of the mind.[22] It establishes an internal link between autonomous rational effort and the shaping of some naturally given ground into cultivated form. This ability of rational endeavor to transform and improve nature implies that humanity possesses a degree of freedom from nature. Thus, in its societal dimension, culture designates, first, the realm of human beings in general, as opposed to nature, as well as a normative ideal to grade the differences between various peoples belonging to that realm.

Accordingly, culture begins to have an objective dimension. It now refers to a second nature, a reality that is higher than mere nature. In its secular meaning, *Bildung* denotes the inner-directed formation of an individual in the image *(Bild)* of a personality prescribed by moral norms. By extension, culture in general becomes synonymous with the totality of *"objectified results* of human creativity by, and due to which the 'natural constitution' of human individuals—their inborn needs, drives and propensities—become modified, developed and supplemented."[23] Better yet, culture in general designates the realm where ideal forms materialize as external objects with a reality or life independent of the individual who created it. No longer just an attitude or way of life, culture in its utopian aspect is an objective reality both opposed to and superior to nature, the realm in which humanity overcomes the blind contingency of nature through reason. The culture concept of philosophical modernity thus carries the immense ethical burden of reconciling facticity and universal normativity. It articulates nothing less than our ability to structure reality according to universal norms and values that are not just given by tradition but are instead rationally justified through time.

For Kant, cosmopolitan culture is precisely the realm in which humanity is able to free itself from the given, understood first as the passions and sensuous inclinations that subject human beings to nature, and second as the finitude of human existence. Human beings are finite moral subjects, creatures of nature who also possess moral autonomy. As natural creatures with passions and sensuous inclinations, we are, like things and animals, creatures of a world merely given to us and are bound by the same arational mechanical laws of causality governing all natural objects. As moral subjects, however, we are self-legislating rational agents. We belong to a transcendent realm of freedom that we create for ourselves, a world encompassing all rational beings governed by universal laws that we prescribe through our reason. The moral world is supersensible and infinite because it is not subject to the blind chance and meaningless contingency that characterize finite human existence.

Kant proposes that we can realize the ideal world of moral freedom in the given world of egotistical strife and unsocial sociability through culture. Culture provides a bridge to the transcendent realm of freedom because it minimizes our natural bondage by enhancing the human aptitude for purposive self-determination. As a form of disciplinary education that curbs our animal inclinations, culture liberates the human will from the despotism of natural desires and redirects human skill toward rational purposes by forming the will in accordance to a rational image.[24] The *society of culture* that grows out of individual efforts is a simulacrum of the universal moral community because it promotes cosmopolitan sociability: "[For we have] the fine art[s] and the sciences, which involve a universally communicable pleasure as well as elegance and refinement, and through these they make man, not indeed morally [*sittlich*] better for [life in] society, but still civilized for it: they make great headway against the tyranny of man's propensity to the senses, and so prepare him for a sovereignty in which reason alone is to dominate."[25] Indeed, culture is our primary means of overcoming human finitude: in view of individual mortality, the moral progress of humanity can be guaranteed only through cultural products that preserve for posterity all the significant achievements of humanity as a moral species beyond the lives of individual actors. Therein lies the normative basis of a cosmopolitan world order. It is the only efficient means for creating this universal society of culture.

This view of culture as the promise of humanity's freedom from or control over the given is not confined to idealist cosmopolitanisms. The same concept of normative universal culture also indelibly marks materialist cosmopolitanism. Defining the given as the changing needs of sensuous human beings to be satisfied by labor *qua* purposive self-objectifying human activity, Marx argued that the economic realm of natural necessity formed by social intercourse could be equitably governed only by a world community of socialized laborers and producers: "Freedom, in this sphere, can consist only in this, that socialized man, the associated producers, govern the human metabolism with nature in a rational way, bringing it under their collective control instead of being dominated by it like a blind power."[26] The erosion of the nation-form (an ideological construct obscuring the universal interests of the proletariat) by the globalization of the market and the capitalist mode of production meant that this community would soon be realized. Universal competition and exploitation would lead to the teleological formation of the proletariat as a universal class that transcends national borders:

> Only this will liberate the separate individuals from the various national and local barriers, bring them into practical connection with the production . . . of the whole world and make it possible for them to ac-

quire the capacity to enjoy this all-sided production of the whole earth (the creations of man). *All-round* dependence, this primary natural form of the *world-historical* co-operation of individuals, will be transformed by this communist revolution into the control and conscious mastery of these powers, which, born of the action of men on one another, have till now overawed and ruled men as powers completely alien to them.[27]

Despite Marx's strong anti-culturalism, the proletarian world community is a materialist version of Kant's society of culture. Just as Kant saw cosmopolitan culture as nature's end for humanity, the proletarian world community is also the sphere in which humanity maximizes its freedom from finitude through rational-purposive self-objectifying activity (labor). This community is also formed by a combination of human action and natural teleology (in Marx's case, world commerce and a globalized mode of production).

We should not presume that a more realistic or mundane universalism necessarily takes the form of cosmopolitanism. The same concept of universal culture also underwrites varieties of nationalism ranging from Hegel's civic patriotism to the different ethno-linguistic nationalisms of Fichte and Herder. The common thread that links all these cosmopolitanisms and nationalisms (Fichte's nationalism is also a cosmopolitanism) is the idea that individuals willingly bind themselves to a collective body as a rational response to human finitude because this collective entity provides a substrate or medium of subsistence for their existence. The transcendence of the givenness of existence can be understood either as the better satisfaction of essential needs through a social contract or in the higher sense of the fulfillment of humanity's moral essence or the prolonging of the effects of moral endeavors beyond one's individual life. Thus, for Hegel and Fichte, individuals willingly die for a patriotic cause because it is only in and through the transindividual body of a national culture, a people, or the state that they can achieve moral freedom, transcend their facticity, and endow their actions with an ethical significance that will endure beyond their mortal lifespan.[28] Hence these philosophical cosmopolitanisms and nationalisms are also secular religions or humanist onto-theologies.

We see the complicity between Marxist cosmopolitanism and nationalism in their offspring, Third World socialist decolonizing nationalism, which regards national culture as the source of political liberation. The following quotation from Amilcar Cabral is representative: "Whatever the conditions of subjection of a people to foreign domination and the influence of economic, political and social factors in the exercise of this domination, it is generally within the cultural factor that we find the germ of challenge which leads to the structuring and development of the liberation movement. . . . [N]ational liberation is necessarily an act of culture."[29] Despite the shift from moral freedom to political liberation, the onto-theological theme of culture as the realm of acts by which we free ourselves from the given is unmistakable in Cabral's suggestion that cultural activity precedes and lays the groundwork for liberation from political, economic, and social oppression.

This utopian culture concept also underwrites the various new cosmopolitanisms discussed in this and previous chapters. The normative value and autonomy from capitalist globalization which they ascribe to cultural hybridity, cosmopolitan *Öffentlichkeit,* the formative power of the imagination *qua* global circulation of mass mediatic images, and various emergent forms of global political culture and social networks is the freedom of cultural activity in the general sense, given a more specific inflection as the spontaneity and freedom of the imagination, social organization, political debate, language, or discourse. It is misleading to distinguish these new cosmopolitanisms from their predecessors by arguing that they are grounded not in abstract universal reason but in multiple and concrete affiliations and attachments. All these cosmopolitanisms are united by the belief in the critical self-reflexivity and autonomy of the human condition as the rational-purposive state of *cultural* existence. This understanding of culture is, however, premised on a complex of unresolved ontological problems. It presupposes that we can use ideal forms to shape the external world according to human values and norms. But the sharp opposition between nature and culture makes this problematic. For if nature is opposed to culture and culture is the becoming-nature of ideas, then how can ideas be realized as external objects and yet remain in accord with human purposiveness? For instance, tradition is arguably a quasi-nature of our own making, an ossification of ideational structures specific to a certain historical moment into immutable givens. The entire Marxist problematic of alienated labor and all that follows from it—commodity fetishism and the reification of social relations into a second nature that oppresses the human producer—is a variant of this problem.

When culture merely designated a process of individual cultivation according to social/moral norms, this problem of culture's power over nature was posed and answered in an obfuscating manner: the causal effects of ideas on *human* nature could be explained by psychological theories of the self-reflexive action (cultural discipline) of human beings as mind-body complexes. The emergence of an objective dimension to culture means, however, that the causality of ideas needs to be extended over nonhuman nature. Crudely put, philosophical modernity resolves this problem by reconciling the nature/culture opposition in a natural-teleological account of culture as nature's final end for humanity. The success of culture as a utopian project depends on an anthropocentric conception of nature as a totality in harmony or accord with human normative interests: because nature is amenable to human purposes, nature itself leads humanity beyond nature. Put another way, the nature of the *anthropos* is to be free of nature. This is the logic behind Kantian and Marxist cosmopolitanism as well as various philosophical nationalisms.

But this reconciliation of nature and culture in humanity remains unconvincing. Insofar as human beings are irreducibly objects of nature and subject to its laws, it is unclear what our cultural activity can effect in us. Put another way, what can we hope to achieve in ourselves through our own makings insofar as we are finite beings, creatures who are given and who come to exist and cease to exist not by our own making? I propose to call this ensemble of problems the aporia of given culture. The aporia is as follows: Culture is supposed to be the realm of human freedom from the given. But because human beings are finite natural creatures, the becoming-objective of culture as the realm of human purposiveness and freedom depends on forces which are radically other and beyond human control. Culture is given out of these forces. Thus, at the same time that cultural activity embodies and performs human freedom from the given, it is also merely given because its power over nature is premised on this gift of the radically other.

The aporia of given culture implies a radical vulnerability that we have not learned to accept. We have seen that philosophical modernity smothers this aporia by recourse to the dogmatic idea that culture is nature's highest end for humanity, an end that has been variously characterized as a cosmopolitical order (Kant and Marx), a national culture (Fichte and Herder), or the ideal state (Hegel). The accounts of linguistic freedom and cultural flux that ground the new hybrid cosmopolitanisms are relays of this dogmatic faith. Because of their profound antinaturalism, theories of hybrid culture do not reconcile the opposition between nature and culture by means of a natural teleology. Hybridity theorists rely, however, on the same anthropologistic opposition between nature and culture/language insofar as they regard indeterminacy as the exclusive feature of social or discursive formations.

Indeed, the canonical culture concept of philosophical modernity takes many other protean shapes in postcolonial cultural studies. The cultural face of national liberation movements is characterized by political claims for local autonomy that are logically similar to the discourse of cultural difference. Because these discourses rely on anthropological definitions of culture, they are often seen as critiques of a universalistic concept of culture. In fact, these affirmations of difference do not seek to retrieve a lost authentic tradition oppressed by universalism. In rejecting the false universalism of cosmopolitan culture, these discourses already desire access to a true universal. The argument for the autonomy of the local presupposes the universal value of autonomy and proposes to apply it to every particular group or collective unit. This desire for a polymorphic universal capable of respecting the particularities of its constituent units sublates the oppositions between the universal and the particular, modernity and tradition. Consequently, political claims for cultural specificity posit the autonomy of cultural identity either in an original state of independence or as an ideal-normative goal: all cultural groups should have equal access to the social, economic, and political forces that constitute the world system and the freedom to direct these forces according to their own interests. They are deemed to possess this freedom from external determinations in the final instance because they are variations of *Kultur,* humanity's vocation to lead itself beyond the merely given.

To phrase my criticism of hybridity theory in terms that will cover all these cases of anthropologistic culturalism, how plausible is the hope that we place in culture's freedom over nature, the primacy of culture's form in the altering of the matter that nature gives us, if culture itself becomes a quasi-nature devoid of the trait of anthropocentric freedom? Cultural studies emphasizes the power of culture in shaping politics, power, and economic systems. Yet, writing on the precarious relationship between feminism and postcolonial cultural reassertions in the contemporary world order, Valentine Moghadam observes that while "cul-

ture may have been originally introduced to overcome some of the heavy
determinism associated with social and economic analysis, . . . since the
latter half of the 1980s it has taken on a weight of its own, reified, even
sacralized."[30] This astute remark echoes Samir Amin's point that the fundamentalist reassertion of cultural identity is the inevitable product of
uneven globalization rather than a solution to it.[31] Taking my cue from
these observations, I want to suggest that the formation of postcolonial
national culture in the late twentieth and early twenty-first centuries
reopens the aporia of given culture and deforms the culture concept
underwriting the nationalisms and cosmopolitanisms of philosophical
modernity, the various new cosmopolitanisms, and the assertions of cultural difference in postcolonial cultural studies, because even as it indicates the unfeasibility of postnationalism, it also performs the impossibility of either celebrating national culture as the vehicle of freedom
from the given or rejecting it as a means of resisting uneven globalization.

In macro-sociological terms, postcolonial national identity-formation
is in part a response to uneven economic globalization.[32] The uneven accumulation of capital and distribution of wealth and resources on a
global scale exacerbates the unequal distribution of political power and
economic resources within decolonized countries. At the same time,
globalization is accompanied by the spread of a political culture which
historically emerged in the West: human rights, women's rights, equality,
democratization. This intersection of cultural change and rapid economic upheaval leads to resentment and resistance on the part of disadvantaged groups who may use "cultural resources to mobilize and organize opposition . . . even though a motivation and cause of opposition is
economic and social disadvantage."[33] Political elites may also draw on
"tradition" or "intrinsic cultural values" to maintain hegemony and justify their actions, sometimes overemphasizing cultural issues such as religion, morality, cultural imperialism, and women's appearance to divert
attention from economic failures and social inequality. As Moghadam
notes with regard to Islamic cultural reassertions, "culture, religion, and
identity are thus both defense mechanisms and the means by which the
new order is to be shaped. Islamist movements appear to be archaic but
in fact combine modern and premodern discourses, means of communication, and even political institutions [and] . . . must therefore be seen as
both reactive and proactive."[34]

It would be precipitous to dismiss all postcolonial national-cultural reassertions as fanaticist pathologies or statist ideologies. Reassertions of national identity are not necessarily religious or confined to Islamic Middle Eastern states. They occur in most postcolonial countries, ranging from weak neocolonial African nation-states to the hyperdeveloping economies of East and Southeast Asia. The united stand by Asian governments at the Vienna Convention in rejecting intervention by Northern states over human rights issues on the grounds of cultural differences is partly a collective assertion of postcolonial national sovereignty in response to the history of colonialism and the inequality of contemporary North-South relations.[35] Moreover, these cultural reassertions are not necessarily ideological constructions of state elites. They also express the interests of disadvantaged social groups that seek to change economic conditions. Thus, although human rights NGOs from the South have rejected the position of Asian states on human rights, they have also been careful to distinguish their criticisms of their own governments from the position of Northern governments by asserting the need to respect cultural differences and the urgency of establishing an equitable global economic order and interstate system. In other words, the New World Order has generated an entire spectrum of popular and official postcolonial nationalisms. Islamic fundamentalist nationalism, which has given rise to the desperate acts of Palestinian suicide bombers and the terrorism of the al-Qaeda network, stands on this spectrum's extreme end. It should be analyzed alongside the Confucian chauvinism that the Singapore government has celebrated as the basis of the East Asian path of global capitalist development.[36] Both forms of cultural identity are product-effects of the larger social text of global capital.

The resistance to global forces promised by contemporary postcolonial rearticulations of national culture is severely curtailed by the fact that they arise in response to economic globalization and can be manipulated by state elites in the indirect service of post-Fordist global capital. Decolonization failed because it merely involved the devolution of state power to local and regional actors, who used this power to attract investment and expand production within a transnational economic system of surplus extraction. Similarly, much contemporary official postcolonial nationalist ideology aims at fostering social cohesion to attract foreign direct investment and providing cheap female labor for multinational-owned industries in Free Trade Zones. Furthermore, postcolonial nationalisms, even popular nationalisms, run the permanent risk of majoritarian oppression because most postcolonial nations are not culturally homogeneous, and their cultural identities are the dubious gift of colonial cartography. They have also been deeply marred by patriarchal oppression. Marie-Aimée Hélie-Lucas, an Algerian feminist, offers us a sense of the difficult double bind of a cultural identity twice given for women in decolonization—given once by colonialism and given yet again by indigenous patriarchy in an aporetic embrace with global capitalism:

> It would have been mean to question the priority of liberating the country, since independence would surely bring an end to discrimination against women. What makes me angrier in retrospect is . . . the brainwashing that did not allow us young women even to think of questioning. . . . It angers me to see women covering the misbehaviour of their fellow men and hiding, in the name of national solidarity and identity, crimes which will be perpetuated after independence.
>
> This is the real harm which comes from liberation struggles. The overall task of women during liberation is seen as symbolic. Faced with colonisation the people have to build a national identity based on their own values, traditions, religion, language and culture. Women bear the heavy burden of safeguarding this threatened identity. And this burden exacts its price.[37]

The aporia is that in the current conjuncture, nationalism cannot be transcended by cosmopolitan forms of solidarity no matter how pathological it may appear in its ineradicably oppressive moments. First, transnational networks are neither sufficiently mass-based nor firmly institutionalized. Proponents of a global civil society or an international public sphere which already exists independently of nation-states must gloss over the fact that we inhabit a decentralized political system in which global loyalty is thin, an ideal vision largely confined to activists and intellectuals.[38] Hence, in order to be effective at the level of political institutions or the people, transnational networks have to work with and through the nation-state to transform it. They have to negotiate with the state in the hope of influencing its political morality and/or mobilize local support into popular national movements that press against the state. As Alexander Colás observes, the nation-state is both a constraining factor and an emancipatory potential in its relation to global networks. These networks are subject to the same constraining social and historical forces that shape other social actors, but "the nation-state is not necessarily at odds with the emancipatory aspirations of cosmopolitanism . . . [and] cosmopolitan political action would actually involve the defense of social and political rights *via* the democratic nation-state."[39]

Second, the necessity of the nation-state as a node that progressive global-local networks must pass through is especially salient in the postcolonial South, where economic poverty is the root cause of economic, social, and political oppression. Although foreign capital–led market growth and development may alleviate poverty when actively regulated by strong host governments to serve official national interests, such as in hyperdeveloping Southeast Asia, rapid economic growth cannot lead to social development or gender equity unless the existing inequitable sociopolitical and economic structures within these nation-states are overhauled. Indeed, hyperdevelopment gives greater legitimation to authoritarian regimes, as in the case of Singapore. In the worst case scenario, as in some African nations, the "development of underdevelopment" produces the Fourth World. My point is that in the absence of a world state capable of ensuring an equitable international political and economic order, economic globalization is uneven. Instead of engendering an emancipatory cosmopolitan consciousness, it produces a polarized world in which bourgeois national development and industrialization in the periphery cannot be evenly distributed because in many countries, these projects are hampered by structural adjustment policies.[40] To alleviate the shortfalls of global restructuring in the South, the state needs to be an autonomous agent of economic accumulation. But it can resist capitulation to transnational forces only if it is transformed into a popular national state. Thus, popular rearticulations of postcolonial national identity are ethically imperative and cannot be dismissed per se as statist ideologies that hinder the rise of a more equitable cosmopolitan consciousness, even though the exclusionary dimension of popular nationalism can always be manipulated by state elites and captured by official nationalism.

Contemporary revivals of postcolonial nationalism, which are instances of negative identification in defense against uneven globalization, should be seen as a weak repetition of the earlier phase of negative identification in decolonization that initially united the people into a nation. This ambivalent necessity of postcolonial nationalism deforms the concept of cultural agency at the heart of old and new cosmopolitanisms. In Marx's version of the culture concept of philosophical modernity, economic forces of production constitute an autotelic realm of necessity that points beyond itself to a realm of human freedom from the given that is based on, but sublates, the realm of necessity—the proletarian world community. The persistence of postcolonial nationalism in contemporary globalization, however, refutes Marx's economistic assumption that transnational forces of production necessarily lead to transnational movements which engender a popular global consciousness, a mass-based loyalty to a transnational body. In his critique of orthodox Marxist cosmopolitanism, Samir Amin points out that peripheralization and the North-South conflict are the two truths of actually existing capitalism. Socialist revolution is not possible at present because "the expansion of capitalism in the periphery . . . ruins the chances of national crystallization and accentuates the fragmentation and atomization of society."[41] Consequently, he suggests that there is "no real alternative to popular national transformation in the societies of the periphery," and that African and Asian popular nationalist socialism are inheritors of the true vocation of Marxism.[42] Amin's vision of a polycentric world departs from the orthodox Marxist idea of the withering away of the state. In his view, strong postcolonial states, and hence popular nationalism, are crucial to resisting recompradorization.[43]

Put another way, postcolonial nationalism is the irreducible stuttering that the permanent threat of peripheralization introduces into the dialectic of global socialism. Therefore, contrary to neo-Marxist critiques such as Partha Chatterjee's and Ranajit Guha's, postcolonial nationalism is not necessarily an ideology imposed from above, a "forced resolution . . . of the contradiction between capital and the people-nation."[44] Postcolonial nationalism is not a contradiction that we can and should transcend in the name of cosmopolitanism, because it does not obey the logic of dialectical contradiction. Both medicine and poison, postcolonial nationalism is a double-edged stricture that uneven globalization makes necessary. By pulling us back from a cosmopolitical realm of freedom into nationalism as given culture, globalization problematizes the Marxist understanding of the given as something we can transcend through normative human action.

Similarly, postcolonial nationalism also reveals the limits of new hybrid cosmopolitanisms. I noted earlier that although Bhabha and Clifford claim that their new cosmopolitanisms are analyses of postcolonial agency in contemporary globalization, their focus is actually transnational mobility *qua* phenomenal analogue for cultural flux and linguistic freedom. For the majority who remain in peripheral space by choice or by necessity, however, the nation-state, whatever its inconveniences, is necessary because postnationalism through migration is not an alternative. But more important, because these rearticulations of national culture are induced by and given from within a global field of economic and political forces, they are not instances of a cultural agency that is unmoored or relatively independent from material forces. They cannot be explained in terms of symbolic flux and linguistic freedom from the given. Instead, the peculiar dynamism of given culture has to be thought from within stasis, in terms of its being mired in a material force field.

The failure of both Marxist and hybrid cosmopolitanisms to account for postcolonial nationalism as given culture should be referred to their common theoretical source: the modern philosophical concept of culture as the realm of freedom from the given. Indeed, Clifford's and Bhabha's privileging of migrant mobility as the type case of hybrid dynamism also repeats Marx's teleological view of economic development. Like Marx, they too regard global economic processes as the positive material condition for disrupting the givenness of naturalized national or local ties. The difference between new hybrid and old Marxist cosmopolitanisms is merely that the former emphasizes the importance of cultural dispersal because it does not regard globalization as leading to a unified world order. Both cosmopolitanisms are premised on the transcendence of the given.

The nontranscendable finitude of postcolonial nationalism in uneven globalization, however, implies that a contemporary revival of "cosmopolitanism" cannot feasibly take the form of an "-ism," the project of a mass-based global emancipatory consciousness, no matter how strategic or compromised. Simply put, "discrepant cosmopolitanisms" do not cover the whole picture. My point here is not merely that transnational migrancy is not identical to postcoloniality. More precisely, although globalization creates a greater sense of belonging to a world because it makes individual lives globally interdependent, it has not, thus far, resulted in a significant sense of political allegiance or loyalty to the world. Unlike nationalism, which is notoriously nonphilosophical or underintellectualized, cosmopolitanism lacks a mass base. Bodies such as Amnesty International and international human rights NGOs are creatures of intellectuals aimed at promoting a wider consciousness of humanity through the power of rational or affective persuasion. They attract allegiance by working at a different level from nationalism. To reach a wider base or to be effective at the level of state policy, these transnational bodies usually have to work through the political morality of the state and through popular nationalism. Especially with regard to the postcolonial nation-state in the current conjuncture, it is unlikely that they can displace the nation, however imperfect it is, as the object of mass-based loyalty. This may be partly because some of these transnational bodies are located in and/or depend on the hegemonic North for funding and can be unwittingly used in various ways to bypass the already beleaguered Southern nation-state and undermine its legitimacy.

But then, as given culture, postcolonial nationalism also deforms the argument of philosophical nationalisms that the nation is a better embodiment of human freedom than a world order. Because it neither respects nor is able to reconcile the divide between nature and culture, stasis and activity, necessity and freedom, the postcolonial nation is not the grasping of the *an sich* as the *für sich* through autonomous social action. On the one hand, this national identity is given, a quasi-nature incarnated in lived bodies through fiscal and technological flows and shifting linkages that are not amenable to anthropocentric self-determination. On the other hand, the postcolonial nation also cannot be deterministically viewed as an immutable epiphenomenon of global forces because it is induced from a *heteronomous* force field. Contemporary articulations of postcolonial national identity are responses to economic globalization, but they are not *entirely* reducible to the interests of state elites indirectly serving global capital. Like a compound formed in a chemical reaction that is not reducible to its different reactants, the postcolonial nation is the volatile product of an unstable gathering together of economic, cultural, and political factors.

The crucial point here is that the body of the postcolonial nation-state is heterogeneous, and globalization can intensify this heterogeneity in positive and negative ways. Although transnational forces are inadequate to engender a mass-based global consciousness, although global capitalism produces weak neocolonial comprador states and authoritarian capitalist regimes in the South, globalization also creates new political opportunities and increased resources for popular mobilization. The national body is the volatile substrate for a tug-of-war between elites and the people. The opportunities and resources offered by transnational networks loosen the hyphen that tethers the nation to the state without actually cutting it. They can weaken the stranglehold of political elites over the nation even as they allow the not quite deterritorialized, popularly rearticulated nation to press against and transform the state. It might therefore be more appropriate to characterize contemporary transnational activity aimed at postcolonial transformation as aporetic cases of postcolonial nationalism in a cosmopolitical force field. It follows from this that postcolonial national culture is a double agent that grows out of, resists, and can also be pulled back into uneven global processes. In the concluding section, I suggest that this risky agency of the national-in-the-cosmopolitical entails a certain responsibility to the given.

The Global Sheaf of the Postcolonial National Body: Responsibility to the Given

The rearticulation of the hyphen between postcolonial nation and state by globalization is determined by how the postcolonial state responds to the fiscalization of the globe. Samir Amin observes that "in the Third World as a whole, the food crisis, the external debt crisis, and the impasses of imported technology have led to capitulation after capitulation before the *diktat* of transnational capital reorganized around the International Monetary Fund and World Bank and the consortia of big Western banks."[45] It is important to emphasize that postcolonial states are not entirely passive. Contrary to appearances, multinational-led foreign direct investment is not necessarily an economic form of extraterritoriality because there is state agency on both sides. For host countries and multinational investors alike, the primary motivation behind foreign direct investment is to maximize fiscal inflow (profits in the case of multinationals, foreign currency in the case of host countries) and to minimize outflow (investment capital in the case of multinationals, foreign reserves in the case of host countries). In addition, host countries embarking on export-oriented industrialization also hope to reduce unemployment, train skilled personnel, and gain access to advanced technology. Obviously it is not possible for both sides to maximize overall inflow and minimize outflow. Host states are in principle able to achieve their desiderata through taxes, trade and currency restrictions, regulations that limit the mobility of foreign capital, and legislation that ensures fair wages and labor conditions. Multinationals, however, can also enlist the states of their countries of origin to pressure postcolonial states in the South to improve conditions for foreign investment. Such diplomatic pressure, together with the global competition for foreign investment and the self-interests of the indigenous economic elite, ensure the utmost flexibility of foreign capital. Indeed, host states have bent over backwards to sacrifice their workers' interests in order to provide cheap labor.

In this scenario, the globalization of trade and production cannot lead to the formation of a world federation of the Kantian type. The implicit hydraulic model indicates the barely visible national limits of multinationals: where profits are repeatedly *repatriated* before being reinvested, and which territorial national or regional economy benefits more from the global flow of money. In times of economic stress, one sees quite clearly that capital flows are partly determined by the economic health of nation-states and state policies designed to foster such well-being. Once again, the postcolonial state is not always passive. Nor does the wide-scale entry and flight of global capital necessarily bring about a denationalization of the state. For instance, when the United States closed its market to labor-intensive goods in the mid-1970s because its economic health was coming under increasing threat, the Singapore state responded to the drop in capital investment in these industries by changing its labor composition and moving into high-tech manufacture to attract new forms of capital.

The active implementation of such fundamental changes of state economic policy necessarily involves a corresponding official project to transform the national body. If this official nationalism is met by a popular counternationalism, then this may cause a rearticulation of the hyphen between nation and state. As Noeleen Heyzer observes with regard to Singapore:

> The internationalisation of the economy . . . has to be explained not only by the structural response of foreign capital, but also by the active official policy. The PAP [People's Action Party] government had always intended that multinationals should form the base of the Singaporean

economy. It was hoped that the internationalisation of the economy, foreign expertise and resources would be harnessed to serve Singapore's national interest. . . . In contemporary Singapore society, the changing social formation results not only from external economic factors but also from the dialectical interplay of factors emanating from the top (i.e. the State) and from factors pushing from below (i.e. worker's participation) with factors at the top tending to dominate increasingly. Essentially, the issue here is how the State controls, decides, arbitrates, dominates and how this affects people at the ordinary level. At the same time, people are seldom totally passive, and certain sectors, at least, provide challenges to the State defined reality.[46]

For those who do not have the option of postnationalism through transnational migrancy, the postcolonial state is not so easily dismissible. Heyzer suggests that in its aporetic embrace with global capital, the postcolonial Singaporean state is at once liberator and oppressor.[47] On the one hand, this embrace generates economic growth and national prosperity with all its trappings: higher standards of living, upward mobility, and consumerism. But on the other hand, in its project of making the nation attractive to multinational investment, the Singaporean state also represses challenges to its official picture of what constitutes the good life, especially meaningful political life. This official nationalizing project computes well-being in terms of increasing the economic wealth of individuals. The widespread inculcation of this idea of well-being curbs popular counternationalizing sentiments by producing a depoliticized population that identifies the nation's well-being with the state's well-being.

The inherent danger of any rearticulation of the hyphen between the postcolonial nation and the state in response to its loosening in economic globalization is that instead of being transformed in the image of the nation-people, the state may gain increased control over the nation-people. The Singaporean administrative state has enjoyed an immense degree of legitimacy because of its high level of economic prosperity. Together with other comparable cases of rapid industrialization in high-growth East and Southeast Asia, the Singaporean economic miracle is often adduced as evidence to refute the theory of the development of underdevelopment. It is, however, crucial to remember that such miracles occur within uneven global capitalism. We will see in Chapter 6 that in the case of Singapore, the burden and the costs of this apparently jointless soldering of nation to state in globalization are borne by a migrant workforce that is either periodically abjected from the proper boundaries of the nation-state or whose assimilation is tightly controlled, even as such workers are crucial to its daily functioning as an indispensable solution to labor shortages.

The precariousness of feminism in weaker Southern states reveals in the most pronounced way how this risky agency of the national-in-the-cosmopolitical requires a radical reconceptualization of freedom. The burden of the illusory autonomy from global-system imperatives claimed by cultural reassertions in the periphery is generally borne by women. Because of the politicization of gender and the family, women play an essential role in the postcolonial project of patriarchal ethno-cultural fundamentalism, which "seeks to meet the needs of international capital with its liberal window dressing ('a modern look') without being culturally imperialized."[48] For present purposes, what is especially interesting is that many women actively participate in these cultural reassertions even as they are also gender activists. The strength of their popular-nationalist conviction is striking in the face of the sacrifices it entails. This cannot be explained in terms of a dichotomy between popular spontaneity and state manipulation through official nationalist ideology. Many Maghrebian states do not have an Islamic government. In Sudan, "Islam is an integral part of the political culture and of popular culture, even though in Sudan, as elsewhere, religion may be manipulated by elites."[49] Cultural reassertions should be understood as part of the popular reformulation of national identity. Alya Baffoun notes that "the persistence of traditional thought and the inability of the political elite to impose a pattern of a society based on a modern rationale are the ways by which the irrational and the mythical become a form of social organization and management."[50] Indeed, Algerian Islamic groups understand their project of the Islamicization of the nation as a popular response to "the failure of the nationalist, modernist, socialistic and secular regimes of the post-independence era of the Arab World."[51] Khawar Muntaz observes that for Pakistani women's rights activists, women who participate in fundamentalist movements are profoundly enigmatic because they reject the concept of gender equality, "see restrictions on women's mobility and curtailment of legal rights as protective measures prescribed by religion (and therefore unquestionable), and condemn women agitating for rights as westernized and un-Islamic. At the same time a number of these women are also professionals, working as teachers and doctors. They demand a ban on polygamy, reject divorce by repudiation, condemn exploitation of women by men—all concerns with which the women's rights activists are also occupied."[52]

Such popular articulations of national identity are patently not instances of the self-conscious reformulation of a community's collective ethical self-understanding through public rational deliberation that Habermas envisions. National identity is clearly a form of internalized or naturalized constraint on feminist interests. Cherifa Bouatta and Doria Cherifati-Meratine observe that Algerian women who espouse women's rights are denigrated for abandoning their own natural and sacred tasks: "They are soulless bodies and souls whose bodies give course to baseness. They are the offspring of France. They want to transgress what is sacred and based in nature and culture."[53] This identity is, of course, neither natural nor freely chosen through rational deliberation. It is induced from within a global force field. Nawal el-Saadawi writes that in the Arab world, "religious and moral appeals and claims" about women's cultural identity conceal "the links between imperialism and conservative religious forces and the economic reasons for expelling women from the wage-labour market and from public life," which include "international struggles over petrol and Arab wealth, Israel's occupation of Palestine, the employment of petrol revenue against the interests of the Arab peoples, spurious dependency projects, more external debt, more unemployment, rising prices and inflation."[54]

But paradoxically, this cultural identity is also not an ideological mystification imposed from above. It is generated through a process of subject-formation that does not respect the distinction between rational form and inert matter, nature and culture, passivity and activity. It is a case of given culture, where cultural identity is not the product of critical self-understanding but a second nature generated from material processes that are not even of the order of the ideational and visible, such as the tracings of the digestive tract by inequalities in food production and consumption or the weaving of the body through superexploitation under the new international division of labor. This second nature cannot be overcome through acts of self-conscious deliberative reason or interpretive hybridity. In the chance and necessity of the current global conjuncture where national identity is given culture, a feminist cannot afford to dismiss the postcolonial nation-state even if she has to criticize it. The link between women and national culture stems from the symbolic role of women and the family in national liberation movements. Both decolonizing national culture and postcolonial feminist consciousness are formed from the popular nationalist spirit, which may conflict with or remain an integral part of feminist goals.[55] Hence, women in the postcolonial nation-state occupy various irreconcilable subject positions. This uneasy fit means that postcolonial feminisms are irreducibly marked by an interminable responsibility to given culture. Hélie-Lucas notes that in Islamic countries, "women's organizations range from participating in the fundamentalist movement, to working for reform within the framework of Islam, and to fighting for a secular state and secular laws. In spite of this wide range of tendencies and strategies, all of them have internalized some of the concepts developed and used by fundamentalists. In particular, they have internalized the notion of an external monolithic enemy, and the fear of betraying their identity—defined as group identity, rather than gender identity in the group."[56] In the face of the mutual exclusivity of being a feminist and being a nationalist in these cases, a gender activism has arisen in Egypt which is not political in a highly organized, self-conscious sense but is instead a form of low-profile pragmatic activism within the milieu of the popular-religious national everyday. Margot Badran observes that "today's feminists in Egypt are women with layered identities, only one of which is feminist. By publicly asserting one identity they might be seen as giving priority to that identity over others, and this they are most unwilling to do."[57]

Similarly, Hélie-Lucas speaks of the haunting hold of the nation as given culture over her position as a feminist in international public space:

> I personally believe in internationalism, also among women's groups, but I am not representative of the opinion of Algerian and Third World women in general. . . . [A]ccusing the West and imperialism is fine, but I don't see how we can get any solution except by identifying with the Left forces, *however limited their awareness is of our situation,* of the evils of international capitalism. . . . But believing in *this kind of inter-*

nationalism, acknowledging all the differences of interest and in wealth and class, and whatever . . . this I don't deny, and I think we have to work on it. . . . I haven't always been like this, either—I have been very *blindly nationalist* in the past.[58]

But to be "this kind of" an internationalist is not to be a postnationalist. It is about being an *unblind* nationalist at the same time, however difficult that may be. Speaking about the struggle of Muslim feminist internationalists for the legal reform of Muslim personal codes, Hélie-Lucas observes "that internationalism in their view *does not transcend or erase their belonging to a cultural-religious compound in which they still want to grow their roots;* nor does it come into conflict with forms of nationalism drawn from the full consciousness of imperialism and memories of the time of colonization."[59] In the face of the persistent threat of peripheralization in uneven globalization, these feminist activists must lovingly inhabit the postcolonial nation-state even as they resist being crushed by the official renationalizing project of the patriarchal state weakened by its aporetic embrace with global capitalism. Conversely, they can remake the state in the image of a popular-feminist counter-nationalism only by linking up with a larger global network, all the while remaining aware that these persistently shifting global alignments can also undermine the postcolonial state that they are trying to save from predatory global capitalism. This is another manifestation of the aporia of given culture: that the re-cathexis of the postcolonial state by popular nationalism must occur both with and against the state, through the cosmopolitical, which can always work in the service of global capitalism. It involves a risky self-inoculation in which the vaccine could also be poisonous.

This responsibility to given culture becomes even more onerous and fraught if we remember that these feminists are not women "at the bottom," women in poverty, or subaltern women. Let us turn to a development-oriented example in which the responsibility of feminist activists to women "at the bottom" must occur through the class-divided nation-state: the attempt to translate growth and alleviation of poverty into social development through popular participation and state regulation. Commenting on the need for advocacy in making the voices of poor women heard and addressed by the market and the postcolonial state,

Gita Sen notes: "In general, the non-governmental sector has been particularly active in South Asia and the Philippines as well as in parts of the Pacific. It has understood the need to empower women and has acted as a vital catalyst that has been able to experiment, innovate and respond flexibly to needs on the ground, providing governments with invaluable inputs when the latter have been able and willing to recognise them."[60]

What is broached here is a progressive rearticulation of the hyphen between nation and state through normative *Öffentlichkeit* in order to achieve social cohesion and change fundamental social, political, and legal structures. Likewise, Heyzer observes that

> the types of state-led development that can have a positive effect on gender equity are those that have invested in social development; . . . [those that have] provided . . . the legal and institutional framework for the regulation of the market so that the entitlements of the poor may be strengthened through better access and protection; those that recognize poor women's productive and reproductive roles; those that recognize women as citizens in their own right and not merely as "dependents," "target groups," or "instruments of development."
>
> For women to hold the market and the state accountable, there must first be a strengthening of poor women's rights . . . to active participation in the public sphere of market and state. In this regard the potential role of education, non-governmental organizations and women's groups in developing the capacity of poor women to define, defend and extend their rights through the empowerment process cannot be understated.[61]

But this effort cannot afford to limit itself to resources from within the nation-state. As Heyzer points out: "The state can intervene to bring about social equity. However, the state itself reflects the interest of powerful organized groups and is subject to pressures by multilateral donor agencies."[62] The danger is that the state can capture these NGOs and turn them into its de facto agencies for service delivery, devolve responsibility to them, and filter (elite) state interests through them, thereby perverting their ideal function of making the state accountable to the nation-people. Thus, the state must be made to recognize the claims of poor women and cultural minorities by pressure from emerging non-elite women's and human rights groups that try to link up with international networks and seek immediate support from international aid donors. Yet such multilateral donor agencies may preach the same policies of world trade liberalization that weaken the postcolonial state, thereby exacerbating existing gender hierarchies and discrimination along lines of culture and religion. Here, where every political decision is a response to the undecidability of its eventual effect, agency is not an assertion of freedom from givenness. Instead, it involves a rigorous responsibility to a condition of miredness within the shifting cosmopolitical linkages that give the postcolonial nation-state and enable the hyphen between nation and state to be rearticulated.

In uneven globalization, a metropolitan cultural politics which seeks to let the subaltern speak, or even to listen and speak to the subaltern woman so that *we can teach her our* ethical and political theories of freedom and clean our hands in the process, seems somewhat absurd.[63] If, however, we want to learn how to respond to the subaltern woman in uneven globalization, we might reverse the charge and see Hélie-Lucas, Heyzer, and others as teaching us the lesson that our response to the subaltern works through an interminable responsibility to the postcolonial nation-state as given culture within a cosmopolitical force field. This responsibility to given culture is (a) prior(i) to all forms of cultural agency that are based on the axiom of humanity's freedom from the given. It is a practical awareness of our structured co-implication with the world, everything that we take for granted when we begin from the claim of an existent condition of freedom which transcends the given. Yet we must presuppose this co-implication in order for our actions to be effective.

What I have broached here is the radical vulnerability of politics to finitude that previous philosophical nationalisms and old and new cosmopolitanisms have always foreclosed. The culture concept of philosophical modernity that became articulated into these different secular religions promised humanity a vocation that would lead it beyond the meaningless anonymity and permanent death of the merely given, the promise of a certain life beyond death through the nation, the ideal state, cosmopolitical culture, cultural hybridization, public rational deliberation, and so on. This foreclosure of the fact that it is in finitude that human beings *qua* finite corporeal creatures are given life informs the culturalism and economism of old cosmopolitanisms and their new hybrid successors in postcolonial cultural studies. Marxist economism suggests that political, social, and cultural forces are embedded in, grow out of, and reflect a material infrastructure. But it also suggests that the contradictions between base and superstructure are resolved by a teleological development of the material base that will point beyond necessity to a realm of cosmopolitan freedom. By contrast, culturalism grants autonomy to cultural forces. Autonomous culture can be regarded either as a unified realm that regulates, controls, or transcends material forces (idealist cosmopolitanism and nationalism) or as a force that outstrips and subverts the tendencies of material forces (varieties of nihilism and aestheticism relying on negative dialectics, of which hybridity theory is an unreflective example). Economism and culturalism are complicit because regardless of whether they reconcile material and cultural forces or assert the freedom of the latter over the former, both regard the vocation of humanity as the transcendence of the given.

The theoretical significance of postcolonial nationalism—the work that it does in the house of theory—is that as given culture in uneven globalization, it is a historical case of the gift of life in finitude. I am speaking here of a life-giving death, a death that gives life. Not a certain life beyond death, but life in a certain kind of death. A spectral life—life perpetually haunted by the spectrality from within that constitutes it. For the processes of globalization are not inimical to the postcolonial nation-state even though they also weaken it. Since the postcolonial nation-state remains a necessary terminal for these processes, they are its condition of (im)possibility. They make up the cosmopolitical sheaf of the postcolonial national body. Both noun and verb, *sheaf* can denote a cluster of disparate strands as well as the process of gathering. The global sheaf of the postcolonial national body is the shifting field within which the nation-state finds itself both dislocated and rearticulated. This field is not the cosmopolis as an ideal horizon of the Kantian type. Nor is it the global capitalist system as a factual totality waiting to be sublated into a global proletarian consciousness. It is definitely not a transnational realm of cultural hybridization unmoored and exhibiting a subversive freedom from the weighty constraints of political and economic determinations. It is a nontranscendable moving ground extending across the globe in which political, cultural, and economic forces are brought into relation. These forces constrain, alter, and bleed into one another without return to form and deform the postcolonial nation-state. Because no single force is thereby able to assert itself as the final determinant that overarches the entire field, the postcolonial nation-state finds itself persistently modulating from being an agent for resisting global capital to being a collaborator of global economic restructuring.

No account of postcolonial political transformation in uneven globalization can in good faith suggest that the postcolonial nation-state has been or can be transcended in the name of a cosmopolitanism or postnationalism. But neither can any popular nationalism seeking to reclaim the postcolonial state choose not to respond to and tap the motility of the cosmopolitical sheaf that gives it body. This means that the postcolonial nation-state is always under negotiation in response to a changing globality and that we cannot calculate absolutely the value of these globalizing processes for the realization of freedom. The most rigorous sense of responsibility to the given is imperative here.

4

Chinese Cosmopolitanism in Two Senses and Postcolonial National Memory

The Chinese were economically successful in South-East Asia not simply because they were energetic immigrants, but more fundamentally because in their quest for riches they knew how to handle money and organize men in relation to money.
Maurice Freedman, "The Handling of Money: A Note on the Background to the Economic Sophistication of the Overseas Chinese"

In the previous chapter I suggested that the popular nation in the post-colonial South is not merely an ideological formation but a collective subject-in-process that is induced by and responds to the uneven force field of globalization. I also noted that such cultural reassertions belong to a continuum that includes the chauvinistic Confucianism claimed by East Asian states as the animating ethos of the East Asian economic model, in which the hyperdevelopment of capital within the framework of flexible accumulation is achieved under the strict and generally repressive guidance of a strong administrative-bureaucratic state. In this chapter I look at the Southeast Asian Chinese diaspora in order to explore in greater detail the processes by which global capital generates a second type of collective subject—this time, cosmopolitan rather than national—in a different part of the postcolonial world. As we have seen, theories of new cosmopolitanisms tend to celebrate diasporic cultures as harbingers and bearers of progressive change and underplay the uneven character of globalization and the ways in which it marks diasporic cultures. I examine two opposed representations of the cosmopolitanism of the Chinese diaspora in Southeast Asian postcolonial national memory and argue that one of these strands of cosmopolitanism is integral to the predatory workings of global capital. I also outline an account of the formation of collective subjects that takes into account their irreducible imbrication in and susceptibility to contamination by the imperatives of uneven globalization.

Diaspora studies has become such a fashionable topic that in the past decade or so there has been growing support within the staid field of China studies for the suggestion that the study of Chinese culture ought to shift its focus from mainland China in favor of a broader, more cosmopolitan definition of "Chineseness" that would include not only the different Chinese states or territories of Taiwan, Hong Kong, and Singapore but also the many overseas Chinese communities scattered throughout the globe. In his influential essay "Cultural China: The Periphery as the Center," Tu Wei-ming, the director of the Yen-ching Institute at Harvard University and a leading voice for the revival of Confucianism in contemporary social ethics, makes the even bolder claim that these various Chinas beyond the mainland proper, what he calls "the periphery," are beginning to displace the People's Republic of China (PRC) as the dynamic cultural center for the articulation of "Chineseness" and "will come to set the economic and cultural agenda for the center, thereby undermining its political effectiveness."[1]

Tu's argument is premised on the dawning of a new era of capitalist accumulation centered on the Pacific Rim. The Pacific Century, he suggests, is heralded by the rise of the four East Asian dragons—South Korea, Taiwan, Hong Kong, and Singapore—in the wake of Japanese economic success.[2] Its significance is twofold. First, it allows Tu to dismiss both Communist China and Western capitalism in favor of a Confucian Chinese modernity that he detects in the East Asian economic miracle.[3] He suggests that *guanxi* or networks/connections capitalism, a form of capitalism that is underwritten by a Confucian humanism and that implies a degree of communitarianism, is superior to Western capitalism because it can alleviate the atomistic individualism and instrumental rationality of the Western Enlightenment.[4] Chinese mercantile culture and its Confucian basis are therefore to be regarded as modular or normatively cosmopolitan.

But second, and more important, Tu's focus on Pacific Rim development leads him to privilege the Chinese diaspora in Southeast Asia as the best example of this alternative model of modernity. The diaspora

Chinese carry the burden of maintaining the Pacific Century because they are a crucial terminal for the transmission of the Chinese *guanxi* capitalist ethos in their part of the world:

> A recent economic phenomenon with far-reaching political and cultural implications is the great increase in intraregional trade in the Asian-Pacific region. The annual volume of $200 billion already exceeds trans-Pacific trade (which is now significantly larger than trans-Atlantic trade). Since the Four Dragons are providing 31 percent of all foreign investments in the countries of the Association of Southeast Asian Nations (ASEAN), notably Malaysia, Indonesia, the Philippines, and Thailand, *the participation of "diaspora" Chinese is vitally important; they are responsible for the largest transfer of capital in this region, exceeding that of both Japan and the United States.* A predictable result is the evolving image of the Chinese. . . . *[T]he image of Chinese as economic animals is likely to be further magnified in Southeast Asia,* changing perhaps from that of trader to that of financier. The Chinese merchant culture underlying Chinese behavior as trader, banker, and entrepreneur adds vibrant color to the impressive reality that the Chinese constitute not only the largest peasantry in the world, but also the most mobile merchant class.[5]

In other words, the diaspora Chinese of Southeast Asia—cosmopolitans in the colloquial sense of rootless merchant sojourners—have become the best exemplars of Chinese cosmopolitanism in the normative sense.

In the aftermath of the 1997 Asian financial crisis, we cannot speak with such confidence of a Pacific Century. Indeed, the fallout from the Asian crisis provides a less benign perspective on Chinese cosmopolitanism in Southeast Asia. The popular unrest in Indonesia on May 14–16, 1998, which led to the resignation of President Suharto, was marked by a spate of anti-Chinese riots. The organized looting and burning of stores beginning in and radiating outward from Jakarta's Chinatown district, which saw 1,200 Indonesian Chinese killed, has been compared to the Nazi *Kristallnacht*. The systematic gang rape of 180 Chinese women reinforced the impression of deliberate ethnic cleansing.[6] These inhumane atrocities were all the more shocking because the uprising was widely regarded as a progressive popular-nationalist revolution against a neocolonial regime and its right-wing dictator.[7] Significantly, transnational Chinese solidarity condemning this anti-Chinese violence was registered from the mainland Communist state, human rights and women's groups in Taiwan and Hong Kong, and other overseas Chinese communities in Southeast Asia.[8]

What makes this tragic picture of the Indonesian Chinese the flipside of Tu's vision of Chinese cosmopolitanism is the shared identification of the overseas Chinese, or more precisely their culture, with global capitalism. But whereas Tu regards Chinese capitalism as the embodiment of a new cosmopolitan ethos, the Indonesian rioters regarded it as neocolonial exploitation.[9] This violence against the overseas Chinese has not been confined to Indonesia. The widespread personification of cosmopolitan capital as "ethnic Chinese" in the various national public spheres of Southeast Asia has a rich history. In Thailand, then known as Siam, a pamphlet titled *The Jews of the East,* the authorship of which is generally attributed to King Vachiravut, appeared in 1914. The contemporary persistence of this conflation of capital and "ethnic Chinese" is best seen in the following anecdote from the Philippines. Since the late 1980s, wealthy Philippines Chinese have been the victims of kidnappings for ransom. When a graduate student from the University of the Philippines was asked if she was disturbed by the spate of kidnappings, she replied, "No, because I am not Chinese and I am not rich."[10]

But is this identification of the cosmopolitanism of the Chinese diaspora with global capital entirely accurate? If it is, does this make the diasporic Chinese the proper targets of popular-national revolutionary action? Does nationalist revolution necessarily involve fanaticist violence against ethnic minorities? There are no simple answers to these questions, no clear-cut line to be found separating the virtuous from the evil. In this chapter I attempt to trace, in as analytical a way as possible, how cosmopolitan capital has become personified by the Chinese diaspora as a result of both historical and contemporary globalization and the policies of colonial and postcolonial regimes in Southeast Asia. I then look at a more positive representation of revolutionary Chinese cosmopolitanism in Southeast Asian postcolonial national memory by turning to the activist narrative fiction of Ninotchka Rosca and Pramoedya Ananta Toer. Although I attempt to reconstruct for a generalist readership some of the necessary background for assessing the ethical complexities raised by the "overseas Chinese" and the violence directed against them, I cannot explore the question of ethical responsibility in any detail. Even though colonial and postcolonial regimes are partly responsible for the historical conflation of the Chinese diaspora with cosmopolitan capital and for instigating anti-Chinese violence in the resurgent national awakening, it is important to consider how it is that both the Chinese and the national awakenings as well as the postcolonial nation-people are susceptible to this contamination by the state. Suffice it to say that "the Chinese question" in postcolonial Southeast Asia cannot be solved by simple finger-pointing.

I begin with an obvious question: In what manner of speaking is the Confucian ethos that Tu detects in contemporary Chinese mercantile capitalism a form of normative cosmopolitanism? The relationship between Confucianism and cosmopolitanism in modern intellectual history has always been troubled. In his sociology of religion, Max Weber had argued that the Confucian ethos was antipathetic to the cosmopolitan vocation characterizing a modern personality. Despite some surface similarities to Protestantism, Confucian rationalism could not give rise to modern economic capitalism because its ultimate goal was adjustment to the world and not salvation from it through rational mastery:

> A true prophecy creates and systematically orients conduct toward one internal measure of value. In the face of this the "world" is viewed as material to be fashioned ethically according to the norm. Confucianism in contrast meant adjustment to the outside, to the conditions of the "world." . . . Such a way of life could not allow man an inward aspiration toward a "unified personality," a striving which we associate with the idea of personality. Life remained a series of occurrences. It did not become a whole placed methodically under a transcendental goal.[11]

Consequently, Chinese culture restricted access to universal norms of the utmost generality that characterized a modern conscience. "The great achievement . . . of the ethical and asceticist sects of Protestantism," Weber argued, "was to shatter the fetters of the sib," leading to the establishment of "the superior community of faith and a common ethical way of life in opposition to the community of blood, even to a large extent in opposition to the family."[12] In contradistinction, Chinese culture remained particularistic and parochial, as evidenced by the traditional domination of sib organizations and the cult of village ancestors in everyday life.[13] Thus, Confucianism, to use Benjamin Nelson's felicitous phrase, obstructed the passage from "tribal brotherhood to universal otherhood."[14]

Joseph Levenson's account of cosmopolitanism in modern Chinese intellectual history reinforces this interpretation of Confucian provincial-
ism. Insofar as Confucianism could no longer meet the intellectual challenges of an encroaching modernity, insofar as it was reduced to the
dogma of unreflective peasants, Levenson argued, it became provin-
cial. It was succeeded by the liberal and iconoclastic anti-Confucian nationalism and cosmopolitanism of the May Fourth modernization movement.[15] This was in turn succeeded by Communist cosmopolitanism in
the 1950s. Chinese communism was anti-imperialist. But it was also
anti-traditionalist. This made Chinese communism cosmopolitan, for it
had a universalistic sense of mission that was similar to the Pauline
spirit of Christian universalism, precisely that which Weber regarded as
the necessary condition of modernity.[16]

If we situate the contemporary revival of Confucianism within this intellectual history, it should be clear that this neo-traditionalism is both a
critique of Western cosmopolitanism and a new form of cosmopolitanism. In Tu's view, the sociological, political, and cultural implications of
East Asian capitalism are as follows: "If, indeed, the 'Sinic World' or
the 'Post-Confucian' region has succeeded in adopting a form of life,
definitely modern, distinctively East Asian—*by implication Chinese as
well*—the sharp dichotomy between tradition and modernity must be rejected as untenable, as useless in analyzing developing countries as in its
application to more highly industrialized or postindustrial societies."[17]
On the one hand, insofar as the East Asian capitalist model is explicitly
non-Western, it is a critique of the rootlessness of (Western) capitalist cosmopolitanism, with its "aggressive anomie, radical individualism,
disintegration of society and vulgarisation of culture."[18] On the other
hand, this neo-Confucian capitalism is also an alternative cosmopolitanism for two reasons: it purports to be an alternative universal model of
global capital, and its bearers are the diasporic Chinese, who, in Tu's
words, constitute "the most mobile merchant class."[19]

The thesis of neo-Confucian capitalism thus has as its fundamental premise a narrative that regards the migration of the Chinese to
Southeast Asia as crucial to the autogenesis of global capital in its East
Asian form. By this, I do not simply mean that the diasporic Chinese
have *historically* emerged as the bearers of East Asian capital. The neo-
Confucianists propose a much more direct link between Chinese Confucian culture and global capital: the suggestion is that a superior form of
global capitalist development necessarily grows out of Chinese culture

once it is freed from the restrictions of the mainland Communist state.[20] One could even say that they regard capital as ontologically proper to Chinese culture, as co-belonging with it, to use a Heideggerian word. This position is dangerous because, ultimately, it further inflames anti-Chinese feeling in Southeast Asia, since this is aroused by a similar historical conflation of the overseas Chinese with global capital. For if the co-belonging of Chinese culture and capital is ontologically inevitable, then the relationship between the overseas Chinese and the native peoples of Southeast Asia can only ever be one between exploiter and exploited.

At this point an examination of the history of the Chinese diaspora in Southeast Asia is instructive, because through it we perceive a more complex relationship to capital that includes the machinations of colonial regimes as well as political forces from mainland China. As we will see, the irrefutable historical link between the Chinese diaspora and capital is not genetic but is instead a spectral process of paradoxical incorporation.

In the first place, the claim that a genetic relationship exists between Confucian values or "Chineseness" and mercantile culture/East Asian development is extremely dubious. As Wang Gungwu has argued, because of the low status accorded to the trader in Confucian China, merchant culture was hard to define within imperial China and became identifiably Chinese only among the overseas Chinese. Moreover, the values of mercantile culture—thrift, honesty, trust, loyalty, and industriousness—are not exclusive to Confucianism.[21] Indeed, there is nothing exceptionally Chinese about the mercantile culture of the overseas Chinese because allegiance to imperial China was minimal. Wang points out that

> as long as the Qing dynasty was weak and unable to protect them and indeed rejected them once they left the shores of China, any loyalty to China [from the overseas Chinese] was itself tenuous. And . . . for most of the time, it was irrelevant since China exercised no influence over any part of Southeast Asia. The only real link with China was to families in their home villages and to that end, good relations had to be maintained with Chinese officials. It was also necessary to maintain the use of Chinese language and such cultural links as would enable them to fit in well when they eventually returned to China or if they should send their children to study in China.[22]

Related arguments can be made about the genetic link between Confucian values and East Asian industrialization: the values of the mercantile Chinese in Taiwan, Hong Kong, and Singapore that enable them to adapt to modern capitalist ways have more in common with traders outside China than with the Chinese literati.[23]

The personification of the mercantilism of the overseas Chinese as "Chinese" can be explained only by referring to the role of colonial regimes in Southeast Asia as instruments or agents of global capital. Before the sixteenth century, overseas Chinese were largely sojourning merchants in foreign ports who traded and returned home. The small minority who married locally and settled were absorbed into native society, and being Chinese was not an issue. As European naval power expanded, however, the Chinese were encouraged to stay and perform specific trading and artisan roles in European-controlled ports such as Manila, Malacca, Batavia, Penang, and Singapore, leading to the formation of distinctively mestizo or *peranakan* Chinese communities, which were replenished with new immigrants.[24]

Generally speaking, the colonial regimes in Southeast Asia dealt with such communities by means of segregational policies designed to produce what John Furnivall has termed a "plural society," a society of different ethnic or racial groups segmented by religion, culture, and language, and held together solely by the self-interest of market forces regulated by alien colonial institutions: "Probably the first thing that strikes the visitor is the medley of peoples—European, Chinese, Indian and native. It is in the strictest sense a medley, for they mix but do not combine. Each group holds by its own religion, its own culture and language, its own ideas and ways. As individuals, they meet, but only in the market-place, in buying and selling. There is a plural society, with different sections of the community living side by side, but separately, within the same political unit."[25] The essential feature of a plural society is that it lacks a general or collective will, either of the native customary variety or the culturally homogeneous society conventionally regarded as typical of European countries prior to the era of mass migration. Furnivall takes this segregation to be a necessary historical consequence of societies formed by labor migration, but it can be argued that plural societies in Southeast Asia were in fact actively fostered by colonial regimes by means of the colonial census.

In his description of Jeremy Bentham's Panopticon as an architectural figure for the surveillance or generalized panopticism that characterizes a society of discipline, Michel Foucault suggests that one of the intended effects of the Panopticon's division into cells is the dissolution of a compact mass into a segregated multiplicity of individuals who can be counted and monitored and made into objects of information: "The crowd, a compact mass, a locus of multiple exchanges, individualities merging together, a collective effect, is abolished and replaced by a collection of separated individualities. From the point of view of the guardian, it is replaced by a multiplicity that can be numbered and supervised."[26] The colonial census can be understood as an apparatus and technique of surveillance and discipline. By dividing and classifying colonial society in Southeast Asia into ethnicized or racialized groups, the colonial census impeded the assimilation of migrants into the native population and prevented the formation of an undifferentiated colonized mass that would be more difficult to regulate and bend toward colonial interests.

The historical conflation of the overseas Chinese with mercantile capital, the culturalization of these merchants as self-consciously Chinese, is a direct consequence of their subjectification through colonial "plural society" policies. Benedict Anderson observes that under the census category *chinees,* the Dutch East Indies Company included

> descendants of immigrants who had settled locally and married local women, adapted to local cultures and even religion, and lost the use of Hokkien or Cantonese—in other words, mestizos of a second, non-Eurasian type. Over the years the Company pursued a general policy of attempting to block or reverse the assimilative process by ruthless legal and administrative means: people it decided were *"chinees"* were compelled to live in restricted residential areas, pay separate taxes, be subject to their "own" authorities, and have their marriage and inheritance practices regulated in distinct institutional niches. Although this administrative segregation collapsed in the first decade of the twentieth century, by which time the steamship and the abandonment of the closed colonial economy had encouraged a substantial new flow of Hokkienese, Cantonese, and Hakka-speaking immigrants, the category of *"chinees"* remained fundamentally in place, even though it "fantastically" covered groups not only speaking the above languages as their mother-tongues, but also Malay, Javanese, Madurese, Balinese, and so forth.[27]

In this way, the Dutch colonial government encouraged Chinese consciousness by making it clear to these migrant merchants that it was their "Chineseness" that gave them a key economic place in colonial society. And by virtue of their adaptability, these merchants affirmed their "Chineseness" as an instrument of profit making. As James Rush observes, "It was the intensity and variety of this quest for livelihood that most thoroughly marked the Chinese, for they were everywhere 'material man.' . . . [W]here the economy was concerned, the Chinese were ubiquitous and essential. . . . From top to bottom, commerce marked the Chinese. . . . As revenue farmers, Chinese merchants were a critical part of the state apparatus."[28]

One should exercise appropriate caution against overgeneralizing about the position of the diasporic Chinese in colonial Southeast Asia. Far from being a politically homogeneous region, colonial Southeast Asia included British Malaya and Singapore, French Indochina, Siam, a semi-independent buffer state between British Burma and French Indochina, the Dutch East Indies, the Spanish (and later U.S.) Philippines, and Portuguese East Timor. Different colonial states practiced different forms of census politics, which altered over the course of history. Thus, depending on the kind of classificatory scheme, the category "Chinese" had a different social position vis-à-vis other census categories that were used to classify Europeans, natives, and other non-indigenous "Asiatics."[29] The differences among these policies have different consequences for ethnic or racial politics even after formal independence. Moreover, "the Chinese" were equally heterogeneous. They came from villages in different regions of the Chinese empire and spoke different languages. It seems absurd to have to point out that not all of them were traders or merchants. They engaged in a variety of occupations and assumed varying sociological positions depending on which colony they migrated to and whether they ended up in densely populated areas, where they were mainly relegated to trade, or less settled regions, where they could engage in agriculture or mining.[30]

Nevertheless, it is possible to make four general observations about the Chinese diaspora in colonial Southeast Asia. First, even though not all overseas Chinese were traders, it was this occupational identity that took hold and that could adversely affect their position throughout Southeast Asia. Second, the colonial situation was a general impediment to complete assimilation. As Wim Wertheim notes:

Inasmuch as a status of inferiority became attached to the position of "being a native," the attraction of complete assimilation within native society decreased accordingly. Though ethnic Chinese, who were considered as more or less foreign elements, suffered from a good deal of discrimination on the part of the colonial authorities, still their position within the colonial setting, which set them apart from native society, was in general more favourable than it would have become after complete assimilation. For ambitious members of the higher strata of local Chinese society the trend became rather to identify themselves with the colonial upper caste.[31]

Moreover, the colonial authorities actively prevented any assimilation via the disciplinary techniques of census enumeration that subjectified these migrants as Chinese. Third, insofar as colonial regimes needed "the Chinese" to fill different economic functions within their respective economies—as traders, but also artisans, lessees of different government monopolies and tax farms, and so on—but also feared the power that began to accrue to them, the colonial state persistently oscillated between protection and repression of the Chinese.[32] Finally, the casting of "the Chinese" as agents of large-scale European enterprises and the main compradors of European capital often aroused economic envy in the native population, which could be incited to aid the colonial state in its oppression of its Chinese subjects. This is exemplified by the 1603 massacre of the Chinese in Manila and the 1740 pogrom against the Chinese in Batavia. In the postcolonial era, it is the economic competition between the indigenous elite and the Chinese that prevents the assimilation of the latter.[33]

What we are witnessing in these twin processes of subjectification and scapegoating of "the Chinese" is precisely the negotiability of "Chineseness." It is a form of mercantile capitalism that becomes "Chinese" via the machinations of the colonial state and not a preexisting Chinese ethos that engenders mercantile capitalism. A fictive ethnic category of the colonial census has become real. This process has political-institutional and social-psychological consequences that continue up to the present. It lays the ground for neo-Confucianist Chinese cosmopolitanism and anti-Chinese sentiment.

How should we understand this process of collective subject-formation? This fabulation cannot be explained by theories of ideological mystification in combination with accounts of Orientalist stereotyping.

Crudely put, ideology refers to a set of ideas foisted upon a subordinate group by a politically dominant socioeconomic group and is lived by the former as natural reality. An expression of the self-conscious interests of the dominant group, ideology functions to organize the whole of society in a way that prevents the subordinate group from knowing its oppression and its material conditions. It thereby obscures the *true* interests of the subordinate group in its social relations with the dominant group.[34] Because ideology generally connotes deception, the concept of ideology necessarily presupposes a distinction between truth and falsehood. What is important here is not the distinction between truth and falsehood per se but the linking of truth to the ontological trait of active self-determination as opposed to a state of *passivity* in which distorted ideas are *imposed* upon consciousness by external historical processes that are contingent because their significance as a concrete totality remains unthematized.[35] It is this dimension of passive acceptance or internalization of an external imposition that allows the concept of ideology to be spliced onto the idea of stereotypes.

This dichotomy between active self-determination and manipulated passivity derives from the modern philosophical conceptualization of freedom as a capacity that is coextensive with the spontaneity of critical-rational human activity. It governs all our theories of subject-formation including definitions of ideology as material practice and theories of social-discursive construction and performativity. It also informs all our normative judgments and evaluations of specific concrete instances of subject-formation. Hence, all the new cosmopolitanisms discussed in previous chapters argue that the various forms of cosmopolitan consciousness they celebrate exhibit a certain autonomy or self-determination. Of course, the capacity for freedom can take many forms. It can be understood as the transcendence of particularistic class or group interests, the contestation of exclusionary social or ethical norms, or autonomy from the imperatives of global capital. Such fetters are essentially regarded as contingent and finite limitations that need to be overcome.

The fabulation of "Chineseness" in the scenario at hand, however, involves a situation in which the ontological distinction between active self-determination and passive internalization of a manipulative idea or norm no longer holds. For although "Chineseness" was a category of the colonial census, it was not simply an ideological stereotype imposed upon these merchants. Nor were they mystified by it. They actively accepted this idea/identity because it suited their interests: they both de-sired and needed its attendant material benefits. The historical co-be-longing of Chineseness and mercantilism is more appropriately under-stood as the *spectralization* of these merchants by colonial capital in the precise sense that Jacques Derrida gives the term, the incarnation of an ideational or phantomatic form in an aphysical body which is then taken on as the real body of a living and finite being: "The spectrogenic process corresponds therefore to a paradoxical *incorporation*. Once ideas or thoughts [*Gedanke*] are detached from their substratum, one engen-ders some ghost by *giving them a body*. Not by returning to the living body from which ideas and thoughts have been torn loose, but by incar-nating the latter *in another artifactual body, a prosthetic body,* a ghost of spirit."[36]

Spectralization is a consequence of the radical finitude of all temporal beings. Simply put, for any present being to exist or be present, its *form*—that which makes it actual and allows it to be materialized—must be able to persist through time so that it can be identified as the *same* throughout all its possible repetitions. This differing-defer-ral (*différance*) of a present being in the living-on of its form, that is, its spectralization, is neither simply active nor passive. It is a type of originary automatism that opens up any present being to alterity, the radical susceptibility to the outside that constitutes all finite beings. This internal vulnerability to iterability/alterity—its pregnancy with the movement of alter-ing—allows a being to alter, change, or transform it-self in time. But by the same token, the spectrality that constitutes any finite being also allows it to be changed, transformed, or altered by an-other in time. Hence, the spectral forms taken on by a finite being in generating and maintaining its life can also entrap it and endanger its life.

What is illuminating about Derrida's idea of spectrality is that it im-plies an account of collective subject-formation that acknowledges orig-inal contamination or the constitutive marking and circumscription of a subject by the field in which it is generated as opposed to the modern philosophical belief in the capacity of human subjects for the overcom-ing or transcendence of finite limitations. This is useful for understand-ing postcolonial national culture and the fabulation of the Southeast Asian Chinese diaspora as cases of given culture.

Historically, the merchants who are today said to embody the Chinese ethos inhabited a situation in which their continued survival required them to respond by taking on the spectral form "Chinese." It *became* them. These merchants had become and were Chinese in the Dutch (British, Spanish, etc.) colonial sense. And their being Chinese, even though it was given to them by their official niche in colonial society and bore little resemblance to the Confucian ethos of their homeland, would henceforth be used to explain, by way of a metalepsis, their daily habits and institutional roles in colonial society. These habits and roles would in turn repeatedly mark them and reconfirm their Chineseness in perpetuity. Their adaptability and political flexibility had made them Chinese, but paradoxically, their identity thereby remained fixed, immutable in its very mutability. The role of the colonial state is decisive in this plural-society type of spectralization. If we simply assume an autogenetic relationship between Chineseness and mercantile capital, we sanction the historical self-representation of the colonial state as protector to the natives against Chinese mercantile capital, thereby dissimulating the fact that the colonial state itself was the most powerful agent of global capital in the age of imperialism.

In the early twentieth century, however, there emerged another type of spectralization of the overseas Chinese that ran counter to this plural-society type of spectralization. Between 1895 and 1911, as China began to modernize in reaction to Western imperialism, the imperial Chinese government started to harness the enterprise and capital of the overseas Chinese to develop its own national resources and industry. Likewise, representatives of the Republican movement and other revolutionary political organizations traveled to Southeast Asia and sought support from the diasporic Chinese by invoking patriotic sentiment.[37] What evolved in the first half of this century was another paradigm of Chineseness that is conventionally described as the *huaqiao* pattern.[38] At the end of the nineteenth century, *huaqiao* was used to refer to a Chinese person or a Chinese community temporarily residing abroad. By the early 1900s it had become a political term with strong emotional overtones. After 1911 it was generally used to refer to all overseas Chinese.[39] The central thrust of this type of spectralization was re-Sinicization. Contrary to colonial policy, which saw the overseas Chinese as eternally Chinese, the assumption was that the overseas Chinese were not Chinese enough and had to be re-nationalized through law, education, and renewed contact with China.

In 1909 the Chinese Nationality Law recognized all overseas Chinese as Chinese nationals by adopting the doctrine of dual nationality. As a result of increased communication links between the Chinese ports and European colonial bases in Southeast Asia (faster and safer shipping, cable and telephone connections), China was brought closer to the overseas Chinese. Political activists from the mainland shared the excitement of a rejuvenating China with the Chinese diaspora. But most important of all was the role of modern Chinese education—the numerous teachers and journalists recruited from China, and Chinese schools—in spectralizing the overseas Chinese with a modern Chinese nationalist identity. This identity was consolidated and strengthened by Japanese expansion in China and the subsequent invasion of Southeast Asia.

These two types of spectralization led to the formation of two quite different types of Chinese cosmopolitanism. As we have seen, the plural-society type engenders a mercantilist cosmopolitanism. *Huaqiao* spectralization, by contrast, produces a fervent patriotism that is also a revolutionary cosmopolitanism. For although this type of spectralization instilled political loyalty toward the Chinese state, this patriotism was not necessarily a form of chauvinism, and it played a part in the stimulation of indigenous nationalism, and, later, communism and socialism in Southeast Asia. Indeed, some of the overseas Chinese identified with indigenous nationalist movements, while others identified with the international struggle against imperialist exploitation.[40] From an intellectual-historical perspective, this is precisely the progressive form of cosmopolitanism that Levenson attributed to Chinese Republicanism and early Chinese communism.

Huaqiao nationalism, however, was very threatening to the colonial regimes and provoked an intensification of the plural-society type of spectralization. On the one hand, this aggressive Chinese patriotism could be demonized as a threat to the native well-being that colonial governments claimed to protect in order to give their presence legitimacy. Conversely, the less politically radical Chinese, whose adaptability to colonialism aroused feelings of contempt and resentment among the native population, could be frightened into helping the Europeans against recalcitrant natives. Once these Chinese were successfully isolated from the native population, the Europeans could ossify the Chinese in their traditional economic skills and encourage their modernization, while the indigenous peoples were left to stagnate.[41] What resulted was the entrenchment of a more complacent, even chauvinistic Chineseness, which, being "largely backward-looking and rarely assertive," allowed the Chinese to fulfill the economic functions allotted to them within the colonial social machine.[42]

Relations between the ethnic Chinese and indigenous peoples in postcolonial Southeast Asia have been governed by this plural-society politics inherited from the colonial era. The specters of Chinese communism and Chinese capitalism are routinely conjured up by authoritarian regimes to secure their domination.[43] This continuing spectralization of the overseas Chinese as the personification of cosmopolitan capital is responsible for anti-Chinese violence in contemporary Indonesia. Contemporary transnationalism has only served to magnify this chauvinistic version of Chinese cosmopolitanism of which the neo-Confucianists are ideologues. The narratives they fabricate within the domains of national and international public discourse obscure the fact that the spectral identity of capitalist merchant-financier does not incorporate many lower-middle-class and working-class diasporic Chinese.[44] When explicitly sanctioned by the state to maintain its legitimacy, as in the case of Singapore, these narratives have discriminatory political consequences. As Aihwa Ong notes, "By claiming the superiority of Confucian-based moral economies, these discourses define a hierarchy of moral and economic performances that coincide with racial difference in Southeast Asia."[45] But most important, these neo-Confucian fables foreclose the fact that the Chinese of the diaspora have become spectralized by postcolonial global capital even as capital also spectralizes the postcolonial nation-state, such that the Chinese can both facilitate the flow between global capital and the postcolonial state and become the scapegoat for the postcolonial state because they alone are identified with exploitative cosmopolitan capital by the native population. As Wang Gungwu observes, being an overseas Chinese today for many entrepreneurs and businessmen has

> nothing to do with becoming closer to China. It [is] . . . a private and domestic matter only manifested when needed to strengthen a business contact or to follow an approved public convention. . . . [T]he *one legitimate reason to be Chinese in the ASEAN open economies is that it is useful for a wide range of trading purposes.* Even nationalistic governments accept that traders and entrepreneurs helping in national devel-

opment may need to act and think like Chinese in order to maximize their effectiveness in certain Chinese-dominated trading areas. . . . *Being Chinese, therefore, may be somewhat disembodied or internalized and is confined to activities of economic benefit to business.* . . . [B]eing Chinese is a legitimate extension of having a profitable . . . enterprise.[46]

I have suggested that the intensified spectrogenic processes that are part of the financialization of the globe have led to the conflation of Chinese diasporic cosmopolitanism with exploitative chauvinism. This conflation has obscured the indelible contributions of revolutionary Chinese cosmopolitanism to the native awakenings of Southeast Asia in postcolonial national memory. In contemporary Southeast Asia, the tight control of many postcolonial states over the economic and political spheres is in part secured by fostering public amnesia through educational policies and media censorship. Within this context, activist literature has become an important agent for reviving postcolonial national memory and for retrieving the history of nationalist revolution that colonial regimes and neocolonial and postcolonial states have tried to obliterate. As the Indonesian writer Pramoedya Ananta Toer has observed, "The New Order [Indonesian regime] is born from stone, without any history. . . . [It] is simply the New Order, victimizing millions of people."[47] But if nationalist historical fiction aims to point the nation beyond its degraded present by looking back into the revolutionary past, much of that past involves the overseas Chinese. I turn to look at how Pramoedya and the Filipina author Ninotcka Rosca try to undo the collective amnesia of their respective nations about the overseas Chinese by reminding us of the importance of *huaqiao* cosmopolitanism.

Rosca's *State of War* (1988) is a novel about memory. Anna Villaverde, the central character, is a mestiza Chinese who joins the resistance against a Filipino dictatorship that resembles the Marcos regime. As the novel unfolds, the reader is given an insight into her lineage. Insofar as Anna's own recollection of her ancestry takes her back into the history of the Filipino nation and its birth, her personal memory also reenacts and symbolizes the Filipino people's collective memory of their struggles against Spanish, American, and Japanese colonialism. There is much nostalgia and yearning by various characters for a forgotten innocent past, a lost presence uncontaminated by colonial culture, a "morning when the archipelago's song was just beginning, in a still-young world of uncharted seas," at "a time when the world was young, the sea was simply the sea, and names were but newly invented."[48] Rosca characterizes the various colonial regimes as blights upon the archipelago's collective memory. They had introduced alien languages and renamed the landscape until the people became so confused about where they were that they no longer knew who they were and where they were heading. Anna puts it this way: "They monkeyed around with language . . . while we were growing up. Monkeyed around with names. Of people, of places. With dates. And now, I can't remember. No one remembers. And even this . . . even this will be forgotten. They will hide it under another name. No one will remember."[49] But since there is no going back, the way out of this confusion is to retrace these successive colonial invasions, and, more important, the various revolutions against them, backward. If one could at least remember how one got to the befuddled present, then one could go forward.[50]

One of the things to be remembered is the role of revolutionary Chinese cosmopolitanism in Philippines history. At a crucial moment of Anna's family history, Anna's part-Chinese grandmother, who has followed Anna's father into the hills to fight against the Japanese after the Philippines has been abandoned by the United States during the Second World War, comes across three Chinese guerrillas who teach the Filipino soldiers combat skills. When she refuses to believe in the guarantee given by one of the nameless Chinamen that her son will be safe, he reproaches her: "You have never trusted us. We were trading with you before the Spaniards came. Your ancestors were buried in porcelain kilned in our land. Yet, at the white man's word, you razed our districts and massacred our uncles. . . . We'll never understand you."[51] When she asks him why he is fighting a Filipino war, he replies: "Some say [we are fighting the Japanese] because of Manchuria. Some say because any ground where our forefathers are buried is hallowed ground. Can you, with your blood, understand that? The others don't; your people do not. So we say because of Manchuria. This country—it has no continuity. It is only a country of beginnings. No one remembers. Not the burial jars at least."[52] This scene is a missed encounter because there is no mutual understanding. Anna's grandmother does not reassure the Chinaman that she understands him, and he is never mentioned again. But it is a fragment of the historical record of a different type of Chinese cosmopolitanism that can be retrieved by the contemporary Filipino reader from underneath the erasures of colonial and postcolonial plural-society politics.

In his Buru Quartet, a portrayal of the birth of Indies national consciousness in the first three decades of the twentieth century, Pramoedya suggests that *huaqiao* cosmopolitanism and Indies nationalism are genetically connected but that this connection has been effaced by the racial enmity instigated by the Dutch colonial government.[53] Minke, the protagonist and narrator of the first three novels, is a fictive version of Tirto Adhi Soerjo, the father of the national awakening. As Pramoedya tells it, Minke was deeply influenced by the Chinese Republican movement, especially by the ideas of Sun Yat-sen, the father of modern China. The first chapter of *Glass House,* the final volume of the quartet, evokes the thriving activity of two emergent nationalisms in the Indies, Chinese and native, from the perspective of Pangemanann, a native member of the colonial secret police who is Minke's nemesis. As a native representative of the colonial regime, Pangemanann is also a proleptic personification of the neocolonial Indonesian state.

Caught between these two waves of awakening, the colonial state attempts to channel them into a less threatening path. Although the national awakening cannot be stopped, it can be blunted and attenuated into a less radical, reactionary form. It can be co-opted. Pangemanann spreads rumors that ignite the anti-Chinese riots. Afraid that Chinese and native organizations will begin to oppose European interests and erode whatever loyalty it commands, the colonial state turns these two groups against each other so that it can attract the loyalty of the Chinese by claiming to be the protector of the Chinese community. At the same time, violence against the Chinese will destroy the international esteem that the native awakening has commanded from the foreign press.[54] The colonial archives record only the enmity between the overseas Chinese and the Indies natives.

The archaeological effort behind the second and third volumes, however, uncovers the Chinese revolutionaries' direct influence on Minke. They show how he develops a national consciousness, first, by emulating Khouw Ah Soe, a Chinese youth movement leader who has come to the Indies to urge the Indies Chinese to modernize, and, later, by learning from Ang San Mei, the bereaved fiancée of Khouw, who becomes Minke's wife. Khouw exemplifies an anti-imperialist Asian model of modernity. He teaches Minke about European imperialism, Japanese modernization, the Philippines' revolution against Spain, and the importance of publishing to the life of a political movement. He also teaches Minke the difference between *huaqiao* cosmopolitanism and mercantile cosmopolitanism. He points out that most of the overseas Chinese work hard to acquire personal wealth and return to China to attract the admiration of others and to rebuild the graves of their ancestors: "They were not like the overseas Japanese, who always returned with some new learning, who humbly set out to learn all they could from the countries where they sought their livelihood, and who took home what they learned as a contribution to the development of their own nation and people."[55] It is precisely the geopolitical scenario of the early twentieth century that induces the urgent need for an alternative spectralization of the overseas Chinese as *huaqiao*. "The children of the overseas Chinese must be prepared to receive a modern education" so that they can be instilled with an "awareness of the need for change; and for a new man with a new spirit, ready to work for his people and his country. . . . If not, the country of his ancestors would be swallowed up by Japan, just as Africa has been swallowed whole by the English."[56]

By stressing the responsibility that the overseas Chinese should feel toward their nation at the same time that he stresses the modular nature of the Chinese youth movement and Chinese nationalism, Khouw also teaches Minke that cosmopolitanism and nationalism are not incompatible and can be mutually reinforcing. The contribution that the *huaqiao* can make to the Indies is precisely to stimulate the native awakening by example. The nationalist awakening of each Asian country has a cosmopolitan or world-historical significance (or at least a significance for all the colonized peoples of Asia), because "every country in Asia that begins to arise and awaken is not just awakening itself, but is helping to awaken every other nation that has been left behind, including China."[57] Likewise, Ang San Mei reminds Minke that all the educated natives of Asia have a responsibility to help awaken their peoples (*bangsa*).[58] The title of the quartet's second volume, *Child of All Nations (Bangsa)*, expresses the related ideas that the nationalism of each colonized people can contribute something to a more cosmopolitan movement against anticolonialism and, conversely, that the revolutionary cosmopolitanism of the overseas Chinese has been crucial to the birth of Indies nationalism.

*   *   *

One cannot, of course, measure in any tangible way the success of such literary attempts at revising the position of the overseas Chinese in Southeast Asian postcolonial national memory. Insofar as such activist literary narratives try to penetrate, influence, and reshape their respective national public spheres (*Öffentlichkeit*) so that the public sphere can in turn press upon and transform the state by inspiriting the latter, activist literature must also be seen as a form of spectralization that runs counter to and must compete with the spectralization of the postcolonial nation-state by global capital. The success of activist literature can be judged only in the *longue durée,* and even then, only with a lot of reconstructive guesswork. But Rosca and Pramoedya at least help to illustrate the analytical line that needs to be drawn between the two types of cosmopolitanism of the Southeast Asian Chinese. To recapitulate, the type celebrated by neo-Confucianists is continuous with the Chineseness generated by the plural-society policies of colonial regimes and their neocolonial and postcolonial successor states. It is recidivist, chauvinistic, immutable, and a cause of the ethnic enmity that has shaped most postcolonial societies in Southeast Asia. In contradistinction, the *huaqiao* cosmopolitanism of Ang San Mei, Khouw Ah Soe, and Rosca's Chinese guerrilla is measured by generous action and self-sacrificing political commitment.

In contemporary globalization, it is clear that *huaqiao* cosmopolitanism has been overshadowed by Chinese mercantilism, to the point where it has almost completely disappeared. The historical decline of *huaqiao* cosmopolitanism occurred because Chinese migration to Southeast Asia ended by 1950. In the 1950s, in response to pressure from the newly postcolonial states of Southeast Asia and also because it was in fact unable to protect the overseas Chinese, the PRC adopted a restrictive definition of *huaqiao* and encouraged the overseas Chinese to settle abroad and become loyal citizens of their adopted countries.[59] Nevertheless, the question that remains is why the political radicalism of *huaqiao* cosmopolitanism failed to survive on a large scale among the overseas Chinese as patriotic commitment to their adopted nations. In other words, was the general decline of *huaqiao* cosmopolitanism, or at least its admirable features, inevitable? Conversely, can this type of cosmopolitanism from a period of anti-imperialist euphoria that is clearly dated be revived in contemporary globalization? The answer to the first question is probably yes; the answer to the second question is probably no.

One must remember that both types of Chinese cosmopolitanism were generated by processes of spectralization at different points in history. They were induced within and by certain conjunctures of capitalist globalization. Historically, the mercantile activity of the overseas Chinese was spectralized as *Chinese* mercantilism by the plural-society policies of colonial regimes that stressed the exploitative nature of Chinese business, even as the Chinese were indispensable to colonial capital. In contradistinction, the spectralization that gave rise to *huaqiao* cosmopolitanism was induced by anticolonial modernization. If these identities are spectral responses to various shapes *(Gestalten)* of the appearance of global capital, then perhaps the analytical line I have tried to draw was always doomed to break down, because one cannot guard absolutely against the spectral inspiriting of the *huaqiao* paradigm by (mercantile-financial) capital.[60] Spectrality is not an imposition from the outside but the constitutive openness of any finite body. Finance capital is profoundly spectral in nature: national modernization and revolution, after all, need to be financed, and those who are able to finance them are the merchant-financiers.

The fiscalization of the globe is part of the era of *postcolonial* capital. I use the phrase to refer to the huge inflows of capital and technology from the two most powerful capitalist economies in the post–Second World War era, Japan and the United States, to Southeast Asia and parts of East Asia under the regime of flexible capitalist accumulation sanctioned by the World Bank and the International Monetary Fund over a sustained period of forty years, in the form of either financial loans, speculative capital, foreign direct investment, or international subcontracting.[61] Whereas neocolonial capital is typified by the development of underdevelopment (to use Andre Gunder Frank's phrase) that characterizes Africa and South America, postcolonial capital is typified by the development of hyperdevelopment by authoritarian regimes in East and Southeast Asia through global financialization.[62] The governments of hyperdeveloping East and Southeast Asia are not merely comprador states in the strict Marxist sense of the word. They are often vocal in their policy disagreements with and ideological opposition to Northern or Western governments. But this hyperdevelopment does not really indicate the emergence of an Asian Pacific hegemony, as the neo-Confucianists claim. The thematic distinction and occasional doctrinal skirmish between crony capitalism and visions of world trade liberalization (transnational capitalism) remain part of the configuration of postcolonial capital, a structure that ultimately rests on and is sustained by the exploitation of the masses of Asian Pacific nations in the name of free trade and development. As the Asian financial crisis clearly indicates, the United States remains the hegemonic economic power in this configuration. The high economic performance of these East and Southeast Asian nation-states is induced largely by the spectrality of finance capital. Since the abandonment of the gold standard and the deregulation of international currency markets, the U.S. dollar has become the universal equivalent for all other currencies, the money of all other regionally or nationally marked monies, even though it can weaken against other currencies in the short term.

The contemporary rise of Chinese mercantile cosmopolitanism must be situated within this larger force field. The Southeast Asian Chinese diaspora has become a crucial conduit of finance capital in larger East Asia. Thus, in the era of postcolonial capital, the Chinese mercantilism of the colonial era has been re-spectralized as *guanxi* capitalism and celebrated by a new class of overseas Chinese literati in collaboration with the official policies of various East Asian states as a Confucian revival and the beginning of a new Pacific era. This can only serve to exacerbate popular anti-Chinese feeling in those parts of Southeast Asia with Chinese minorities despite the fact that some indigenous ASEAN leaders have begun referring to their countries as "East Asian."[63]

Ironically, the PRC is now appealing to the *huaqiao* paradigm again to attract foreign capital and expertise from the Chinese overseas to facilitate its own development—but this time, development in the image of Singapore, Hong Kong, and Taiwan.[64] Thus, it would seem that what was initially a spectral identity that arose in order to allow China to defend itself against Western imperialism finds itself possessed by the opposite type of spectralization. The revived *huaqiao* paradigm is now a means for China to open itself up to capitalist globalization with all its attendant contradictions. In Special Economic Zones such as Xiamen and Shenzhen, where the new *huaqiao* managers and businessmen mistreat mainland workers, especially women workers, the chauvinism of mercantilist Chinese cosmopolitanism is felt in full force in the ancestral homeland.[65] Such phenomena exemplify and attest to the spectral power of finance capital to conjure up concrete forms of Chinese cosmopolitanism that can monstrously supplement and usurp even the putative geographical origin of Chineseness.

II

Human Rights and the Inhuman

5

Posit(ion)ing Human Rights in the Current Global Conjuncture

The practical discourse of human rights claims the burden of safeguarding the most fundamental features and conditions of our humanity. Insofar as this universalistic vocation can conflict with the state's governance of its citizens, human rights discourse is the other way of giving a human face to globalization. This is why new theories of cosmopolitanism invariably point to human rights NGOs as an example of the new cosmopolitanism. The need to institutionalize human rights discourse at the level of international relations became more urgent after the Second World War, during which human rights violations by the totalitarian Nazi regime were so extreme that they were regarded not simply as crimes against individuals but as crimes against humanity as a whole. Hence, the general tenor of human rights discourse is moralistic. Violations brought into the phenomenality of public light via the global mass media also tend to be of the most extreme or exceptional kind, such as genocide or massacre. When aligned with neoliberal arguments about the power of globalization to unify us into a common humanity, the moral universalism of human rights discourse can, paradoxically, be used to justify economic globalization as a form of postcolonial civilizing mission. It can legitimize the predatory expansion of global capital as a fundamental mechanism for spreading the rule of law and the recognition of civil liberties purportedly ignored by "traditional" political cultures and "despotic" regimes outside the North Atlantic. This process of moralistic finger-pointing conveniently elides the less visible violations of human rights occurring in non-exceptional quotidian settings outside the hegemonic North Atlantic that are directly caused by globalization.

In the second part of this book I outline an account of the normativity of human rights that acknowledges their contaminated nature without reducing them to ideological reflections of global capitalism.

In the current conjuncture of global capitalism, the deployment of human rights discourse by various key actors on the stage of international politics takes the general form of a performative contradiction. Existing human rights discourses claim a normative force that is unconditional. Yet within the international frame of their invocation, these practical claims become radically contaminated and stretch the theories of normativity that have so far governed our understanding of human rights to the point where they become untenable. Does the contaminated normativity of human rights necessarily lead to nihilism, cynical pragmatism, or relativism? Or can normativity be both unconditional and contaminated at the same time? In this chapter I suggest that the theoretical significance of the internationalization of human rights—the work that it does in the house of theory—is that it enjoins us to think of normativity as a response/responsibility to original contamination.

Orientations

Human rights are a crucial part of politics and international relations, ethical and political philosophy, law, and even comparative history and anthropology if we are concerned with the cultural or historical origins of the concept. I begin with several preliminary clarifications to orient the reader to my approach. First, the debate over human rights in international relations should be wrenched away from the common but mistaken approach that juxtaposes the plurality of cultures with the universal validity that makes human rights normative. This view suggests that if human rights are inalienable entitlements which should belong to all individuals for the sole reason that they are human, then irresolvable tensions inevitably arise from the fact that individuals also exist as members of a plurality of collectives called "cultures," which have their own unique norms and rules. Such an argument can function to expose universalizing modes of thought as cultural forms of imperialism that serve the interests of a hegemonic culture. Thus, unwittingly or consciously, critiques of the ideological abuse of the doctrine of universal human rights are influenced by the early Karl Marx's critique of the formalism of bourgeois civil rights.[1] They argue that the Universal Declaration of Human Rights (1948) sets forth a vision of rights that "reveal[s] a strong Western bias" and regards "human rights ahistorically and in isolation from their social, political, and economic milieu."[2] Phrased even more sharply, the Declaration, *qua* doctrinal basis for the U.S. government's drive for international human rights, is denounced as a mask for *Realpolitik* because it incorporates "all human beings across nations and cultures into an abstract universal community of which the U.S. government is the champion."[3]

This is also the view of many Asian governmental actors in contemporary global politics. For instance, in his statement at the Vienna World Conference on Human Rights titled "The Real World of Human Rights," the foreign minister of Singapore argued that "the extent and exercise of rights . . . varies greatly from one culture or political community to another . . . because [rights] are the products of the historical experiences of particular peoples."[4] He cautioned against a harmful universalism, an artificially imposed and stifling unanimity, "which is used to deny or mask the reality of diversity." This staged resistance to Northern or Western imperialism is representative of the position of Asian states on human rights (see the Bangkok Declaration adopted by ministers and representatives of Asian states). The ostensible opposition between universalism and cultural relativism expressed here is also the insular focus of the greater part of cultural studies and postcolonial discourse analysis.

We would, however, be wrong to interpret this scene in terms of the sterile opposition between universalism and cultural relativism, for at least two reasons. First, the critique of the historical limits of the Western concept of human rights is also a universalistic argument that remains within a human rights framework. Far from being monolithic, the concept of human rights includes first-, second-, and third-generation rights.[5] The Asian governmental position on the cultural limits of the Western vision of human rights is invariably linked to an argument about the need to subordinate political and civil rights to the right to development. It thus depends on an assertion of the universal right to self-determination of all peoples. Second, the claim to cultural difference by Asian states is itself questionable since the figured face of statist cultural difference is not identical to the cultural diversity of its peoples. The very governments that claim to be the custodians of Southeast Asian cultures are responsible for the destruction of the cultures of indigenous peoples who stand in the way of the deforestation and mining projects of state-supported capitalist development. Therefore, the question should not be whether universal human rights exist or not. Instead, we should focus on the nature and limits of the normative claims being made by various actors—Northern and Southern states and NGOs—when they appeal to human rights within the theoretical framework of established human rights discourse.

A third reason makes the attempt to move beyond the question of universalism versus cultural relativism particularly important. Prior to the Asian financial crisis of 1997, the spectacular economic growth of the Asia-Pacific region led to the rise of the "East Asian" path of development as a competing model of global capitalism.[6] China's current breathtaking rate of economic growth is gradually eroding the power of American influence in Asia.[7] Both then and now, some Asian conglomerates are outperforming U.S. and European multinationals in private sector investment in the Asia-Pacific region.[8] The message in the business pages of the *New York Times* then was that U.S. companies should "plug themselves into local conditions" by "finding the right partner, someone to guide you through the maze of Asia," much as Ariadne guided Theseus.[9] (But then we know what befell Ariadne once she had served her purpose.) After the correct moans and groans were made about East Timor, the Clinton administration wooed then-President Suharto of Indonesia for support for market-opening progress at the APEC (Asia-Pacific Economic Cooperation) meeting in Osaka: "'He's our kind of guy,' a senior Administration official who deals often on Asian policy, said. . . . '[T]his is the kind of relationship we want to have with China.'"[10] This oddly conjugal vocabulary, which is also evident in the negotiations leading to China's entry into the WTO, indicates that what is at stake in the elaborately media-staged skirmishes between states over international human rights is not really Western or Northern imperializing universalism versus Eastern or Southern cultural difference. The two poles of that binary opposition are complicitous. The fight is between different globalizing models of capitalist accumulation attempting to assert economic hegemony.[11] The coding of this fight in terms of cultural difference diverts our attention from the subtending line of force of global capital that brings the two antagonists into an aporetic embrace *against* the possibility of other alternatives of development, feminist or ecologicalsubalternist. Hence, any analysis of the normative claims of appeals to human rights within established discourse ought to ask: What do we mean when we posit human rights? How are these various positings positioned in or by the current global conjuncture?

As I argue in the concluding section of this chapter, the irreducible imbrication of all claims to human rights within the force field of global capitalism requires us to rethink the understanding of normativity that is the basis of currently existing human rights discourse. Here, let me offer a schematic working definition of "normativity" for a non-specialist readership. Simply put, normativity is that which confers the status of norm upon a maxim of action or a desired state of affairs. It is the being-normative of norms, that which makes a norm normative. Thus, normativity is that quality that makes us regard ourselves as obligated to bring about a certain state of things or as being bound—etymologically, *obligation* derives from *ligature*—by an imperative commanding or restraining a certain course of action.

In contemporary Western thought, there are different criteria for the rational determination of different sources of normativity just as there are different types of normativity. The common analytical distinctions are between legal, ethical, and moral normativity. According to legal positivism (the dominant position in analytical jurisprudence), a specific rule is legally valid if it conforms to an internalized, rationally accepted set of social standards that operates within a territorial political community.[12] Such conformity makes the rule a rule of law because its enforcement by coercive mechanisms will be upheld by popular social sanction. Yet as morally evil laws such as Nazi laws illustrate, legal normativity is distinguishable from ethical and moral normativity because it is concerned only with the day-to-day operations of a legal system and not with the moral value of that system beyond the minimum content of natural law that is fundamental to the social life of a particular political community, for instance, some prohibition on killing, provision of basic resources and protection of property, and so on.[13]

By contrast, the normativity of morality is unconditional. After Kant, a maxim is said to possess moral force, to be morally binding, only if it is universally valid for all rational creatures or humanity in general. But as Hegel astutely pointed out in his critique of Kant, the problem with the unconditional, atemporal, "pure" normativity characterizing morality (*Moralität*) is twofold. First, because it is articulated at such an abstract level of universality, the moral law is deprived of all determinate objective content. Second, the abstraction "humanity," the collective carrier and agent of morality's norms, cannot be politically effective because it is not embodied in a sociocultural institutional context in which meaningful action can take place. Hence, in Hegel's view, morality risks degenerating into the bad infinity of destructive absolute subjectivism whose type case is the Terror of the French Revolution. The third type of normativity—the ethical—can be seen as a bridge that mediates between mere legality and abstract universal morality. As distinguished from morality, ethical normativity (*Sittlichkeit*) refers to binding substantive forms of ethical self-understanding that are arrived at through consensual procedures of law enactment and political decision making. Thus, at the same time that the procedural consensus of their articulation (procedural justice) reflects universal rationality, ethical norms also express and give objective embodiment to the concrete life of a political community, thereby reconciling the universal and the particular. The ethical realm has also been characterized as the political morality of the state or its (national) public sphere (*Öffentlichkeit*).[14] It is the site where morality can exert an influence over the political and legal processes of the state. The important point to note, however, is that notwithstanding their differences, these three types of normativity all compute normativity in terms of *rational* obligation. Legality, morality, and ethical life are respectively determined by and express legal-political rationality, universal reason, and the ethical self-understanding of the national political community. Indeed, legality, morality, and ethics are interrelated and form a continuum only because they share this rationalist determination of normativity.

This working taxonomy of normativity helps us position the practical discourse of international human rights more exactly. The anomalous status of international human rights instruments is well known. On the one hand, they are regarded as part of public international law.[15] They are commonly invoked to justify humanitarian intervention in areas under the jurisdiction of sovereign states on the grounds of illegality under the provisions of international treaties. Thus, their normativity would appear to be legal in nature. "Public international law" is, however, a misnomer. Within the current interstate system, where nation-states largely retain their sovereignty and there is no supranational executive body capable of enforcing decisions independently of the compliance of individual states, public international law cannot be law in the strict sense. On the other hand, to the extent that humanitarian interventions also invoke the universality of human rights, they might be seen as examples of moral normativity. Yet, unlike moral claims, human rights claims have a normative force that is institutionally grounded. Since these claims are codified in the UN Charter and other international covenants and resolutions, human rights claimants can rightfully expect to rely on the limited policing mechanisms which are available to ensure that the claimed rights are being observed. Consequently, it may be more appropriate to regard international human rights practical discourse as expressing a kind of political morality on an international scale.[16] Indeed, transnational human rights NGO networks regard themselves as forming an international public sphere (*Öffentlichkeit*). Primarily deriving its normative force from quasi-formal codifications that center on and elaborate the Kantian principle of moral respect for humanity, such an emergent transnational *Sittlichkeit,* or ethical community, seeks to influence the actions of particular states.

We see from the foregoing that theories of political morality of modern German philosophy are far from obsolete. They have become institutionalized and continue to exert a tenacious influence through the operational logics of states and other collective actors. As I will later suggest, Asian states asserting sovereignty in defense against foreign intervention over human rights issues take a position that is not unlike Hegel's communitarian critique of Kant's cosmopolitanism. The claim that transnational human rights networks constitute an international public sphere should therefore be understood as a response to a Hegelian communitarian critique of neo-Kantian human rights talk. Yet these philosophies of normativity also find themselves deformed in their historical performance in contemporary globalization. I will show that arguments about the existence of an international public sphere or transnational political morality are implausible because they are grounded in a rationalist conception of normativity that the actually existing capitalist world system renders untenable. But against neo-Hegelian statism, I will also suggest that international human rights have a very real normative force and do not merely take "the form of an ought-to-be [*des Sollen*]."[17] The question, then, is how to think this normative force, how to philosophize otherwise.

One final clarification about the genre of my argument: The preferred mode of philosophical discourse on human rights is deontological talk. But formal philosophizing inevitably ends up confirming the rationalist determination of normativity that we should question because it presupposes ideal rational actors. Hence, I have chosen to approach the philosophical question of normativity by way of a sociohistorical analysis of the human rights practices of finite institutional actors within the text of global capitalism. It should, however, be clear that I am not suggesting that human rights practical discourse in global capitalism is bereft of any normative element. That would be a lapse into sociological determinism and historicist relativism. My wager is that normativity should be thought outside both historicist relativism and rationalist-teleological conceptions of history.

The Three Voices of Existing Human Rights Practical Discourse and Their Philosophical Basis

Existing human rights practical discourse can be divided into three voices. What I call the first voice is the position of governments in constitutional democracies in the economically hegemonic North. The second voice refers to the position of Asian governments. The third voice refers to the position of human rights NGOs in the South. My taxonomy is meant to be heuristic. Its immediate frame of reference is the assertion of cultural difference by Asian governments in response to charges of human rights violations. I have not considered the position of former Eastern bloc countries in a post–Cold War scenario, although it is arguable that they have been assimilated into the South. My concern here is with the universal validity of human rights in general, the normative force claimed by the three voices of human rights. This is not quite the same as the validity of specific human rights. The latter refers to the determinate negative or positive rights laid out in conventions, covenants, or declarations. The former refers to something more primary and more difficult to determine: the right to human rights. Obviously, any articulation of why the constitution of human beings gives them a right to rights will influence the specific rights that flow from this universal entitlement. The crucial point is that unlike specific rights, which can be challenged, the right to rights is not contestable because it has no specific historical, political, or cultural content.

The United States prides itself on having contributed to international human rights discourse the most famous articulation and justification of the idea of rights: the justification of rights by natural law in the preamble to the Declaration of Independence. But in fact, as Louis Henkin points out, universal human rights reflect no particular political philosophy: "International human rights instruments do not affirm rights as 'natural.' They do not necessarily assume that a person is originally, or in principle, autonomous, that rights antecede society and government. . . . As justification for human rights, they simply assert truths—or rhetoric—that no one has bothered to question. Rights derive from the 'inherent dignity of the human person.'"[18] The phrase "dignity of the human person" comes from the Preamble and Article 1 of the Universal Declaration of Human Rights. The Preamble begins with the statement that the recognition of "the inherent dignity and of the equal and inalienable rights of all members of the human family is the foundation of freedom, justice and peace in the world." Article 1 elaborates this inherent dignity in terms of an anthropological thesis: "All humans are born free and equal in dignity and rights. They are endowed with reason and conscience and should act towards one another in a spirit of brotherhood."

The minimal philosophical justification of the human entitlement to rights in these sections of the Universal Declaration seems to be as follows: Humans are born with an inherent dignity. This is, however, not a natural justification of human rights. Since rights come into existence only via political instruments that specify and protect them, dignity by itself is not the source of rights. Dignity is rather some contentless human attribute that is the basis of freedom in the world. The second sentence of Article 1 introduces "reason" and also "conscience" for the first time. The three terms, "dignity," "freedom," and "reason," are related as follows: Because dignity is contentless, it involves a practical orientation. Reason is the operator of normative human action (because humans "are endowed with reason and conscience," they "should act") that protects and fleshes out dignity by specifying determinate rights via political instruments. Now, precisely because dignity is contentless, the work of reason is open-ended and interminable, and this links reason to freedom. Freedom is the ideal state of not being blindly constrained. Reason co-belongs with freedom because it constitutes the persistent ability to question and transform the external situations in which we find ourselves. In other words, human rights are the enterprise by which reason persistently affirms human dignity. We are entitled to them because we are born with dignity but also, more important, because we possess the rational capacity needed to reaffirm dignity. The open-ended nature of the human rights enterprise is expressed in the exhortatory nature of the Declaration, which involves a pledge by all signing nations to achieve a non-exhaustive common standard.[19] This open-endedness is also reflected in the subsequent increase in human rights instruments and in ongoing debates about different views of human rights.

I have suggested that the normative force of human rights belongs to the realm of political morality rather than morality per se. But the axioms of political morality are derived from morality. Thus, whether self-consciously or by historical osmosis, the philosophical justification of human rights found in the Declaration is indebted to Kant's definition of the dignity of man in his second formulation of the categorical imperative. Seeking a law for moral action that would be universally valid for all rational creatures, Kant resorted to the postulate of human dignity as something that is an end in itself. For Kant, inclinations can have only a conditional or relative validity. The object of an inclination constitutes a merely subjective end because it appeals to sensuous desire. In contradistinction, dignity is an objective end because it is of absolute or intrinsic worth. Hence, respect for dignity can serve as a universal law for moral action:

> Now I say that the human being and in general every rational being *exists* as an end in itself [*Zweck an sich selbst*], *not merely as a means* [*Mittel*] to be used by this or that will at its discretion; instead he must in all his actions, whether directed to himself or also to other rational beings, always be regarded *at the same time as an end*. All objects of the inclinations have only a conditional worth [*Wert*]. . . . Thus the worth of any object *to be acquired* by our action is always conditional. Beings the existence of which rests not on our will but on nature, if they are beings without reason, still have only a relative worth, as means, and are therefore called *things*, whereas rational beings are called *persons* because their nature already marks them out as an end in itself, that is, as something that may not be used merely as a means, and hence so far limits all choice (and is an object of respect [*Achtung*]). These, therefore, are not subjective ends, the existence of which as an effect of our action has a worth *for us*, but rather *objective ends*, that is, beings the existence of which is in itself an end, and indeed one such that no other end, to which they would serve *merely* as means, can be put in

place, since without it nothing of *absolute worth* would be found anywhere; but if all worth were conditional and therefore contingent, then no supreme practical principle for reason could be found anywhere.[20]

What is interesting for us is that Kant proceeds to distinguish between dignity *qua* end-in-itself and merely subjective ends by means of a mercantile metaphor even though, technically speaking, human practical action is ontologically prior to historical commerce because it is the "rationality" behind historical commerce, trading, or commodification. In the kingdom of ends *(im Reiche der Zwecke)* constituted by human action, Kant writes:

> Everything has either a *price* [*Preis*] or a *dignity* [*Würde*]. What has a price can be replaced by something else as its *equivalent;* what on the other hand is raised above all price and therefore admits of no equivalent has a dignity.
>
> What is related to general human inclinations and needs has a *market price* [*Marktpreis*]; . . . . but that which constitutes the condition under which alone something can be an end in itself has not merely a relative worth, that is, a price, but an inner worth [*einen innern Wert*], that is, *dignity.*[21]

As an intrinsic worth, dignity transcends all relative values, all exchange, all equivalence, and has no market price. Hence, any being with dignity cannot be treated instrumentally, as the means to another end.

Although narrower in scope than Kant's universal moral law, the philosophical justification of the right to human rights inherits these axiomatic oppositions between absolute and relative worth, dignity and market price, and the philosophical baggage that goes with them. We will see that human rights discourse literalizes the quasi-metaphorical opposition between dignity and market price. The important point here is that as a result of this Kantian legacy, "dignity" in the Declaration is not identical to the civil and political liberties that are invoked by the United States when it accuses Singapore or China of violating human rights. Dignity subtends every specific human right but is not reducible to any specific right because it is its philosophical ground. The concept of dignity refers to nothing less than the peculiar nature of human nature *qua* rational nature to be free of natural or arbitrary human constraint, the leitmotif of philosophical modernity. This means that all visions of specific human rights are open to contestation if they are found to obstruct the affirmation of dignity.

This separation of dignity from specific rights indicates that the official Asian position on human rights set out in the Bangkok Declaration (1993) and the individual statements by Asian ministers at the Vienna Conference (1993) do not depart from the normative framework of established human rights discourse. The universality of human rights derives from the shared condition of being human, that is, being endowed with dignity and reason. Dignity and reason constitute the common ground for the civil and political liberties associated with Western constitutional democracies as well as the questioning of this vision of human rights by Asian governments as myopic and narrow because it does not live up to the spirit of international cooperation specified in the UN Charter and fails to take into consideration the economic problems and cultural specificity of Asian societies. There is thus a tacit agreement by both sides that there is some positive thing called "human dignity" that must be affirmed and protected even if there is disagreement about the best way to protect it. For instance, the official Singapore position is that "poverty makes a mockery of all civil liberties," that "economic growth is the necessary foundation of any system that claims to advance human dignity," that "order and stability are essential for development," and, hence, that "good government is necessary for the realization of all rights."[22] Even the additional claim to cultural diversity of nations is not, on its face, cultural relativist since Article 29, section 1, of the Universal Declaration stipulates that "everyone has duties to the community in which alone the free and full development of his personality is possible."[23]

Indeed, the official Asian position or second voice seems eminently reasonable in its insistence that "the promotion of human rights should be encouraged by co-operation and consensus, and not through confrontation and the imposition of incompatible values." Not entirely without justification, Asian governments accuse Northern governments of using a double standard and of applying a limited vision of human rights as a power ploy to sabotage the economic success of East Asia. Emphasizing "the interdependence and indivisibility of economic, social, cultural, civil and political rights," the Asian governments claim to be the voice of reason and seek to resist intervention by Northern governments over human rights issues by reaffirming the principles of respect for national sovereignty and territorial integrity.[24]

Asian governments therefore argue that communitarian values and national-territorial integrity are necessary conditions for the concrete maximization of human dignity. Thus, where the first voice is isomorphic with neo-Kantianism, the second voice more or less expresses a version of Hegel's statist-communitarian critique of Kantian moral politics. For Hegel, morality is merely universal reason in its subjective and abstract form. The nation-state is universal reason in its objective actuality: "The nation state [*das Volk als Staat*] is the spirit [*Geist*] in its substantial rationality and immediate actuality, and is therefore the absolute power on *earth;* each state is consequently a sovereign and independent entity in relation to others. The state has a primary and absolute entitlement to be a sovereign and independent power *in the eyes of others,* i.e., *to be recognized* by them."[25] Thus, "the immediate existence of the state as the ethical substance [*sittliche Substanz*], i.e., its right, is directly embodied not in abstract but in concrete existence, and only this concrete existence, rather than any of those many universal thoughts which are held to be moral commandments, can be the principle of its action and behaviour."[26] Consequently, Hegel argued that Kant's idea of a world federation of states, the historical model for the UN *qua* human rights enforcer, could never be fully actualized. Resting "on moral, religious, or other grounds and considerations, [such a federative agreement between states] would always be dependent on particular sovereign wills, and would therefore continue to be tainted by contingency."[27] Likewise, Asian governments counterpose the concrete or actual universality of the national political community against the false abstraction of "humanity" that Northern governments arrogantly deploy. Singapore's statement at the Vienna Convention is titled "The Real World of Human Rights."

Let us now consider how the third voice circumvents this statist-communitarian argument that the sovereign nation-state alone is the concrete embodiment of universality. In a formal response to the Bangkok Declaration, human rights NGOs in the Asia-Pacific region have distanced themselves from both official positions. Like the second voice, the third voice also advocates a holistic and integrated approach to human rights and affirms the right to self-determination of all peoples. Yet it deploys these claims against Asian governments that violate human rights. In sketchy summary, the third voice stresses that a holistic approach to human rights means that one set of rights cannot be used to bargain for another. It asserts that all governments must observe the right of peoples to freely determine their political status and pursue their economic, social, and cultural development and specifically mentions indigenous groups within Asia-Pacific nations which are denied the right to self-determination because they have not been recognized by their governments. But what distinguishes the third voice of human rights discourse from the first voice is its attribution of the poor state of human rights to the current global economic order. These NGOs connect domestic oppression to international exploitation by pointing to the collaboration between local elites, transnational corporations, and international aid agencies. They reject the capital-intensive and inherently wasteful statist view of development and argue for a more humane "balanced and sustainable development" that maximizes the social development of the people.[28]

The heterogeneity of this third voice is most evident in the feminist claim that the international human rights movement reiterates conceptual biases in focusing on the public realm as the primary site of human rights violation.[29] Feminist NGOs have asserted the need to consider all violence against women as a human rights issue, regardless of the public or private status of the perpetrator. They have proposed a more flexible theory of culture as an antidote to the abuse of women in patriarchalized national culture.[30] They have also criticized statist development for the additional reason that growth policy–oriented models of development are incompatible with the rights of women in development because such models seek to integrate women into state-centric plans of economic growth instead of addressing systemic economic, political, and ideological biases against women.[31] In sum, the third voice articulates a new universalism that is mindful of systemic economic inequality, genuine cultural diversity, and gender. It does not regard the advocacy of human rights as an encroachment upon national sovereignty. Indeed, the Bangkok NGO Declaration claims an entitlement to international solidarity that transcends national borders to protect human rights throughout the world: "We are entitled to join hands in solidarity to protect human rights world-wide. International solidarity transcends the national border to refute claims of State sovereignty and of non-interference in the internal affairs of the State."[32]

But notwithstanding the immense doctrinal differences among them, all three voices share the same normative framework. All existing human rights practical discourses are grounded in the Kantian notion of moral respect for dignity as an end in itself and something of absolute worth. Thus, they all exhibit three key characteristics. First, because the point of departure is the concept of human dignity as the supreme value that transcends all material interests or empirical inclinations, each vision of human rights is seen to be separate from the realm of particularistic political or economic interests. Each of the three voices within existing human rights practical discourse discredits its opponent by pointing out that the opponent's vision of human rights is in fact contaminated by its particular site of emergence, that it is an ideological mask for some insidious particularistic interest: Northern domination or global capitalism in the case of the first voice; industrializing Oriental despotism or statist capitalist development in the case of the second voice. Each of the three voices claims to be the pure voice of reason representing genuine universality in which respect for human dignity can be maximized: the autonomous individual (the first voice); a community of nations that respects cultural differences and the right to development (the second voice); and a polymorphous global community within an equitable international economic order that is genuinely sensitive to sexual difference and cultural diversity (the third voice). Second, this separation of genuine universality from particularistic interests in turn implies a distinction between material reality and rational form. Here, practical primacy is accorded to rational form. It is presumed that a holistic system of rights in which human dignity is respected embodies a total rational form for the ordering of social and collective interaction between individuals and states and in interstate relations. Respect for dignity also involves a practical injunction for the persistent rational transformation of existing institutional structures. Through the act of respect, the enjoined agents are elevated beyond their particularistic interests into a state of rational universality, simultaneously (trans)forming themselves and their world according to a moral image prescribed by reason alone.

Finally, each of the three voices claims that through the prescription of rational form, critique is able to change institutional structures that oppress or fail to foster human dignity. A lot of faith is placed in both the neutrality and the paramount effectivity of the good conscience/reason of various institutional actors, that is to say, the political morality of states in the act of interpreting the appropriate rights or restrictions necessary in a given situation, or international public opinion as the moral conscience keeping state authoritarianism in check and guiding state policy toward sustainable development.[33] As Dieter Henrich succinctly notes, such a theory of normativity views the world as a field that is bereft of norms. The world is not itself a source of norms but instead a field to be shaped by norms that only *rational* human agents can bring into play. Any positing of human rights within the current framework of human rights discourse tacitly presupposes the negotiation between an ideal world-image and the existing world situation onto which that rational world-image is projected and which will accept that world-image as universally valid. In other words, what is envisioned is an ideal or rational universality that is anterior to historical human interaction but has to be flexible enough to accommodate the diversity and singularity of its global constituent actors in order to be realized as a concrete universality.[34]

This theoretical framework easily leads to a Habermasian proceduralist account of normativity that models international relations in the image of constitutional-democratic procedures that are accorded quasi-transcendental status. In progressive literature on the topic, many argue that a multilateral international forum is the way to go in a shrinking world of information command and borderless economies. The third voice of human rights, the international network of human rights NGOs, has been represented, and has represented itself, as a transnational political morality or *Sittlichkeit*. Effectively, these claims about the existence of a global civil society or an international public sphere in which the right of peoples to self-determination is respected imply that the discrepancy between communitarian and neo-Kantian rational images of the world is in the process of being historically eliminated by post–Cold War globalization.

Global Capitalism as a Case of Original Contamination

Human rights NGO networks may dream of living in an undivided but also diverse world. The essential problem with the normative framework of human rights practical discourse, however, is that it cannot account for the original contamination of the three voices by virtue of their constitutive inscription within the force field of global capital. In the existing framework, different visions of human rights are explained in terms of a progression toward a more encompassing totality. Each successive voice criticizes the preceding vision for being contaminated by particularistic interests and sees its vision of human rights as subsuming and transcending (in German, *aufheben:* to destroy and preserve at the same time) the preceding vision. This drive toward self-purification—or what amounts to the same thing, this denial of inscription, of being part of an uncontrollable network of forces—is another manifestation of the notion of pure human dignity that exists outside equivalence, exchange, and market price. To reiterate, because dignity is contentless, it can be given content only by rational action. The open-ended nature of the human rights project is said to reside in the power of reason to take changing world contexts into account in its articulation of a moral world-image. In the first and last instance, this rational world-image is anterior to politics and economics although it must subsume them in its concrete realization. This is, of course, a literalization of the Kantian quasi-metaphorical opposition between dignity and market price. Each voice of human rights discourse claims to be the pure voice of reason representing genuine universality and to serve as an external check on particularistic interests and material forces.

But what if the globalization of capital is uncontainable? What if it establishes a de facto, oppressive universality that cannot be transcended by normative action? What if, all claims to the contrary, normative institutional action finds itself reinscribed within a weave that includes the very particularistic material forces it seeks to transcend or check precisely because it is generated by this weave of forces? More specifically, if the three voices of human rights are complicit or cannot differentiate/extricate themselves from one another by virtue of their constitutive imbrication in global capital, then their original contamination means that the normativity of human rights can no longer be thought in terms of an ideal universal form that is grounded in the co-belonging of pure human dignity and reason. We would then need to rethink normativity otherwise, from the ground up.

The contamination of the first voice by global capital is obvious enough. For instance, when the United States conceptually relates human rights issues to trade negotiations by presupposing that human rights and commercial/industrial growth are causally dependent, this link means that the latter can sometimes override the former as a result of lobbying by corporations.[35] Furthermore, the first voice can also serve Northern economic hegemony indirectly. It can cover up the scandalous open secret that the resource-intensive and inherently wasteful macro-policies of economic development and market economy–led linear models espoused by international development agencies and financial institutions such as the World Bank and International Monetary Fund force some countries of the South deeper and deeper into debt, thereby maintaining an unjust global economic order controlled by a handful of elites, transnational corporations (TNCs), and Northern states. In the current conjuncture, these Bretton Woods institutions are inadequate to prevent the erosion of the technological and economic bases of power of the Group of Seven nations in the face of East Asian economic success. The World Trade Organization, which was established after the Uruguay round of GATT negotiations, is the main institutional structure for the execution of an elaborate plan to reorganize global production and production capacities by vastly extending the scope of rules for the protection of intellectual property rights throughout the world by means of multilateral agreements that link these rights to trade. The most notable of these agreements is the Trade-Related Aspects of Intellectual Property Rights (TRIPS) agreement, which is part of "a policy of 'technological protectionism' aimed at consolidating an international division of labour whereunder Northern countries generate innovations and Southern countries constitute the market for the resulting products and services."[36] The TRIPS agreement is effectively a "neo-mercantilist" attempt to destroy the emergence of competition from outside the hegemonic North.[37] By restricting access to key technologies and pursuing aggressive policies to open up foreign markets in Asian and Latin American NIEs (newly industrialized economies) via export promotion and reciprocal market access, industrialized countries seek to control industrial development in the South and to expand the space and freedom of TNCs at the same time. They seek to produce a global division between knowledge-rich and knowledge-poor countries, recolonizing the latter by permanently blocking them from acquiring the knowledge and capacity to accumulate wealth. It is, of course, not a nice thing to steal the ideas of others, especially when these ideas can lead to great profits. But then, no Northern government is suggesting that the wealth accumulated by Northern countries after centuries of colonial and imperialist theft be returned to the South.

Indeed, the global expansion of intellectual property protection can also be a legalized form of late capitalist theft. As Vandana Shiva points out, international patent and licensing agreements facilitate a new era of bio-imperialism since they are used by Northern-based transnational pharmaceutical and agribusiness corporations to monopolize the biological resources of the Third World, which can be developed into drugs, food, and energy sources. Shiva argues that "the U.S. has accused countries of the Third World of engaging in 'unfair trading practice' if they fail to adopt U.S. patent laws which allow monopoly rights in life forms. Yet it is the U.S. which has engaged in unfair practices related to the use of Third World genetic resources. It has freely taken the biological diversity of the Third World to spin millions of dollars of profits, none of which have been shared with Third World countries, the original owners of the germ plasm."[38] Furthermore,

> with worldwide patent protection, agribusiness and the seed trade are trying to achieve truly global reach. While the rhetoric is agricultural development in the Third World, the enforcement of strong patent protection for monopoly ownership of life processes will undermine and underdevelop agriculture in the Third World in a number of ways. . . . Patent protection displaces the farmer as a competitor, transforms him into a supplier of free raw material, and makes him totally dependent on industrial supplies for vital inputs like seeds. Above all, the frantic cry for patent protection in agriculture is for protection from farmers, who are the original breeders and developers of biological resources in agriculture. It is argued that patent protection is essential for innovation—however it is essential only for the innovation that brings profits to corporate businesses.[39]

The negative consequences of the globalizing/universalizing of intellectual property protection should therefore be seen in a continuum with the curious homology between the first voice's use of human rights universalism to justify encroachments upon the national sovereignty of the developing South and the attempt of the postindustrial North to increase the freedom of TNCs from regulation by host governments. Political freedom and the liberalization/freeing of trade go hand in hand. The former secures assent for the globalizing of market mechanisms and the continuing fiscalization of the globe. Needless to say, the global spread of free-market mechanisms cannot lead to generalized development. It only exacerbates world polarization and leads, in some cases, to the formation of comprador states that subordinate development to the requirements of transnational capitalism and adjust their economies to global restructuring. The compradorized state is no longer capable of actively shaping its own society and political morality. This handicapping of democratic national projects in the periphery from the start gives the lie to the neoliberal sermon that the global spread of free-market mechanisms will lead to global democratization.

The inequality of North-South relations is partly responsible for a seemingly undivided stand by Asian countries on human rights. The second voice's catechism on the right to development, however, is just as contaminated by global capitalism. For systemic reasons, the spectacular economic growth of some East Asian countries is not evenly distributed to every sector. Most of their governments are no longer comprador regimes in the strict Marxist sense. They are vocal in their policy disagreements with and ideological opposition to the North or the West. Yet their high economic performance, essential to their continued legitimation, depends on their willingness to accommodate transnational capital. These governments acquiesce in the exploitation entailed by profitable foreign investment: poor laboring conditions and low pay in Free Trade Zones compared to those in the countries of origin of TNCs. Indeed, the richer Asian countries are now investing in their poorer neighbors and preaching a competing "Asian" model of free trade there. In a visit to Manila in 1992, Lee Kuan Yew, former prime minister of Singapore, urged the Philippines to model itself after the economic policies of Indonesia, Malaysia, and Thailand, saying, "You will have to further liberalise the trade and investment regulations to stimulate activity."[40] Thus, the real audience of the continuing human rights debate between Asian and Western governments is the disenfranchised in Asian countries whom their governments are trying to convince about the virtues of their authoritarian path to capitalist development. It is the disenfranchised who are caught in the aporetic embrace between a predatory international capitalism and an indigenous capitalism seeking to internationalize.

I come now to the most counterintuitive and politically incorrect part of my argument: the contamination of human rights NGOs. This third voice tries to extract itself from the miasmic complicity between domestic oppression and international exploitation by claiming the normative status of an international public sphere or, what is not quite the same thing, a global civil society. In topographical terms, both "civil society" and "public sphere" refer to zones that exhibit autonomy in relation to the territorial state. They are thus sites of struggle between dominant and counter-hegemonic forces. The normative status of civil society simply comes from this autonomy from the state that allows it to represent society to the state and to alleviate pressures that come from state institutions. By contrast, the concept of the public sphere (*Öffentlichkeit*) is formulated by abstracting a universally valid procedural framework for the rational-critical articulation of norms from various historical manifestations of autonomy in relation to the state. The public sphere grows out of civil society but is not reducible to it. Its more exacting normativity comes from the rational universality of the procedures through which social norms are articulated. Thus, in contemporary social theory, "public sphere" is another name for the site where the substantive forms of ethical self-understanding that bind a territorial political community are generated from consensual rational procedures of political decision making and law enactment.

The normative status accorded to civil society and the public sphere has been challenged on various grounds, especially with regard to their claims to autonomy from the state and the rational transcendence of particularistic interests.[41] What is important for us is that the compromised nature of these normative phenomena become even more pronounced when they are generalized on a global scale.[42] For the claims by human rights NGOs to the normative status of a global civil society or an international public sphere are contaminated at various levels. First, the vocabulary of civil society or public sphere presupposes a state-versus-society topology within a territorially bounded entity, where "civil society" or "public sphere" represents the "nation" side of the nation-state. Ideally, a global civil society or public sphere would transcend national interests because it would be the autonomous site of mediation between humanity and a global political order. But as I argued in Chapter 2, human rights NGOs do not possess the requisite autonomy. In the first place, transnational social movements occur in a decentralized political system where no supranational executive body independent of the compliance of nation-states for the enforcement of its decisions exists, and where mass-based loyalty to the world of humanity is insignificant. Thus, civil society institutions are constrained by and have to rely on the agency of nation-states and are largely defined in terms of national bases.[43] Furthermore, Martin Shaw points out that social movements have very little leverage on the state and even less impact on interstate relations because they rely more on cultural pressure than on elaborate institutional connections with the political system.[44] At best, social movements with global networks can make national civil societies more globally aware. Indeed, even when NGOs invoke formal international human rights instruments to make their claims on behalf of humanity, these claims are always channeled through specific national sites, against specific nation-states.

This means that human rights NGOs have to negotiate with shifting interstate relations within an unequal global economic order. Their claims are thus irreducibly susceptible to co-optation by competing states on both sides of the North-South divide the very moment they are articulated. In fighting against state violations of human rights, NGOs from the South are precariously balanced between, on the one hand, relying on Northern sources for funding and the risk of co-optation by the international media and the expansionist economic interests of wealthy postindustrial countries and, on the other hand, criticizing statist models of development in the South without jeopardizing the ambivalent need for the nation-state as an agent of accumulation in defense against transnational capital. Simply put, NGOs are always part of the linkages of global capital as they invest state-formations and are effective only by virtue of being so.[45]

I should stress that I am not suggesting that human rights NGOs articulate universal ideals that are subsequently contaminated in their implementation. I am suggesting that these ideals are always already conditioned by the force field within which they are invoked. These ideals are posited only in their violation. Consequently, the recognizability of these ideals depends on what counts as oppressive in a given historical conjuncture. We must therefore learn to see that human dignity itself is a product-effect. This is apparent enough in the observation that any assertion of right is limited by its positionality. Take, for example, the feminist right to cultural difference. The need to assert the right to cultural self-determination as integral to human dignity is a by-product of unequal North-South relations. It has been contested by feminist groups in the South seeking to assert women's rights as human rights. These groups seek to establish a feminist right to cultural self-determination in opposition to the patriarchal statist model of cultural difference that obstructs possibilities of gender reform. Yet, even here, it is impossible to locate a pure voice of feminist cultural difference. As Arati Rao observes, much feminist leadership is urban, well educated, middle class, and often government paid. "Since the responsiveness of the state to women's well-being remains debatable, we must remain critical of the relationship between governments and those women's groups permitted to flourish freely."[46] Therefore, "when women's groups or individual women talk about culture, we must remind ourselves that *there can never be a purportedly popular notion of culture that is unmediated by the positionality of the speaker;* we must look at claims for exemption [from human rights issues] on cultural grounds in relation to the axes of class, ethnicity, race, sexuality, and age, and so on."[47]

This argument about the contamination of the subject of rights should be made at an even more fundamental level that goes beyond a critical analysis of positionality. The politics of positionality or location implies a distinction between an inauthentic or dominant institutional position and a repressed but residual authentic voice that is retrievable by an exhaustively universal vision of human rights. The point I am making is that an irreducible because systemic contamination occurs in the very court of claims in which the voice of the oppressed can be heard, although it is in this court alone that justice can be done, and we cannot not want this justice-in-violation. The impossibility of locating a pure voice of the subject of oppression or a genuinely popular voice, and therefore of any vision of human rights claiming an all-encompassing universal validity, is especially salient in the assertion of aboriginal rights by "tribals" in Southeast Asia. As Benedict Anderson observes, "in most cases their humble wish is to be left alone." But they are compelled to defend against the encroachment of nation-states and the forces of global capital on their way of life by staging a collective identity and demanding rights in the name of that identity:

> Their very isolation leaves them unacquainted with the ceremonies of private property, the techniques of coalition politics and even the organizational methods needed for modern self-defense. The irony is that typically, they are not ethnic groups; to survive they may have to learn to think and act as such. . . . Yet, the costs of going ethnic, that is, participating in ethnic majority politics and economics within the nation-state, are not to be underestimated. . . . These [ethnic] identities . . . occlude and submerge non-ethnic local identities in the very process of attempting to defend them. Such identities may, under ill-starred circumstances, invite conscious oppression rather than malign neglect, but they also open the way to developing a necessary political and economic bargaining power.[48]

The dilemma of "going ethnic" illustrates that rights accrue only when the subject claiming them is a collective subject endowed with institutional epistemic recognition. Put another way, rights claims are contingent on the performative positing of a subject of rights within and by a given conjuncture although this performative is then necessarily taken to be a constative declaration about and by a preexisting subject. Jacques Derrida makes the same point in a different context when he observes that "this obscurity, undecidability between . . . a performative structure and a constative structure . . . is essential to the very positing or position of a right as such."[49] Human rights NGOs often make the observation that "one of the major issues is how to overcome the barrier of ignorance on the part of the rural poor about their rights, including the right to organize [, because] to make matters worse, the poor do not know they are poor."[50] Without dismissing the necessity and importance of the project of politically educating "the rural poor," it is nevertheless important to note that what we are witnessing is a performative-constative ruse by which the rural poor begin to think of themselves as such, in terms of a collective identity capable of articulating *their* human rights. They are being taught to make cognitive sense of their exploitation by global capital even as the project of consciousness-raising is necessarily part of the same systemic violation. They are constituted as an institutionally recognizable collective, which they were previously not, so that they can have leverage as the subjects/objects of institutional decision making. Yet, this fabulation also reduces them to the accountable data of sustainable development policies that may disrupt their old ways of life even further. This is the crisis. No easy claims of historical relativism or nihilism here, but the sobering acknowledgment that in global capitalism, this is the only way to help them and the only way for them to help themselves.

Normativity in Original Contamination: Global Capitalism Is a Text, Not a Totality

It may be fruitful at this point to situate the performance of human rights practical discourse in contemporary global capitalism in relation to the two main competing theories of international society in intellectual history: cosmopolitanism and realism. We have already encountered cosmopolitanism in the concepts of international public sphere and global civil society. Clearly, the contaminated normativity of international human rights claims can no longer be explained in terms of the Kantian idea of cosmopolitan right. As I suggested earlier, in the current interstate system, no international public sphere or global civil society in the full sense has come into existence. None of the three voices of human rights can represent universal humanity. Although they can be complicit with one another, the hegemonic North, the weak neocolonial states in the South, the economically high-performing Asian NIEs, and human rights NGOs in both the North and the South clearly do not share identical interests.

In international relations theory, the alternative to a cosmopolitanist conception of international society is realism. Hedley Bull represents a more moderate example. As one commentator observes, Bull cautioned that "'cosmopolitanist ideas can determine our attitudes and policies in international relations only to a limited extent' since states were 'notoriously self-serving in their policies.' Having suggested that a commitment to basic human rights underpin any cosmopolitanist world culture, he pointed again to the continuing lack of agreement among states as to what is meant by human rights, and the dangers of subverting coexistence by pursuing partial conceptions of justice."[51] Hegel offers an even stronger philosophical articulation of realism. He argued that the normativity of international society would never go beyond a mere "ought to be." Hence, "the broadest view of these [international] relations will encompass the ceaseless turmoil not just of external contingency, but also of passions, interests, ends, talents and virtues, violence [*Gewalt*], wrongdoing [*des Unrechts*], and vices in their inner particularity. In this turmoil, the ethical whole itself—the independence of the state—is exposed to contingency."[52]

Hence, in its most cynical version, a realist account of international society is a relativism that emphasizes the historical contingency of state action toward other states. In the face of the ineluctable historicity (*Geschichtlichkeit*) of moral-political norms, Hegel could assert the rational-universal normativity of state action only by resorting to a teleology of world history. He argued that the institutionalization of certain norms coincided with the direction of world-historical progress and that these norms retained their universal validity in later stages of development. Such world-historical norms cannot be revoked even though they can be modified.[53] The nation-state that embodied the world spirit of a certain epoch would lead all other states, and its actions would have universal normative force. Thus, "it is through this dialectic [of the finitude of national spirits] that the *universal* spirit, the *spirit of the world,* produces itself in its freedom from all limits, and it is this spirit which exercises its right—which is the highest right of all—over finite spirits in *world history* as the *world's court of judgement.*"[54] Furthermore,

> the nation [*Volk*] to which such a moment is allotted as a *natural* principle is given the task of implementing this principle in the course of the self-development of the world spirit's self-consciousness. This nation is the *dominant* one in world history for this epoch. . . . In contrast with this absolute right which it possesses as bearer of the present stage of the world spirit's development, the spirits of other nations are without rights, and they, like those whose epoch has passed, no longer count in world history.[55]

We clearly cannot follow Hegel's rationalist impregnation of the contingency of historical events with teleological significance. The neocolonial ideology of development deployed by the IMF and the World Bank under the leadership of the Group of Seven nations is world history in its misdestination, or *destinerrance.* Indeed, both the United States in its self-staging as the champion and defender of human rights and the authoritarian governments in the South that justify human rights violations in the name of the right to development try to endow their actions with normative force by exploiting weaker variations of the same teleological argument. The question is whether in the face of the irreducible contamination of human rights in global capitalism (a case of ineluctable historicity) we must give up their normativity and reluctantly embrace cynical realism if we reject a teleological solution to historical contingency.

The situation is not as bleak as it seems. For if idealist universalism is unrealistic, cynical realism is equally unrealistic, given the very real normative power that human rights exert on various types of actors notwithstanding the fact that their normative basis cannot clearly be separated from global-systemic imperatives and particularistic tendencies. To be a concrete agent in history is, after all, to be influenced by historically existing ideals and norms, no matter how contaminated they are. The task is rather to rethink the normativity of human rights claims within the original contamination and violence of global capitalism, within ineluctable historicity. It is to accept that our principles of rational action are irreducibly conditioned by what they seek to alleviate and transform even as we cannot *not* invoke these principles because they condition us in turn. But this will require a radical break with the theory of normativity behind human rights practical discourse, which, in claiming exhaustive universal rationality, has always taken as axiomatic the co-extensiveness of ethico-political change with the prescription of a total rational form by the human agent to historico-material forces.

Indeed, all existing theories of normativity regard normative force as something that issues from and expresses self-present reason and define rational normative activity as the elimination, regulation, or transcendence of historical contingency. The struggle of normative reason to transcend historicity can take different forms. In neo-Kantian human rights discourse, it involves the prescription of an ideal total form, for example, a holistic system of rights maximizing respect for human dignity, that is distinct from and even transcendent to historical reality, but that functions as a regulative or asymptotic horizon of the Kantian type, a guiding thread for the transformation of reality. Or, following Hegel, normative reason can be reconciled with historical contingency: it can transcend the contingent by actualizing itself in history through autonomous action that affirms the ethical institutions of the nation said to embody the spirit of world history. Reason's struggle to transcend historical contingency can even take the form of Fredric Jameson's neo-Marxist argument that human rights, like the ideals of other progressive social movements, are necessarily compromised so long as they are articulated in global capitalism. The full realization of human rights would then be premised on the transcendence of the capitalist world system. The first step toward transcendence would then involve an aesthetic of cognitive mapping that enables us to imaginatively outline global capital into the form of an oppressive social totality in urgent need of transformation.[56]

But we can no longer rely on these rationalist accounts of normativity if we want to make cognitive sense of the normative force that human rights can exert in their very contamination by global capital. This is because the normativity of human rights is coextensive with their historical contingency. I have already suggested that the irreducible contamination of the subject of human rights indicates that we can no longer theorize the normativity of rights claims in terms of the rational universality of a pure, atemporal, and context-independent human dignity that is ultimately separated from economics or politics. But more important, however hard it may be for leftist critics to accept, this irreducible contamination also indicates that we may never be able to transcend global capital. For the very constitution of a subject entitled to rights involves the violent capture of the disenfranchised by an institutional discourse that inseverably weaves them into the textile of global capitalism. Human rights are generated as concrete rights at the level of bodily needs and materialized through institutional practices as part of a complex of processes by which global capitalism continually sustains and reproduces itself through the production of human subjects with rights. Our interconnectedness within global capitalism thus generates a real and unequal universality that caricatures the ideal universality presupposed by conventional human rights discourse. Rights are not, in the original instance, entitlements of intersubjectively constituted rational social agents but violent gifts, the necessary nexuses within immanent global force relations that produce the identities of their claimants. Yet they are the only way for the disenfranchised to mobilize.

From the foregoing we can see that the normative force of human rights issues from the material linkages that make up the global capitalist system without either being reduced to these forces (historicist relativism) or being able to transcend them (varieties of neo-Hegelianism and neo-Marxism). In his reflections on the aporias of justice and the gift, Jacques Derrida has articulated an account of normativity that is explicitly distinguished from the Kantian and Hegelian accounts of normativity underpinning cosmopolitan and realist accounts of international relations. I want to suggest that his idea of justice can help us arrive at a more adequate understanding of the contaminated normativity of human rights.[57] As we have seen, Kant's idea of a cosmopolitan federation is an ideal horizon that is only tenuously connected to present actuality. Hegel's critique of Kant, however, is animated by the argument that the state's political morality constitutes an "ought" that already "is," a sphere in which normativity and actuality are reconciled and historical contingency is transcended. Insofar as any account of normativity involves an understanding of how a norm is related to the present, these two institutional models of normativity are characterized and underwritten by different temporal relations. In Kant's case, the cosmopolitan federation is an ideal horizon, an infinitely deferred and asymptotic future end that functions regulatively as a guiding thread, whereas for Hegel, the ideal state is a sphere of normative facticity where justice is immanent to the present. In Derrida's view, however, justice is not so much a mode of time as the movement of temporalization or the giving of time itself.

Against Hegel, Derrida argues that it is unjust to regard justice as being exhausted by or reduced to its present historical forms or determinations. This is because justice must remain fundamentally open to unpredictable future circumstances: "The deconstruction of all presumption of a determinant certitude of a present justice itself operates on an infinite 'idea of justice,' . . . [which] seems to me to be irreducible in its affirmative character, in its demand of gift . . . without economic circularity, without calculation and without rules, without reason and without rationality."[58] But, unlike Kant's idea of the cosmopolitan federation, this infinite idea of justice is not a projected ideal form that has a limited effective relation to present actuality. Justice is not a transcendent exteriority that can function only as an ideal horizon. It demands an immediate intervention into and transformation of the present: "I would hesitate to assimilate too quickly this 'idea of justice' to a regulative idea (in the Kantian sense) . . . or to other horizons of the same type . . . (. . . eschato-teleology of the neo-Hegelian, Marxist or post-Marxist type). . . . As its Greek name suggests, a horizon is both the opening and the limit that defines an infinite progress or period of waiting. But justice, however unpresentable it may be, doesn't wait. It is that which must not wait" (FL, 965, 967). To be just, justice must not be either simply immanent in or transcendent to the historical present. Hence, justice must paradoxically be immanent and transcendent at the same time. To be just, justice must give itself to the historical present. But in the same instance, it must withdraw itself or be effaced from the present. Thus, justice must (and can only) give itself in its own violation, contaminate itself by appearing in the present.

What is important here is Derrida's suggestion that the source of normativity—its condition of possibility—can only be the absolute surprise or chance of the event that reopens and keeps time and history going. Justice ought not to be exhausted by rational action in the present. But at the same time, it must have an effect on the present through rational action. This persistent, sheer possibility of the transformation of historical actuality can therefore issue only from a contingency original to and constitutive of the historical present: the historicity of history. Normative reason is born in an unconditional response to this original contingency, but since historicity is constitutive of finite reason, reason cannot cognitively master, eradicate, or transcend it. The radical historicity or finitude of reason thus refers to reason's constitutive inscription within an unstable and shifting field of historical forces that it cannot control or transcend. But at the same time, this moving base also holds the ineradicable promise of ethical transformation because it exceeds and cannot be captured by the hegemonic forces of any given historical present. In this sense, normativity is both unconditional and coextensive with historicity, which is precisely why normativity cannot be reduced to existing norms or their historical conditions:

> Justice remains, is yet, to come, à venir, it has an, it is à venir, the very dimension of events irreducibly to come. . . . Perhaps it is for this reason that justice, insofar as it is not only a juridical or political concept, opens up for l'avenir the transformation, the recasting or refounding of law and politics. "Perhaps," one must always say perhaps for justice. There is . . . no justice except to the degree that some event is possible which, as event, exceeds calculation, rules, programs, anticipations and so forth. Justice as the experience of absolute alterity is unpresentable, but it is the chance of the event and the condition of history. No doubt an unrecognizable history . . . for those who believe they know what they're talking about when they use this word, whether it's a matter of social, ideological, political, juridical or some other history. (FL, 969, 971)

This is precisely the structure of justice-in-violation that characterizes the unconditional but contaminated normativity of human rights in their historical contingency. For as we have seen, human rights are double-edged but absolutely necessary weapons that are given to the disenfranchised by the global force relations in which they find themselves mired in a given historical conjuncture. On the one hand, we should be able to account for the historical conditions that determine and impose limits on any invocation of human rights so that we can calculate the effectiveness of human rights claims in a given situation. On the other hand, because they are in-history, these contextual conditions are subject to radical mutability. A mutation in historical conditions will cause a corresponding change in the effectivity of human rights. At the same time, the contaminated normativity of human rights can be a factor in bringing about and inflecting a mutation in historical conditions.

This view of normativity in historical contingency is not a historicist relativism that reduces normativity to a ruse of hegemonic power. First, conjunctures have an immense stability. Second, no collective institutional actor can predict when and how a given conjuncture will mutate. Thus, although some actors may be invested with hegemony by the current state of affairs, no single actor can be said to have exhaustive mastery over it.

But by the same token, human rights are also not inevitably strategic instruments or ideological fictions available for progressive or reactionary use. The normative force and effectivity they have are given by the mobile force relations that make up the global capitalist system. Human rights are not *our* instruments as rational actors, for we are their product-effects rather than their originators. Neither progressive nor capitalist forces can choose either to embrace or to repudiate human rights, for they are given to us as finite historical actors by existing historical forces, and they constitute us. What we *can* do is calculate their effectiveness in situations we can envision and act accordingly. Derrida puts it this way:

> It is a matter . . . of responding faithfully but also as rigorously as possible both to the injunction or the order of the *gift* . . . as well as to the injunction or the order of meaning (presence, science, knowledge): *Know* still what giving *wants to say, know how to give* . . . know how the gift annuls itself, commit yourself [*engage-toi*] even if commitment is the destruction of the gift by the gift, give economy its chance. For finally, the overrunning of the circle [of economy] by the gift, if there is any, does not lead to a simple, ineffable exteriority that would be transcendent and without relation. . . . [I]t is this exteriority which puts the economy in motion.[59]

Thus, as we have seen, although the three voices of human rights discourse can be complicit, the line of force that joins them together and in the service of the global capitalist economy can also mutate to separate their interests and pit them against one another and against capitalism. In the shifting global force field nothing is etched in stone, and progressive forces must learn to tap this motility.

It follows from this that human rights are not just part of an ideological structure that needs to be re-embedded within the systemic totality of global capital by immanent critique. Neo-Marxist understandings of human rights are continuous with rationalist theories of normativity that prescribe an ideal totality or world image onto material reality. Global capitalism has undoubtedly brought about material interconnectedness on a world scale. But contra Jameson, the contaminated normativity of human rights practical discourse suggests that global capitalism is not a totality but a textual network, a sheaf of differential processes. The conditioning power of human rights on our rational actions and their ambivalent effects indicate that the global relationality that enables each agent to act and to affect others is marked by a randomness that cannot be entirely harnessed by either hegemonic or emancipatory interests: the randomness of the shifting linkages that sustain global capital. And this chance of economy means that although global capitalism is a formation with great extension and deep penetration, "it" cannot be enclosed as a cognizable totality. Since it is also a product-effect of force relations that overflow it, there are points of weakness generated within "it" that "it" cannot account for. This radical alterity immanent to global capitalism makes totality impossible because it opens the structure up into a general textuality at the very moment when totalization occurs.[60] The positive effects of human rights arise from these unpredictable points. But by the same token, these neuralgic points are not spatially exterior to the formation. They are part of it, conditioned by its historical determinations, and do not present a visible historical or imaginary limit to it. They do not make up an external present site from which we can (imagine and) transcend capitalism as a totality. This is why human rights are originally contaminated, pulled back into the particularistic forces they seek to transcend or check in their very movement of transcendence.

Let me be more concrete: the globalization of market mechanisms and production requires the creation of a technologically educated laboring and administrative class in the South. But the requisite globalization of education and technological know-how also leads to the formation of a stratum of activists. In response to the proliferation of new needs, these human rights NGOs make claims that are provisionally against the interests of global capitalism. Yet, as I have suggested, these provisional points of resistance are also reinscribed into the text of global capitalism: witness the co-optation of "sustainable development," "environmentalism," and "international civil society" by the IMF and World Bank. Thus, what gives a particular vision of human rights more normative validity and historical effectivity depends on the constellation of forces at a given conjuncture rather than an ideal or imagined horizon of all-inclusive universality which that vision has managed to grasp.

I have argued that the unconditional normativity in original contamination of human rights arises from their inscription within the text of global capitalism and not from a self-present exteriority grasped by enlightened reason or neo-Marxist cognitive mapping. Such an approach deprives human rights claims of absolute rational justification, since by viewing normativity as arising out of the radical alterity of the global force field, it sunders the co-belonging of normativity with reason and presence. But then what are the theoretical alternatives? A dogmatic idealism of human rights is disproved by "the real world of human rights." At the same time, an outright realist dismissal of human rights denies their very real enabling force in the current conjuncture. Given that the transcendence of global capitalism is not in imaginary sight, we have no choice but to take the risk of conjuring with and against the inhuman force field of global capitalism as it induces changing forms of human dignity.

6

"Bringing into the Home a Stranger Far More Foreign"

Human Rights and the Global Trade in Domestic Labor

The material processes that we call globalization touch the heart and core of what it means to be human. On the one hand, the globalization of production and financial networks bring peoples in different parts of the world closer together. Transnational media and telecommunications networks promise to unite us into a common humanity. On the other hand, insofar as these processes are profit-driven and obey the "inhuman" imperatives of capital accumulation, they also raise the deepest anxieties about the continuing preservation of our humanity. This understanding of globalization as a set of processes that can have inhuman consequences if they are not regulated by humane influences is, of course, not new. It repeats a time-honored analytical schema whereby the entropy characterizing human interaction and social endeavor requires a higher normative force to hold it in check, for instance, moral sentiment (Adam Smith), socialized labor (Marx), or critical reason (the Frankfurt School). The intensified debates about human rights in recent years are driven by this logic. As a normative system for ordering the totality of interactions between collective actors such as states and groups organized around particular interests, and between collective actors and individuals, as well as relations between individuals, a universal human rights regime confers a human face on our globalizing world. It enables us to figure the global as the human.

Accordingly, contemporary theory links globalization to the actualization of humanity in at least three ways. In the liberal account, the liber-

alization of world trade and the globalization of production in the post–
Cold War era are conducive to the worldwide institutionalization of universal human rights because the global spread of market mechanisms is
necessarily accompanied by the spread of the rule of law and democratic
culture, and the introduction of a "modern" mode of production erodes
traditional *Gemeinschaft*-type social structures in which the rights of the
rational individual are sacrificed to habitual collective duty. In the current academic climate, where nationalism is often dismissed as a right-
wing patriarchal ideology, this is a widely accepted account of globalization: globalization is good and national parochialism is bad for human
rights in general and women's human rights in particular. This narrative
can be found in academic cultural studies in Arjun Appadurai's argument for a postnational global order. It is also present in social policy, for
example, in the entrepreneurial-corporatist internationalism informing
large sections of the Platform of Action of the UN Fourth World Conference on Women, held in Beijing, in 1995.

The other two approaches acknowledge the unequal character of
globalization but still consider it as contributing to the actualization of
universal humanity. It is argued that although globalization leads to increased inequality, it is nevertheless the crucible for the formation of
new geographical spaces in which transnational political institutions
and human rights regimes can flourish and lay the groundwork for
global citizenship. Saskia Sassen's influential work on global cities is the
best example of this second position.[1] Alternatively, there is a more leftist, post-Marxist position that theorizes an emergent globalization from
below that is immanent to capitalist globalization, namely, new social
movements that are global in scale and that show the obsolescence of
both the sovereign state and popular nationalism. The best representative of this position is Michael Hardt and Antonio Negri's book, *Empire*.
Hardt and Negri argue that the multitude of migrant labor constitutes "a
new geography": "The cities of the earth will become at once great de-
posits of cooperating humanity and locomotives for circulation, temporary residences and networks of the mass distribution of living humanity."[2] This multitude needs to be organized into a truly universal and
positive political power, beginning with the demand for "global citizenship," the demand that "the existent fact of capitalist production be recognized juridically and that all workers be given the full rights of citizenship. In effect this political demand insists in postmodernity on the

fundamental modern constitutional principle that links right and labor, and thus rewards with citizenship the worker who creates capital."[3]

But how exactly does globalization enable the actualization of humanity? And is the humanity engendered in this manner capable of harnessing global capital and checking its excesses? A crucial part of the answer seems to rest on the impact of transnational migration. In each of the aforementioned ways of figuring the global as the human, transnational migration, especially the flow of labor, is a fundamental motor for the actualization of humanity because it is seen as leading to the erosion of particularistic national ties and borders, even to the erosion of state sovereignty itself, and, thus, to the formation of borderless solidarities in the distant future, whether these take the form of a postnational order, the global city, or the multitude.

In this chapter I challenge the axiomatic link between transnational migration and the actualization of humanity by considering the human rights of migrant female domestic labor in rapidly developing Southeast Asia.[4] I make two arguments based on this examination. First, the migrant female domestic worker's human rights can be effectively protected in the present and near future only by affirming the importance of political citizenship or membership in a nation-state. For such rights to be claimed successfully, labor-sending states need to have a strong bargaining position and the political will to demand just treatment for their workers. The penetration of the state apparatus by popular-national forces is crucial to the formation of this political will. Second, the inherently aporetic character of these rights claims within the larger theater of competitive development puts into question the analytical schema that opposes the initiatives of humane regulation to the forces of global capital. I suggest that the human being *qua* possessor of the right to human rights is not, in the primary instance, the victim, the alienated originator, and then the resistant subject who is opposed to and seeks to regulate the inhuman forces of global capital. The human being is instead the *différance* inscribed within the inhuman force field that he or she seeks to transcend and overcome.

The chapter is divided into four sections. The first outlines the global-systemic framework that has led to the acceleration of labor migration across the Southeast Asian region and the feminization of labor migration. In the second section I examine the normative validity of existing international legal and quasi-legal instruments for protecting the human rights of female migrant workers and argue that they are ineffective in the absence of nation-state-based activity and cooperation. The third section focuses on the inhuman treatment of migrant female domestic labor in hyperdeveloping Singapore, a wealthy Southeast Asian city-state with aspirations of being a cosmopolitan global city, and examines the various biopolitical technologies that regulate such workers and their employers. In the fourth section I show how this heavy reliance on foreign domestic labor undermines even as it enables the articulation of purportedly humane social formations and political projects that are underwritten by the axiom of the rational human individual as a free consensual agent, for example, cosmopolitan society in Singapore, Philippine national development, and the emerging subject of global feminism staged by the Beijing Conference.

It should be evident that my argument is different from many recent social-scientific studies of female migrant labor in Southeast Asia. These have focused on the sentimental and at times sensationalist documentation of the foreign maid's suffering, the deformation of the family unit through transnationalization, and her heroic strategies of resistance.[5] The world is a cruel place. But what else is new? Pathos is undoubtedly important, just as it is important to imagine a world without suffering from which we can criticize the degraded present. These studies have much to teach us, and I have learned from some of them. My point of departure stems from the fact that their devotion to the retrieval of voices and the redescription of complex material has sometimes come at the expense of conceptual thought. Fieldwork provides a mask of concrete specificity. Yet, many of the conclusions in these studies are informed by a priori concepts and ethical ideals that bear the trace of the most dogmatic of humanisms. A quick example suffices to make my point. The preface of a collection of sensationalist fictive short stories about Filipina maids in Singapore glosses the attitude of employment agencies toward maids in terms of a thematic opposition between profit and humane empathy, a popular cultural version of Rousseauist pity or Smithian moral sentiment: "To an agent, dealing with a maid's problem is merely handling a case. The agents are so concerned with the absolute dollars and cents that they have forgotten that a Filipino maid, too, is a human being."[6] A valuable scholarly study of female domestic workers in neighboring Malaysia concludes its informative analysis by recycling exactly the same opposition in the more intellectual register of socially committed ethical appeal:

> The many different peoples and cultures in Malaysia offer the opportunity to construct an alternative vision of development that need not necessarily sacrifice humanity for material progress and wealth. Yet, economic and social preparations for capturing transnational markets and capital, thus material wealth, threaten to bring about the reverse. . . . At the close of the twentieth century, a key challenge remains for all—to strive to build and maintain societies in which "service" is given to humanity, not to capital.[7]

The same unquestioned humanism informs the obligatory distinction between social development and mere economic development in social policy. I have chosen instead to broach the idea of the inhuman that is not reducible to humanity because it constitutes humanity. My argument is, therefore, primarily a theoretical argument about the nature of human freedom. I have, however, drawn on social-scientific research and informal fieldwork because the abstraction and insularity of orthodox philosophical discourse prevents genuine engagement with contemporary social, economic, and political structures and processes.[8]

One final caveat: I have not fixed my glance on Singapore in order to single out the city-state unfairly and cast aspersions on the inhumanity of its institutions. To the contrary, what is interesting about Singapore is precisely its exemplarity as a remarkably successful case of hyperdevelopment within the framework of flexible capitalist accumulation. The dizzying rapidity of change in the Singapore state's strategies for ascending the hierarchy of the new international division of labor by attracting global capital and upgrading from a manufacture-based economy to an economy based on higher value-added services, knowledge, and technology allows us to see the inhuman face of globalization in the highest relief.[9] The Singaporean case is not abnormal. It is not a pathological aberration. The Singapore state repeatedly shows a keen willingness to copy and imitate successful socioeconomic models, policies, and strategies and to adopt the latest theoretical ideas in order to maintain a competitive edge in capital accumulation. It is as though the state's policy makers have been instructed to read Saskia Sassen's account of the global city so that Singapore can become a successful one. To take another example, as though in direct response to the argument in the United States that gay people are part of a creative class that stimulates economic development, the Singapore government lifted its restriction on hiring homosexuals as part of a broader plan to indicate that Singapore was a diversity-tolerant society and encouraged the creative lifestyles found in cities whose entrepreneurial dynamism it sought to emulate.[10] Singapore thus embodies the values and imperatives at work in the operations of global capital artificially speeded up as in a computer animation model that simulates natural motion in exaggerated fashion. Because of its uneven nature, rapid development in the Asia-Pacific region leads to the exploitation of foreign workers from poorer neighboring countries. As one earlier study observes, "The question must no longer be whether the rapidly developing countries of the region should admit foreign manpower, but rather on what terms these workers should be admitted, what rights they should have and the longer term welfare measures to which they should be entitled."[11] However, the ruthlessly competitive nature of the global market for human capital places the humanity of migrant workers under erasure. The Singaporean situation is a telling object lesson about the inhuman way of developing the human condition in our current global conjuncture.

The Transnational Trade in Domestic Labor and the Global Development of Humanity

The accelerated increase in the passage of guest workers is a key feature of our times. The material conditions for its intensification in Southeast Asia arise directly out of a broader structural change in the system of capital accumulation that we now understand under the related rubrics of "the new international division of labor" and "flexible" or "disorganized global capitalism."[12] Simply put, technological innovations enabled the decomposition of production processes. At the same time, the high costs of labor and infrastructure in the established industrial centers meant that the valorization and accumulation of capital could be greatly improved by transferring production elsewhere. Hence, transnational corporations engaged in certain types of manufacturing, such as textiles, computers, and electronics, sought to maintain and increase profitability by relocating certain industrial production processes to developing countries with lower labor costs either through foreign direct investment or international subcontracting, even as research and development and technical and managerial control remained in the center. Various East and Southeast Asian countries responded positively to this tendency of transnational corporations to relocate and "outsource." They used their comparative advantage—whether in terms of a large and cheap labor force or skills, technical abilities, infrastructure, and low taxes—to carve out a niche in this new international division of labor, thereby basing their development on "outward looking, export-oriented industrialisation (EOI) strategies."[13]

The impact of these largely state-sponsored strategies of industrial development through economic globalization on East and Southeast Asian growth was dramatic. They created the pre-1997 "economic miracle" of the East Asian newly industrialized economies of South Korea, Taiwan, Hong Kong, and Singapore.[14] The pattern was repeated again and again, and hyperdevelopment quickly spread to the tiger economies of Southeast Asia (Malaysia and Thailand), which were recipients of U.S. money and Japanese, South Korean, and other intra-Asian capital flows. This integration into the new international division of labor led to improvements in the material well-being of many countries. But as a sharp testament to the relentlessly uneven and brutally competitive character of capitalist development, it also created a regional divide within Southeast Asia. For some countries were able to adapt to the regime of flexible accumulation and harness foreign capital flows for their development, while others were unable to do so for a variety of reasons.

Singapore is a notable example of a successful high-growth country.[15] National Semiconductor chose Singapore as its regional center. By the 1970s, because of rising labor costs and the availability of highly qualified personnel in Singapore, National Semiconductor's Singaporean plant was already upgrading to the production of more complex semiconductors and subcontracting the assembly of less sophisticated and lower-cost types of semiconductors to independent producers in other parts of Southeast Asia, for instance, the Philippines.[16] Indeed, in 1979, the Singapore state prudently realized that the country's economic growth could be maintained only by actively moving away from labor-intensive production (and direct competition with neighboring countries with lower wages) and upgrading to even higher-value-added forms of production based on sophisticated scientific technology, skills, and knowledge.[17] From 1981 onward, it was an important site for the assembly and testing of disk drives in plants owned by U.S.-based computer companies such as Apple and Seagate. By the mid-1980s, Singapore was a major world exporter of disk drives.[18] Within twenty years it was producing one third of the world's disk drives and was favored over Hong Kong as a "hub" for investment in the most technologically advanced processes of semiconductor production. The city-state's continuing drive to maintain its competitive edge at the global level was best expressed by its trade and industry minister in 2001: "For Singapore, the new wave of globalisation presents an acute challenge. In anything and everything we do, we must achieve international standards to be competitive. It is not good enough now to be the best in South-east Asia; we must go beyond that. Either we compete globally, or we are not in the game."[19] This drive informs an ensemble of state initiatives that range from becoming a major center of research and development in high technology, to making Singapore a cosmopolitan global city that can attract and mobilize human talent from around the globe, to, most important, fostering Singapore-based multinationals that can take their turn in playing the outsourcing game and taking advantage of lower labor costs elsewhere.

In contradistinction, low-growth countries in the region that had unsuccessfully adopted the path of export-oriented industrialization under the neoliberal policies of the World Bank and IMF and had to rely on the export of commodities (e.g., the Philippines) were economically crippled by low commodity prices, high balance-of-payment deficits, large foreign debt, and massive unemployment.[20] The situation became worse for such oil-importing countries after the OPEC raised oil prices in 1973. As an indication of the vast economic gap in the region, Singapore's electronic products and exports in 1990 were $14.885 billion and $19.774 billion, respectively, whereas those of the Philippines were only $2.050 billion and $1.574 billion, and Indonesia's electronic products and exports amounted to an even more paltry $1.269 billion and $157 million.[21] In 1994, Indonesia and the Philippines had per capita incomes of $880 and $950, respectively, whereas Singapore's per capita income was $22,500.[22]

This divide between high- and low-growth countries is the precipitating condition for the acceleration of labor migration in Southeast Asia. The success or failure of each case of development through economic globalization appears disconnected because it is rooted in historical, economic, sociological, and political factors specific to each country. As far as labor power is concerned, however, the structural change in the logic of capital accumulation connected various countries in the region as moments within the same dynamic. For as countries such as Singapore and Malaysia undergo a transformation in their workforce because of rapid industrialization, they experience a shortage of low-skilled manual labor. Because it is economically sounder for them to turn elsewhere for cheap sources of lower-end industrial and domestic labor, they begin to import migrant labor from their less developed neighbors to perform what are sometimes called the 3D jobs, "dirty, dangerous, and demanding." By contrast, the Philippines actively exports workers overseas because of the inability of its economy to absorb the labor of its citizens. Hence, for each case of successful development through state-sponsored globalization, there seems to be another case of state-driven exportation of labor, as if this interconnection were an outcome dictated by an unseen law of the global economy. The traffic in migrant labor is, of course, not necessary to development in any absolute sense. But it was encouraged by many states as a means of development and contributed to the economies within its circuits. As Stella Go observes:

> As greater economic interdependence is fostered among countries in the Asian region through trade and investment, a transnational space is created for the circulation not only of goods and capital, but of labor as well. . . . The migration of Filipinos and other foreign workers into the more developed countries in the Asian region and the world is a phenomenon that serves the economic ends of both the labor-sending and the labor-receiving countries. For the Philippines, it is one way of addressing the unemployment and underemployment problems of the country as well as its foreign exchange needs. For the labor receiving countries in the region, it is vital for their continued economic growth and development. For countries like Taiwan and Korea, foreign labor is necessary to bolster their declining small and medium-sized enterprises (SMEs), while for countries like Singapore, Hong Kong and Japan, foreign workers are in demand in service occupations such as entertainers and domestic helpers.[23]

What is striking here is the systematic link between labor emigration and development and its aggressive institutionalization through national state policy with the sanction of international bodies. The World Bank's 1991 *World Development Report* observed that labor migration could aid in curbing unemployment and reducing the worldwide disparity in income. Migrants returning from more advanced countries also contributed to the diffusion of technology.[24] The 1995 report, titled *Workers in an Integrating World,* described migration as "an important economic and social safety valve" that allowed "labor to relocate to areas where it was more scarce" and stressed the efficiency gains it created, particularly in the form of higher wages for migrant workers, foreign exchange remittances to sending countries, the possible stimulation of capital investment, and lower production costs in receiving countries.[25] These observations were merely a formal tabulation of assumptions already at play since the 1970s, when less developed countries such as the Philippines, Sri Lanka, Pakistan, Bangladesh, and India began exporting labor in response to the massive increase in demand by the oil-rich Middle East. The ministries of labor and manpower of these countries set up administrative bodies, for example, the Philippine Overseas Employment Administration (POEA) and the Sri Lanka Bureau of Foreign Employment (SLBFE), to promote and regulate labor migration. In the Philippines, the Marcos regime regarded the export of labor as a matter of "national interest" and embarked on its aggressive labor export policy, citing the alleviation of chronic unemployment and the relief of the balance-of-payments deficit as the two key economic benefits.[26] The Philippines is one of the world's largest labor exporters, second only to Mexico by the turn of the twenty-first century. In 1997, the number of overseas contract workers (OCWs) from the Philippines was estimated at 6.1 million.[27] By December 2001, the estimated figure had risen to 7.4 million, representing close to 10 percent of the population and 21 percent of the total labor force.[28] Their contribution to the Philippine economy is indispensable. Remittances by OCWs totaled U.S.$7.4 billion in 2003 and amounted to slightly over 8 percent of the gross national product and 19 percent of the overall export of goods and services.[29] The U.S.$18 billion brought into the country through remittances from 1975 to 1994 was roughly four times larger than the total amount of foreign direct investment for the same period.[30] Hence, what was initially a temporary measure to increase foreign exchange inflow and reduce unemployment was now cynically represented by the Philippine state as a long-term means for achieving economic growth and national development.

Both moments of this dynamic of development within the framework of economic liberalization which I have outlined—state-sponsored globalization through EOI and the normalization of labor exportation by the state to cope with global economic pressures—directly intensify the feminization of labor. Strictly speaking, "the feminization of labor" refers to the entry of more and more women into low-paid work in multinational manufacturing production and the service sector in response to family hardship.[31] Female labor is preferred in export-oriented industries and newly established industrial zones because in comparison to men, women workers are cheaper, and perceived as more flexible (more amenable to part-time or home-based work or piece-rate contracts, more subservient to managerial authority, less prone to unionization, and easier to dismiss and replace), and because of their greater manual dexterity, the latter being especially important in the textiles and electronics industries.[32] Such labor ensures the international competitiveness of a country as a destination for foreign capital investment in low-value-added manufacture. The greater mobility of capital under the WTO depresses women's wages further and worsens their working conditions by increasing competition between workers in different developing countries.[33] But the feminization of labor should also be extended beyond paid employment to include the situation whereby, as a result of the intersection between a patriarchal sex/gender system and uneven development, the structural adjustment programs of many postcolonial states (forced cuts in basic services and in investments in human development in response to the burden of foreign debt) are largely supported by shifting the responsibility for social services from the state to women without compensation.

The specific modality of the feminization of labor that concerns us here is that of transnational labor migration. This involves the increasing migration of Asian women from the late 1970s onward in response to the growing international demand for workers to fill low-status "feminized" occupations—domestic helpers, workers in restaurants and hotels, entertainers, and so on. Much of this increased demand is generated by another gender dynamic within high-growth economies: the entry of middle-class women with sufficient training into white-collar employment at the same time that the surplus young female labor that had been the traditional source of paid domestic work for middle-class households had been completely absorbed into industry and other non-domestic services. Consequently, live-in foreign domestic helpers were required to take care of the functions of the home. In 1975, women represented 30 percent of OCWs from the Philippines. By 1994, the percentage share had doubled.[34] Most of the Filipina OCWs in the service sector are domestic workers, so much so that they have been the subject of popular discourses of shame concerning their country's exportation of its female citizens and also apotheosized in state ideology as "heroines of the Philippine economy."[35] As Lin Lean Lim and Nana Oishi observe, the flexible movement of Asian women, "often a family survival strategy, was given added impetus by the negative impacts of structural adjustment programs in their home countries . . . [as well as] the active role of governments and private intermediaries in promoting their migration."[36] The 1997 Asian financial crisis exacerbated the situation. Labor-exporting countries have become more competitive with one another in their aggressive search for labor markets to assist in offsetting the massive outflow of foreign exchange in the wake of financial panic.

It is important to emphasize that what is at stake in these outward-looking development and labor migration policies of high- and low-growth states in Southeast Asia is nothing less than the cultivation of the full humanity of their citizens through national growth. All state actors (and international bodies such as the IMF and the World Bank) insistently claim that such growth and cultivation can be achieved today only through economic globalization. Indeed, one of the justifications for exporting labor is that it serves as a form of individual and national pedagogy. It is suggested that migrants will undergo a form of *Bildung* overseas. They will learn new skills and gain work experience and will return to impart this training, thereby enhancing the technological and knowledge resources of the nation and facilitating its development. But why does the cultivation of humanity rely on patently inhuman techniques? And what are the implications for rethinking some of the key powers and traits we associate with humanity such as freedom? For it is clear that women migrant workers are made to shoulder the burden of development or lack thereof in their nation-states and the actualization of the humanity of their fellow citizens. Hence, it is within the feminized space of transnational labor created by globalization—a mutating interface between the sex/gender systems of different nation-states—that the figure of the human being in postcolonial national development takes shape and the meaning of being-human is rearticulated. Let us now consider the complex normative validity of the human rights of migrant workers from this perspective.

Using Other People: The Human Rights of (Female) Migrant (Domestic) Workers

The widespread adoption of labor-export policies by low-growth states as a means of national development and the cultivation of the humanity of their citizens has made the protection of migrant workers' rights more urgent than ever. The main cause of the mistreatment of migrant workers is the very nature of their status as workers imported by the host country because they will gladly fill jobs local people shun. Traditionally, the protection of migrant workers has been largely left to the domestic law of host countries because international law sets only minimal standards for the treatment of aliens, such as the guarantee of the right to a fair trial, humane treatment in prison, and protection against arbitrary seizure of property. Host states can and often do discriminate against migrant workers in favor of their own citizens, and migrant workers rarely have the same rights that a citizen has through national laws. Consequently, the doctrine of universal human rights has been crucial in the affirmation of migrant workers' rights.

Although we think of human rights in terms of conventions, covenants, or declarations, we saw in the previous chapter that the universal validity of specific human rights issues from the universal entitlement or absolute right of all human beings to rights by sheer virtue of their ontological constitution as human. This right to rights is unconditional because it transcends all specific historical, cultural, or political content. Specific human rights merely elaborate what it means to be human by giving determinate content to the human being's general right to rights. In the neo-Kantian doctrine of the Universal Declaration of Human Rights, the normative force of human rights depends on a rigorous separation of the human and the nonhuman. As we saw in the previous chapter, Kant argued that the supreme principle for all moral action is the imperative to treat every human being not as a means but as an end, on the grounds that the human being *qua* rational creature is an end in itself.[37] If another human being is treated as a means, if his or her ontological status as an end in itself is disregarded, human freedom is violated because our ontological constitution as ends in themselves is what gives us the capacity for freedom, our inherent dignity, and other related traits we associate with human freedom. There is therefore a moral prohibition on the instrumentalization or technologization of human relations, the regarding of any human being as a tool or instrument to be used to pursue another's end.

It is, of course, impossible to avoid instrumentality in human relations altogether. In pragmatic action, which makes up the bulk of human relations, human beings are routinely treated as useful means. The purpose of human rights is the establishment of a juridical or quasi-juridical framework, backed up by sanctions, for the circumscription and regulation of human relations so that people can act according to their self-interests and freedom of choice *as long as* their actions do not deprive others of the same freedom that they ought to have because of their humanity.[38] Thus, Kant states that there is only one fundamental right: "*Freedom* (independence from being constrained by another's choice [*Willkür*]), insofar as it can coexist with the freedom of every other in accordance with a universal law, is the only original right belonging to every man by virtue of his humanity [*Menschheit*]."[39] Such innate freedom necessarily implies "innate *equality*, that is, independence from being bound by others to more than one can in turn bind them."[40]

As human beings, we are all entitled to more specific rights because we are born with dignity and possess the freedom and rational capacity needed to reaffirm our dignity. The *universality* of human rights thus indicates something more than the complete inclusiveness of a right at the level of application or even a set of pre-given attributes that are common to all human beings. Precisely because *humanity* is defined in terms of the rational ability to question and transform the external situations and contingent circumstances which are given to us, the universality of our entitlement to rights is essentially normative or ideal. It issues from the capacity for universal reason that is coextensive with freedom and that distinguishes humanity from the inhuman. The inhuman refers to forces or circumstances that are blindly given to or imposed on us from the outside, all that is merely contingent and does not possess universal necessity because it does not originate from our reason. The violation of human rights is viewed as the result of inhumanity, whether this takes the form of individual cruelty, institutional violence, or, for the more theoretically savvy, the vicissitudes of global capitalism or the system (Habermas). These inhuman forces can, however, be humanized or transcended (*aufgehoben*) by human rational work because they are aberrations or deviations from our humanity. Insofar as the content of specific human rights have universal validity and moral necessity, they make up a total rational form for regulating social interaction between states and individuals and enable us to mitigate the forces that constrain us from fully realizing our capacity for freedom. Transnational human rights groups are described as *humane* agencies precisely because they attempt to safeguard the basic conditions necessary for achieving the optimal state of freedom that co-belongs with the project of humanity.

The universal right to rights of all human beings thus presupposes a strict demarcation between humanity *qua* possessor of rational freedom and the inhuman as well as the ability of the human subject to transform or remake the inhuman world in the image of ideal rational forms that it prescribes for the world. The belief that human beings can rationally transform and overcome the contingent limitations of the material conditions of their given existence through the purposive regulation of an ideational norm or image (*Bild*) is simply a practical extension of the power of transcendence implied by human dignity. All the different human rights regimes—existing human rights instruments *and* the various positions taken by governments in the North, states in the developing South, and the international civil society of human rights NGOs with respect to these instruments—share the same normative framework. They maintain that this border separating humanity from the inhuman must be rigorously policed and that the inhuman should be humanized through international human rights instruments. As we saw in my analysis of the Asian values debate, they differ only in how they figure the inhuman, for instance, oppressive regimes, institutions, and practices that will disappear with the global spread of the market; the monstrous totality of unfettered neocolonial global capital; or the complicity between right-wing postcolonial regimes and the hegemonic North. These different representations of the inhuman shape the content of specific human rights.

Human rights doctrine is therefore continuous with the concept-metaphor of *Bildung* that informs the purported attempts of postcolonial states to cultivate the humanity of their citizens through economic development. Many postcolonial constitutions affirm the right to full employment and other labor rights as human rights of the socioeconomic kind. The legitimacy of many postcolonial states is directly tied to their ability to uphold the socioeconomic rights of their citizens. For example, Article 13, section 3, of the Philippine Constitution (1986) provides that "the State shall afford full protection to labor, local and overseas, organized and unorganized, and promote full employment and equality of employment opportunities for all." Low-growth countries, however, face a profoundly troubling dilemma. On the one hand, they hope to achieve full employment for their citizens. On the other hand, this and the nation's economic development can occur only if the state actively engages in exporting its workers. Because workers' rights are difficult to protect beyond the sending state's sovereign boundaries, the humanizing projects of national development and the cultivation of the humanity of citizens are paradoxically undercut by the primary technical means *(techne)* the state deploys to achieve such goals. The hope, however, is that this inhuman *techne* can be humanized through another instrument, namely, the protection of the migrant worker's rights as human rights when he or she is abroad. Human rights are thus a moral trump card in the justification and legitimation of state action.

What, then, is the normative force behind the protection of migrant workers' human rights, and how effective are these instruments? Today, we find an increasing number of international resolutions concerning migrant workers' rights, such as the 1990 UN International Convention on the Protection of the Rights of All Migrant Workers and Members of Their Families and the two main International Labor Organization (ILO) conventions on migrant workers.[41] But their usefulness in protecting the type of migrant worker that concerns us, namely female domestic workers, is circumscribed by their scope and implementation. First, despite the explicit emphasis on the equal treatment of male and female migrant workers, the male worker remains the implicit norm of the migrant worker.[42] Consequently, the 1990 UN Convention does not address the particular needs of migrant women who are remunerated at lower rates, subjected to poor working conditions without the possibility of unionization and security, and rendered vulnerable to different forms of violence as a result of the specific nature of women's work and patriarchal representations of women, for instance, sexual abuse or exploitation, forced prostitution, and violence against women.[43] As we shall see, domestic workers are in an especially precarious situation because they are isolated in their respective households and closed to public scrutiny. Second, the UN Convention is based on the principle of "equal treatment." Its provisions attempt to ensure that migrant workers are not discriminated against and have the same protection as that afforded to indigenous workers by national legislation.[44] But this "equal treatment" approach is irrelevant in the area of domestic workers because indigenous domestic workers are also generally not protected by the labor laws of host countries because of the patriarchal-ideological prejudice that reproductive work is "private" in character and was traditionally unpaid.[45]

Moreover, any attempt to establish minimum standards for the treatment of migrant workers based on the principles and provisions of existing UN and ILO conventions and recommendations faces the more profound obstacle of implementation. In a world of sovereign states, the execution of standards articulated in international documents depends on the action of individual states. These standards are binding only on states that have ratified the documents, something that is likely to occur only if a given state already has equitable labor policies for its own nationals. Thus far, these instruments have been ineffective because they have not been ratified by major labor-receiving states.[46] Until these instruments gain wider ratification, migrant workers' rights are not recognized and are not concretely activated as universal human rights by labor-receiving states. Hence, although international law recognizes migrant workers' rights as universal rights that can be claimed by every individual, in the current conjuncture, the most feasible avenue for protecting them in cases of abuse lies with the individual worker's nation of origin.

There is another way of giving the migrant worker's rights a universal grounding. Through a combination of diplomatic channels, economic negotiations, and moral pressure, a labor-sending nation-state can urge labor-receiving states to view the rights of its overseas workers as an extension of its collective *right to development,* thereby imbuing these rights with the normative force of third-generation human rights.[47] The human right to development links the socioeconomic rights of individual citizens to the collective economic rights of their nations, that is, the economic well-being of nations conceived in analogy with an autonomous organic human body striving to maximize its capacity for life and self-fulfillment. It is suggested that national development is crucial to the welfare of a nation's citizens and that individual worth and dignity are meaningless if a nation cannot satisfy the basic needs of its citizens, such as adequate food, clothing, and shelter. Hence, the attainment of collective economic rights is indispensable to the fulfillment of individual-based human rights.[48] A developing nation-state ought to be able to reasonably expect (and demand) the cooperation of developed nations in assisting its development because this is in the interests of humanity as a whole. This human right can be extended to migrant workers on the grounds that their individual development and the fulfillment of their individual rights are indivisible from and premised on the national development of the sending country. At the same time, a sending country has a collective economic right to protect the rights of migrant workers because they are crucial to its development. Indeed, it has been argued that the complex interdependence created by economic globalization makes the protection of migrant workers' human rights a matter of mutual economic interest to both labor-exporting and labor-importing countries.[49]

Understood in this way, migrant workers' human rights not only explicitly define being-human in terms of the capacity for development. They also imply that state action is crucial to achieving humanity's full potential. This is especially so in the difficult task of reaching bilateral agreements that follow the internationally established guidelines for minimum standards of treatment.[50] The administrative bodies set up by labor-exporting states for regulating the recruitment of overseas workers and the labor attachés working in embassies in labor-importing countries play an increasingly important role in protecting migrant workers, especially in monitoring compliance with existing bilateral treaties. The crucial point here is that within the framework of uneven global development, the protection of migrant workers' rights cannot take the form of an unqualified endorsement of globality. Contra liberal accounts of globalization, even though less developed nations derive economic benefits from transnational labor migration, globality is not the concrete shape of universal humanity because the migrant worker's human rights can be protected only through the nation-state's universal human right to development. Yet, anchoring them to the latter also does not completely protect them. For the right to development inevitably comes up against an internal limit: the inherently competitive character of development in an uneven world economy. Despite the emphasis of the Declaration of the Right to Development on concerted cooperation among developing countries to promote rapid development, the right to development of one nation in the postcolonial South often clashes with that of another. The mistreatment of migrant workers occurs so frequently because many labor-exporting governments do not have the will to demand fair treatment for their workers for fear of losing their market share to others. The global economic downturn has worsened this aggressive competitiveness and lack of solidarity among labor-exporting countries. As Lim and Oishi observe, "More countries have attempted to break into the international market for migrant workers and to export their 'cheap and docile' labor to a limited number of increasingly choosy host countries."[51] In the zealous scramble to carve out a market niche, states inevitably sacrifice the protection of their migrant workers. We must therefore ask: How can the right to development be fully human/ humanized? Because it is the basis for the human rights of migrant workers, we can also rephrase the question this way: Can the migrant worker achieve humanity in the current new international division of labor? The solution cannot be found at the level of international legal instruments alone. Instead, the migrant worker's human rights (and humanity) take shape at the intersection of various political technologies, negotiations, and calculations of labor-exporting and receiving states and other collective actors participating in the global traffic in labor. I will now consider these processes in greater detail by focusing on the migrant domestic worker's human rights in Singapore. As we shall see, the articulation of the foreign domestic worker's (FDW) humanity renders untenable the secure boundary between the human and the inhuman that informs much critical-emancipatory thought and progressive practical discourse.

The Biotechnologies of Foreign Domestic Workers

The cultivation of human capital has always been crucial to Singapore's hyperdevelopment. The city-state's ongoing ambitions to upgrade to a non-labor-intensive, knowledge-based economy by becoming the high technology and financial center for Asia and the primary Asian hub of transnational capital investments in high-value-added manufacture and services has intensified governmental development of Singapore's business and human resource capabilities. The state has formulated a complex foreign labor policy to facilitate the upgrading of its "indigenous" human resources.[52] The more glamorous or "marketable" part of this policy involves the gathering of "global talent." For instance, the state has set up a recruiting agency called Contact Singapore, with a global network of offices in cities such as Boston, Chicago, London, Sydney, Chennai, Hong Kong, and Shanghai.[53] Contact Singapore's motto is "Singapore. Your world of possibilities." It has launched an international print and Web ad campaign that features examples of global talent who have been attracted to Singapore. One ad quotes Richard Tomlin, an English banker who is the vice chairman of UBS Warburg in Asia, saying, "Like Singapore, I believe people are the greatest assets." Another ad featuring Adekunle Adeyeye, a Nigerian nanotechnology researcher who was at Trinity College, Cambridge University, before becoming an assistant professor at the National University of Singapore, begins with a quote: "Doing research in Singapore is like playing in the top league" (Figure 1).

The state hopes that some of this "foreign talent" will become integrated, develop loyalties to Singapore, and settle there. But even those highly skilled expatriates who do not stay permanently will make a lasting contribution by transferring skills and professional expertise to the local population, thereby improving the quality of Singapore's human capital in the long term. As its deputy prime minister noted in 1998: "For this nation to keep growing, a continued inflow of talent is essential. Without this inflow, Singapore cannot be a cosmopolitan society, or support the diverse activities and services which make us relevant to the world. . . . Hence, our systematic policy is to attract a broad spectrum of foreign talent, ranging from skilled workers to professionals, from all round the world. Some will come to work for a time, before moving on. But we hope a fair proportion will eventually sink roots and make this their home and nation."[54] To attract such talent to linger or settle permanently, the government launched an aggressive campaign to market Singapore as a city with a thriving cosmopolitan culture and creative lifestyle. This attempt to make Singapore a "Global City for the Arts," an exciting destination for arts tourism and an arts business hub, mirrors the ambition to become a financial and technological hub.[55] The cultural component of state-sponsored globalization is therefore state-sponsored cosmopolitanism. This is a ferocious caricature of the hybrid migrant cosmopolitanism we have learned to celebrate in contemporary cultural studies.

The second arm of the foreign labor policy involves the importation

"Doing research in Singapore is like playing in the top league."

Dr Adekunle Adeyeye, a soccer enthusiast, made his big career move to the National University of Singapore as an Assistant Professor.

"I was struck by Singapore's educational excellence, economic vision and technological edge on my first visit in 1997. When I returned in 2000, I brought my wife because I am here to stay."

A top student in his homeland, Adeyeye spent eight exciting years at Trinity College, Cambridge University, where he was the first Nigerian to be elected as a research fellow. Moving to Singapore enables him to further his groundbreaking research in nanotechnology.

Adeyeye's work has endless applications, ranging from the computer and automotive to medical industry. All of which adds to his delight with the scientific advances he has made. Above all, he is also thrilled that Singapore's rising prominence as a high-tech hub is a magnet to world-class companies and scientists.

If you want to be exploring new frontiers in the research arena, visit www.contactsingapore.org.sg/time today. It could be a win-win situation for you and Singapore.

Singapore. Your world of possibilities.

Contact Singapore

OFFICES: BOSTON • CHICAGO • SAN FRANCISCO • LONDON • SYDNEY • CHENNAI • HONG KONG • SHANGHAI • SINGAPORE

1. "Doing research in Singapore is like playing in the top league." Advertisement for recruitment of foreign talent by Contact Singapore. *Source: Time* magazine, November 18, 2002, p. 14.

of short-term low-skilled or unskilled workers to fill menial jobs that are crucial to the economy and the reproduction of social life but are shunned by the local workforce as it is upgraded to meet the needs of a progressively capital-intensive economy. FDWs, a significant component of this lower tier of migrant labor, fulfill an additional function. To augment the professional and skilled worker sector, the Singapore government encouraged educated middle-class women to join the workforce even as it sought to reverse the declining birth and marriage rates of such women. Women in developed economies shoulder a double burden. They are expected to contribute to national economic growth but also to fulfill the roles of wife and mother, with the attendant responsibilities for household management ascribed by masculinist society.[56] The Singapore state made accessible a pool of live-in foreign domestic helpers who could take care of household chores and child care needs. As the female labor force participation rate, especially that of married women, increased dramatically, the number of foreign maids also catapulted from 40,000 in 1988 to more than 140,000 in 2001, with a 19 percent increase between 1998 and 2001 alone.[57] Hence, another kind of cosmopolitanism coexists with the high-end cosmopolitanism of talented professionals as its polar opposite: the cultural practices of the underclass foreign domestic helpers who are the disavowed support of the aspiring global city, a form of culture that the local population generally regards as annoying babble. As part of the reproductive sphere, these migrant workers are crucial to the sustaining of social and civil life. But they are not recognized as "foreign talent." They are merely "foreign workers" to be used and discarded rather than integrated into the social fabric of the city-state. Indeed, these two poles of cosmopolitan labor have distinctly different legal statuses. Members of the higher tier hold "employment passes" and enjoy liberal benefits and conditions of employment designed to induce them to take up permanent residence and even citizenship, whereas those in the lower tier merely hold temporary "work permits" that must be renewed every two years for a maximum stay of eight years and are subject to stringent legal restrictions.

This set of strategies for the cultivation of human capital is an instance of what Michel Foucault has called bio-power, or the power over life. Foucault coined the term to refer to a new type of political power that came into being in the seventeenth century and served as an indispensable mechanism in the development of capitalism.[58] Instead of functioning repressively, the central task of bio-power is the administration of human life as a resource that can be attached to the apparatus of production or adjusted to broader economic processes. Foucault distinguished between two basic forms or poles of bio-power: discipline and government.[59] The former refers to a form of social control directed at individual bodies. Techniques of discipline, which emanated from extrastate institutions such as factories, schools, and hospitals, served a twofold function. As a form of cultivation or formation, they augmented and optimized the capacities of bodies at the same time that these were rendered docile so that they could be tethered to and integrated into the production machine and their forces extracted as labor power.[60] Disciplinary techniques thus constituted "an anatomo-politics of the human body."[61] Government, by contrast, refers to a mode of power that regulates the life of the population. The population is viewed as a system of living beings with biological traits (such as propagation, births and deaths, the level of health and life expectancy) that can be analyzed and known through specific scientific knowledge and rational technologies. It can therefore be modified, altered, and managed through policy interventions that aim to increase the state's economic resources and forces.[62] Such technologies of regulation and control constituted "a biopolitics of the population."[63]

The inherently productive character of bio-power can be understood in at least three senses. Most obviously, bio-power increases the capacities and aptitudes of individual bodies through investment and valorization and enhances the quality of the population as an efficient economic resource. But it is also productive because instead of being a coercive instrument for the maintenance of social relations that is located at the superstructural level, bio-power operates within the social body and the sphere of economic processes. It operates within the sphere of the forces and relations of production as their indispensable *constitutive* force. Indeed, one can say that techniques of bio-power articulate the economic base and political, legal, and ideological superstructures into a seamless web or network. In Foucault's view, "they also acted as factors of segregation and social hierarchization, exerting their influence on both these movements, guaranteeing relations of domination and effects of hegemony."[64] But most important, what bio-power produces is a form of being that is essential to production itself: the human subject with a free consensual will capable of labor, exchange, and other forms of social interaction and cooperation.[65] Industrial society presupposes that the individual body is the repository of labor power, which, measured in units of time, is a commodity that an individual exchanges for a wage. The individual is deemed to undertake this exchange *freely* and *willingly* because he fulfills his *human needs* through such compensation. Labor power and labor time are constituted through techniques of discipline, which subjectify the individual as a member of a system of means and ends.[66] But the human subject of needs is also not a natural given. It is constituted through governmental technologies or biopolitics. For instance, welfare policies can shape the population by affecting birthrates, health, and the distribution of the population. Such technologies thoroughly invest human life and shape its basic needs. As Foucault puts it: "The population is the subject of needs, of aspirations, but it is also the object in the hands of the government, aware vis-à-vis the government, of what it wants, but ignorant of what is being done to it. Interest as the consciousness of each individual who makes up the population, and interest considered as the interest of the population as a whole regardless of what the particular interests and aspirations may be of the individuals who compose it: this is the new target and the fundamental instrument of the government of population."[67]

It is important to distinguish government, a terminal form of power, from governmentality, the heterogeneous assemblage of institutions, technologies, calculations, and tactics that are the conditions enabling the exercise of government. As we shall see, this distinction is crucial because it implies that even non-state actors and entities such as NGOs and civil society rely on and are part of the web of governmentality. One can say that bio-power enables the maximization of the state's resources by organizing the population into a *bios*, a system of means and ends in which the contribution of each member is reciprocated with benefits and rewards that are not merely monetary.

The deployment of technologies of bio-power for the betterment of human life through economic development in Singapore has oppressive consequences. As we saw, the cultivation of human capital for postindustrial hyperdevelopment involved a policy of importing low-level migrant workers to support the enhancement of the local workforce by increasing the participation of highly educated women. What sustains this component of the greater project as its necessary condition is the production of two different but constitutively interdependent subjects: the liberal middle-class professional woman and the docile FDW. The latter's work makes the former's employment possible. Singaporean women can join the workforce only if the burden of reproductive labor is transferred elsewhere. Hence, in order to attach educated middle-class women to the professions and high-value service industries, migrant women have to be tethered to the Singaporean home *qua* machine for the reproduction of society and human capital so that the forces of their bodies can be extracted as reproductive labor. The pervasiveness of this double tethering, which is also a dependency, is obvious. Many middle-class workingwomen in Singapore regard foreign maids as a necessity rather than a luxury, so much so that a 1996 academic study suggested that, "the maid culture has become a way of life in Singapore."[68] Thus, if the sex/gender system, in Gayle Rubin's words, "determines that a 'wife' is among the necessities of a worker," then in the postindustrial hyperdevelopment of Singapore, a foreign maid is widely viewed as one of the necessities of a wife so that she can work for the betterment of the country's economy.[69]

This situation represents an important modification of Foucault's account of bio-power. When Foucault formulated the concept to explain the rise of industrial capitalism in Europe, he did not envisage that postindustrial hyperdevelopment outside the North Atlantic would require the mass deployment of human bodies engaged in *reproductive* labor and, more important, that the labor power in question would be a revolving pool of temporary labor consisting of *foreign* bodies that are emphatically barred from becoming part of the permanent population. Such bodies do not need to be cultivated and augmented in the same way as those belonging to the permanent labor force. They do not need to be subjectified as members of the population because their presence is only temporary. Their absorption into the permanent workforce is to be vigorously prohibited because it is not of any value to the receiving country. When exhausted, their forces can always be replenished by substituting other temporary migrants. As Noeleen Heyzer and Vivienne Wee observe, "Because of their transient immigration status, foreign domestic workers are treated by the receiving governments as needed but undesirable aliens who have to be controlled stringently, with only their labour to be extracted and the rest of them as persons to be restricted."[70] This is, therefore, a form of labor whose constitution involves discipline and regulation, but *without either increasing/enhancing workers' bodily forces through concerted training or any subjectification.* As members of the indigenous population, middle-class women workers are repeatedly bound to the project of hyperdevelopment through subjectifying processes that not only enhance the individual's skills through training but also induce a sense of belonging through social recognition and the emotional reward of striving toward a higher goal that transcends mere economic self-interest. As Singapore's prime minister stated in 1997:

> We aim to maximise the talents and abilities of all Singaporeans, not just the best and brightest, but every individual. Not everyone is equally talented. But every person has some useful ability. Our education system must therefore not only groom our top talent, but also recognise and develop a range of skills and abilities at every level. . . . Not everyone can perform equally well. But every person who tries his best should have his contribution recognised. Every Singaporean has a contribution to make to his job, his company, his community and his country. But equally, he has a responsibility to keep himself employable and productive through continuous learning, and to play his part to the best of his ability.[71]

In contradistinction, FDWs, who can never hope to become citizens of Singapore and are not part of its *bios*, are constituted as quasi-subjects to be utilized as means. Their only subjective incentive to be attached to the Singaporean economic machine is financial remuneration. The human rights abuses suffered by FDWs have this biopolitical formation as their structural basis. The problem is primarily one of concrete structural conditions that are inherently conducive to the widespread dehumanization of FDWs and only secondarily a matter of the personal cruelty or pathology of individual employers. The latter is merely a product-effect or extreme symptom of the former.

For an outside observer, the frequency of local newspaper reports about the abuse and dehumanization of FDWs by their female employers and their voyeuristic headlines (Figure 2) are a strange and striking attestation to the FDW's importance in the Singaporean public imagination:

> "She Tortured Maid with Clothes Peg." Faridah Abdul Fatah was angry with her maid for waking up late. So she decided to teach Miss Sugiarti Sugino, 22, a lesson that the young woman would not forget in a hurry. She clipped eight clothes pegs to the maid's ears and then yanked them

off one by one. She wanted to humiliate her. But that was not all that she did. (*Straits Times*, November 7, 2000)

"Abused Maid Speaks: My Seven Months of Horror." "She told me that since I had cut the mooncake wrongly, she could not eat the mooncake and she had better eat my breast." (*Straits Times*, March 20, 2002)

"Maid Told to Burn Herself and Hit Head with Slippers. She Said Her Financial-Controller Employer Inflicted Such Punishments on Her for Not Doing Her Work Well." An 18-year-old maid was made to squat and stand 100 times with her hands crossed over her chest, holding her ears, as punishment for not doing her work properly. . . . The maid, Miss Mani Nagavalli, was also told to burn herself with a heated ladle for not cleaning a container, which had flour on it, carefully. When she pressed the ladle on her wrist twice and cried out in pain, her employer walked away after noting the burn marks. (*Straits Times*, July 11, 2001)

"I Had to Cut Lawn with Pair of Kitchen Scissors." Economics graduate Marissa was made to cut her wealthy former employer's lawn with a large pair of kitchen scissors. The lawn measured about 50 sq m, and Marissa says she was forced to do the work every week from 10 AM to 2 PM without any protection from the rain or sun. The Singaporean couple she was working for refused to hire a gardener or buy a lawn mower. Marissa, not her real name, eventually developed an allergic rash because of the grass cutting, and decided that enough was enough. She quit after seven months. (*Straits Times*, December 16, 2001)

The number of officially recorded abuse cases is actually very small, given the large number of FDWs (140,000 in 2001) in Singapore. The state has also zealously prosecuted such cases and imposed increasingly severe penalties on offenders. The cases brought into the phenomenality of the public gaze, however, are only the most extreme manifestations of a deeper rationality stretching from state administrative agencies to commercial employment agencies and individual employers that regards migrant workers as tools or means in the employer's quest for economic advancement and the larger project of national development.[72]

The deployment of this rationality within the transformation of the family structure and the sex/gender system of Singaporean society as a result of the entry of women citizens into different levels of socioeconomic and public life is best indicated by the title of a popular book published in 1993 in the genre of entertaining instruction, "To Have and to Hold: How to Have a Maid and Keep Her."[73] Oblivious to the irony of violating Kant's categorical imperative, the author announces in the preface that "this book looks at the foreign maid issue from the perspectives of viewing it lightly to seriously thinking how to maximise the use of the maid in the house." The proliferation of such "how-to" guides to "managing" a maid extends the rhetoric and tactics of managerial administration into the household. It indicates a certain commercialization of the home, the introduction of economic imperatives of utility and labor

Wednesday, March 20, 2002 : THE STRAITS TIMES

PRIME NEWS

'SHE TOLD ME THAT SINCE I HAD CUT THE MOONCAKE WRONGLY, SHE COULD NOT EAT THE MOONCAKE AND SHE HAD BETTER EAT MY BREAST.'

— Miss Kusmirah, whose woman employer took to biting her breasts repeatedly to punish her

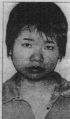

Keloid scars on her hands bear testimony to the cruelty Miss Kusmirah endured at the hands of her ex-boss Chow (above).

WANG HUI FEN

ABUSED MAID SPEAKS

My seven months of horror

She was cut, burned, beaten and bitten. Teenage maid suffered employer's abuse until her badly injured nipple fell out

By WONG SHER MAINE

INDONESIAN maid Kusmirah Mujadi knew that life with Jennicia Chow Yen Ping was going to be tough when she suffered her first beating just three days into the job.

But the 19-year-old never expected to be running away seven months later with a bloody trail on her T-shirt marking where Chow had bitten her excruciatingly hard on the nipple the night before.

Miss Kusmirah also left the Woodlands Circle flat on that pre-dawn morning with angry keloid scars on her arms and a host of other permament reminders of the cuts, burns and beatings meted out by Chow during the seven unhappy months spent in her employment.

A more humiliating reminder would come days later when her nipple fell off because it was so damaged from Chow's repeated bitings.

Speaking to The Straits Times yesterday, Miss Kusmirah, now 20, recalled how her nightmare started soon after she began work on Marit last year.

"She scolded and beat me from the start. I didn't know why she did it, even though I kept saying sorry. I thought maybe she was insane," Miss Kusmirah said, in a mixture of Malay and English.

Chow, who lived in the flat with her insurance agent husband and three-year-old daughter, would frequently abuse Miss Kusmirah for not doing her work properly.

The 30-year-old used a cane, a knife, a hot oven rack, boiling water, scissors and the back of a chopper to carry out her cruelty.

The petite maid, who is about half a head shorter than Chow at just under 1.5 metres, said she was also made to work long hours, seven days a week. She slept on the kitchen floor and ate leftovers.

She could not escape because Chow, then a customer relations officer at a private hospital, locked her inside the flat when she went to work.

Chow also threatened to send her back to Indonesia if she complained to anyone.

But greater humiliation was to come.

During the Mooncake Festival in September, Chow got angry when Miss Kusmirah did not cut the mooncake properly.

Said Miss Kusmirah, who is well-endowed in spite of her slight frame: "She told me that since I had cut the mooncake wrongly, she could not eat the mooncake and she had better eat my breast."

She dared not fight back as Chow was brandishing a knife, threatening to cut her nipple off. That was the first time Chow bit Miss Kusmirah's breasts.

After that, it happened regularly. Chow would sometimes bite Miss Kusmirah's breasts through her T-shirt; sometimes she would lift up her shirt and bra so she could bite her bare skin.

Miss Kusmirah said that Chow's husband was never around to witness this bizarre behaviour.

She took her solitary chance to flee at 6.50 am on Oct 18 when she saw the house key lying on the table. The family was sleeping.

Chow, said to have been chronically depressed, was on Monday sentenced to five years in jail, for what was described as the worst case of maid abuse seen here.

Miss Kusmirah, now staying at a dormitory in the Indonesian embassy, has re-ceived counselling.

Wearing lipstick and with her short nails varnished, Miss Kusmirah, who was sporting a chin-length bob, was cheery enough at the start of yesterday's interview.

But her face turned sombre and her eyes grew glassy when she recounted her time under Chow's roof. Tears welled up in her eyes when she lifted the long sleeves of her sunshine yellow baju kurung to unveil the dark ugly keloid mass on her left elbow.

The eldest daughter of farmers from central Java said she is still haunted, especially at night, and sometimes bolts out of bed at 3 am like she had to do when she was Chow's maid.

What would make her happy now, she said, is "to go back home."

2. "Abused Maid Speaks: My Seven Months of Horror." *Source: Straits Times*, March 20, 2002, p. 3, © Singapore Press Holdings Ltd. (SPH). Permission required for reproduction.

efficiency into its functioning. Employers are taught to reasonably expect "that all the work that needs to be done is done. In order to avoid having a situation where you feel cheated that your maid hasn't put in a day's work, here's what you can do. . . . Experience and commonsense will tell you that it is better to over-supervise or over-monitor (no matter how much a workaholic she is) than to feel short-changed later."[74] The foreign maid is thus the wife of the wife. But she is also an employee to be managed in order to increase her efficiency, just as the woman professional's efficiency in her workplace has to be increased. The advancement and development of the professional woman human being thus involves a certain inhumanity: the bringing into the home of a foreign stranger who is dehumanized because she inherits the feminized chores of the wife and mother without any of their human-redemptive aspects.

Such guidebooks are a commercial supplement to the official guides distributed by the Ministry of Manpower as part of an information kit accompanying applications for FDW work permits. The prose of these official documents is more tempered and cautionary. For instance, potential employers are advised to consider other child care alternatives. Nevertheless, there is a clear continuity in the objectives of household and state with respect to the FDW. One finds at the state level the same managerial vocabulary and economic cost-benefit calculations, the same rationality that views the FDW as a mere means to achieve another's economic self-interest and material well-being. The employer is advised to "consider if you are able to provide for, maintain and properly manage the worker during her stay with you. . . . There is also the additional risk that the worker may abscond and your losing the $5,000 security bond." At the same time, however, the state also invests the commercial relation of employment with the aura of warmth and felicity usually reserved for the intimate sphere of marriage: "The Ministry wishes you a pleasant and happy relationship with your foreign domestic worker."[75] This commercialization of the family unit and this making-intimate of a labor relation occur because the Singaporean state has largely abdicated to the family the economic responsibility for the social reproduction of human capital that welfare states of developed countries have generally assumed. It has repeatedly asserted that the employment of FDWs is a "private" decision of individual households and should thus be left to "free-market" mechanisms. By consigning such employment to the private sphere, the state benefits from hidden savings of funds it would otherwise have to invest in family care and other social services, for instance, the costs of establishing and running a child care infrastructure with appropriately trained caregivers and food, or providing facilities for care of the handicapped and elderly.[76] As Noeleen Heyzer and Vivienne Wee astutely argue: "In the disappearance of unpaid female labour in the home, the alternative of paying for available and affordable migrant female labour remains the economic responsibility of the family, especially that of the working woman. It is in this sense that in the receiving countries, development processes are being subsidised by a genderised international class structure—by the labour subsidy of female migrant workers and by the income subsidy (and therefore also a labour subsidy) of middle class women."[77] The displacement of the costs and burdens of social reproduction from the state to migrant women from poorer countries means that economic success within the new international division of labor generates and is sustained by an international division of domestic labor.

But even as the Singapore state indirectly deploys the labor power of FDWs, it refuses to treat such employment as a genuine labor relation that deserves government protection. For although a labor relation is one of economic utility, the science of management views the worker as more than a mere means because of the need to increase labor efficiency. Moreover, terms of employment are never only a matter of consensual agreement between two private parties. Since labor is connected to the basic needs of human beings who are members of the population, work conditions are subject to government regulation and protection, for instance, the establishment of maximum hours of the working week, minimum pay, paid leave, sick leave, and so on. The Singapore state's refusal to provide fuller regulation of the working conditions of FDWs stems from the fact that unskilled migrant workers are always already viewed disadvantageously in comparison to highly skilled migrants and the local population. They are beings with a lesser status, on whom the state does not need to expend resources and care. Although the Ministry of Manpower acknowledges the important economic and social contributions of FDWs to Singaporean society, these are not enough to warrant their full integration into the Singaporean *bios*.[78] In response to a question about the state's foreign labor policy, an official of the ministry drew a telling contrast between the compatibility of high-end migrant workers with the local population and the incompatibility of FDWs:

It is a question of "how do you judiciously manage the growing population [of FDWs]." . . . They [professional and educated migrant workers] don't create social problems. They don't fall down from a height. You don't have the problem of housing them. You don't have the problem of them not being able to assimilate and integrate into our local population. They are more global in their thinking. A different *breed* of people come and work in Singapore [as FDWs]. That's fine with us. But these people leave their countries, many of them, invariably from rural areas. Some of them have never even seen a high-rise block, and here, they are working in a high-rise apartment and you have people falling down when they hang clothes, when they clean windows, and then we have a maid problem.[79]

Excluded from the system of means and ends that the state wishes to enhance through the integration of professional and educated migrant workers, FDWs are viewed in terms of sheer technical utility: as mere means to the ends of others, without any ends of their own that need to be taken into account in the state's calculations. Hence, what we have is a form of governmental regulation without the welfare of the *bios*. Instead of being the objects of *productive* regulatory techniques, FDWs need to be policed to mitigate what the state euphemistically refers to as "social costs": the negative consequences that their presence inflicts on Singaporean society, problems ranging from congestion of public space to strained bilateral relations with labor-exporting countries over their abuse by the local population.[80] Here, too, much of the policing is delegated to employers. The two main state mechanisms are the foreign worker's levy and the bond. The levy is a pricing mechanism used to regulate the demand for foreign workers. It is a monthly cost borne by employers of foreign workers in addition to the worker's salary. The figures are reviewed and adjusted regularly according to changing market circumstances. It is a two-tier scheme designed to discriminate between skilled and unskilled foreign workers, encouraging retention and recruitment of the former and dampening demand for the latter. In November 1997, the levy for unskilled foreign construction workers was increased by S$30 to S$470, and that for FDWs was increased by S$15 to S$345, whereas that for skilled foreign workers in the construction, marine, manufacturing, and service sectors was cut by half (from S$200 to S$100).[81] The levy is high relative to the disgracefully low salaries of FDWs in Singapore. The starting salaries for Indonesian FDWs as of

2002 ranged from S$230 to S$250, and new FDWs from the Philippines were paid between S$320 and S$350. The move reflected the state's policy of encouraging the inflow of talented foreigners who could help Singapore maintain its economic competitiveness and its attempt to curb overreliance on low-cost unskilled workers whose increasing numbers would prevent the upgrading of the local construction industry and the development of professional domestic and child care services, and cause a whole array of "social problems." As an official of the Ministry of Manpower stated in an interview:

> We have 900,000 to 1 million households. If every one of them were to have a domestic worker, we would have 1 million FDWs. I mean, can you imagine the social implications? We are talking about 1 million FDWs alone. What about foreign construction workers and other foreign workers? The situation is not tenable. That will also have an impact on the way our children are raised, dependency problems of FDWs, bilateral problems that will invariably arise from time to time with the exporting countries. So there are social and management issues we have to grapple with, so we can't allow the population of FDWs just to rise. We can't allow the situation where every household who wants a FDW can have one.[82]

Increasing the levy also makes FDWs cost-prohibitive for less affluent households. This removes another impediment to the upgrading of human capital: it makes it unfeasible for unskilled housewives to take up low-grade jobs in the workforce. As another Ministry of Manpower official put it: "If we encourage women with low skills to hire maids to look after their families so that they can take up low-paying jobs, we will merely be replacing one group of unskilled workers with another. The Government's objective is primarily to encourage women with higher skills to remain in the workforce and to have children."[83] The levy is a constant issue of contention in the national media and a major source of tension between the domestic worker and her employer. It is widely perceived by Singaporean women to be a means of lining state coffers at the expense of "the working class."[84] In fact, the costs are largely borne by the FDW. Although a higher levy effectively reduces the income of the woman employer who must factor in this additional cost as a condition of her employment, it is often passed on to the FDW in the form of a lack of wage increases or even salary deductions. The rising costs of employing an FDW also lead employers to expect "to get more out of their maids."[85]

Whereas the levy reduces the number of FDWs, the security bond—S\$5,000 which employers are required to pay to the state—is an instrument for ensuring that the behavior and movement of FDWs is firmly policed and restricted by their employers during the term of their employment. An FDW is granted a work permit subject to various conditions.[86] The most repressive of these conditions are the prohibition of marriage to a Singapore citizen or permanent resident during her stay and the prohibition of pregnancy. The FDW is also required to submit to a medical examination for pregnancy and sexually transmitted diseases once every six months, and is repatriated immediately if the test results are positive. Since the bond is forfeited if any of these conditions are violated, the mechanism transfers the monitoring of workers to the site of the household, where it can be performed most effectively and zealously by employers to prevent the possibility of any "illegitimate" activities even before the FDW enters into public space.

These governmental mechanisms contribute to the systematic dehumanization of the FDW by articulating two principles or maxims of conduct that have become deeply ingrained in the subjectification of the middle-class woman employer. The FDW's lesser status as a being to be excluded from the Singaporean *bios* is repeatedly reinforced through state education of the public via the print media about the gravity of the social problems FDWs cause. Such pedagogical messages also emphasize that the personal choice of an individual employer to hire an FDW has inflicted social problems on the *public*. One representative statement from the Ministry of Manpower reads: "The management of a large number of FDWs and finding amicable solutions to the various problems, for example, resolving disputes between FDWs and their employers, dealing with runaway FDWs or errant employers and preventing illegal deployment of FDWs require substantial costs which are not only borne by the employers of FDWs, but also by the public."[87] Two lessons are imparted to employers. First, FDWs are a necessary but undesirable presence. Second, the employer has a responsibility to mitigate the social problems they cause. Indeed, it is almost a public duty of the employer to control the behavior and movement of her foreign maid. From the start, therefore, the FDW is viewed as a minor or delinquent, someone without a full moral personality who needs to be trained, corrected, and policed so that she will not err. This is a constant theme sounded by employers and employment agencies. One employment agent observed, "Most employers think that it is the second nature of maids to tell lies."[88] Another agent noted that "the agent is the guardian, protector, brother, and father of the maid."[89] A secondary school teacher who employed an Indonesian FDW, felt that an employer should act like a guardian: "Since they [FDWs] are on their own here, we should protect them as our child, because they are under our care. If they lose their money, if someone threatens their lives etc. We should protect them against harmful people and advise them not to go out with other foreigners such as construction workers."[90]

The ethico-practical structure put in place is one of control and management from a standpoint of benevolent superiority. Such control is inevitably justified as a form of pastoral care for the FDW's moral welfare. While it may be partially motivated by concerns that the FDW may squander her hard-earned income on frivolous purchases or be led astray by predatory foreign construction workers, it can also modulate into excessive control and unrealistic demands for efficiency, especially given the deeper economic conditions that make the importation of FDWs necessary in the first place. As one employment agent observed: "The employer feels they have to make the maid work very hard because they have paid the levy. On the other hand, I think also because our whole society—Singapore is driving for productivity and good work, for performance. So this will also indirectly affect the mentality of people here. Everybody is driving for that, you see, so maybe it will drive down to the maid also."[91] This obsession with productivity can easily end up in abuse if one takes into account the fact that the female employer has to contend with both economic and workday pressures and the social-moral pressure to be a good wife and mother. The conduciveness of the ethical structure of benevolent superiority to abusiveness is amplified when it intersects with individual racism and cultural chauvinism in Singaporean society, as clearly evidenced by the fact that many exclusive private clubs ban maids from their premises (Figure 3).[92]

FDWs, for their part, are placed in the debased position of non-personhood. Employers who want to maximize their economic usefulness and are fearful of losing the bond engage in constant surveillance of maids, their working and eating habits, their social activities, and their use of the phone. Children are often the chief watchers. They are en-

Are Singaporeans behaving Like the white Raj?

The furore over the banning of foreign maids from dining in social clubs and swimming in condominium pools has sparked off charges that some Singaporeans are behaving like their former British colonial masters. Have they inherited the colonial mentality? What lies behind this psyche of superiority? SUSAN LONG *looks for the answers.*

'A maid's work is not defined by set hours or product delivery, but this intangible called the quality of "care" or "help".'
— Prof Brenda Yeoh

'As a maid, I feel if they don't want me there, I don't want to be there either. I think it's true, Singaporeans are behaving like British colonials.'
— Madam Gloria Liklyan

'Money talks here. People with big cars and branded suits are bound to be served better than a person in a short-sleeved shirt in a boutique.'
— Mr Robert Lim

FORUM LETTER KICKED OFF DEBATE

IT ALL started when Straits Times Forum letter-writer Gim Leng Monksfield wrote about her experience dining with a Sri Lankan family friend at the Singapore Cricket Club.

She was approached by the waiter and captain, who both asked: "Is she a maid?"

Her anecdote ignited a flurry of letters lambasting Singaporeans' treatment of foreign maids and construction workers.

Some say that while Singaporeans complain about racial discrimination when they are in Western countries, they are guilty of this very same shoddy treatment of people from poorer countries here.

The letters are still streaming in.

ADAM LEE

3. "Are Singaporeans Behaving Like the White Raj?" *Source: Straits Times*, August 2, 2000, p. 52, © Singapore Press Holdings Ltd. Permission required for reproduction.

couraged by their parents to carry tales about their maids, and are even rewarded for doing so.[93] As a caregiver who may not command the respect of her wards, the FDW finds that her work is not reciprocated by the emotional rewards and recognition that constitute the subjectifying and human-redemptive dimension of mothering. The minimal pastoral care an FDW receives from her employer or agent is only a subordinate process aimed at making her more efficient and submissive so as to enhance the middle-class professional woman's subjectification.

Employment agencies often hand out a list of rules to FDWs about appropriate conduct. One representative list (available in both Malay and English) consisted of imperatives and prohibitions addressed to the FDW with the aim of fostering docility and unquestioning submissiveness. The FDW is forbidden to express any disgruntlement with employers and wards, and is told to follow the employer's orders without any argument.[94] One rule expressly forbids taking part "in any activities or organization which is related your religion [sic]," although there is a concession that the FDW is "allowed to pray before you sleep." The FDW is supposed to sign this list as an indication that she has accepted these "house rules" and has understood that her failure to observe them may lead to dismissal. The Malay version stresses that these rules are for the FDW's benefit *(kebaikan)* and safety *(keselamatan)*. The FDW is told that it is in her interest to observe these rules because her employer will be happy with her work and give her presents and bonuses, and will not scold her if she follows instructions and orders well. An English supplement with the heading, "How to Succeed Working with Your Employers," adds that it is the FDW's duty to earn the employer's trust and "get them to like you. You can achieve these [sic] by trying to please them always by following instructions carefully and taking initiative to be useful in the house. Work hard and well and your stay will be a rewarding one." A list of codes of behavior follows. The FDW is advised that diligence is a cure for homesickness. She is told to be constantly courteous to "soften and prevent any friction. Therefore always practise: smiling and be happy." She is also instructed never to "answer back when [the] employer is angry. Say 'Sorry' even if you think you are right." Since FDWs often become dissatisfied with their working conditions when they discuss them with other, more experienced FDWs who are savvier about the market, the supplement also contains additional advice aimed at preventing such communications. The FDW is told not to make many friends ("Have 2 to 3 good friends will be good enough"), and not to "simply trust another experienced maid, especially your neighbour's maid." She is also told not to "compare with others and try to renegotiate your terms [of employment] or even tell your employer that others are getting a higher salary or more off-days and easier work than you."

The variety of handbooks published by local presses that are addressed to both maids and their employers, instructing the former about good behavior and the latter about proper techniques of management, indicate that similar techniques and rules are crucial to the employer's subjectification.[95] The submissiveness of the FDW is a fundamental component of the employer's formation as a productive middle-class member of the Singaporean population. Even the more lenient guidebooks that acknowledge that an FDW's day off is something that the employer should not try to regulate since it falls outside the work period advise a less obtrusive form of control. It is noted that Christian employers bring their Filipina maids to church to minimize their exposure to "bad" company and because they hope that "the church environment will instil in the maid the importance of spiritual things."[96] Curfews are deemed advisable because of concerns that "the longer the maid is out the more [money] she might spend or the greater likelihood that she might engage in activities not beneficial to her welfare."[97] Employers are also advised to make subtle inquiries about the FDW's activities during her day of rest as a way of "letting her know you care about her even when she's out of the house."[98] The less benevolent handbooks engage in crude, almost racist speculations about the attributes and abilities of maids according to their nationality. For example, "Filipino maids, given their cheerful outlook and colourful lifestyle, tend to be extroverts. . . . The downside of Filipino maids is their higher incidence of love affairs. Their more open personalities are usually the root cause. . . . The North Indians have little social networking here and are a demure lot. Their less aggressive personalities make them good followers of instructions" (see Tables 1 and 2).[99] They give advice on how to "handle" maids from different countries so that they do not take advantage of the employer's generosity and friendliness and become uncontrollable. As one guidebook puts it: "Treating a maid extremely well does not necessarily lead to our desired objective. Familiarity may deteriorate into contempt of authority. All that is required is to treat them fairly and reasonably."[100]

But who decides what constitutes "fair and reasonable treatment"? Employment agencies repeatedly complain that employers have exaggerated expectations about the performance of FDWs and are impatient and intolerant about their need to adapt to a new cultural and social milieu with unfamiliar modes and standards of housekeeping. This highly demanding ethos and the environment of constant surveillance is fertile breeding ground for abusive behavior. Felice Banyaga, a thirty-five-year-old Filipina domestic worker who, in 2001, had been working in Singapore for sixteen years, said that even though they are not physically abused, many FDWs feel debased in Singaporean society: "They [the employers] think, 'You are only a servant.' For them, it is like so low. They look down on us very low. In their mind, because they have money, they can employ [a new maid] every time if we cannot meet their needs and requirements. They will grumble and are not happy, and scold you. A servant is a wet rag, something you step on and you use to clean. It is demeaning. Very low, you should always be in a kitchen."[101] Joanna Elias, a thirty-seven-year-old Filipina who had worked in Singapore for nine years, said that on their days off, FDWs feel that Singaporeans "don't like us to be around because they look down on us." In her employer's home, she felt monitored all the time: "The employer wants you to work for every cent they pay you. The only rest you get is in the toilet, when you go and just sit there. When you first come here, you are alienated and you feel homesick because the employer doesn't make you feel welcome. There are many prohibitions. Some employers don't let you open the fridge. Some lock the front door when they leave."[102]

But worse still, the nebulous socio-legal status and ambiguous site of paid housework render maids especially vulnerable to poor treatment. Unlike foreign construction workers, domestic workers are not governed by the Employment Act. The Singaporean government has repeatedly insisted that the employment of domestic labor involves a private contract between worker and employer and that the conditions of service and wages should be determined by the free market rather than by labor legislation. The excuses given for this policy are the sacrosanct privacy of the home and the impracticality of enforcement. The state maintains that the household cannot and should not be regulated like a

Table 1 Comparison of attributes of foreign maids

Category of maids	Expected salaries S$	Appearance	Education background	Religion	Experience
Filipinos	$300–$350. Those with poor English get lower.	Fair to light brown.	High school, college grads, nursing cert, midwife courses, teaching qualification, secretarial certs.	Catholics/ Christians.	Work in Singapore, Malaysia, Saudi Arabia, Taiwan, Hong Kong, Philippines.
Indonesian (Native)	$230–$240. Those that can handle simple English get slightly more.	Fair to light brown.	SD (Primary-6 years), MP (Sec-9 years), SMA (College-12 years).	Mostly Muslims, 10% Christians.	Work in Singapore, Malaysia, Saudi Arabia, Indonesia.
Indonesian (Chinese)	$300–$400	Fair, oriental looking.	Majority illiterate. Some can speak and write Mandarin. Teochew and Hokkien (esp Kalimantan region) speaking.	Buddhists/Taoists.	Same as above.
North Indians	$300–$350. University grads get more.	Fair, oriental looking.	Grade 8, high school, and college. Some are university grads.	Buddhists/ Hindus. Some are Christians.	Mainly come from managing own homes. Only recently worked in Singapore and Hong Kong.

Category of maids	Expected salaries S$	Appearance	Education background	Religion	Experience
South Indians	$200-$250. University grads get more.	Dark brown.	Mostly primary and secondary (Grade 8). Some are university grads.	Hindus.	High demand in Middle East (eg: Saudi Arabia).
Sri Lankans	$200-$250. Overseas experience gets $240-$300.	Light brown.	'O' and 'A' levels.	Mostly Buddhists. Some Hindus/ Christians.	Work in Saudi Arabia.
Thais	$280-$350. Those who speak dialects get $350-$400.	Fair.	Primary to secondary.	Buddhists.	Work in Singapore, Hong Kong, Malaysia, Taiwan and Saudi Arabia.

Source: Maids Handbook: An Essential Guide to Hiring and Keeping a Foreign Domestic Helper (Singapore: Raffles, 2000), p. 27.

Table 2 Comparison of abilities of foreign maids

Category of maids	Languages	Cooking	Housework	Baby/Child care	Aged care
Filipinos	Good comprehension of English.	Able to cook with recipe book. Good at yellow rice, bee hoon and roast pork.	Good at house work, especially cleaning, packing and tidying.	Most love newborn and get along well with kids.	Those with nursing backgrounds do well.
Indonesian (Native)	Poor in English. Those with more experience and better educated speak better.	Muslims do not eat pork but can handle it. Good at spicy and curry dishes.	Good at heavy-duty housework as most are from farms.	Some have worked as babysitters. Others gained experience working in hospitals.	Same as above.
Indonesian (Chinese)	Most can handle dialects. Riau region and the older maids can speak Mandarin.	Good at cooking Nonya and Chinese dishes.	Good, but need to be motivated. Need more supervision and guidance initially.	Can take care of newborn and kids.	Able to speak dialects raises the success rate.
North Indians	Fair command of English. But university grads speak well. Speak Tamil/Tibetan/Nepalese.	Can cook fried rice, fried noodles and momo (dumpling).	Good, but need guidance as they come from very different living environment.	Experience comes from handling their own children.	Average.

Category of maids	Languages	Cooking	Housework	Baby/Child care	Aged care
South Indians	Poor to fair in English. But university grads speak reasonably well. Speak Tamil and dialects.	Good at curry and spicy dishes.	Do not prefer big house. House-keeping standards generally lower. Most come from extremely poor families	Average.	Average.
Sri Lankans	Fair to good command in English. Speak Tamil or Sinhalese.	Good at curries and fried vegetables.	Same as above.	Not recommended unless with experience.	Average.
Thais	Young maids have fair comprehension of English, but not the older ones. Able to pick up Chinese dialects fast.	Thai and Chinese style but a lot sweeter and spicier.	Generally good.	Same as above.	Those that can speak dialects handle better.

Source: Maids Handbook: An Essential Guide to Hiring and Keeping a Foreign Domestic Helper (Singapore: Raffles, 2000), p. 28.

workplace. It would be impractical to define minimum working hours because the nature of the maid's work makes it difficult to distinguish between her personal tasks and household chores. As an official from the Ministry of Manpower puts it:

> It is very difficult to enact rules to govern relationships at home. You are basically interfering into how a household runs and manages itself. How do you regulate how many hours a maid should work? In an office, you can see a person working. But maids have breaks in the afternoon. When the employer is not at home and the child is asleep or at school, she may not be working. If you regulate this and say that she can only work eight hours and after that she should be held overtime, then can you imagine? By the time you go home, the maid will be asking for overtime. Who is going to wash the dishes and serve you food after 8 P.M.?[103]

The government has therefore staunchly rejected proposals for a standard employment contract for maids and employers, emphasizing instead the importance of bilateral contracts that spell out the terms and conditions of employment.[104]

The government's contradictory logic is revealing. The basic philosophical principle it deploys at various levels is that of the liberal doctrine of the free consensual subject. First, all employment contracts are a matter of mutual agreement between the involved parties, and the state should leave the terms of such agreements to be governed by free-market principles. Second, even if labor legislation governs the minimum conditions of employment in public spaces such as offices, factories, and construction sites, the location of domestic labor is unique, and the freedom of the employer as an individual personality to live his or her private life within the household as he or she chooses prevents state regulation of this particular type of work. Finally, the FDW is also a free individual who has the ability to consent or refuse to work in a given household. It is assumed that she has freely chosen to accept the terms and conditions of employment even if they are not spelled out in advance. But this insistence on the free consensual subject masks the ubiquitous operations of biopolitics. For the consensual subject is always already a product of biopolitics. Both the need to import FDWs and the desire to export them are generated by the biopolitics of development, and these techniques irreducibly condition the consensual actions of individual employers and FDWs. In addition, the insistence of the state that the private sphere of the family should be distinguished from the public realm of work as a site that should not be subject to government intervention obfuscates the fact that it has already intervened in this intimate sphere by encouraging educated mothers and wives to join the workforce. The sacrosanct privacy of the home is thus an ideological ruse that gives an illusory sense of personal freedom to the individual employer although his or her individual subjectivity and very life as a member of the population are already thoroughly penetrated by the two poles of bio-power. The separation of public and private spheres is moreover contradictory because its affirmation with regard to the employer's household is simultaneously a cancellation of that very distinction for the FDW for whom the employer's household is both a workplace and the place where she lives her "private life" for the duration of her contract. Precisely because there is no clear physical distance between workplace and private space for the foreign maid, the unequal power relationship between employer and domestic worker persists at every moment in the lives of FDWs.

By refusing to regard the FDW as a genuine employee with clearly defined basic working conditions, the Singapore state exacerbates her vulnerability. Overseas employment bureaus and embassies of sending countries may design standard contracts governing the terms and conditions of employment and recruitment by employment agents aimed at preventing exploitation of their female migrant workers. But such contracts are easily sidestepped since an FDW can obtain a work permit without going through the relevant authorities in her home country or accredited recruitment agencies. She will then be deemed to have assented to excessive recruitment fees and harsh and exploitative terms of employment of her own "free will." As long as the maid is bound to the employer by a variable contract that does not follow any guidelines about minimum wages and tolerable working conditions, abuses can be regulated only through soft mediation by the Ministry of Manpower, self-interested employment agents, and the well-meaning but generally ineffective care of the embassies of sending countries. Moreover, this environment fosters a culture of fear and self-suppression in FDWs similar to battered women's syndrome. A newspaper article reported that Filipina domestic workers who were aware of the standard contract set by their embassy said that they would not use it as a basis to seek redress if their employers did not observe its terms because they feared losing their job.[105] Similarly, although the Ministry of Manpower guidebook for FDWs clearly states that abuse by an employer is punishable by law, an FDW may be unwilling to report abuses because she needs the income and is afraid of being blacklisted by employment agencies and barred from returning to Singapore.

The Inhuman in the Human

The technologies that craft the liberal middle-class professional woman and the docile FDW clearly have inhumane effects. They replicate the unevenness of the global capitalist system micrologically within the intimate sphere of the bourgeois conjugal family, a site that Habermas describes as the hallowed space for the cultivation of the universal ideals of humanity, but which has here become the quotidian site of potential and actual violence.[106] This violent exploitation extends into civil society since the traffic in foreign domestic labor, which is an integral part of social life that is factored into socioeconomic planning, is now a huge and profitable business with its own professional associations. The inhumanity of global capital thus marks from within and undermines the Singaporean state's ambitions to generate a cosmopolitan, civilized, and humane society through hyperdevelopment. As Hing Ai Yun observes:

> Family, community and society are also eviscerated in the process. As for the employing party, the huge imbalance of power provides much opportunity and space for eliciting the many forms of extreme and indecent patterns of behavior so maligned by a state ambitious to move Singapore forward to become a more gracious and civilized society. It is not conceivable that the state can play a leading role in creating the gracious Singapore society because of its complicity in generating and gaining from a whole new world of criminal and undesirable activities tied to the trade in foreign labor.[107]

The Singapore state has responded to the increasing local and international public debate about abused FDWs in two ways. It has attempted to impress upon employers that FDWs are not a long-term or sustainable solution to the household's domestic needs because of the social costs and other problems arising from a dependency on foreign labor. It has also attempted to reduce reliance on FDWs through measures intended to increase the availability of affordable alternatives such as professional child care and domestic cleaning services, a Baby Bonus scheme to help offset the cost of having more children, a Third Child Maternity Leave grant, and measures to enable more familial care through the promotion of pro-family work practices.[108] The state has also undertaken a very limited cosmetic rehumanization of the FDW. It has laid most of the blame on the inhumane actions of individual employers through severe punitive measures and public statements about the government's commitment to ensuring that employers fulfill their obligation of treating maids in "a decent and humane way."[109] Identical rhetoric about "just and humane treatment," the prohibition of physical violence, and the duty of the employer to "create harmonious relations and working conditions," has made its way into employment contracts used by agencies. But such attempts are merely cosmetic because they place the welfare of FDWs solely in the hands of individual employers who are punished if they err. As Singapore's labor minister put it in 1998, "The Government wants to send a very, very strong signal to employers that their maids' well-being and welfare are in their hands."[110] Focus is therefore effectively deflected from the root source of the FDW's dehumanization: the fact that the labor-importing state takes no responsibility for her welfare since she is excluded from the national *bios*. The true motive for this cosmetic rehumanization of the FDW—national self-interest rather than genuine feelings of solidarity as part of humanity—is ironically divulged in the official guidebook for employers: "The Government takes a serious view of employers who ill-treat or abuse their foreign workers. Such actions are cruel and inhumane, and they undermine Singapore's efforts to be a gracious society. Our international image as a country and as a people will be tarnished. Singapore's relations with foreign governments can also be seriously affected."[111]

It is important to emphasize here that we cannot confine the charge of inhumanity to the Singaporean state. The borderline between the human and the inhuman cannot be fixed as the territorial border between host and labor-exporting countries. Labor-exporting states are not blameless for the inhuman treatment suffered by FDWs. The migration of Filipina FDWs does not simply occur out of their personal choice. Internalized gendering and syndicated businesses in the Philippines based on the trafficking in women play a systematic role in their export. The Marcos and Aquino regimes aggressively promoted labor exportation as a solution to chronic unemployment and the major source of foreign exchange. Sending remittances back home is a necessary condition of overseas employment under Philippine law. Under Article 23 of the Labor Code and Executive Order 857, every contract worker has to remit a portion of earnings to her beneficiary in the Philippines through the Philippine banking system. All officially processed labor contracts for domestic workers include a provision mandating that they remit 50 percent of their base salary. The limited-validity passports of OCWs can be renewed only if proof is provided that the remittance requirement has been complied with; noncompliance will cause an individual to be removed from the list of workers eligible for overseas employment.[112] The Overseas Workers Investment (OWI) Fund Act passed under the Aquino regime formalized the policy of improving economic growth by "tapping the unofficial and informal remittances" of OCWs.[113] Indeed, to facilitate the formal remittance process, the Overseas Workers Welfare Administration (OWWA) of the Philippine Labor Department has entered into the remittance business through partnerships with overseas banks that offer special exchange rates and eliminate commission fees. Hence, despite its rhetoric of protection, the Philippine state's labor migration policy focuses primarily on the economic rationale for labor migration and not on the social dysfunction that arises from it.[114]

The most notable social cost is the fracturing of the family in the Philippines: FDWs leave behind motherless children; husbands start second families, often with the money remitted by the wife abroad. Hence, as Arnel de Guzman, executive director of an established NGO, Friends of Filipino Migrant Workers (KAIBIGAN), notes, the Philippine state can also be seen as a violator of the human rights of its own citizens: "The aggressive export of labor is not the ultimate solution. In fact, with such a policy, but without doing anything to revitalize the economy, without going into genuine agrarian and aquatic reforms, without embarking on genuine light to heavy industrialization, without the political will to do all these, the rights of migrant workers can never be adequately protected. On the contrary, such a situation breeds human rights violations on the level of the individual, the community and the nation."[115]

The borderline between the inhuman and the human also cannot be fixed as that between despotic Asian regimes and the liberal West, as some U.S. coverage of the hanging of Flor Contemplacion (discussed in Chapter 7) suggests.[116] For the violations of the human rights of FDWs can also be linked back to the United States, the champion of human rights on the world stage. The Philippines was a U.S. colony. Its economy, already severely damaged by the Second World War, was further hampered by the economic concessions extracted by the departing colonial masters. The corrupt Philippine oligarchy thrived under these conditions from 1954 to 1972, and Washington gave its full support to the Marcos regime.[117] More important, there is a fundamental complicity between neoliberalism and the biopolitics of postcolonial development through labor exportation. Structural adjustment programs justify the large-scale exportation of labor as a way of improving a less developed country's human resources.

The deformation of the intimate sphere of the family in Singapore and the Philippines resulting from the interface between their sex/gender systems in uneven development certainly marks the eruption of the inhuman as the condition of both the possibility *and* the impossibility of humanity in these societies. But can the humanity of the FDW within postcolonial Asia be asserted through humanizing forces that are more global in reach, such as the international feminist solidarity exemplified by the Platform for Action of the Fourth World Conference on Women (the Platform), held in Beijing in 1995?[118] Unfortunately not, because the Platform also presupposes and relies on the same biopolitical technologies that have led to the dehumanization of FDWs. The entry of Singaporean women into white-collar work is precisely the upward mobility narrative of woman in the developed or hyperdeveloping nation that the Platform celebrates. Generally speaking, the Platform incorporates some of the language of the Covenant on Economic, Social, and Cultural Rights and includes provisions regarding the right to work, the right to earn a living, the right to protection, and the right to fair treatment in the workplace. There are also sections explicitly concerned with the elimination of violence against women migrants and the right to sustainable development. Like other progressive projects of transnational sorority, however, the Platform's basic vision is to rectify inequality vis-à-vis *men* within the implicit framework of national advancement and development.

The Platform necessarily presupposes but disavows the competitive nature of development. In place of acknowledging the harsh realities of global exploitation, it gestures toward a benign internationalism forged out of the enlightened, benevolent, and, it is hoped, soon-to-be-feminized mutual self-interest of nation-states, each striving to maximize its own well-being without encroaching on other nation-states in post–Cold War globality. Despite its note of caution about the power of transnational corporations, paragraph 11 offers an optimistic view of that post–Cold War globality: "The end of the cold war has resulted in international changes and diminished competition between the super-Powers." Consequently, "international relations have improved and prospects for peace among nations have increased." The characterization of women's equality and right to development as a valuable human resource and target of biopolitical cultivation in the interests of the felicitous development of the *nation-state* is most obvious in paragraph 159: "In countries that are undergoing fundamental political, economic and social transformation, the skills of women, if better utilized, could constitute a major contribution to the economic life of their respective countries. Their input should continue to be developed and supported and their potential further realized." Paragraph 41 expresses the Platform's benign internationalism: "The advancement of women and the achievement of equality between women and men are a matter of human rights and a condition for social justice and should not be seen in isolation as a women's issue. They are the only way to build a sustainable, just and developed society. Empowerment of women and equality between women and men are prerequisites for achieving political, social, economic, cultural and environmental security among all peoples."

It has been suggested that the Platform promotes "a slightly expanded identity for women that mandates the embracing of free market ideology in addition to maternity."[119] In uneven development, it is the transitory migrant worker, especially the migrant domestic worker, who sustains the advancement and entrepreneurial spirit of her more privileged fellow Southeast Asian sister. As paragraph 118 implies, the Platform can understand violence against women only as something perpetrated by men. It cannot explain the fact that in Singapore, abused FDWs are mostly oppressed by women employers. The same fracture of the collectivity "women" compromises transnational sisterhood. Even though paragraph 154 recognizes the contribution of women migrant workers such as domestic workers to the economies of both sending and receiving countries, global sorority was not strong enough to secure more support for the Philippines' call for the ratification of the 1990 convention on migrant workers' rights. Of the 132 countries participating in the

Beijing Conference, only five countries (Bangladesh, India, Pakistan, Sri Lanka, and Thailand) responded positively, and they were all labor-exporting countries. As Carmela Torres notes, "Despite the liberalized trade among countries and moves to liberalize trade in services and movement of personnel, many of the richer countries which are expected to host migrant workers and their families tend to be protectionist in their attitude towards migrant workers."[120]

What this competitiveness reveals is the inherently aporetic character of development. At the global level, the interests and ends of states, and their agencies and the actions of employers and individual workers in the processes of economic development and labor migration constitute and are in turn conditioned by the larger structural mechanisms of capitalist accumulation. Obviously, these actors are free consensual agents who make conscious choices. But they are placed in a position to make choices because they inhabit a dynamic field of imperatives and strategies that have as their ultimate end the articulation of a hierarchical division of economic development and labor. In the first place, export-oriented industrialization is premised on a hierarchy of capital, skills, technology, and labor.[121] Moreover, while it is possible for a country to upgrade itself and ascend the international division of labor in a given sector, its success limits the opportunities for similar upgrading by other countries unless it upgrades further and vacates its slot in the economic hierarchy. Each state desires to ascend the hierarchy, and the success or failure of its policies determines the slot it will take up. Hence, the pervasive economic vocabulary about the importance of "carving a niche." A country's position will shape its society, and this will in turn condition the actions of individual citizens, such as a worker's decision to seek overseas employment. In all this, one senses most acutely the competitive anxiety driving capitalist development. If even "advanced" Singapore feels that its future survival depends on trying to ascend the hierarchy, less developed countries must feel this anxiety more intensely.

The theoretical issue raised here is whether the right to development can be fully human/humanized in an uneven world. Since this right is the basis for the human rights of migrant workers, we can also put it this way: Can the migrant worker fully achieve humanity? The sad prosaic answer to these related questions has to be no. Aggressive competition in the name of development legitimates the mistreatment of migrant workers. Labor-importing parties stress that however poor the working conditions of FDWs, they receive higher remuneration and are economically better off than they would have been if they had not left their home countries. Labor-exporting states stress the contributions of migrant workers to their home economies, the fact that it is better to be employed overseas than not employed at all, and the value of the skills they will learn abroad. We can offer more salutary answers to these questions if we associate the competitiveness of development with the inhuman totality of global capital as a determinate *Gestalt* and argue that the right to development can be humanized and the migrant worker can achieve full humanity with the transcendence of global capitalism. This axiom of post-Marxist, progressive leftist thought shares the motif of human transcendence with the doctrine of human rights notwithstanding Marx's critique of the abstract nature of civil and political rights. The basic structure of righting inhuman wrongs is juridical and presupposes the originality or primacy of the free human subject. The idea that one is free to pursue one's interests provided one does not constrain the freedom of others to do the same presupposes the liberal subject with freedom of choice. In post-Marxism, the concrete human being as subject of labor and basic needs possesses the capacity for transcendence. The functioning of bio-power, however, puts into question the human capacity for freedom, namely, the ability to transcend the instrumental-technical use of human beings through regulation. For the free subject itself is a product of technologies of bio-power and is constitutively imbricated within an inhuman field of means and ends. It is subjectified as a member of a hierarchical system of means and ends through disciplinary techniques. The interests and basic needs that supply the content of specific human rights are products of governmental techniques.

It is important to stress that although biopolitical *technai* have inhumane consequences, they also enable humanizing efforts at both the national and international levels. We have focused on the bio-power of labor-receiving states, but the sending state also cultivates and enhances the capacities of migrant workers through the exercise of bio-power so that they can achieve their full humanity. OWWA runs programs abroad and within the Philippines to assist in reintegrating returning workers into the Philippine economy by teaching them new skills, fostering entrepreneurship, and planting in them the idea of self-employment. In this way the remittances are diverted from consumption to investments and capital formation that will benefit them and the national economy in the long run.[122] National development is a necessary means to achieving "humanity," for instance, the full protection of the migrant worker's human rights. The more difficult thing to grasp is that because these humanizing endeavors are part of a biopolitical complex, they also dehumanize OCWs by regarding them as *means* to development.

A radical equivocation thus marks the human right to development. This right links the economic rights of individuals to the economic well-being of their nations, conceived in analogy with an autonomous organic body striving for self-fulfillment. But development is competitive and requires an active opening-up of the national body to the global capitalist system. Hence, a developing nation-state such as the Philippines needs to attach itself to inhuman prostheses in order to protect, augment, and cultivate the humanity of its citizens. The state claims that it needs to export labor so that it can develop. It needs to bind itself to global capital in the hopes that the Philippines can replicate the success stories of Taiwan and South Korea. Its purported hope is that economic growth and foreign investment will, in due time, create jobs that will absorb returning migrants and make further labor emigration unnecessary. Unfortunately, there is no guarantee that this humane future will come to pass. Meanwhile, the Philippines has ironically exported so much of its skilled labor that it has to import workers in certain sectors, such as welders and metalworkers, to cope with internal demand.[123] And far from enabling migrant workers to upgrade their skills, when skilled women are forced to work as domestic helpers overseas, they find that their skills become eroded because they are not utilized. It is unlikely that FDWs will acquire new and more valuable skills abroad because they do not work in positions that will expose them to new technologies. In many cases, the hard-earned foreign exchange is not wisely invested but fuels wasteful consumption of imported luxury goods that leads to inflation. The very real danger of a chronic dependency on the part of society (as opposed to the state) on remittances from OCWs can also lead to decreased agricultural production for both domestic use and export. Indeed, one can even say that the inhuman has possessed society or the people, stunting the possibility of social and political transformation. As Arnel de Guzman notes, in the 1970s, "revolution used to be an option [an alternative to the dire economic situation]. Now, it's foreign work."[124]

In the final chapter, we will see how the human rights of female migrant workers *qua* universal norms can be generated only from within the field of inhuman force relations that make up global capital.

7

Humanity within the Field of Instrumentality

In the previous chapter we saw how various projects underwritten by the idea of freedom as the human capacity for the transcendence of inhuman forces through rational regulation (Singapore's attempt to establish a civil, cosmopolitan society, Philippine national development through labor exportation, the Beijing Conference Platform for Action) are disrupted by the inhuman consequences of capitalist globalization for foreign domestic workers. This conventional discourse of human transcendence also informs most activism and socially committed scholarship. We commonly oppose the human to inhuman forces that oppress and degrade humanity, such as social engineering or capitalist accumulation. The aporias of development, however, indicate a constitutive marking of the inhuman within the human that renders indeterminate the borderline between the two terms. They force us to acknowledge that what we know as human has always been given to us by an inhuman temporality and spacing that we cannot fully grasp or control.

The Human in the Inhuman

The understanding of the inhuman that I am proposing should be rigorously distinguished from humanistic critiques of rapid development as creating an empty shell or a mechanically efficient economic machine without a human soul or heart. My point, rather, is that the soul or humanity is generated by inhuman techniques. As a product-effect of the inhuman, the human is always haunted and possessed by it. But because we intuitively grant priority to the human, this original contamination has always been viewed as a fall from a prior presence, whereby our humanity is threatened or eroded by the inhuman. Yet, as Rousseau, Kant, Hegel, and Marx realized, there is something inherently inhuman within the very essence of humanity insofar as the human capacity for transcendence or self-uplifting, the human *spirit,* to use a Hegelian phrase, necessarily implies competition and inequality.

I have merely attempted to locate the inhuman way of being human in the technologies of bio-power that enable the actualization of humanity through economic development. Instead of regarding the inhuman as an attribute, effect, or consequence of the global capitalist system *qua* product of alienation from our humanity, it would be more accurate to situate global capitalism as the terminal form of microphysical and biopolitical technologies, tactics, and strategies that stretch across labor-exporting and receiving nations. These techniques are indispensable to the smooth functioning of global capitalism. They serve the building of national economies in the competitive pursuit of development and constitute a complex that exceeds the cruel personal attitudes of individuals or the institutional ethos of collective actors. The latter is what we commonly refer to as inhumane behavior. It is inhumanity in the restricted or derived sense, the consequence of a lapse from common human decency or universal goodwill toward other human beings, a feeling that supposedly issues from some pure reserve of humanity within us. What is at work here, however, is a form of inhuman production that cannot be regulated and transcended because it is the condition of possibility of humanity. It forms the concrete human being and all its capacities at the most material level. We can call this "the inhuman" in the general sense, a form of inhumanity that is not secondary to or derived from the human because humanity itself is its product-effect. These techniques are not always conducive to the achievement of humanity. But their inhuman character exceeds their inhuman consequences. It lies in the fact that these technologies cannot be traced back to an individual human subject or a centralized collective subject as their origin because they constitute the concrete human being and enable collective agency. Although these technologies are intentional and involve calculation, their effectiveness for the achievement of humane ends is radically unpredictable.

My point is not simply that existing human rights instruments are practically ineffective because we live in a particularistic, unjust, and competitive world. My more sobering argument is that the normative framework of human rights discourse, which is based in the doctrine of human reason's capacity to transcend the inhuman, cannot adequately comprehend the perverse processes that lead to the constitutive marking of the inhuman within the human. We assume that FDWs innately possess human rights, and we appeal to them as trump cards to humanize global processes. But in fact, such rights are generated from the inhuman web of bio-power. Their protection depends on the same technologies of bio-power that facilitate national development. First, the human rights of FDWs are pedagogically induced. Migrant workers have to be educated about these rights, instructed by national and international benevolent agencies that they have rights that need to be protected. In turn, the protection of FDWs' rights by labor-exporting countries will make state policies of labor exportation more acceptable to the people. The same can be said of efforts on the part of labor-receiving countries such as Singapore to safeguard migrant workers' rights. Projecting a humane image in the international public sphere is crucial to attracting foreign investment and expertise. This constitutive imbrication of human rights in bio-power does not inevitably lead to futility. Just as technologies of bio-power cannot be controlled for the pursuit of humane ends, they also exceed the terminal hegemonic forms (e.g., the state or the bourgeoisie) whose power rests on them. Since we have never known a human condition that has been purged of the inhuman, instead of seeing the inhuman as a fall from an ideal humanity, we should ask: How does the inhuman force field sustaining global capital induce effects of humanity, and how are these effects contaminated? In this concluding chapter I focus on two related examples of the emergence of the human from the inhuman: the public outrage and mobilization of a critical public sphere in the Philippines that challenged the state's labor-exportation policies after the hanging of Flor Contemplacion, and the ongoing attempt of civil society forces in Singapore to push through institutional reforms that can serve as a basis for the protection of the human rights of female migrant workers.

The Specter of Flor: Popular-Nationalist Counter-*Bildung* in the Philippines

On March 17, 1995, the Singapore government hanged a Filipina maid, Flor Contemplacion, for the murder of her friend Delia Maga, another

Filipina maid, and a four-year-old Chinese boy who was Maga's charge. The event caused a great deal of public outrage in the Philippines which in turn seriously jeopardized the cordial relations between Manila and Singapore and slowed the accelerating pace of Singaporean investment in the Philippines. What is pertinent here about the case is not whether Contemplacion was guilty of the murder (as the Singapore legal system claimed) or whether she was framed by the boy's father but the fact that the hanging catalyzed a period of public outrage and mourning in which the Filipino popular nation began to question the humanity of its state's policy of exporting labor, and, indeed, of the paradigm of neoliberal free-market development practiced by Singapore, which the regime of Fidel Ramos was keen to adopt as a model for the development of the Philippines.

In the five years prior to the incident, bilateral relations between the two countries had been extremely cordial. Goodwill reached an all-time high by the first quarter of 1995. The Ramos regime was keen to increase the Philippines' share of manufacturing that Singapore industries had been relocating to lower-cost countries within Southeast Asia. This is precisely the same ideology of national self-making through export-oriented development that Singapore had adopted in the 1960s which had made it an Asian economic tiger. Singapore encouraged this modeling process because it would facilitate the entry of Singaporean capital into the Philippines. In his visit to Manila on November 17, 1992, Lee Kuan Yew, the former prime minister of Singapore, urged the Philippines to follow the "proven path" to economic growth, emphasizing the importance of economic liberalization: the establishment of good infrastructure and the relaxation of trade and investment regulations through the reduction of tariff and non-tariff barriers and the provision of attractive packages for foreign investors. "If you can create these conditions you will fill your country once again with jobs, with hope," Lee preached. "The misery Filipinos created for themselves was what held things back: constant threat of coups and instability. It is not enough to have sympathy. It is more important to have confidence of others in your capacity to guarantee them their security and their lives. . . . But that [peaceful transition of power] by itself cannot satisfy the basic needs of the people: Freedom, human rights, democracy, when you are hungry, when you lack development, when you lack basic services, does not add up to much." In Lee's version of the ideology of self-making, material growth and the fulfillment of the economic rights of a nation's members through regional economic cooperation is given greater priority than civil liberties. This does not bode well for Filipino workers. Lee regards them as a means to national development: "All you have to do is establish stable political and economic conditions and you can capitalize on the resourcefulness, the drive, the education, the skills of your own Filipinos."[1]

Investment from Singapore steadily increased between 1992 and 1995, backed by concerted efforts of the Ramos regime.[2] Total bilateral trade amounted to S$3.6 billion in 1994, up 19.1 percent from the previous year, making the Philippines Singapore's fifteenth-most-important trading partner. The trade balance highly favored Singapore since the value of its exports to the Philippines was twice that of its imports. Economic ties between the countries were represented by both regimes as a close friendship and a complementary partnership, a synergy between a country rich in human and natural resources (the Philippines) and a technologically advanced country (Singapore), "a joint effort" that would help ASEAN ascend the hierarchy of the international division of labor by making it "more attractive than other economic areas, [thereby] benefit[ing] the individual members."[3]

The Contemplacion incident generated a completely unexpected popular-national force in the Philippines that interrupted these convivial relations. The hanging could not have happened at a worse time for Ramos. Philippine general elections were scheduled for May 8. Widespread public outrage in the Philippines quickly gathered momentum. Communist guerrillas threatened to exact "revolutionary justice" against responsible Filipino officials and warned of threats to the safety of Singaporean diplomats in the country if Contemplacion was executed.[4] When Singapore denied Ramos's appeal for clemency and his request for a retrial, church, human-rights, and feminist groups were outraged. A demonstration of 1,500 people occurred outside the Singapore embassy, which also received many abusive and threatening phone calls.[5] Following the hanging, 2,000 people participated in a nighttime prayer vigil outside the embassy. The mayor of Davao City, the fourth-largest city in the Philippines, burned a Singapore flag, and its city councilors resolved to ban the sale and distribution of Singaporean products.[6] In the face of this anti-Singapore sentiment, Singapore's prime minister postponed a scheduled April visit to the Philippines. But popular outrage was also directed at the Ramos regime. For the incident took on a significance larger than its empirical facticity. Through her sufferings and subsequent death, Contemplacion became an icon for the plight of all overseas Filipino workers caused by the labor-export policy of their state and its failure to safeguard the rights of workers who are so crucial to the nation's economic development. Media reports and editorials in the Philippines variously described her as the "Flower of National Rage," a national martyr, and a "national saint."[7] In response to the popular uproar, the Ramos government established a commission headed by retired Supreme Court judge Emilio Gancayco to investigate the judicial findings. It subsequently recalled and sacked diplomats and labor attachés from its embassy in Singapore and demanded the resignation of the foreign secretary. It also temporarily banned the deployment of more domestic workers to Singapore and offered to repatriate any Filipina maids wishing to leave Singapore. Ramos further promised to cut ties with Singapore if the commission's findings pointed to a miscarriage of justice.

Media sensationalism and the manipulations of opportunistic opposition politicians certainly amplified popular anti-Singaporean sentiment and outrage at the Philippines state. Yet the outrage undoubtedly represents a clear dehiscence between the popular nation and the state. Not only was Contemplacion repeatedly identified with the people as their personification in an individual body (one article ran under the title "The Martyr That Is the Philippines"). She was also repeatedly likened to Benigno Aquino, whose assassination had catalyzed the popular-nationalist EDSA uprising that led to the downfall of the Marcos regime.[8] The suggestion was that the incident could trigger a popular-nationalist revolution against the Ramos regime. The Philippine foreign secretary, Roberto Romulo, noted that "the nation is in mourning for Mrs. Flor Contemplacion and is demanding the full disclosure of the facts of her case."[9] Even Ramos conceded that this was a serious test that involved the health of the national body and could jeopardize his government: "It's my neck on the line. . . . We want to get to the bottom of this . . . because we have many things at stake here, and first is our economic growth and sustainable development."[10] It was as though the hanged body of Flor Contemplacion (and the mutilated body of Delia Maga) simultaneously exemplified the victimage of all overseas contract workers and personified the mutilated body of the Filipino nation.

How can we understand the transformative efficacy of this public outrage? As the Filipino people became metamorphosed into a collective subject that demanded accountability from and sought to inspirit the state, there was a scramble both within the state administration and in society to deflect responsibility by pointing a finger at the inhumanity of other parties, their failure to safeguard the basic human rights of OCWs. The gesture of finger-pointing presented itself as a humanizing act that places the accuser firmly within the party of humanity. Thus, the Gancayco Commission criticized Singaporean society for its lack of humane feeling: "We echo the message we have been hearing from Filipino OCWs employed as domestic helpers that their Singaporean employers generally treat them like machines and not as fellow human beings. Apparently, Singapore has ceased to be a caring and humane society because of its sudden affluence. We hear them talk of economic rights and not of human rights. We hope that the martyrdom of Flor Contemplacion shall awaken them from such insensitivity and lack of concern for others." But it also attempted to mitigate the Ramos regime's broader collective responsibility to all OCWs by identifying and filing administrative and/or criminal charges against specific individuals in the diplomatic corps and the labor administration who had been negligent in the performance of their duties or exercised bad judgment in the affair.[11] An editorial in the *Manila Chronicle* similarly denounced Singapore's inhumanity, associating this with its profit-making drive: "Singapore has presented herself to the world as a powerful formula for prosperity. . . . But prosperity too should be measured by the capacity of a society that has produced it to be human and to be compassionate. Singapore with her many years of economic success seems to have produced less and less souls and more and more automatons. With her growing affluence, her citizenry and government have become straight-laced and arrogant." The Philippines, by contrast, is a society of "imperfect but perfectible human beings, with our flaws and follies, but also with our indestructible hope that we could be better. . . . [W]e will make one thing truly work: to articulate universal outrage over the unjust execution of Flor Contemplacion. . . . Let us summon the collective strength to teach a nation of hangmen a lesson in justice and mercy, universal values that should be forever above dollars and cents, law and order."[12] Such humanizing pedagogy is, however, also a popular-nationalist counter-*Bildung* that asserts the humanity of ordinary Filipinos against the directives of official *Bildung,* especially its tactics of development through labor exportation, which are viewed as equally responsible for the plight of Filipina domestic workers abroad. Thus, Fermin Adriano writes in the *Manila Chronicle*:

> in the long run, OCWs must be gradually eliminated as one of the cornerstones of our economic strategy. While in the short term, the potential gains they bring to the economy are, at face value, enormous, their long-term costs, both social and political, to the people at large, simply outweigh the possible benefits they bring the nation. . . . [I]t will necessitate a singleness of purpose among our leaders and people in terms of developing our economy so that there will be no more need to send our workers abroad. . . . Flor did not die for them but for the ordinary Filipinos so that all will realize that no matter how economically deprived and poorly educated they are, they too, are human beings.[13]

Prima facie, all of these gestures express a belief in the human capacity for transcendence. They claim to draw a clear dividing line between the human and the inhuman to enable the better regulation of the latter. On closer examination, however, all these humanizing efforts spring from and are irreducibly inscribed within inhuman technologies. For they do not reject the fundamental axiom that development is the best way to actualize the humanity of the Filipino people. Rather, popular anger is directed against the failure of their state's particular strategies of development to live up to its promises, namely, the fact that the state celebrates female OCWs as national heroines who make a vital contribution to the economy even as it fails to protect their rights. Thus, newspaper editorials comment on "the utter frustration of a people with a government that has made a foreign policy of abandoning its nationals to maltreatment, prejudice and abuse in foreign geographies," and "the inexhaustible capacity of our foreign service to be insensitive to the plight of our workers overseas."[14] Another article urges: "Isn't it about time government opened its eyes to the plight of our brothers and sisters abroad and did something about it? Isn't it about time that the Filipino began to feel that he is protected by his government before another Flor Contemplacion dies?"[15] Far from breaking with the technologies of governmentality, such cries lament the fact that the Philippines state does not engage in enough government and urge the intensification of biopolitics. Nor does the humane feeling these cries express lie outside governmental technologies. Humanity is the necessary subjective pendant produced by these technologies to justify their continued functioning. Here the outpouring of humane feeling is optimized because, as a result of the inherently unequal character of development, the Filipino people have not been adequately invested with bio-power. Instead of being humanized, they have become dehumanized. The Contemplacion episode arouses so much outrage because her corpse is the iconic concretization of the manifest falsity of the state's promise to cultivate the humanity of its citizens through export-oriented development. The promise ends in its exact opposite: the utter dehumanization of the bodies of Flor Contemplacion and Delia Maga in death.

Here one also witnesses the radically undecidable character of governmental technologies. They can have inhumane effects, but since they also produce humanity, their inhumane effects will in turn generate demands for more humanity. In the public canonization of Flor as a national martyr, her body, utterly dehumanized by the global traffic in domestic labor, becomes rehumanized to the point that it inspirits and forces a rehumanization of the Philippine state and this particular circuit of capital accumulation. In order to appease the people, the Ramos regime passed the Migrant Workers and Overseas Filipinos Act (1995). Styled as a "magna carta" for OCWs and others in the Filipino diaspora, the act was composed after consideration of suggestions from all sectors involved in labor migration and recommendations from the Gancayco Commission. What is important is the government's attempt to reevaluate the basis of its entire overseas employment program by shifting from promoting labor migration to making a concerted effort to protect the basic rights of overseas workers, enhance their welfare through closer attention to the social costs of labor migration, and reaffirm a commitment to creating local employment opportunities that would remove the need for emigration. Hence, the policy section of the act explicitly asserts: "The State does not promote overseas employment as a means to sustain economic growth and achieve national development. The existence of the overseas employment program rests solely on the assurance that the dignity and fundamental human rights and freedoms of the Filipino citizen shall not, at any time, be compromised and violated."[16]

Of course, this humane spirit is never completely actualized and is necessarily transient. The Gancayco Commission had recommended the phasing out of all deployed domestic workers by 2000. But the state did not adopt this recommendation. On July 15, 1995, Senator Blas Ople observed: "It is in our interest that normal relations be restored with Singapore. Beyond the emotions generated by the Contemplacion case, Philippines-Singaporean relations are very important to the Philippines and ASEAN. At some point differences must be allowed to lapse into history and we want to begin anew."[17] Nevertheless, this humanizing moment within the relentless processes of global capitalist development occurs because these processes are sustained by the repeated generation of humanity by inhuman technologies of governmentality. Without this humanizing moment, the governing regime would have been hampered by social unrest and would have failed to serve as a terminal within the global capitalist system.

The Contemplacion incident has had some long-term effects for the protection of FDWs in Singapore. First, the Singapore state realized that in order to protect Singaporean foreign investments in labor-sending countries such as the Philippines and Indonesia, it could not afford to arouse international ill will and had to maintain a decent international public image. It has therefore zealously publicized and prosecuted the most extreme cases of maid abuse. Second, in response to the widespread hysteria among Filipina FDWs over the hanging, the Singapore state began to offer a limited measure of subjective reward to FDWs via public statements of appreciation, free concerts and cultural events, and the encouragement of limited forms of vocational training in order to prevent future problem cases.[18] This has led to a devolution of preventive pastoral care to non-state elements. What is important is that such elements have converged and aligned to seek affirmation for the human rights of FDWs and to cultivate their humanity even if many of them do not deploy the language of human rights. These forces are essentially of three different types: foreign missions of labor-exporting states, church groups in Singapore, and NGOs that are part of an emerging local civil society. Let us briefly consider these agents.

Diplomatic Care as Official Humanizing Pedagogy

The Philippine embassy in Singapore has attempted to provide more pastoral care for Filipina domestic workers following the Contemplacion affair. Since many of the problems FDWs encounter stem from extremely disadvantageous terms of employment, it has attempted to provide increased regulation of the recruitment process. In fact, labor-sending states have tried to document and monitor the deployment of workers by establishing lists of employment agencies accredited by administrative bodies governing overseas employment. Hence, Filipina domestic workers recruited through approved agents are protected by a standard contract with terms of employment the POEA deems to be fair. Many agents choose not to be accredited, however, because of higher costs. They evade this documented process by having FDWs enter Singapore on tourist visas and apply for work permits on the basis of "in-principle approval" documents that they obtain from the Singapore state. The majority of FDWs take this route to avoid paying bureaucratic costs for official documentation from their home countries.[19] This makes them extremely vulnerable to exploitation from recruiters. Since they are not protected by standardized employment contracts, they pay exorbitant recruitment fees and acquiesce to appalling terms of employment.[20] They also do not have the advantage of participating in the pre-departure orientation seminar offered by the POEA that acquaints FDWs with the local culture and work practices of their countries of destination as well as their rights. The POEA has responded to this situation by setting stricter guidelines for accreditation and banning nonaccredited agents from entering the Philippines.[21] The Philippine embassy in Singapore also conducts post-arrival orientation seminars for employees who arrive through the "tourist" channel. Other foreign missions have taken action on the specific problems encountered by their workers. The Indonesian embassy has responded to the comparatively large number of Indonesian domestic workers who fall to their deaths from high-rise apartments by advising employers to show more concern for the safety of their employees. It also issued a temporary ban on sending more domestic workers.[22] All missions also engage in soft mediation to resolve daily employment disputes in a conciliatory manner.

What is noteworthy about these efforts is the conscious avoidance of the vocabulary of human rights in favor of the language of negotiation and diplomatic conciliation. A labor officer in the Sri Lankan High Commission observed that mentioning human rights would not be of much help: "You can fight for human rights in your own country but not in a foreign country. In the media here, no one speaks of human rights. If a country tries to enforce human rights requirements, demand for domestic labor from that country will drop. We have no hand in this. It is beyond our limits. It is a governmental matter. We will lose our market share if we make too many demands."[23] And yet, what foreign missions are trying to protect and cultivate is precisely the humanity of FDWs. Two things are noteworthy. First, sending states play a crucial role. The labor attaché of the Philippine embassy observed with some bitterness and condescension that "in Manila, they [workers who enter as tourists] avoided the government, they didn't mind their government. They would disregard their government. They say they don't need the government, but when they have problems, they will come."[24] Second, the protection of migrant workers' rights is in a tense relationship to the imperatives of profit making and economic development that is neither one of simple opposition nor one of continuity. The economic development of the labor-sending country is premised on sacrificing its workers' human rights. Any attempt to protect such rights must always be balanced against the need to maintain or increase the market share in FDWs. But such sacrifice can occur only to a certain degree and for a limited period of time. If the dehumanization of these workers becomes excessive and permanent, the country will deplete the human capital on which its development depends. Hence, both the Philippine embassy and the Sri Lankan High Commission in Singapore try to cultivate and enhance the humanity of their FDWs to endow their time abroad with lasting value, in anticipation of their future repatriation.

Bio-power is also deployed here, but it consists primarily of techniques of discipline directed at the individual to impart the importance of diligence, teach her new skills, and inculcate habits of frugality and saving money as future capital. This discipline is inseparable from the patronizing attitude of the upper class toward the lower classes. As the labor attaché at the Philippine embassy puts it, the FDW "has to save her money. You come here to earn money and to learn new experiences. You should appreciate the experience. I always tell the worker: you came here to earn and to save money. A poor person has to work doubly hard. If you see a rich person working hard, you have to work twice as hard because you are poor. I don't want people to be wasting their resources."[25] Her counterpart at the Sri Lankan High Commission elaborated on the need for pedagogy:

> The maids get three diseases. First, they forget the objective of coming here, that they are here to earn money for the betterment of their lives. Second, they get a telephone disease. In Sri Lanka, there are very few telephone facilities in the villages. The maids make local calls here to their friends and boyfriends and also international calls back to Sri

Lanka. They get caught by their employer and are asked to pay for these phone calls. Third, they catch the boyfriend disease. In my counseling, I tell them to set apart $100 a month to send back home. This is the targeted amount that they should save. . . . This should be put in a fixed deposit and be viewed as a pension. You can get a 12 percent interest on this investment. . . . You can also get an overdraft for which you are charged 15 percent interest. I advise them to use this to invest in a house or other property. They will have an aim and they won't run away. They will tolerate hardship and won't get into bad habits if they have this aim.[26]

As part of this official-national pedagogy, vocational classes are offered to teach FDWs English, computer skills, hairdressing, dressmaking, and cookery during their days off. Some foreign missions have also encouraged banks from their home countries to link up with foreign exchange agencies in Singapore to facilitate the secure transmission of funds from workers.

Such disciplinary techniques are forms of pastoral care that enhance the individual capacities of FDWs and provide the subjectification denied them by the Singaporean state. The humanization they bring about, the humanity-effects they generate, are integral to the profit imperatives of economic development. Money-saving and transmission schemes maximize the remittance of foreign exchange. Skills-development programs provide a legitimating alibi for the policy of exporting labor by adding value to workers as human capital when they rejoin their national *bios*. Such programs also reduce the incidence of "social problems" caused by FDWs by regulating their leisure time. Indeed, such projects of humanization are welcomed by the Singaporean state because it is relieved of the responsibility and burden of having to do more for the welfare of FDWs. Significantly, the Sri Lankan labor attaché speaks of the consultation meetings between the different foreign missions, employment agencies, and the Singaporean Ministry of Manpower in the language of commercial enterprise: "This is a joint venture between governments, agencies, employers, employees. It is a joint operation. We must play an important role in making this venture a success."[27]

Humanization through Religious Faith: The God Industry

The urgent need to serve the needs of the mainly Catholic community of Filipina domestic workers was made very clear to local churches after the Contemplacion incident, but there were also broader Catholic directives from outside the country in response to the increasing numbers of itinerants such as refugees and migrant workers that resulted from the intensification of globalization. The Singapore state has encouraged these pastoral efforts, which range from small-scale fellowship groups to ministries that organize special services and masses for a Filipino congregation as a form of supplementary humanization of FDWs.[28] This devolution of care reveals the original roots of governmental technologies in religious pastoral work. Once the demand for such religious work for the Filipino migrant community was established, it became easier for people in the God industry—pastors and church workers of various denominations from the Philippines—to enter Singapore to work for various churches with the aim of fostering the emotional, psychic, and spiritual well-being of maids.[29] The Ministry of Manpower has welcomed this effort. One official remarked:

> We want the community to come out and help. Government supports this kind of community-based approach. If you are a religious worker, you can come to work in Singapore quite freely. What we have done is to encourage the NGOs, the community, and the religious organizations to come together. You really need a "many hands" approach. One hand cannot do everything. I think that is happening. I just came back from a workshop organized by the Catholic Church, an international workshop for female migrant workers. These are things that we encourage. Many maids do community and social work. We are happy with that sort of situation. If there is a demand for religious workers, they can come in. You can come in quite freely as a religious worker. We have not been a hindrance to the Filipino Church, the Catholic Church, when they want to bring in these people.[30]

In this spirit, the state has donated a building to the Philippine embassy to house a community center that offers a skills program which enables interested maids to upgrade their skills by learning nursing aid, baking, computing, and English.

Such religious pastoral work is invariably represented in apolitical terms. It does not seek to solve the structural political and economic problems that have led to the increase in migrant workers but only offers a panacea to the ills of material worldly existence through spiritual transcendence. The Archdiocesan Commission for the Pastoral Care of Migrants and Itinerant People (later abbreviated to the Commission for Migrants and Itinerant People, or CMI), a Catholic body formed in June 1998, under the capable directorship of Bridget Lew offers the clearest articulation of this theme of transcendence common to church groups of all denominations. After a succinct discussion of the causes and consequences of labor migration in Asia in the first issue of its magazine celebrating the Jubilee of Migrants and Refugees, we find the following conclusion: "Christianity teaches us that the migrant, no matter how poor, how disheveled and how unlike us, has the capacity to develop and share a spiritual richness, which springs from the very trials of being uprooted. The Jewish exodus from Egypt, the plight of the Holy Family, the wandering ministry of Jesus and the travels of the apostles and their successors illustrate this important point: that in welcoming the migrants in our midst, we can share in a spiritual growth."[31]

Christian pastoral work, therefore, also provides subjectification and humanizing relief to the FDW. But unlike that offered by foreign missions, the subjective relief is not generated through belonging to a territorialized national community. Instead, the FDW's humanity is affirmed through her membership in a spiritual community (the church) that transcends ethno-national barriers and offers universal hospitality. In his homily during the celebration of Mass for the Jubilee of Migrants and Refugees on June 2, 2002, Pope John Paul II stressed the importance of connecting this ethos of acceptance to positive laws:

> In the Church, . . . there are no strangers or sojourners, but fellow citizens with the saints and members of the household of God. . . . Indeed, the Christian community is called to spread in the world the leaven of brotherhood, of that fellowship of differences which we can also experience at our meeting today. Certainly, in a complex society like ours which is marked by many tensions, the culture of acceptance must be joined with prudent and far-sighted laws and norms, which allow the most to be made of the positive aspects of human mobility and to provide for its possibly negative aspects. This will ensure that every person is effectively respected and accepted. Even more in the era of globalization, the Church has a precise message: to work so that this world of ours, which is often described as a "global village," may truly be more united, more fraternal, more welcoming. Here is the message which this Jubilee celebration is meant to spread everywhere: always put man and respect for his rights at the centre of the phenomena of mobility.[32]

In a similar spirit, the CMI describes its primary objective as follows: "In welcoming them [the displaced in our societies] we expose the causes of displacement, work toward conditions for a more human living in community, experience the universal dimension of the Kingdom and appreciate new opportunities for evangelisation and intercultural dialogue." The suggestion here is that we can become more human through religious faith because Christianity provides an ethical basis for persuading people to respect the human rights of others. This is further justification for the importance of evangelizing migrants. Evangelization will widen the spiritual community and humanize the world through "build[ing] a communion of communities of faith, hope and love."[33]

Prima facie, such pastoral care is not passive ideological indoctrination. First, migrants are accorded an active part in the spiritual community since their unique experiences and hardships equip them to evangelize. Hence, many church groups stress the importance of grooming members within migrant worker communities to carry out pastoral and missionary work. "It is my dream," writes Bishop Ramon Arguelles, chairman of the Episcopal Commission for the Pastoral Care of Migrants and Itinerant People, "that all Catholic migrants, in their simple and humble way, may become evangelizers in the receiving country."[34] Another church representative writes, "The aim of evangelization is to empower migrants to be evangelizers among their fellow workers. In the papal document, 'Evangelization in the Modern World,' Christians are reminded that "when Jesus ministered to the people, the weak and the poor were evangelized, became his disciples, formed the great community of those who believe in him. The man who has been evangelized becomes himself an evangelizer. This is every Christian's essential mission and function."[35] Second, the human feeling that this pastoral care seeks to affirm is not an ideological fiction because it is materially produced in two ways. Techniques of discipline induce in the FDW a sense of belonging to a universal community. At the same time, pastoral and missionary work directed at the larger society is viewed as an effective mechanism for humanizing the FDW's social position in the eyes of the Singapore state and people insofar as it persuades them of the importance of providing hospitality to strangers. The active participation of FDWs in their subjectification and recognition as human is further encouraged through extended analogies with the migrant experiences of Jesus and Pope John Paul II. The CMI takes Jesus' comment from Matthew 25:35 as its motto: "I was a stranger and you welcomed me."[36] Bridget Lew, director of CMI, explained the motto's significance: "Like Christ, migrants are also itinerant people. . . . Thus, hospitality should be given to strangers and their rights should be protected. These rights include the human dignity of the human person because he is a child of God."[37] Similarly, Pope John Paul II is described as "the first migrant pope. Our role model of a migrant, a witness, a defender, a supporter, a comforter, a servant of Christ."[38]

In Christian doctrine, the ethical basis for respecting migrants' human rights is the association of human dignity with divinity. As Father Conor Donnelly of the Filipino Catholic Community of Singapore puts it: "Materialism tells us that man is only matter and as such he does not really 'matter.' Christianity tells us that every man has dignity because he has a soul, and that soul was created in the image and likeness of God, has an eternal destiny and was redeemed by Christ. Every man therefore is important. Materialism tells us to value things and use persons. Christianity tells us to value persons and use things."[39] Here one sees clearly the theistic origins of the neo-Kantian doctrine of transcendence in human rights discourse. Yet despite the repeated insistence on the transcendent nature of the human soul, it is actually a myriad of material technologies functioning at various levels that secures (or attempts to secure) the human dignity of migrant workers. Many local churches conduct special services for Filipino fellowships led by Filipino pastors and priests. In his regularly scheduled radio program, Father Angel Luciano, a chaplain of the Filipino migrants of Singapore, gives guidance to the Filipino community. He also writes an advice column in the *Pinoy Bulletin,* a monthly publication for Filipina maids. Father Luciano has also cooperated with the CMI to establish an outreach program meant to include FDWs of other nationalities through contact with Filipina workers in his congregation. "The aim is to create more apostles to minister to each other—if possible, one in every HDB [Housing Development Board] flat," he remarked.[40] Other non-Catholic churches such as the Bartley Christian Church and the Touch Community rely on more intense cell-group structures and Bible-reading groups to "inform and educate its members to do the work of the ministry" and to create a tight-knit community of faith "characterized by caring and nurturing relationships."[41] Among all these church groups, the CMI and its director, Bridget Lew, has most actively undertaken the task of direct case-to-case ministration of migrant workers encountering severe hardships and bad employment relations in an attempt to provide pastoral care for their physical, emotional, and spiritual needs. The CMI established a twenty-four-hour hotline and has served as a mediator between FDWs, agents, employers, foreign missions, and the Ministry of Manpower to obtain the necessary relief for the worker in question. It has also set up counseling clinics in accessible public locations, liaised regularly with foreign missions, collaborated in the establishment and running of skill-development centers, and planned occasional commemorative events to celebrate the contributions of migrant workers.

Like the foreign missions, most of these church groups do not deploy the discourse of human rights, although they are committed to the concept. Instead, they try to affirm the humanity of FDWs by convincing employers, agents, and the Singapore state that the humane treatment of foreign workers will lead to better and more efficient service, cause fewer "social problems," and improve Singapore's international public image. For instance, although Father Luciano believes that "one of the aims of pastoral care is to make the maids aware of their rights and how to exercise them through all the legal means prescribed by the Ministry of Manpower in cooperation with the Philippine embassy," his public appeal to employers to allow their domestic help to attend Christmas celebrations was based not on the right to have a day of leave but instead on the reasoning that "this will surely reduce their loneliness . . . and they will be able to serve you better in the future."[42] Bridget Lew of the CMI succinctly expressed her wariness about the use of human rights discourse:

> We cannot solve all the problems, but we can do our best to alleviate them by teaching the employers to have human respect for the dignity of maids. We work with the government. We call MoM [the Ministry of Manpower] for advice and then the embassies. It is important that all parties understand that we want to reach an amicable solution in the interests of all parties. *Educating maids about their rights is generally useless because they subjugate these rights out of a desperate need to keep their jobs.* They feel beholden to both the employer and agent for the job. The free-market situation is suitable for commodities. But we are talking about human beings. . . . Our vision is not to keep the maids here but to give them hope to return to their home country with a good livelihood. If they stay here out of economic incentives, they will forget the social evils that follow. . . . We don't want to use the press because of the sensitivity of the issue. We work in a consultative manner. My idea is to engage interested groups to have a win-win situation. We

don't want to make use of the pressure of public opinion. The Singapore government should see that helping maids is good for the image of the country because maids are part of the infrastructure.[43]

The comment is interesting because even though it subscribes to the common opposition between humanity and commodification or profit making, it points out that because the Singapore state views the outright assertion of human rights as antagonistic, it is an ineffective way of safeguarding humanity. Instead, the means deployed are precisely the strategies of business management: networking and liaising beyond the church so that migrant workers will receive support from secular bodies, coordinating the different activities of pro-migrant worker groups, and consulting and negotiating with the government and embassies of sending countries in order to convince all parties, including the migrant worker, that a humane outcome will serve their economic self-interest. It is important to emphasize that such techniques do not merely protect preexistent human rights. Rights related to minimum employment conditions for domestic helpers are not enforceable because they do not have state recognition. Insofar as these techniques achieve the same result without formal state codification of such rights, they are a de facto actualization of labor rights in a concrete situation. In other words, these rights would merely be abstract without these techniques, which produce the rights or the effects that flow from their assertion.

Yet because these techniques are the same techniques of capital accumulation, they are also reversible. Pastoral care by church groups can modulate in the opposite direction as well, since any outcome is regarded as a means to self-interested ends. In the first place, its effectiveness is limited by the position of the church vis-à-vis the state, which is not pro-Christian. In addition, such pastoral care can easily become an instrument that aids employers in policing and managing an FDW's leisure time during her day off. As one pastor pointed out: "The employers tell me to tell the maid to be involved with fellowship activities and to return home early to make the curfew. They want me to encourage [maids] to be involved with church activities and not to be involved with friends, going to questionable places, and getting into trouble."[44] The line between such management and the use of biblical doctrine to instill submissive forbearance in the present, which is made more palatable by the hope of future redemption, is a fine one, especially given the importance of the concept-metaphor of "service" in Christian doctrine. As one FDW observed in a CMI publication: "I initially viewed my work as a way out of my family's impoverished situation. Later I realized that it is a calling and I felt privileged to have met so many families . . . from many racial and cultural backgrounds and beliefs. It is a calling and a challenge to love people despite their diverse situations. Being a maid is my way of serving other people. It is where I continually experience joy."[45]

Another FDW who had worked as a primary school substitute teacher in the Philippines consoled herself through an analogy with Christ: "I am a servant and I don't want to be a servant forever. But I accepted it because although I'm a teacher, the pay as a servant is better. As a Christian, it is okay to be a servant because God serves us and we are not servants in God's eyes. Even God himself serves us. Christ died for our sins. For me I consider myself a Cinderella. Someday I will be my own person because the money I'm saving now is for a bright future."[46] The same message was driven home in gatherings of the fellowship group. In a sermon following a cell-group meeting the pastor focused on Luke 1:38, where Mary describes herself as "the maidservant of the Lord," and stressed that Mary was grateful to be used by the Lord.[47] He asked the group to be happy and grateful for the blessings they had received in everyday life. The cell-group meeting the following week was devoted to a discussion of verses from Ephesians 6 and passages from Samuel 1 and centered on the theme of the accountability of members of the cell to their leader. Ephesians 6:5–8 reads:

> Servants, be obedient to them that are *your* masters according to the flesh, with fear and trembling, in singleness of your heart, as unto Christ;
> Not with eyeservice, as menpleasers; but as the servants of Christ, doing the will of God from the heart;
> With good will doing service, as to the Lord, and not to men:
> Knowing that whatsoever good thing any man doeth, the same shall he receive of the Lord, whether he be bond or free.

Joanna Elias, the leader of the cell group, offered the following comment: "The more you refuse what the leader says to you is more on the rebellious side of your spirit. But if you submit to the leader, the leadership, or even to your Ma'am and Sir, your boss, it is pleasing the Lord because it is all in the Bible that you have to obey. That's the big word, 'obey.' If you go against the 'obey' word, that will be rebellion, and whether you like it or not, if you obey, it is pleasing the Lord."[48]

Governmentality and the Feminist Conscience of Civil Society

In addition to religious voluntary welfare organizations, nongovernmental groups oriented toward social and political advocacy, particularly around feminist issues, have also expressed concern about the dehumanization of FDWs. The Association of Women for Action and Research (AWARE), the most visible and successful of these groups, has extended its ongoing efforts at eliminating violence and discrimination against women to include the abuse of FDWs. Some of its members have stressed that such abuse imparts the wrong social and ethical values to children and undermines Singapore's attempt to be "a civil, humanistic society." Despite its exclusively middle-class composition, AWARE presents itself as the feminist conscience and vanguard of societal forces. Some of its members are alert to the fact that the abuse of FDWs by their female employers is a setback to the feminist cause because it contradicts the principles of egalitarianism and the empowerment of women that are fundamental to feminism.[49] These feminists situate the problem of domestic abuse within the broader hierarchical social structures, value systems, and attitudes in Singaporean culture that breed authoritarian elitism and callous treatment of the economically less fortunate at all levels of Singaporean life. In the words of one letter to the editor: "The culture of abuse in the private space cannot be isolated from the wider culture. The overarching ideologies of patriarchy and Confucianism and the resultant hierarchical structure and effect on the status of women, class and race prejudice, the family-unfriendly corporate culture—all these have a direct impact on our perception of foreign domestic workers, housework, abuse and the formulation of public policies."[50] In comparison to religious groups, these social advocacy groups are political in orientation. Their focus is not on direct service to needy FDWs on a case-by-case basis or broader welfare enhancement. They are interested instead in changing public consciousness and state practice through conscientious education/*Bildung* to bring about a structural shift toward better treatment of FDWs.

In January 2003, members of AWARE and other societal elements joined forces with members of the CMI, other church groups, and individuals interested in improving the conditions of FDWs in a broad alliance that presented itself in civil society terms. This alliance, which called itself TWC2, was modeled after the Working Committee of Civil Society (TWC), an alliance that attempted to create a critical civil society by identifying present and future roles for societal activities. TWC2 drew on this momentum, focusing it on improving the welfare of FDWs, with the hope that the FDW issue would also serve to further consolidate and galvanize civil society. As articulated by its chairperson, Braema Mathi, a nominated member of parliament, TWC2's concrete goal was for the public and the state to regard foreign workers as people who have come to Singapore to earn a living and who should be given all the benefits available to Singaporean workers and foreign talent.[51] To achieve this goal, TWC2 organized a whole range of activities and campaigns to increase public awareness of the plight of FDWs and to educate and transform public consciousness. It also initiated discussion with relevant state authorities and within parliament about the necessity of institutional and statutory reforms that establish a legal basis for the protection of FDWs' rights, such as a proposed amendment of the Employment Act to cover domestic workers that would authorize a standard contract and a government scheme for the accreditation of all employment agencies.

These activities are animated by the same neo-Kantian theoretical principles that sharply oppose humanity to profit, money, or capital. TWC2's governing theme, "Dignity Overdue: Respecting the Rights of Maids," suggests that household work is labor, the universal activity by which human beings achieve self-sustenance. It should not be subjected to "inhuman or degrading treatment" and should be accorded the respect due to other forms of labor because it possesses the dignity appropriate to all human endeavor. Two additional reasons are given for this specific focus on the welfare of domestic workers. First, their contributions "to the economic and social well-being of Singapore must be recognized and valued."[52] Second, in the larger campaign to eliminate violence against women, special attention must be given to the FDW because "she is the most vulnerable woman in our homes. She is a guest worker, here at our invitation, to support our families and earn an honest living for their [sic] own families."[53] TWC2 thus clearly places the humanity of FDWs beyond pecuniary or economic interests. Mathi expressed this succinctly in a comment on employers who monitor the movements of their FDWs and deny them a day off out of fear of losing their posted bond: "Why should that $5,000 dictate how you treat another human being?"[54] By urging the public and the state to confer upon FDWs a sense of belonging that had so far been denied to them, TWC2 was also attempting to subjectify FDWs through social recognition.

TWC2 clearly understands its efforts at humanizing FDWs and the Singapore nation-state in terms of an intensification of civil society participation in important sociopolitical issues. It is implied that the development of civil society as a space of freedom or autonomy from the state is a teleological good that comes with the global spread of modernity because strong civil society structures facilitate the achievement of humanity. Contra Hardt and Negri's understanding of globalization, it is important to note that this mobilization of progressive humanizing forces is not a form of transnationalism from below. It is patently driven by a form of popular nationalism. TWC2's exhortation to improve the welfare of FDWs is almost always directed at fellow *nationals* by Singaporeans concerned about the appalling treatment of FDWs. It is almost always an expression of *national* shame by citizens who care about the image of their country and want their nation to be a responsible people. Thus, TWC2's members have stressed in the national press that "the current state of the foreign domestic worker in Singapore is a source of national embarrassment," and that "it is our national obligation to safeguard the welfare of foreign domestic workers."[55] Similarly, Constance Singam of TWC2 noted that "the abuses committed by some, along with the lack of policies and legislation to protect the rights of maids, do not speak well of our society and government. . . . The abuse of maids also affects Singapore's relationships with its Asean partners. It will reinforce the perception of Singaporean arrogance towards those who are different."[56]

On closer examination, however, this understanding of (national) civil society as a space of autonomy from state imperatives and an indispensable mechanism for the achievement of human freedom becomes questionable. For TWC2's claim to represent the universal interests of humanity, here exemplified by the humanity of the domestic worker, is troubled by a tension between its various arguments. Unlike the universalistic argument from the inherent dignity of all labor *qua* human activity, TWC2's other two arguments—the vulnerability of maids and their contributions to the Singapore economy—are utilitarian arguments based on the particularistic interests and situation of employers in general because they have decided to import guest workers and have benefited from their labor. This appeal to various forms of self-interest to justify better treatment of FDWs is radically at odds with the idea of the sacrosanct dignity and inherent freedom of all human labor, the transcendent status of labor that elevates it above all particularistic interests, because it involves calculations about the benefits and consequences of domestic work. It is suggested that FDWs should be treated with greater consideration because they have been placed in a vulnerable position when Singaporeans choose to import them. They should be treated better because it is a fitting return for what they have contributed to the national economy. And they should be treated better because otherwise Singapore's international image will be tarnished, and this will affect foreign business and trade relations. In all these calculations of appropriate ethical conduct, the FDW remains imbricated in a chain of technical or means-ends relationships. She remains an instrument or means in a field of generalized instrumentality.

What we see in these attempts to rehumanize the FDW is a diffusion of the same technologies of bio-power that produce the middle-class professional woman subject beyond the domain of state institutions. Only now, a small degree of the humanity previously accorded only to the middle-class employer as a member of the Singaporean *bios* is extended to the FDW to mitigate the inhumane effects of these technologies. The same technologies that dehumanize the FDW are now partially reversed to reaffirm her humanity. The progressive solutions proposed by elements of civil society are inevitably circumscribed because they rely on the same corporatist-management techniques and administrative strategies for controlling maids. For example, the conventional understanding of labor rights is based on the liberal idea of the free human agent who enters into a consensual service contract. Accordingly, the most common well-meaning solution stresses the importance of respecting FDWs as professionals who provide a much-desired service and should be recognized by the state as full employees with legal rights under labor law. Yet this liberal doctrine clearly has negative consequences. First, as we have seen, the idea of the maid as a free agent who willingly submits to poor working conditions through a contract is a fiction the Singapore state relies on to justify its failure to protect her rights. Second, the elevation of the FDW to employee status facilitates the transposition of a corporatist rhetoric of managerial supervision into the household and reinforces the idea that the maid is someone who needs to be "managed." As Claire Klaus, the general manager of Panglobal Relocation Services, a consultancy firm for relocating expatriates, put it: "The employer has a supervisory function. . . . As a ma'am, you still have a management function, and if you don't want to do that, don't blame the maid if things go wrong. The supervisory function has to be there all the time. It is wrong to invite the maid to be part of the family. You need to show up unexpectedly in the house, call from wherever you are to see if the phone line is available and if she comes to the phone. Have your neighbor check in on the maid or call her from abroad if you are on holiday."[57]

Because these technologies are the fundamental rationality and underlying support of civil society, there are fundamental nodes of overlap and convergence between governmentality and the liberal institutions of civil society. Accordingly, civil society interests have become curiously aligned with state interests. Whereas the state has always encouraged the activity of voluntary welfare organizations because they supplement its existing social welfare schemes, it has been more ambivalent toward political advocacy groups, which it regards as oppositional. TWC2, however, raised enough public awareness that the state began to acknowledge some of its initiatives because they were useful for fostering a good international public image, which was important for attracting international investment and expatriate workers. While the government has maintained that legislative change and a state-endorsed standard contract is not the answer, it established a special division within the Ministry of Manpower to attend to the welfare of FDWs, supported schemes for the accreditation of employment agencies, and began initiatives for first-time employers to attend an orientation course on the management of maids and the penalties for abuse. New FDWs are also required to attend a class informing them of their rights and course of action if employers make unreasonable demands that compromise their safety.[58] The government and the Association of Employment Agencies have also appropriated TWC2's humanizing vocabulary. There is less frequent public use of "free-market" rhetoric. The term "maid" has also been replaced by the more respectable "domestic worker." The government has openly acknowledged the pragmatic rationale for these shifts. When it prohibited employment agencies from displaying FDWs in their office windows, the Ministry of Manpower issued a statement: "The general public perceives this as employment agencies attempting to display foreign domestic workers much like other commodities. Some have even drawn similarities between such display and that of undesirable occupation in the vice trade. This has created international disrepute for Singapore as we are perceived not to have accorded foreign domestic workers basic human dignity."[59]

This appropriation of the progressive language of civil society is part of the state's general attempt to engage with civil society forces initially announced in 1997 as part of its vision for Singapore in the twenty-first century. The prime minister drew a distinction between "hardware," or material wealth, and "heartware," or social development, and announced the state's commitment to fostering the latter:

> Singapore 21 is about what the people of Singapore want to make of this country. More than a house, Singapore must be a home. The Government can provide the conditions for security and economic growth. But in the end, it is people who give feeling, the human touch, the sense of pride and achievement, the warmth. So beyond developing physical infrastructure and hardware, we need to develop our social infrastructure and software. In Sony corporation, they call this "heartware." We need to go beyond economic and material needs, and reorient society to meet the intellectual, emotional, spiritual, cultural and social needs of our people.
>
> Our concept of competitiveness must therefore recognize that the robust and successful societies of the future will be those that place people at the centre. Countries and societies which can develop and mobilize their people, and serve the human needs, goals and aspirations of their citizens will have a lasting edge. Singapore must be such a society.[60]

This pledge to be a more open and consultative government was renewed by Deputy Prime Minister Lee Hsien Loong, who called for active participation in the building of a "civic society."[61]

It would be comforting to view this shift as the gradual enlightenment of the state by civil society *qua* representative of human interests. This would mean that the state assimilation of civil society initiatives, merely co-optative rhetoric at present, will gradually lead to genuine transformation. Hence, the progressive Singaporean intelligentsia has repeatedly insisted on the importance of a more politicized, critically engaged vision of civil society than the softer consultative and collaborative model of "civic society" outlined by the state.[62] This distinction between progressive and conservative models of civil society is another way of drawing a boundary between the human and the inhuman. The former is seen as people-oriented and motivated by a sense of humanity, whereas the latter's conciliatory character is conducive to the pragmatic imperatives of a capitalist market economy that disregards humanity. What this neat opposition glosses over is the fact that humanity itself is a form of capital. The state requires the participation of civil society because its successful functioning is based on human capital, and civil society is precisely the domain for the articulation and formation of the people's interests through governmental technologies. The common substrate that sustains state and civil society alike is precisely the techniques or means-ends relations that we have already detected in TWC2's utilitarian arguments. This field of instrumentality joins civil society to the state. It enables civil society interests to penetrate the state. But by the same token, it also allows the state to capture civil society initiatives for its own ends in the same way that the Singapore state has always copied strategies from outside to serve the ends of its economic development.

This confirms Foucault's counterintuitive argument that civil society, which received wisdom celebrates as a space of autonomy from the state, is a product-effect of governmentality insofar as the subject of needs is always already shaped by bio-power. What this means is that liberalism is itself a modulation within governmentality. It is a form of government that seeks to minimize government in the name of society.[63] What we see in the Singaporean case is precisely a complex combination of the two technologies of strong government and liberalism. The Singapore state makes strategic nods to the liberal rhetoric of the free market. But this is also a form of social control that endows the state and other actors such as employment agencies with a rapacious capacity to absorb external criticism and incorporate and rechannel "oppositional" humane ideas to further the pursuit of economic self-interest. In other words, because civil society is the crucible for the articulation of human interests, its initiatives are inherently undecidable and vulnerable to state co-optation. All the humanizing endeavors of civil society can have inhuman consequences. At the macrological level, the development of Singaporean civil society is itself premised on Singapore's economic success within the hierarchy of the international division of labor. Indeed, many of the civil society arguments on behalf of FDWs have hierarchical implications from the start. FDWs, who can never be part of the Singapore *bios,* are not members of and equal participants in its civil society. At best, they are only objects of benevolence, the recipients of goodwill from civil society because the end of their existence in Singapore is to make life easier for its citizens. The most that can be done is to safeguard their welfare during their stay and to upgrade their skills so that they can have better job opportunities when they return home.

Furthermore, the justification for eliminating the employment of FDWs betrays the pride that civil society elements take in Singapore's advanced economic status and its corollary, an implied disdain for its less advanced neighbors. As one commentator has suggested, "Singapore needs to wean itself off its unnatural dependence on live-in domestic help. No other developed economy is so reliant on live-in maids."[64] Another remarks that "Singapore would be better off if it had fewer foreign maids. It is a First World country, and yet Singaporeans, even lower-middle-class Singaporeans, live like Third World pashas, with servants at their beck and call. . . . [We should get] rid of this ludicrous hangover from our Third World past—our love affair with cheap servants."[65] The various models of alternative child care and work arrangements reveal a clear desire to emulate more "advanced" forms of social life found in the developed countries of Europe and America because they characterize the telos of the modern, civilized nation that Singapore wants to be. This is a kind of competitiveness or desire for superiority at a symbolic, civilizational level: an advanced society also has advanced domestic labor relations.

Since the material condition of civilizational superiority is economic competitiveness, the push to establish advanced domestic labor relations easily modulates into the position that Singaporeans must treat FDWs well so that they can continue to enjoy their superior economic status and standard of living. Hence, one also finds arguments that justify decent treatment by appealing to economic interests: it is economically sound to be good to FDWs because they will repay the kindness of employers by working harder, and their continued presence will also make Singapore more attractive to high-value expatriate workers. A manager of a maid agency welcomed a mandatory rest day for domestic workers, saying, "Our maid salaries are less than half those in Hong

Kong and Taiwan, so we need other incentives to motivate the maid to work harder."[66] Another writer supported a gratuity scheme that would provide maids with a lump sum payment at the end of their contract on the grounds that

> looking forward to a gratuity could . . .result in a better work attitude.
> . . . The scheme could, in addition, buy greater goodwill from neigh-
> bours such as the Philippines and Indonesia, where a significant part of
> their national earnings come from the remittances of their citizens, in-
> cluding maids, working abroad. Without our maids, Singapore would
> be less attractive to the families of foreign talent. So, it is in our own in-
> terest that we take better care of our maids and get them to continue
> coming here to work. . . . We have to show our neighbours we care for
> their citizens and not regard them as mere serfs.[67]

In this well-meaning latter-day version of the transformation of serfs into consensual wage labor, FDWs are always means or tools. They "help Singaporeans enjoy a better quality of life. They do things which most Singaporeans would squirm at or now regard with utter contempt, from looking after the elderly and the infirm to washing cars and windows."[68]

The foregoing indicates that contrary to TWC2's claims, the welfare of FDWs can never transcend the circuit of money and commodification. The brutal fact is that the FDW is brought to Singapore because her employer's time and effort are seen as more valuable and important than hers. This is why she is paid to perform tasks shunned by her employer. In this scenario, the middle-class feminist lament that "my liberation rides on the back of those other women who have come here to toil, sometimes for as long as 16 hours a day," that "it is still the FDW in my home whose work gives me time for family, continual education, skill development, leisure and meaningful work," is a self-indulgent and meaningless piety that serves to salve an uneasy conscience.[69]

What is to be done to give full due to the FDW's human dignity? The only genuine solution is for employers to desist from hiring FDWs. But this is impossible. The complete elimination of FDWs will lead to much higher costs in reproductive labor, a less comfortable style of life, and the dampening of economic productivity. The true crisis comes in recognizing that regardless of the personal goodwill of the individual Singaporean citizen, one *cannot not* be imbricated within the exploitative hierarchical structure of the international division of labor and the division of reproductive labor that sustains it because they are crucial to Singapore's economic success. To say simply, "The market has chosen, so unless competitive alternatives can be found, foreign maids are here to stay," is to abdicate responsibility by affirming the exploitative institution one is criticizing—the market—as a God who must be obeyed.[70] Given that the liberation of middle-class women in competitive postcolonial development is necessarily contaminated, the feminist effort to provide relief and protection to FDWs must be supplemented by the persistent questioning of the problematic character of the very form of development that has benefited feminism. Otherwise, all such efforts degenerate into the complacent appeased conscience of the liberal subject who can congratulate herself on being a decent employer.

Human Transcendence and the Field of Instrumentality

From a theoretical angle, the emergence of progressive efforts at rehumanizing FDWs in Philippine popular nationalism and among Singaporean civil society elements and their inevitable circumscription by the inhuman technologies on which they depend should lead to the sobering acknowledgment that all efforts to affirm and protect the human rights of FDWs neither transcend inhuman economic imperatives nor elevate the humanity of FDWs beyond instrumental relations. In both cases, what occurs is merely the displacement of instrumentality from one site and level to another, a redistribution of the abusive consequences of treating persons as means to the ends of others so that the abuse does not become overly concentrated in a given location and cause the entire system to break down. There is no solution to the instrumentalization of human relations since this is rooted in the very nature of economic development within the structure of capitalist accumulation. One needs to distinguish among at least three types of instrumental relations that occur at different strata of global capital formation in this scenario: the means-ends relations of employers and foreign workers within the household; the more general relations of the global exploitation of cheap labor within the hierarchy of the international division of labor; and the constitution, deployment, and regulation of human capital by labor-sending and receiving states and other actors through techniques of bio-power. The means-ends relations within the household sustain and reproduce the competitive and uneven nature of national economic development. What mediates between these two types of instrumental relations as their obscured template and connecting substrate are techniques of bio-power. The unevenness of the first two types of instrumentality is merely the inequality of the technical relation projected within the household and writ even larger in a global frame.

How can we articulate ethical principles of human action in view of this field of instrumentality? The neo-Kantian imperative to respect human dignity proscribes the treatment of human beings as means because it violates the autonomous character of humanity. Given the necessity and unavoidability of instrumental relations in human life, how can we respond to the moral imperative to treat human beings as ends in themselves? Faced with totalitarian bureaucratic domination and the late-capitalist commodification of the cultural sphere, the Frankfurt School tried to reconcile these antithetical principles by introducing a hierarchical bifurcation within the genus of technical relations. Max Horkheimer and Herbert Marcuse defined instrumental reason as the technical ability of human reason to master, adapt, and use external nature as a mere means to the human subject's ends. Instrumental reason is marked by three fundamental features. First, insofar as it is concerned with calculating the appropriateness of means for the achievement of subjective ends, instrumental reason elevates the (individual and collective) subject's self-preservation into the ultimate criterion for judging the reasonableness of ends. Horkheimer writes:

> If it concerns itself at all with ends, it takes for granted that they too are reasonable in the subjective sense, *i.e.* that they serve the subject's interest in relation to self-preservation—be it that of the single individual, or of the community on whose maintenance that of the individual depends. The idea that an aim can be reasonable for its own sake—on the basis of virtues that insight reveals it to have in itself—without reference to some kind of subjective gain or advantage, is utterly alien to subjective reason, even where it rises above the consideration of immediate utilitarian values and devotes itself to reflections about the social order as a whole.[71]

The goal of self-preservation thus becomes an unquestioned and absolute end. Second, insofar as external reality is reduced to objects to be manipulated for the purpose of the subject's self-preservation, that is, to mere means, instrumental reason involves a radical disrespect for objects. Third, instrumental reason effects a sundering of the subject from the objective context of its activities and existence. In Marcuse's view, this separation of subject from object leads to an irrationalist conception of society in which existing social relations and conditions are viewed as unquestionable by reason. They must be accepted because they further the incontestable end of self-preservation.[72]

This ascendancy of instrumental reason is linked to fundamental processes of alienated life under capitalism such as the money form or the technological process. In Horkheimer's view, the disrespect for objects continues the reduction of all things into quantitative terms under the process of commodification, whereby money is the universal equivalent. "In the face of such leveling [by economic reality], the proper being of an object is no longer taken into account. Cognition thus becomes that which registers the objects and proceeds to interpret the quantified expressions of them. The less human beings think of reality in qualitative terms, the more susceptible reality becomes to manipulation. Its objects are neither understood nor respected."[73] For Marcuse, it is the technological process itself—the mechanization and rationalization of industrial production in the interests of economic efficiency—that creates a "technological rationality." He writes: "The technological power of the apparatus affects the entire rationality of those whom it serves. Under the impact of this apparatus, individualistic rationality has been transformed into technological rationality. It is by no means confined to the subjects and objects of large scale enterprises but characterizes the pervasive mode of thought and even the manifold forms of protest and rebellion. This rationality establishes standards of judgment and fosters attitudes which make men ready to accept and even to introcept the dictates of the apparatus."[74]

Even though it is indispensable to the development of the material conditions of human freedom, instrumental reason, if left to itself, inevitably leads to the domination of nature and humanity. It culminates in the violent domination of nature and a passive mentality that is conducive to authoritarianism and totalitarianism because it cannot develop and articulate universal values that enable us to evaluate critically and discriminate between different ends. Instrumental reason is human only insofar as artifice/*technē* requires intelligence. It is in fact inhuman because in itself, it cannot lead to, and indeed is inimical to the achievement of, what is proper to humanity: moral freedom. Hence, instrumental reason dehumanizes us. In Horkheimer's words: "It seems that even as technical knowledge expands the horizon of man's thought and activity, his autonomy as an individual, his ability to resist the growing apparatus of mass manipulation, his power of the imagination, his independent judgment appear to be reduced. Advance in technical facilities for enlightenment is accompanied by a process of dehumanization. Thus progress threatens to nullify the very goal it is supposed to realize—the idea of man."[75] Accordingly, instrumental reason is characterized by heteronomy and dependency:

> As interiority has withered away, the joy of making personal decisions, of cultural development, and of the free exercise of the imagination has gone with it. Other inclinations and goals mark the man of today: technological expertise, presence of mind, pleasure in the mastery of machinery, the need to be part of and to agree with the majority of some group which is chosen as a model and whose regulations replace individual judgment. Advice, prescriptions, and patterns for guidance replace moral substance.[76]

What is broached through the topos of dehumanization is precisely the inhuman moment or dimension of human reason. It leads Marcuse and Horkheimer to the thought of a limitless field of instrumentality akin to that which I have delineated in globalizing Southeast Asia. Hence, Marcuse writes: "Business, technics, human needs and nature are welded together into one rational and expedient mechanism. . . . There is no personal escape from the apparatus which has mechanized and standardized the world. It is a rational apparatus, combining utmost expediency with utmost convenience, saving time and energy, removing waste, adapting all means to the end, anticipating consequences, sustaining calculability and security."[77] Similarly, Horkheimer speaks of the transformation of every sphere of life into an instrumental field: "The total transformation of each and every realm of being into *a field of means* leads to the liquidation of the subject who is supposed to use them. This gives modern industrialist society its nihilistic aspect. Subjectivization, which exalts the subject, also dooms him."[78]

In the work of the Frankfurt School, however, the unfreedom and heteronomy of this inhuman field of instrumentality is always diagnosed in opposition to and in derivation from an optimal realm of human freedom. Instrumental reason is always thought under the philosophical sign of alienation, or which is the same thing, the quasi-theological sign of a fall. What can lead us back to true freedom and enable us to restore or achieve our humanity is the formulation of universal values through the higher *technē* of moral self-cultivation. This is the preserve and vocation of critical reason. Unlike instrumental reason, critical reason is associated with the human capacity for transcendence. The cultivational processes of critical reason are a special form of *technē* directed at our mental capacities. It is therefore a self-instrumentalization that lifts us beyond the realm of mere instrumentality through the inculcation of universal values that facilitate the practice of moral freedom.

But this mesmerizing motif of human transcendence loses its pertinence in the global field of instrumentality I have analyzed. For the human, while it is certainly not a mere ideological fiction, is also not a concrete a priori that exists outside and independently of instrumentality. The human is instead materially constituted by instrumentality. The exploitation and abuse of FDWs stem from the instrumental character of their relations with states, employers, and other parties. Yet one cannot transcend this field of instrumentality because humanity itself is produced by technologies of bio-power. The power of transcendence proper to humanity can be understood in terms of human capacities and needs and the will to express them in the juridical form of rights, or in terms of self-cultivation, *Bildung,* and even critical reason. The processes that generate this power, however, are part of the subjectifying or humanizing aspect of bio-power. This is why the humanizing moment is necessarily circumscribed. As we have seen, the subjectifying process cannot be applied globally or uniformly to every person. Bio-power cannot produce humanity in every person at one and the same time because the technical relation is based on inequality and the hierarchical division of means and ends. At any given point there can only be competing attempts to generate humanity in a specific location and at a specific level within the field of technical relations.

Yet, paradoxically, it is also from this field of instrumentality that a certain responsibility to the humanity of FDWs comes into presence as a result of a complex and sensitive series of negotiations between the mobile, conflicting interests of different forces. In the Singaporean example, the various groups making up TWC2, the foreign missions of sending countries that are aligned with it, and the Singapore public and state to which it addresses its appeals have interests that are not coextensive with one another, although they overlap and coincide at certain points. Whereas the CMI is a voluntary welfare organization motivated by the spirit of Christian charity, some feminist members of TWC2 are concerned by the patriarchal benevolence of church groups, whose activity is premised on a structure of dependency and protection. These members feel that it is more important to empower people and to convey their interests to the state through advocacy work and the raising of public awareness via the media so that charity will no longer be required. Nor are the interests of the various groups purely benign. Foreign missions of labor-exporting states have two contradictory objectives. On the one hand, they want to protect *their* citizens working abroad partly out of patriotic reasons, but also for reasons of internal political legitimacy. But on the other hand, even if this wish to protect foreign workers is formalized, in the absence of genuine commitment to create local employment and to phase out labor exportation, labor-sending states will not aggressively demand protection because they want to maximize their market share for foreign workers.

The human rights of the female migrant worker are thus generated from mobile and shifting scales of solidarity. They are the product-effects of interminable political negotiations, or, as Foucault would say, "tactics." These rights are only a rationalization or ideational codification, a provisional terminal point of different force relations that are always shifting. Once they become institutionalized, they will influence or invest this field of relations as concrete ideals to be held up by civil society forces pressing against and making demands on labor-exporting and importing states for legislative change. But these ideals cannot govern the mutations of this field from a transcendent position. I am speaking of an entirely provisional and contingent emergence of universal human norms from an inhuman force field.

My analysis of this inhuman field should be distinguished from the Frankfurt School's analysis of administered late capitalist society as a field of means in two respects. First, this field is not an alienated totality the genesis of which can be traced back to the homogeneous and homogenizing spread of a type of rationality (instrumental reason) that is defective and needs to be regulated by a superior type of rationality (critical reason). Second, it follows that the heteronomy of this field of instrumentality is not the determinate, dialectical opposite of freedom that can be sublated and transcended. This heteronomy is instead the very condition of (im)possibility of human freedom in two ways. Instrumental processes generate the capacities of the rational human being who is free and has rights at the same time that they subjectify him or her. But more important, while these processes lead to subjugation and control, the alignments and connections between them that produce these effects of hegemony are also shifting and unpredictable. This incalculable randomness is the inexhaustible opening of freedom since it makes any given hegemonic state inherently unstable and susceptible to reversal, disruption, and transformation. But by the same token, since it cannot be mastered by the calculations of progressive political or technological reason, it also leads to the interminable circumscription of all effects of freedom that it makes possible.

Instead of lamenting the horrendous ways in which human labor is commodified and the humane institution of the family is deformed and perverted by global capitalism, we should examine how the technologies sustaining global capitalism both enable and disenable the actualization of humanity. My insistence on the generative character of the technologies sustaining capitalist globalization should not be mistaken for the neoliberal argument that the global spread of the market system is to be welcomed despite its patently negative consequences because, through the dissemination of the formal rule of law and human rights discourses, it leads to the actualization of humanity. I have argued that these legal and quasi-legal mechanisms are inadequate and that national mobilization remains important for protecting the FDW's universal human rights. I have also suggested that these rights do not exist a priori but are generated and actualized by a field of generalized instrumentality that produces and sustains the human subject and its various collective forms. The human rights and humanity of the female migrant worker do not preexist inhuman forces. They come into presence, into the phenomenality of enlightened public reason, as an aftereffect within the inhuman force field that subtends the various collective and individual actors. Human rights are points of resistance immanent to this inhuman field. They only appear as a priori, as a pure presence that has been threatened, repressed, or eroded by the inhuman forces from which they are derived and which interminably circumscribe them, through a metalepsis. In fact, the small contaminated victories of human rights are not the determinate negation of the inhuman but its *différance,* the other

of the inhuman "different and deferred in the economy of the same."[79]
Instead of regarding human rights as a barrier issuing from the human
capacity for reason that holds the inhumanity of global capital in check
or enables us to transcend it, we should understand their unconditional
but contaminated normativity as arising from the alterity within the inhuman force field of global capital and learn to track how this inhuman
field induces effects of humanity.

Notes

Introduction

1. Immanuel Kant, *Kritik der Urteilskraft*, in *Werkausgabe*, ed. Wilhelm Weischedel, vol. 10 (Frankfurt am Main: Suhrkamp, 1968), §60, p. 300; translation from Kant, *Critique of Judgment*, trans. and ed. Werner S. Pluhar (Indianapolis: Hackett, 1987), p. 231.
2. Frantz Fanon, *The Wretched of the Earth*, trans. Richard Philcox (New York: Grove Press, 2004), p. 55.
3. Kofi A. Annan, "Common Values for a Common Era," *Civilization* (June–July 1999): 75.
4. "East Asia" here refers to both Northeast Asia (China, Japan, Korea, Taiwan, and Hong Kong) and Southeast Asia. This division of the South in contemporary globalization comes from Samir Amin, *Obsolescent Capitalism: Contemporary Politics and Global Disorder* (London: Zed, 2003), pp. 17–21. Amin's account is slightly dated and seems to refer to the 1960s–1990s. Currently, only China is hyperdeveloping. Some political regimes in Southeast Asia are post-socialist (Vietnam, Laos, Cambodia, Myanmar) and some post-authoritarian and selectively developmentalist (Singapore, Thailand, and Malaysia), while others attempt to fashion a developmental state within the framework of a formally democratic political system (Thailand and Indonesia). My thanks to Caroline Hau for this observation.
5. Immanuel Kant, *Anthropologie in pragmatischer Hinsicht*, in *Werkausgabe*, ed. Wilhelm Weischedel, vol. 12 (Frankfurt am Main: Suhrkamp, 1968), p. 674; translation from Kant, *Anthropology from a Pragmatic Point of View*, trans. Mary J. Gregor (The Hague: Martinus Nijhoff, 1974), p. 183.
6. Immanuel Kant, *Grundlegung zur Metaphysik der Sitten*, *Werkausgabe*, ed. Wilhelm Weischedel, vol. 7 (Frankfurt am Main: Suhrkamp, 1968), p. 61; translation from Kant, *Groundwork of the Metaphysics of Morals*, in *Practical Philosophy*, trans. and ed. Mary J. Gregor (Cambridge: Cambridge University Press, 1996), p. 80.
7. Hannah Arendt, *The Origins of Totalitarianism* (San Diego: Harcourt,

269

1968), p. 293. See also Étienne Balibar, "'Rights of Man' and 'Rights of the Citizen': The Modern Dialectic of Equality and Freedom," in *Masses, Classes, Ideas: Studies on Politics and Philosophy Before and After Marx*, trans. James Swenson (New York: Routledge, 1994), pp. 39–59; and Balibar, "Is a Philosophy of Human Civic Rights Possible? New Reflections on Equaliberty," trans. James Swenson, *South Atlantic Quarterly* 103, nos. 2–3 (Spring–Summer 2004): 311–322.

8. Max Horkheimer and Theodor W. Adorno, *Dialektik der Aufklärung*, in Horkheimer, *Gesammelte Schriften*, vol. 5, ed. Gunzelin Schmid Noerr (Frankfurt am Main: Fischer, 2003), p. 26; translation from Horkheimer and Adorno, *Dialectic of Enlightenment*, trans. Edmund Jephcott (Palo Alto: Stanford University Press, 2002), p. 2. Hereafter *DA*, with page references first to the German edition, then to the translation.

9. *DA*, pp. 18–19/xvi, emphasis added.

10. *DA*, p. 21/xviii, emphasis added.

11. See, for instance, Jürgen Habermas, *Theory and Practice*, trans. John Viertel (Boston: Beacon, 1973), pp. 168–169; *Knowledge and Human Interests*, trans. Jeremy J. Shapiro (Boston: Beacon, 1971), chap. 3; and *Legitimation Crisis*, trans. Thomas McCarthy (Boston: Beacon, 1975), chap. 1.

12. Ernst Cassirer, *An Essay on Man: An Introduction to a Philosophy of Human Culture* (New Haven: Yale University Press, 1944), p. 228.

13. On bio-power as power over life, see Michel Foucault, *The History of Sexuality*, vol. 1, *An Introduction*, trans. Robert Hurley (New York: Vintage, 1980), pp. 138–145.

14. See Michel Foucault, "Technologies of the Self" and "The Ethics of the Concern of the Self as a Practice of Freedom," both in *Ethics: Subjectivity and Truth*, vol. 1 of *Essential Works of Foucault, 1954–1984*, ed. Paul Rabinow (New York: New Press, 1997), pp. 224–225 and 298–301, respectively.

15. Ferdinand de Saussure, *Course in General Linguistics*, trans. Wade Baskin (New York: McGraw-Hill, 1966), pp. 73–74.

16. Ibid., p. 76.

17. Jacques Derrida, *Of Grammatology*, trans. Gayatri Chakravorty Spivak (Baltimore: Johns Hopkins University Press, 1976), p. 47.

18. Jacques Derrida, "Force of Law: The 'Mystical Foundation of Authority,'" in *Deconstruction and the Possibility of Justice*, ed. Drucilla Cornell, Michel Rosenfeld, and David Gray Carlson (New York: Routledge, 1992), p. 27.

19. Foucault, *The History of Sexuality*, 1:93–94.

20. The exaggerated charge of antihumanism is not confined to the American reception of post-1968 French thought. Ironically, the French pathologization of "antihumanism" also involves nationalist xenophobia: nam-

ing it as a continuation of the pernicious legacy of German thought in France. Derrida is Heidegger reincarnated in France, Foucault is the second coming of Nietzsche, Lacan is the French Freud, and so on. See Luc Ferry and Alain Renault, *French Philosophy of the Sixties: An Essay on Antihumanism,* trans. Mary Schnackenberg Cattani (Amherst: University of Massachusetts Press, 1990).
21. For the idea of universalizing Asia, see Pheng Cheah, "Universal Areas: Asian Studies in a World in Motion," *Traces* 1, no. 1 (2001): 37–70.

1. The Cosmopolitical—Today

1. See Partha Chatterjee, *Nationalist Thought and the Colonial World: A Derivative Discourse?* (London: Zed Books, 1986); and Ranajit Guha, *A Construction of Humanism in Colonial India,* Wertheim Lecture (Amsterdam: Centre for Asian Studies, 1993).
2. Pheng Cheah and Bruce Robbins, eds., *Cosmopolitics: Thinking and Feeling beyond the Nation* (Minneapolis: University of Minnesota Press, 1998), was the first sustained discussion of some of these new cosmopolitanisms and their relation to nationalism. This chapter is a revised version of my introduction to *Cosmopolitics.* More recent collections about cosmopolitanism include Steven Vertovec and Robin Cohen, eds., *Conceiving Cosmopolitanism: Theory, Context, and Practice* (Oxford: Oxford University Press, 2003); Daniele Archibugi, ed., *Debating Cosmopolitics* (New York: Verso, 2003); and Carol A. Breckenridge et al., eds., *Cosmopolitanism* (Durham: Duke University Press, 2002).
3. For a concise attempt at a historicist-sociological critique of the new cosmopolitanism, see Craig Calhoun, "The Class Consciousness of Frequent Travelers: Toward a Critique of Actually Existing Cosmopolitanism," *South Atlantic Quarterly* 101, no. 4 (2002): 869–897.
4. For methodological critiques of the nation-state as container, see Saskia Sassen, "Spatialities and Temporalities of the Global: Elements for a Theorization," *Public Culture* 12, no. 1 (2000): 215–232; and Ulrich Beck, "Toward a New Critical Theory with a Cosmopolitan Intent," *Constellations* 10, no. 4 (2003): 453–468.
5. See Benedict Anderson, *Imagined Communities: Reflections on the Origin and Spread of Nationalism,* rev. ed. (London: Verso, 1991), chap. 4; and Anderson, *The Spectre of Comparisons: Nationalism, Southeast Asia, and the World* (London: Verso, 1998), chap. 1.
6. Jean Le Ronde d'Alembert, "Cosmopolitain, ou cosmopolite," in *Encyclopédie ou Dictionnaire raisonné des Sciences, des Arts, et des Métiers* (Paris, 1751–1765): "Asking an old philosopher where he was from, he answered,

'I am [a] cosmopolitan, that means a citizen of the universe.' 'I prefer,' said another, 'my family to myself, my fatherland to my family, and humankind to my fatherland.'" My thanks to Nicole Fermon for helping with the translation.

7. Jean-Jacques Rousseau, *Discourse on the Origin and the Foundations of Inequality among Men* (1766), in *The Discourses and Other Political Writings,* ed. and trans. Victor Gourevitch (Cambridge: Cambridge University Press, 1997), pt. 2 (33), p. 174.

8. Imanuel Kant, "Idee zu einer allgemeinen Geschichte in weltbürgerlicher Absicht," in *Werkausgabe,* ed. Wilhelm Weischedel, vol. 11 (Frankfurt am Main: Suhrkamp, 1968), p. 47; translation from Kant, "Idea for a Universal History with a Cosmopolitan Purpose," in *Political Writings,* ed. Hans Reiss (Cambridge: Cambridge University Press, 1991), p. 51. Hereafter IUH, with page references first from the German edition, then from the translation.

9. Immanuel Kant, "Über den Gemeinspruch: Das mag in der Theorie richtig sein, taugt aber nicht für die Praxis," in *Werkausgabe,* 11:172; translation from Kant, "On the Common Saying: 'This May Be True in Theory, but It Does Not Apply in Practice,'" in *Political Writings,* p. 92.

10. Immanuel Kant, "Zum ewigen Frieden: Ein philosophischer Entwurf," in *Werkausgabe,* 11:203n; translation from Kant, *Toward Perpetual Peace: A Philosophical Project,* in *Practical Philosophy,* trans. and ed. Mary J. Gregor (Cambridge: Cambridge University Press, 1996), p. 322n. Hereafter *PP,* with page references first from the German edition, then from the translation. Cf. Kant's discussion of cosmopolitan right, *The Metaphysics of Morals,* §62, in *Practical Philosophy,* pp. 489–490. Hereafter *MS.*

11. Because of Kant's insistence on the inviolability of state sovereignty and the important role of the state in the moral-cultural education of its citizens, his idea of cosmopolitan right remains very limited. The cosmopolitan community is a federation of states and not of world citizens, and the ultimate purpose of "a cosmopolitan system of public political security [*weltbürgerlichen Zustand der öffentlichen Staatssicherheit*]" is to bring about lasting peace so that states can devote their time and efforts to the cultural education of their citizens and increase their aptitude for morality instead of wasting their resources on expansionist war efforts (IUH, pp. 44–47/49–51). Consequently, the scope of cosmopolitan right is limited to the provision of hospitality. This is "the right of a foreigner not to be treated with hostility because he has arrived on the land of another." It is a mere right to visit and not a right of a guest (*PP,* pp. 213–216/328–329). The protection of individual rights that we call "human rights" does not fall under cosmopolitan right but is left to the civil constitution of each

state (see *PP*, pp. 204–206/322–324). Matters concerning relations between states such as the principle that a state has no right to use its citizens to make war against other states are also not governed by cosmopolitan right but fall under the right of peoples (*Völkerrecht*) (*MS*, §55, pp. 483–484).

12. *PP*, pp. 226/328.

13. *PP*, pp. 216–217/330–331.

14. Immanuel Kant, *Kritik der Urteilskraft*, §83, in *Werkausgabe*, 10:392; translation from Kant, *Critique of Judgment*, trans. and ed. Werner S. Pluhar (Indianapolis: Hackett, 1987), p. 321. Hereafter *CJ*, with page references first from the German edition, then from the translation.

15. *CJ*, §60, p. 300/231.

16. See Lord Acton, "Nationality," in *The Nationalism Reader*, ed. Omar Dahbour and Micheline R. Ishay (Atlantic Highlands, N.J.: Humanities Press, 1995), pp. 108–118.

17. Allen Wood points out that *Toward Perpetual Peace* was written after the Treaty of Basel in March 1795, which ended the War of the First Coalition between the monarchical states of Europe and France and can be read as an implicit defense of republican France as the potential leader of a peaceful cosmopolitan federation. Allen Wood, "Kant's Project for Perpetual Peace," in *Cosmopolitics*, ed. Cheah and Robbins, p. 59.

18. *MS* (first published January 1797), §53, p. 482.

19. For a succinct account of the Westphalian system as one of international anarchy and an alternative account of global civil society, see Ronnie Lipschutz, "Reconstructing World Politics: The Emergence of Global Civil Society," *Millennium: Journal of International Studies* 21, no. 3 (1992): 389–420.

20. Giuseppe Mazzini, *The Duties of Man*, in Dahbour and Ishay, *Nationalism Reader*, pp. 91–94.

21. Friedrich Meinecke, *Cosmopolitanism and the National State*, trans. Robert B. Kimber (Princeton: Princeton University Press, 1970), p. 94: "Cosmopolitanism and nationalism stood side by side in a close, living relationship for a long time. And even if the idea of the genuine national state did not come into full bloom within such a relationship, the meeting of these two intellectual forces was by no means unfruitful for the national idea."

22. Karl Marx, *Manifest der Kommunistischen Partei* (February 1848), in *Marx/Engels Gesamtausgabe*, ed. Vladimir Adoratskij, ser. 1, vol. 6 (Berlin: Marx-Engels Verlag, 1932), p. 529, emphasis added; translation from Marx, "Manifesto of the Communist Party," in *The Revolutions of 1848: Political Writings*, vol. 1 (Harmondsworth: Penguin, 1973), p. 71. Hereafter *MCP*.

23. See Marx, "Draft of an Article on Friedrich List's Book, *Das nationale System der politischen Ökonomie*," in Karl Marx and Friedrich Engels, *Collected Works,* vol. 4 (New York: International Publishers, 1975), pp. 265–293, esp. pp. 280–281. For a more extended discussion, see Roman Szporluk, *Communism and Nationalism: Karl Marx versus Friedrich List* (New York: Oxford University Press, 1988).

24. *MCP,* pp. 84 and 85.

25. *MCP,* p. 84.

26. For a concise summary of the national question in socialist cosmopolitanism, see Alejandro Colás, "Putting Cosmopolitanism into Practice: The Case of Socialist Internationalism," *Millennium: Journal of International Studies* 23, no. 3 (1994): 513–534.

27. Vladimir Ilyich Lenin, *The Right of Nations to Self-Determination* (New York: International Publishers, 1951), pp. 24–25.

28. But in his concise and detailed account of cosmopolitanism and nationalism in Latin America, Noël Salomon distinguishes cosmopolitanism from internationalism, arguing that the former is supranational and has a negative meaning whereas the latter affirms nationalism. See Noël Salomon, "Cosmopolitism and Internationalism in the History of Ideas in Latin America," *Cultures* 6 (1979): 83–108.

29. Sun Yat-Sen, *San Min Chu I: The Three Principles of the People,* trans. Frank Price (Shanghai: China Committee, Institute of Pacific Relations, 1927), p. 89.

30. Frantz Fanon, *The Wretched of the Earth,* trans. Richard Philcox (New York: Grove Press, 2004), p. 98.

31. Saskia Sassen, *The Global City: New York, London, Tokyo* (Princeton: Princeton University Press, 1991), p. 6. Sassen's notion of "global control capability" is clearly limited to forms of management and control of production that have become relatively autonomous forms of production in themselves. It does not refer to political control or social management. The suggestiveness of the term "control," however, has led Michael Hardt and Antonio Negri to splice this economic notion of global control to Deleuze's idea of a society of control (formulated in a revisionist interpretation of Foucault's idea of biopolitics) to suggest the existence of a global society of control without exteriority, which they call "Empire." See Michael Hardt and Antonio Negri, *Empire* (Cambridge, Mass.: Harvard University Press, 2000).

32. Sassen, *The Global City,* pp. 127 and 327.

33. See Saskia Sassen, *Globalization and Its Discontents* (New York: New Press, 1998), pp. xxviii–xxix.

34. Saskia Sassen, *Cities in a World Economy,* 2nd ed. (Thousand Oaks, Calif.: Pine Forge Press, 2000), p. 140.

35. Sassen, *Globalization and Its Discontents,* p. 200.
36. Ibid., pp. 21–22.
37. Ibid., p. 193.
38. Ibid., p. 194.
39. Ibid., p. 214.
40. Sassen, *The Global City,* pp. 336–338.
41. Sassen, *Cities in a World Economy,* pp. 111–112.
42. Saritha Rai, "As It Tries to Cut Costs, Wall Street Looks to India," *New York Times,* October 8, 2003. See also Amy Waldman, "Despite Widespread Poverty, a Consumer Class Emerges in India," *New York Times,* October 20, 2003.
43. Arjun Appadurai and Carol Breckenridge, "Why Public Culture?" *Public Culture* 1, no. 1 (Fall 1988): 5.
44. See Arjun Appadurai, "Disjuncture and Difference in the Global Cultural Economy," *Public Culture* 2, no. 2 (Spring 1990): 14–15.
45. Arjun Appadurai, "Patriotism and Its Futures," *Public Culture* 5, no. 3 (Spring 1993): 418.
46. Ibid., p. 412.
47. See Arjun Appadurai, "Grassroots Globalization and the Research Imagination," *Public Culture* 12, no. 1 (2000): 1–19.
48. Appadurai, "Patriotism and Its Futures," p. 421.
49. Appadurai, "Grassroots Globalization," p. 6.
50. Sassen, "Spatialities and Temporalities of the Global," p. 215.
51. This and the previous quotation are from Michael Mann, "Nation-States in Europe and Other Continents: Diversifying, Developing, Not Dying," *Daedalus* 122, no. 3 (Summer 1993): 138–139. See also Sassen, *Globalization and Its Discontents,* pp. 199–200.
52. Giovanni Arrighi, "Lineages of Empire," in *Debating Empire,* ed. Gopal Balakrishnan (London: Verso, 2003), pp. 32–33.
53. The analytical distinction is between Marx's theory of the capitalist mode of production on a world scale (presupposing a truly generalized world market that integrates commodities, capital, and labor, and results in global homogenization) and capitalism as an existing world system (leaving labor unintegrated and leading to polarization). See Samir Amin, *Re-reading the Postwar Period: An Intellectual Itinerary,* trans. Michael Wolfers (New York: Monthly Review Press, 1994), p. 74. See also Amin, "The Social Movements in the Periphery: An End to National Liberation?" in *Transforming the Revolution: Social Movements and the World-System,* ed. Samir Amin et al. (New York: Monthly Review Press, 1990), pp. 96–138.
54. Samir Amin, *Empire of Chaos* (New York: Monthly Review Press, 1992), pp. 10 and 46.
55. Amin, *Re-reading the Postwar Period,* p. 211.

56. Amin, "The Social Movements in the Periphery," p. 137.

57. Anthony D. Smith, *Nations and Nationalism in a Global Era* (Cambridge: Polity Press, 1995), p. 24.

58. João Pedro Stedile, "Brazil's Landless Battalions: The Sem Terra Movement," in *A Movement of Movements: Is Another World Really Possible?*, ed. Tom Mertes (New York: Verso, 2004), p. 43.

59. Long-distance nationalism in postcoloniality is the flipside of minority ethnic politics in the North. As Benedict Anderson notes, "That same metropole which marginalizes and stigmatizes [the ethnic minority] simultaneously enables him to play, in a flash, on the other side of the planet, national hero." Anderson, *The Spectre of Comparisons*, p. 74.

60. For critiques of the concept of global civil society in international relations theory, see M. J. Peterson, "Transnational Activity, International Society, and World Politics," *Millennium: Journal of International Studies* 21, no. 3 (1992): 371–388; and Martin Shaw, "Civil Society and Global Politics: Beyond a Social Movements Approach," *Millennium: Journal of International Studies* 23, no. 3 (1994): 647–667. Peterson cautions us against regarding international society as a larger version of civil society because it operates in a decentralized political system where loyalty to the world as a whole is insignificant. Shaw points out that civil society institutions are defined largely in terms of national bases, and that social movements have little impact on interstate relations because they rely on cultural impact instead of connections within the political system. He suggests that global civil society is more potential than actual and that, at best, social movements with global networks make national civil societies more globally aware.

61. Gayatri Chakravorty Spivak, *A Critique of Postcolonial Reason* (Cambridge, Mass.: Harvard University Press, 1999), pp. 375, 381.

2. Postnational Light

1. The most prominent example from analytical philosophy is John Rawls, *The Law of Peoples* (Cambridge, Mass.: Harvard University Press, 1999). See also Ian Shapiro and Lea Brilmayer, eds., *Global Justice, Nomos 41, Yearbook of the American Society for Political and Legal Philosophy* (New York: New York University Press, 1999).

2. Jürgen Habermas, "Kants Idee des ewigen Friedens: Aus dem historischen Abstand von 200 Jahren," in *Die Einbeziehung des Anderen: Studien zur politischen Theorie* (Frankfurt am Main: Suhrkamp, 1996), pp. 192–236; translation from Habermas, "Kant's Idea of Perpetual Peace: At Two Hundred Years' Historical Remove," in *The Inclusion of the Other: Studies in Political Theory*, ed. and trans. Ciaran Cronin and Pablo De Greiff (Cam-

bridge, Mass.: MIT Press, 1998), pp. 165–201. Hereafter *IO,* cited parenthetically in the text with page references first from the German edition, then from the translation.

3. For instance, Brian Barry observes that "cosmopolitanism is a moral outlook, not an institutional prescription. . . . [C]ontemporary cosmopolitanism . . . is a moral stance consisting of three elements: individualism, equality and universality." Brian Barry, "Statism and Nationalism: A Cosmopolitan Critique," in Shapiro and Brilmayer, *Global Justice,* p. 35.

4. This and the preceding sentence are a close paraphrase of Habermas's essay "Aus Katastrophen lernen? Ein zeitdiagnostischer Rückblick auf das kurze 20. Jahrhundert," in *Die postnationale Konstellation: Politische Essays* (Frankfurt am Main: Suhrkamp, 1998), pp. 86–88; translation from Jürgen Habermas, "Learning from Catastrophe? A Look Back at the Short Twentieth Century," in *The Postnational Constellation: Political Essays,* trans. and ed. Max Pensky (Cambridge, Mass.: MIT Press, 2001), pp. 54–55. Hereafter *PC,* cited parenthetically in the text with page references first from the German edition, then from the translation.

5. While not all formerly colonized countries are part of the South and not all countries of the South are postcolonial, my implicit point of reference is to postcolonial countries in the South. Hence, I use the shorthand phrase "postcolonial South."

6. For a discussion of Kant's extended analogy between moral freedom and the self-recursive causality of the organism, see Pheng Cheah, *Spectral Nationality: Passages of Freedom from Kant to Postcolonial Literatures of Liberation* (New York: Columbia University Press, 2003), chap. 2.

7. For Habermas's arguments about the co-originality of private and public autonomy and the internal link between democratic legitimation and human rights, see his "Remarks on Legitimation through Human Rights," chap. 5 of *PC,* esp. pp. 170–177/113–118; and *Between Facts and Norms: Contributions to a Discourse Theory of Law and Democracy,* trans. William Rehg (Cambridge, Mass.: MIT Press, 1996), chap. 3, hereafter *BFN.*

8. On the public sphere, see Jürgen Habermas, *The Structural Transformation of the Public Sphere: An Inquiry into a Category of Bourgeois Society,* trans. Thomas Burger (Cambridge, Mass.: MIT Press, 1989). On the critique of Marx for ignoring the specificity of communicative action and failing to develop a science of man, see Habermas, *Theory and Practice,* trans. John Viertel (Boston: Beacon, 1973), pp. 168–169; and *Knowledge and Human Interests,* trans. Jeremy J. Shapiro (Boston: Beacon, 1971), chap, 3. On the autonomy of the political and democratization, see *Theory and Practice,* pp. 232–235. *Legitimation Crisis,* trans. Thomas McCarthy (Boston: Beacon, 1975) is a severe qualification of Habermas's general belief in the autonomy of the political.

9. For Habermas's detranscendentalized revision of Kantian autonomy, see *IO*, chap. 1, esp. pp. 45–50/30–34.

10. See *BFN*, "Postscript," and *IO*.

11. *BFN*, p. 451. See Habermas's discussion of the logical genesis of a system of rights from the principle of democracy through rational discourse in *BFN*, pp. 118–131.

12. Benedict Anderson, *Imagined Communities: Reflections on the Origin and Spread of Nationalism*, rev. ed. (London: Verso, 1991).

13. For a discussion of these and other key features of Anderson's theory of nationalism, see my "Grounds of Comparison," in *Grounds of Comparison: Around the Work of Benedict Anderson*, ed. Pheng Cheah and Jonathan Culler (New York: Routledge, 2003), pp. 1–20.

14. Habermas describes German citizens as "the sons, daughters, and grandchildren of a barbaric nationalism." *PC*, p. 156/103.

15. Jürgen Habermas, "The European Nation-State and the Pressures of Globalization," *New Left Review*, no. 235 (May–June 1999): 47.

16. This celebration of the welfare state should be contrasted with Habermas's earlier ambivalent discussion of the welfare state in *The Structural Transformation of the Public Sphere*, especially his point that the social welfare state compromises the autonomy of the public sphere of civil society and leads to "a staged and manipulative publicity displayed by organizations over the heads of a mediatized public" (p. 232).

17. Karl Marx and Friedrich Engels, *Manifest der kommunistichen Partei* (1848), in *Marx/Engels Gesamtausgabe*, ed. Vladimir Adoratskij (Berlin: Marx-Engels Verlag, 1932), pp. 530–531; in English, Marx and Engels, *Manifesto of the Communist Party*, in Karl Marx, *The Revolutions of 1848: Political Writings*, vol. 1, ed. David Fernbach (Harmondsworth: Penguin, 1973), pp. 72–73. I have modified the 1888 translation by Samuel Moore by adding a deleted sentence from the German version as indicated in brackets.

18. G. W. F. Hegel, *Lectures on the Philosophy of World History. Introduction: Reason in History*, trans. H. B. Nisbet (Cambridge: Cambridge University Press, 1980), p. 48.

19. "Globalization processes are not just economic. Bit by bit, they introduce us to *another* perspective, from which we see the growing interdependence of social arenas, communities of risk, and the networks of shared fate ever more clearly." *PC*, p. 87/55.

20. See *PC*, pp. 110–116/71–76.

21. See *PC*, pp. 105–110/68–71.

22. Theodor W. Adorno, *Negative Dialectics*, trans. E. B. Ashton (New York: Continuum, 1973), p. 163.

23. Immanuel Kant, "Zum ewigen Frieden: Ein philosophischer Entwurf," in *Werkausgabe,* ed. Wilhelm Weischedel, vol. 11 (Frankfurt am Main: Suhrkamp, 1968), p. 203n; translation from Kant, *Toward Perpetual Peace: A Philosophical Project,* in *Practical Philosophy,* trans. and ed. Mary J. Gregor (Cambridge: Cambridge University Press, 1996), p. 322n.

24. Albrecht Wellmer, "Models of Freedom in the Modern World," *Philosophical Forum* 21, nos. 1–2 (Fall–Winter 1989–90): 230.

25. Cf. *IO,* pp. 239/204–205: "Feminists, minorities in multicultural societies, peoples struggling for national independence, and formerly colonized regions suing for the equality of their cultures on the international stage are all currently fighting for such claims. Does not the recognition of cultural forms of life and traditions that have been marginalized, whether in the context of a majority culture or in a Eurocentric global society, require guarantees of status and survival—in other words, some kind of collective rights that shatter the outmoded self-understanding of the democratic constitutional state, which is tailored to individual rights and in that sense is 'liberal'?"

26. Samir Amin, *Empire of Chaos* (New York: Monthly Review Press, 1992), p. 40.

27. Samir Amin, *Delinking: Towards a Polycentric World* (London: Zed Books, 1990), pp. 12–13.

28. Ibid., p. 13.

29. Folker Fröbel, Jürgen Heinrichs, and Otto Kreye, *The New International Division of Labour: Structural Unemployment in Industrialised Countries and Industrialization in Developing Countries,* trans. Pete Burgess (Cambridge: Cambridge University Press, 1980), p. 10. Hereafter *NIDL,* cited parenthetically in the text.

30. Saskia Sassen, *Globalization and Its Discontents* (New York: New Press, 1998), pp. 119–120.

31. Deutsche Entwicklungsgesellschaft, *Geschäftsbericht, 1966,* cited in *NIDL,* p. 169.

32. These points are drawn from *NIDL,* pt. 3.

33. Habermas, "The European Nation-State and the Pressures of Globalization," p. 59.

34. Jürgen Habermas, "Beyond the Nation-State? On Some Consequences of Economic Globalization," in *Democracy in the European Union: Integration through Deliberation?* ed. Erik Oddvar Eriksen and John Erik Fossum (London: Routledge, 2000), p. 34.

35. For a thorough discussion of the link between neoliberalism and the rise of NGOs, see Michael Edwards and David Hulme, eds., *Beyond the Magic Bullet: Non-governmental Organisations: Performance and Accountability* (Lon-

don: Earthscan, 1995) and Edwards and Hulme, eds., *NGOs, States, and Donors: Too Close for Comfort?* (New York: St. Martin's Press, 1997).

36. One can always point to the various World Social Forums as positive instances of global social movements that challenge neoliberalism, but it is unclear what their political efficacy is and whether they satisfy Habermas's criteria for democratic legitimation and cosmopolitan values. Many of these activists claim affiliation with anarchistic principles and the nationalism of oppressed peoples, and their activities are not directed at the military and political apparatuses of globalization. They are also against the centralized form of institutional organization that characterizes Habermas's vision of democratic self-steering. For a discussion of these movements, see Tom Mertes, ed., *A Movement of Movements: Is Another World Really Possible?* (New York: Verso, 2004).

37. David Hulme and Michael Edwards, "Conclusion: Too Close to the Powerful, Too Far from the Powerless?" in *NGOs, States, and Donors*, p. 277.

38. See Jürgen Habermas, "Further Reflections on the Public Sphere," in *Habermas and the Public Sphere,* ed. Craig Calhoun (Cambridge, Mass.: MIT Press, 1992), esp. pp. 442–452. Hereafter FR, cited parenthetically in the text. The remainder of my discussion reconstructs the arguments in this essay.

39. Perry Anderson, *In the Tracks of Historical Materialism* (London: Verso, 1983), pp. 64–66.

3. Given Culture

1. Jean-François Lyotard, "Universal History and Cultural Differences," in *The Lyotard Reader,* ed. Andrew Benjamin (Oxford: Blackwell, 1989), p. 319.

2. In his case for paralogical/local legitimation by way of the *petit récit,* Lyotard invokes the Casinahua as a primitive model that precedes the violent imposition of a universal/cosmopolitical narrative. See Jean-François Lyotard, *The Differend: Phrases in Dispute* (Minneapolis: University of Minnesota Press, 1988), pp. 152–161.

3. For instance, as in the pious lament that the problems of constitutionalism in decolonization arise because decolonized space is inadequate to the world-historical ideal of constitutionalism as realized in the West. For some of the arguments in this debate, see R. N. Spann, ed., *Constitutionalism in Asia* (New York: Asia Publishing House, 1963); *Constitutionalism* (special issue), *Nomos* 20 (1979); Lawrence Beer, ed., *Constitutionalism in Asia: Asian Views of the American Influence* (Berkeley: University of California Press, 1979); and Louis Henkin and Albert

Rosenthal, eds., *Constitutionalism and Rights* (New York: Columbia University Press, 1990).

4. James Clifford, *The Predicament of Culture: Twentieth-Century Ethnography, Literature, and Art* (Cambridge, Mass.: Harvard University Press, 1988), p. 95. Hereafter *PC*, cited parenthetically in the text.

5. In his genealogy of the term "culture," Clifford points to a strong continuity between the concept of high culture as the elevated domain of human value and the anthropological definition of culture. *PC*, p. 235.

6. *PC*, p. 95.

7. See *PC*, pp. 15, 246, 250, 274.

8. "The Postcolonial Critic: Homi Bhabha interviewed by David Bennett and Terry Collits," *Arena* 96 (1991): 50–51.

9. The subject of a proposition (*énoncé*) is a psychic unity constituted in language on the uttering of the pronoun "I." It is an empty and assignable slot that presupposes a material para-linguistic speaker (the subject of enunciation) from which it is split. See Emile Benveniste, *Problems in General Linguistics,* trans. Mary Elizabeth Meek (Coral Gables: University of Miami Press, 1971), pp. 224–226; Michel Foucault, *The Archaeology of Knowledge,* trans. A. M. Sheridan Smith (New York: Pantheon, 1972), pp. 102–105.

10. Homi Bhabha, "Of Mimicry and Man: The Ambivalence of Colonial Discourse," in *The Location of Culture* (New York: Routledge, 1994), p. 86. Hereafter *LC*, cited parenthetically in the text.

11. "Hybridity is the revaluation of the assumption of colonial identity through the repetition of discriminatory identity effects. . . . It reveals the ambivalence at the source of traditional discourses on authority and enables a form of subversion, founded on that uncertainty, that turns the discursive conditions of dominance into one of intervention." Homi Bhabha, "Signs Taken for Wonders," in *LC*, p. 112.

12. "The displacement of symbol to sign creates a crisis for any concept of authority based on a system of recognition. . . . Hybridity [enables] . . . other 'denied' knowledges [to] enter the dominant discourse and estrange the basis of its authority." *LC*, p. 175.

13. Edward Said, *Orientalism* (New York: Random House, 1979). Compare Homi Bhabha, "The Other Question: Stereotype, Discrimination, and the Discourse of Colonialism," in *LC*, p. 72; and James Clifford, "On *Orientalism*," in *PC*, p. 264.

14. "No return to a pure Wampanoag tradition was at issue, but rather a reinterpretation of Mashpee's contested history in order to act—with other Indian groups—powerfully, in an impure present-becoming-future." James Clifford, "Identity in Mashpee," in *PC*, p. 344.

15. Homi Bhabha, "Postcolonial Authority and Postmodern Guilt," in *Cultural Studies,* ed. Lawrence Grossberg, Cary Nelson, and Paula Treichler (New York: Routledge, 1992), p. 59.

16. James Clifford, "Traveling Cultures," ibid., pp. 107–108. Hereafter TC, cited parenthetically in the text.

17. Homi Bhabha, "The Postcolonial and the Postmodern: The Question of Agency," in *LC,* pp. 172, 173.

18. This is purportedly nothing less than "a general intervention within the field of modernity . . . both as an epistemological and political project." Bhabha, "Postcolonial Critic," p. 49.

19. See Homi Bhabha, "DissemiNation: Time, Narrative, and the Margins of the Modern Nation," in *LC,* pp. 139–170.

20. Suffice it to say that in his account of colonial ambivalence, Bhabha's attribution of subversive powers to the vicissitudes of colonial representation relies on too narrow an understanding of the historical project of colonialism, which involves more than the establishment of civility and cultural authority through the deployment of colonial symbols.

21. See Bhabha, "Postcolonial Authority," p. 59; and Homi Bhabha, "'Race,' Time, and the Revision of Modernity," in *LC,* p. 245. This closet idealism is appropriately disguised as the self-proximate ipseity of the ever-changing human body (Clifford) or as the subaltern's "affective inscription at the point of human enunciation" (Bhabha, "Postcolonial Authority," p. 59), but in both instances the hybridized body is a cultural sign in free flux, the site of autonomous dispersal and reinvention, and the ultimate act of human freedom.

22. The discussion that follows relies heavily on the scholarly work of the Budapest School philosopher György Márkus. See György Márkus, "Culture: The Making and the Make-up of a Concept (An Essay in Historical Semantics)," *Dialectical Anthropology* 18 (1993): 3–29.

23. Ibid., p. 18.

24. Immanuel Kant, *Kritik der Urteilskraft,* in *Werkausgabe,* ed. Wilhelm Weischedel, vol. 10 (Frankfurt am Main: Suhrkamp, 1968), §83, p. 390; translation from Kant, *Critique of Judgment,* trans. and ed. Werner S. Pluhar (Indianapolis: Hackett, 1987), p. 319.

25. Kant, *Kritik,* §83, p. 392; Kant, *Critique of Judgment,* p. 321.

26. Karl Marx, "The Trinity Formula," chap. 48 of *Capital: A Critique of Political Economy,* vol. 3, trans. David Fernbach (Harmondsworth: Penguin, 1991), p. 959.

27. Karl Marx and Friedrich Engels, *The German Ideology* (Moscow: Progress Publishers, 1976), p. 59.

28. Compare Johann Gottlieb Fichte, "What Is a People in the Higher Meaning

of the Word, and What Is Love of Fatherland?" Eighth Address, in *Addresses to the German Nation,* trans. R. F. Jones and G. H. Turnbull (New York: Harper and Row, 1968); and G. W. F. Hegel, *Elements of the Philosophy of Right,* trans. H. B. Nisbet, ed. Allen W. Wood (Cambridge: Cambridge University Press, 1991), §§325–328.

29. Amilcar Cabral, "National Liberation and Culture," in *Unity and Struggle: Speeches and Writings,* trans. Michael Wolfers (New York: Monthly Review Press, 1979), p. 143.

30. Valentine M. Moghadam, "Introduction: Women and Identity Politics in Theoretical and Comparative Perspective," in *Identity Politics and Women: Cultural Reassertions and Feminisms in International Perspective,* ed. Valentine M. Moghadam (Boulder, Colo.: Westview Press, 1994), p. 6. Hereafter *IP.*

31. Samir Amin, *Eurocentrism* (London: Zed, 1988), pp. xi, 124, 134, 135.

32. For a more detailed elaboration from which my sketch is drawn, see Moghadam, "Introduction," pp. 6–11.

33. Ibid., p. 8.

34. Ibid., p. 11.

35. For example, the former Malaysian prime minister, Dr. Mahathir Mohamad, has suggested that to rid itself of its "colonialised" mentality in its dealings with Western countries over social issues such as human rights abuses and corruption, Malaysia should "set up a body like Europe Watch to monitor the Europeans' index on racial discrimination, immorality and corruption." See "PM: We Can Also Tell Off the West," *The Star* (Kuala Lumpur), June 5, 1996. See Chapter 5 for a more elaborate discussion of the positions on human rights of Asian governments and NGOs from the South.

36. In the next chapter I discuss Confucian chauvinism as a form of Chinese cosmopolitanism. See, for instance, Lee Kuan Yew's lecture on June 17, 1996, at Ludwig-Maximilians University, Munich, "Asia: How It Became a Dynamo of World Economies," reprinted in *Straits Times,* June 18, 1996; and Pang Gek Choo, "East Asian Growth Depends on Its Keeping Culture of Hard Work: SM," *Straits Times,* June 18, 1996.

37. Marie-Aimée Hélie-Lucas, "Women, Nationalism, and Religion in the Algerian Liberation Struggle," in *Opening the Gates: A Century of Arab Feminist Writing,* ed. Margot Badran and Miriam Cooke (Bloomington: Indiana University Press, 1990), p. 107.

38. See M. J. Peterson, "Transnational Activity, International Society, and World Politics," *Millennium: Journal of International Studies* 21, no. 3 (1992): 377.

39. Alexander Colás, "Putting Cosmopolitanism into Practice: The Case of So-

cialist Internationalism," *Millennium: Journal of International Studies* 23, no. 3 (1994): 533.

40. See Samir Amin, *Empire of Chaos* (New York: Monthly Review Press, 1992), pp. 38–44.

41. Samir Amin, "The Social Movements in the Periphery: An End to National Liberation?" in *Transforming the Revolution: Social Movements and the World-System,* ed. Samir Amin et al. (New York: Monthly Review Press, 1990), p. 124.

42. Ibid., p. 124. See also Samir Amin, "The Asian and African Vocation of Marxism," chap. 4 of *Delinking: Towards a Polycentric World* (London: Zed, 1990).

43. Amin, "Social Movements in the Periphery," p. 127.

44. Partha Chatterjee, *Nationalist Thought and the Colonial World: A Derivative Discourse?* (London: Zed, 1986), p. 169.

45. Amin, "Social Movements in the Periphery," p. 114.

46. Noeleen Heyzer and Yao Souchou, "The State, Industrialization, and Women in Singapore," in *Transnationals and Special Economic Zones: The Experience of China and Selected ASEAN Countries,* ed. Theresa Cariño (Manila: De la Salle University Press, 1989), pp. 69–70.

47. Ibid., p. 70.

48. See Sondra Hale, "Gender, Religious Identity, and Political Mobilization in Sudan," in *IP,* p. 147.

49. Ibid., p. 150.

50. Alya Baffoun, "Feminism and Muslim Fundamentalism: The Tunisian and Algerian Cases," in *IP,* p. 174.

51. Cherifa Boutta and Doria Cherifati-Merabtine, "The Social Representation of Women in Algeria's Islamist Movement," in *IP,* p. 187.

52. Khawar Mumtaz, "Identity Politics and Women: 'Fundamentalism' and Women in Pakistan," in *IP,* p. 230.

53. Cherifa Bouatta and Doria Cherifati-Meratine, "The Social Representation of Women in Algeria's Islamist Movement," in *IP,* p. 195.

54. Nawal el-Saadawi, "The Political Challenges Facing Arab Women at the End of the Twentieth Century," in *Women of the Arab World: The Coming Challenge,* ed. Nahid Toubia (London: Zed, 1988), p. 19.

55. See Kumari Jayawardena, *Feminism and Nationalism in the Third World* (London: Zed Books, 1986).

56. Marie-Aimée Hélie-Lucas, "The Preferential Symbol for Islamic Identity: Women in Muslim Personal Laws," in *IP,* p. 398.

57. Margot Badran, "Gender Activism: Feminists and Islamists in Egypt," in *IP,* p. 207. The sentence preceding the quotation is a paraphrase of Badran.

58. Marie-Aimée Hélie-Lucas, "Bound and Gagged by the Family Code," in

Third World—Second Sex, vol. 2, ed. Miranda Davies (London: Zed, 1987), p. 11, emphasis added.

59. Marie-Aimée Hélie-Lucas, "The Preferential Symbol for Islamic Identity: Women in Muslim Personal Laws," in *IP,* p. 402, emphasis added.

60. Gita Sen, "Poverty, Economic Growth, and Gender Equity: The Asian and Pacific Experience," in *Gender, Economic Growth, and Poverty: Market Growth and State Planning in Asia and the Pacific,* ed. Noeleen Heyzer and Gita Sen (Kuala Lumpur: Asian and Pacific Development Centre, 1994), p. 50.

61. Noeleen Heyzer, "Introduction: Market, State, and Gender Equity," ibid., p. 25.

62. Ibid., p. 24.

63. Cf. Gayatri Chakravorty Spivak, "Can the Subaltern Speak?" in *Marxism and the Interpretation of Culture,* ed. Lawrence Grossberg and Cary Nelson (Urbana: University of Illinois Press, 1986), pp. 271–313.

4. Chinese Cosmopolitanism in Two Senses and Postcolonial Transnationalism

1. Tu Wei-ming, "Cultural China: The Periphery as the Center," in *The Living Tree: The Changing Meaning of Being Chinese Today,* ed. Tu Wei-ming (Palo Alto: Stanford University Press, 1994), p. 13. "External China" and "Greater China" are other names for these Chinas outside China. For "External China" *(Waihua Zhengce),* see Wang Gungwu, "External China as a New Policy Area," in *China and the Chinese Overseas* (Singapore: Times Academic Press, 1991), pp. 222–239. The concept of "Greater China" is discussed in a special issue of *China Quarterly,* no. 136 (December 1993). The three distinct themes subsumed under this rubric are the rise of a transnational Chinese economy, the rise of global Chinese culture, and the project of a reunified Chinese state. See, in that issue, Harry Harding, "The Concept of 'Greater China': Themes, Variations, and Reservations," pp. 660–686.

2. For Tu, as for many others, the Pacific Century is markedly Chinese. Cf. David Shambaugh, "Introduction: The Emergence of "Greater China," *China Quarterly,* no. 136 (December 1993): 653, who suggests that in the twenty-first century, Greater China will overtake Japan as the dominant economic power in East Asia, and will be the world's leading trader and possess the world's largest foreign exchange reserves.

3. For Tu, most mainland Chinese intellectuals are in crisis because they view the Confucian heritage of traditional Chinese culture as incompatible with modernity and modernization. The emergence of the Asian dragons is a

godsend because it indicates that Confucianism not only is compatible with capitalist modernization but can in fact lead to a better path of capitalist development. However, the link between Confucianism and East Asian capitalism remains ambiguous. There is a weaker thesis that East Asian capitalism indicates that Confucianism does not impede capitalist development and also a stronger thesis that Confucianism is a necessary and sufficient condition of East Asian capitalist success.

4. Tu, "Cultural China," pp. 32–33.

5. Ibid., p. 8, emphasis added. From the historical fact that the Southeast Asian Chinese are the facilitators of intraregional trade in the Asian Pacific, Tu spuriously infers that they are the best example of the ethos of Chinese mercantilism. He also conflates the Confucian ethos with Chinese mercantilism. For a similar argument, see Ronald Skeldon, "Migrants on a Global Stage," in *Pacific Rim Development: Integration and Globalisation in the Asia-Pacific Economy,* ed. Peter J. Rimmer (St. Leonards: Allen and Unwin, 1997), pp. 222–239.

6. Anti-Chinese violence was not confined to the capital but also occurred in other towns on Java. For more details on the role played by the Indonesian army in instigating anti-Chinese violence, see John McBeth, "Shadow Play," *Far Eastern Economic Review,* July 23, 1998, pp. 23–27; I. Sandyawan Sumardi, "Mass Rape in the Recent Riots: The Climax of an Uncivilized Act in the Nation's Life," report by Tim Relawan untuk Kemanusiaan (Volunteers for Humanity), Jakarta, July 13, 1998; and "Condition of Our Shared Life: The May 1998 Tragedy in Indonesia," report by Tim Relawan untuk Kemanusiaan, Jakarta, July 28, 1998. My thanks to Douglas Kammen for giving me access to these Jakarta sources.

7. The uprising has been described as "a national reawakening" and "another independence day" (*Far Eastern Economic Review,* June 4, 1998, p. 21) and also as "Indonesia's May Revolution" (ibid., May 28, 1998, cover).

8. The Chinese foreign minister, Tang Jiaxuan, expressed official concern about the situation of Indonesian Chinese and called upon the Indonesian government to punish the rioters. He placed emphasis on the indelible contributions of the Chinese Indonesians to Indonesia's economic development and social progress. See "Indonesia Called On to Punish Rioters," *China Daily,* August 5, 1998, p. 1.

9. In 1998 ethnic Chinese made up 3.5 percent of the Indonesian population. Yet they owned nine of the top ten business groups and controlled more than 80 percent of the assets in the top three hundred groups. Thirteen of the top fifteen taxpayers in Indonesia were ethnic Chinese. Even the less prosperous Chinese were a target of resentment because they controlled most of the local economic activity. See Salil Tripathi and Ben Dolven,

"Shattered Confidence: Ethnic-Chinese Hold the Key to Economic Revival," *Far Eastern Economic Review,* May 28, 1998, pp. 20–23; and Margot Cohen, "Turning Point: Indonesia's Chinese Face a Hard Choice," ibid., July 30, 1998, pp. 12–18.

10. Jacqueline Co, "'Democracy' at Work in Crime," *Tulay,* December 4, 1995, cited in Caroline S. Hau, "Kidnapping, Citizenship, and the Chinese," *Public Policy* 1, no. 1 (1997): 62. Hau's article is a brilliant analysis of the conflation of the Chinese and capital in the contemporary Philippines.

11. Max Weber, *The Religion of China: Confucianism and Taoism,* trans. Hans H. Gerth (Glencoe, Ill.: Free Press, 1951), p. 235. For a fuller discussion of Weber's position on Confucianism and its place within his sociology of religion, see Wolfgang Schlucter, "World Adjustment: Max Weber on Confucianism and Taoism," in *The Triadic Chord: Confucian Ethics, Industrial East Asia, and Max Weber,* ed. Tu Wei-ming (Singapore: Institute of East Asian Philosophies, 1991), pp. 3–52.

12. Weber, *The Religion of China,* p. 237.

13. Weber suggests that Chinese religion as a whole, whether represented by the personalist principle of Taoist mysticism or the impersonal rationalization of Confucian bureaucracy, repeatedly ties the individual to the sib and prevents the rationalizing of religious-practical ethics. Ibid., pp. 236–237.

14. See, for instance, Benjamin Nelson, "Civilizational Complexes and Intercivilizational Encounters," in *On the Roads to Modernity: Conscience, Science, and Civilizations. Selected Writings by Benjamin Nelson,* ed. Toby Huff (Totowa, N.J.: Rowman and Littlefield, 1981), pp. 80–106. In its initial formulation in comparative sociology, the issue of Confucian rationalism is tied to the question of modern science *qua* universal world science. The un-cosmopolitan, parochial nature of Chinese culture is used to explain why a universal science developed only in the West. Later this cultural explanation is inserted into the discursive domain of political economy and used to secure theories of underdevelopment. Capitalist modernization is then explicitly coded as Westernization.

15. See Joseph R. Levenson, *Revolution and Cosmopolitanism: The Western Stage and the Chinese Stages* (Berkeley: University of California Press, 1971), pp. 2–5. Cf. Myron Cohen, "Being Chinese: The Peripheralization of Traditional Identity," in Tu, *The Living Tree,* pp. 101–102.

16. See Levenson, *Revolution and Cosmopolitanism,* p. 25: "Though Chinese left home in great numbers, no one had any Confucian pretensions to be bearing out a Word. Now, however, the new China was a Word for the world, beginning with all its Bolivias. China commends itself as a model of revolution. The model applies, allegedly, because all 'peoples" (i.e., all victims of imperialists) are brothers." Nelson makes a similar comment about

the Cultural Revolution and Maoist thought, which he regards as crucial to the spreading of the new universalities of nation and peoplehood that will undermine traditional particularisms (*On the Roads to Modernity,* p. 91).

17. Tu, "Cultural China," p. 7, emphasis added. Note that in the quoted passage the different nations of East Asia are homogenized into "the 'Post-Confucian' region," which is then conflated with Chineseness.

18. Wu Teh Yao, "Opening Remarks," in Tu, *The Triadic Chord,* p. xviii. As the prefatory remarks to the Proceedings of the 1987 Singapore Conference on Confucian Ethics and the Modernisation of Industrial East Asia, these words have the weighty tone of a manifesto. See also, in the same volume, Wu Teh Yao, "The Confucian Concept and Attributes of Man and the Modernisation of Industrial Asia," pp. 397–413.

19. Tu, "Cultural China," p. 8.

20. The literature on this topic is voluminous and comes from numerous conferences sponsored by U.S. think tanks and East and Southeast Asian states since the mid-1980s. See, for instance, Peter L. Berger and Hsin-Huang Michael Hsiao, eds., *In Search of an East Asian Development Model* (New Brunswick, N.J.: Transaction Books, 1988); and Hung-chao Tai, ed., *Confucianism and Development: An Oriental Alternative?* (Washington, D.C.: Washington Institute Press, 1989). For critical views of this argument that are attentive to the text of global capital, see Arif Dirlik, "Confucius in the Borderlands: Global Capitalism and the Reinvention of Confucianism," *boundary 2* 22, no. 3 (Fall 1995): 229–273; and Aihwa Ong, *Flexible Citizenship: The Cultural Logics of Transnationality* (Durham: Duke University Press, 1999).

21. See Wang Gungwu, "The Culture of Chinese Merchants," in *China and the Chinese Overseas* (Singapore: Times Academic Press, 1991), pp. 181–197.

22. Wang Gungwu, "The Chinese as Immigrants and Settlers: Singapore," ibid., p. 172.

23. See Wang Gungwu, "Little Dragons on the Confucian Periphery," ibid., p. 312.

24. See Wang Gungwu, "Among Non-Chinese," in Tu, *The Living Tree,* p. 129.

25. J. S. Furnivall, *Colonial Policy and Practice: A Comparative Study of Burma and Netherlands India* (New York: New York University Press, 1956), p. 304.

26. Michel Foucault, *Discipline and Punish: The Birth of the Prison,* trans. Alan Sheridan (Harmondsworth: Penguin, 1979), p. 201.

27. Benedict Anderson, "Recensement et politique en Asie du Sud-est," *Genèses* 26 (April 1997): 68–69. The "translation" is from Anderson's original English manuscript.

28. James Rush, "Placing the Chinese in Java on the Eve of the Twentieth Century," *Indonesia* (1991): 17–19, special issue, "The Role of the Indonesian Chinese in Shaping Modern Indonesian Life."

29. For an insightful discussion of the various censuses of the Spanish Philippines and the Dutch East Indies, see Anderson, "Recensement et politique en Asie du Sud-est." Anderson notes that in the Philippines, the word used to refer to those whom the English called Chinese, the French *chinois,* and the Dutch *chinees* was the nonracial term *sangley,* which comes from the Hokkien word *sengli,* meaning "trade" (p. 62, note 8).

30. See W. F. Wertheim, "The Trading Minorities in Southeast Asia," in *East-West Parallels: Sociological Approaches to Modern Asia* (Chicago: Quadrangle Books, 1965), pp. 39–82.

31. Ibid., p. 47.

32. Ibid., pp. 54–55.

33. Ibid., pp. 76, 78. Cf. Allen Chun, "Pariah Capitalism and the Overseas Chinese of Southeast Asia: Problems in the Definition of the Problem," *Ethnic and Racial Studies* 12, no. 2 (April 1989): 254.

34. The classic formulation comes from Karl Marx and Friedrich Engels, *The German Ideology* (Moscow: Progress Publishers, 1976), p. 42.

35. This becomes clear in Lukács's suggestion that the "falseness" of bourgeois class consciousness is not simply empirical or veridical in nature but "implies a class-conditioned *unconsciousness* of one's own socio-historical and economic condition." Georg Lukács, *History and Class Consciousness,* trans. Rodney Livingstone (Cambridge, Mass.: MIT Press, 1971), p. 52. Lukács adds that classes unable to organize society in accordance with their interests "are normally condemned to passivity" (p. 52).

36. Jacques Derrida, *Specters of Marx: The State of the Debt, the Work of Mourning, and the New International,* trans. Peggy Kamuf (New York: Routledge, 1994), p. 126.

37. See, for instance, Prasenjit Duara, "Nationalists among Transnationals: Overseas Chinese and the Idea of China, 1900–1911," in Ong and Nonini, *Ungrounded Empires,* pp. 39–60.

38. See Wang Gungwu, "The Origins of Hua-Ch'iao," in *Community and Nation: China, Southeast Asia, and Australia* (St. Leonards: Allen and Unwin, 1992), pp. 1–10; Wang, "Patterns of Chinese Migration in Historical Perspective" and "Southeast Asian Huaqiao in Chinese History-Writing," in *China and the Chinese Overseas,* pp. 1–21 and 22–40, respectively. Sun Yat-sen characterized the *huaqiao* as "the mother of the revolution." Wang, *China and the Chinese Overseas,* p. 246.

39. See Wang, *China and the Chinese Overseas,* p. 176: "The term Huaqiao became closely linked with the expanding emotions about the Chinese na-

tion and the new republican state which all patriotic Chinese were called upon to support."

40. See Wang Gungwu, "The Study of Chinese Identities in Southeast Asia," in *China and the Chinese Overseas,* pp. 200–201.

41. Wang, *China and the Chinese Overseas,* p. 138.

42. Ibid., p. 199.

43. For instance, in 1966 the Indonesian government prohibited use of the Chinese language. Chinese schools were shut, Chinese characters were forbidden, and Chinese newspapers were banned following accusations that the Beijing-supported Indonesian Communist Party was behind the October coup. All ethnic Chinese became suspect. Suharto's aim was to depoliticize the ethnic Chinese so that they could devote themselves to moneymaking. For a more thorough discussion, see Benedict Anderson, "Old State, New Society: Indonesia's New Order in Comparative Historical Perspective," in *Language and Power: Exploring Political Cultures in Indonesia* (Ithaca: Cornell University Press, 1990), p. 116; and James Mackie, "Towkays and Tycoons: The Chinese in Indonesian Economic Life in the 1920s and 1980s," *Indonesia* (1991): 83–96.

44. For a discussion of the heterogeneity of the diasporic Chinese in Malaysia, see Donald Nonini, "Shifting Identities, Positioned Imaginaries: Transnational Traversals and Reversals by Malaysian Chinese," in *Ungrounded Empires: The Cultural Politics of Modern Chinese Transnationalism,* pp. 203–227.

45. Ong, *Flexible Citizenship,* p. 72.

46. Wang, "Among Non-Chinese," pp. 131–132, emphasis added.

47. Chris GoGwilt, "Pramoedya's Fiction and History: An Interview with Pramoedya Ananta Toer," *Kabar Seberang* 24/25, *Essays to Honour Pramoedya Ananta Toer's Seventieth Year* (1995): 14.

48. Ninotchka Rosca, *State of War* (New York: Norton, 1988), pp. 336–337, 192.

49. Ibid., p. 149.

50. Anna's great-grandmother puts it this way: "Soon we will forget everything . . . and if we forget, how are we to proceed?" Ibid., p. 186.

51. Ibid., p. 291.

52. Ibid., p. 292.

53. For an extended study of the Buru Quartet, see Pheng Cheah, *Spectral Nationality: Passages of Freedom from Kant to Postcolonial Literatures of Liberation* (New York: Columbia University Press, 2003), chaps. 6–7. The third and fourth volumes give an account of the anti-Chinese boycotts and riots of 1921, and the enmity between the Chinese and the Sarekat Islam, the most important organization within the native awakening. For a brief ac-

count of the events that culminate in the suspension of the Sarekat's activities on August 10, 1912, see Takashi Shiraishi, *An Age in Motion: Popular Radicalism in Java, 1912–1916* (Ithaca: Cornell University Press, 1990), pp. 45–48.

54. See Pramoedya Ananta Toer, *Rumah Kaca* (Kuala Lumpur: Wira Karya, 1990), pp. 124–125; Pramoedya, *House of Glass*, trans. Max Lane (Victoria, Australia: Penguin, 1992), p. 117.

55. Pramoedya Ananta Toer, *Child of All Nations*, trans. Max Lane (New York: Penguin, 1996), p. 85.

56. Ibid., p. 87.

57. Ibid.. Khouw also describes the Filipinos as "great teachers for the other conquered peoples of Asia. They were the founders of the first Asian republic" (p. 88).

58. Pramoedya Ananta Toer, *Footsteps*, trans. Max Lane (Victoria, Australia: Penguin, 1990), p. 52.

59. The PRC became more wary of the term *huaqiao* after the Bandung Conference of 1955 and has distinguished between foreign Chinese and overseas Chinese, that is, foreign nationals of Chinese descent and the small number of Chinese nationals who live abroad. Taiwan, however, has retained the broad sense of *huaqiao*. See Wang, *China and the Chinese Overseas*, pp. 223, 287–290. For a schematic account of the relationship between the PRC government and the Chinese overseas up to the present period, see Wang Gungwu, "Greater China and the Chinese Overseas," *China Quarterly*, no. 136 (December 1993): 938–939.

60. Cf. Wang Gungwu's interesting argument that mercantilism has always been the fundamental feature of Chinese emigration, and that *huaqiao* cosmopolitanism was only a temporary blurring of this basic pattern that reemerged as dominant with the decline of the latter. Wang, *China and the Chinese Overseas*, pp. 10–12. For an account of the spectacular contemporary use of overseas Chinese voluntary associations to create and maintain transnational business networks as well as strengthening the ties of the Southeast Asian Chinese with their ancestral hometowns, which are the sites of foreign investment, see Hong Liu, "Old Linkages, New Networks: The Globalization of Overseas Chinese Voluntary Associations and Its Implications," *China Quarterly*, no. 155 (September 1998): 582–609.

61. For a succinct general description of these inflows to Southeast Asia and their contribution to the financial crisis of the late 1990s, see Benedict Anderson, "Sauve Qui Peut," in *The Spectre of Comparisons: Nationalism, Southeast Asia, and the World* (London: Verso, 1998), pp. 299–317.

62. Andre Gunder Frank, *Capitalism and Underdevelopment in Latin America* (New York: Monthly Review Press, 1969).

63. It is interesting to observe that Chinese mobilization in post-Suharto Indonesia seeks to reverse the previous three decades of de-politicization and discrimination. The Partai Reformasi Tionghua Indonesia took pains to distance itself from ethnic Chinese tycoons and conglomerates that lived off Suharto's largesse. "The party's economic proposals include establishing cooperatives and holding companies involving both Chinese and pribumis. These would be vehicles for transferring business skills to pribumis, for example through apprenticeship and mentoring programmes." Cohen, "Turning Point," p. 14. Is this a partial revival of the generosity of *huaqiao* cosmopolitanism?

64. In his famous visit to South China in January 1992, Deng Xiaoping had called for the construction of a few Hong Kongs. After 1992, overseas Chinese investment, which had earlier been concentrated in the South China economic periphery, expanded into the interior provinces of Hubei and Sichuan and the Northeast beyond Beijing. See Wang, "Greater China and the Chinese Overseas," pp. 930–931.

65. Aihwa Ong notes this and other contradictory views of the overseas Chinese held by mainlanders in *Flexible Citizenship*, pp. 46–48.

5. Posit(ion)ing Human Rights in the Current Global Conjuncture

1. See, for instance, Karl Marx, "On the Jewish Question," in *Early Writings* (Harmondsworth: Penguin, 1975), pp. 211–241. For an incisive discussion of Marx's critique of rights, see Claude Lefort, "Politics and Human Rights," in *The Political Forms of Modern Society: Bureaucracy, Democracy, Totalitarianism* (Cambridge: Polity Press, 1986), pp. 239–272.

2. Adamantia Pollis and Peter Schwab, "Human Rights: A Western Construct with Limited Applicability," in *Human Rights: Cultural and Ideological Perspectives,* ed. Pollis and Schwab (New York: Praeger, 1979), p. 17.

3. Marnia Lazreg, "Human Rights, State, and Ideology: An Historical Perspective," in Pollis and Schwab, *Human Rights,* p. 34.

4. Statement by Wong Kan Seng, Minister of Foreign Affairs of the Republic of Singapore, Vienna, June 16, 1993, reprinted in *Human Rights and International Relations in the Asia Pacific,* ed. James Tang (London: Pinter, 1995), p. 243.

5. First-generation rights are primarily civil and political rights. They are basically negative rights that protect the individual from arbitrary state action and are associated with Western liberal democracies. They are said to have their roots in the French and American revolutions and are articulated in the Universal Declaration of Human Rights and the International

Covenant on Civil and Political Rights. Second-generation rights are social, economic, and cultural rights. They are positive rights associated with socialist states and are said to have their roots in the socialist revolutions of the early twentieth century. They are specifically articulated in the International Covenant on Social, Economic, and Cultural Rights. The covenants were not ratified by the UN General Assembly until 1966. Third-generation rights are summed up under the right to development and are rooted in post–Second World War anticolonialist revolutions, which led to decolonization in the period from 1947 to 1974. The right to development is implicit in Articles 55 and 56 of the UN Charter and Articles 22 and 27 of the Universal Declaration of Human Rights. In June 1979 the UN Commission on Human Rights resolved that the right to development is a human right. Most developed countries (Denmark, Finland, Germany, Iceland, Israel, Japan, Sweden, and the United Kingdom) abstained from voting on the Declaration on the Right to Development. Canada and Australia adopted a compromise position and voted in favor. The United States voted against it. For an overview of the politics involved in the ratification of these rights and their pertinence in a cold war and post–Cold War scenario, see Brenda Cossman, "Reform, Revolution, or Retrenchment? International Human Rights in the Post–Cold War Era," *Harvard International Law Journal* 32, no. 2 (Spring 1991): 339–352. For a discussion on how the right to development relates to the other two types of rights, whether the right to development is an instrumental or third-generation right or a resultant/consequential right, and whether it refers to the development of the individual or the state, see R. N. Treverdi, "Overview of International Human Rights Law in Theory and Practice: Its Linkages to Access to Justice at the Domestic Level," in *Access to Justice: The Struggle for Human Rights in South-East Asia,* Harry Scoble and Laurie Weisberg, eds. (London: Zed, 1985), pp. 27–30.

6. On contemporary Asian capitalism, see Ruth McVey, ed., *Southeast Asian Capitalists* (Ithaca: Cornell Southeast Asia Program, 1992); and McVey, "Asia's Competing Capitalisms," *The Economist,* June 24, 1995, pp. 16–17.

7. Jane Perlez, "Asian Leaders Find China a More Cordial Neighbor," *New York Times,* October 18, 2003.

8. See Edward Gargan, "An Asian Giant Spreads Roots," *New York Times,* November 14, 1995, pp. D1, D4; and Gargan, "Asia Guide Calls Local Partners Key to Success," *New York Times,* November 14, 1995, p. D4.

9. James Rohwer, author of *Asia Rising: Why America Will Prosper as Asia's Economies Boom,* quoted in *New York Times,* November 14, 1995, p. D4.

10. David Sanger, "Real Politics: Why Suharto Is In and Castro Is Out," *New York Times,* October 31, 1995, p. A3.

11. James Tang rightly observes that "the post–Cold War confrontation between East Asia and the West over human rights . . . has to be understood in the context of the spectacular economic development in the Asia-Pacific region." He notes that "some East Asian states seem to have drawn the conclusion that the East Asian model of development has proved to be more successful than the Western model" and have asserted "that their political systems and economic policies are better than the Western political models, and can offer an alternative vision of the values needed for a better world." See James Tang, "Human Rights in the Asia-Pacific Region: Competing Perspectives, International Discord, and the Way Ahead," in *Human Rights and International Relations in the Asia Pacific*, p. 2.

12. See H. L. A. Hart, *The Concept of Law* (Oxford: Clarendon Press, 1961).

13. On the relation between law and morals in legal positivism, see ibid., chap. 9.

14. For elaborations of political morality and public sphere, see, respectively, Ronald Dworkin, *Law's Empire* (London: Fontana, 1986), chap. 6; and Jürgen Habermas, *The Structural Transformation of the Public Sphere* (Cambridge, Mass.: MIT Press, 1989).

15. "Public" in "public international law" is a sociological term designating the realm of state activity as opposed to the private realm of the actions of individuals. The sociological use of the term should not be confused with the normative notion of the public sphere (*Öffentlichkeit*), which lies resolutely within the private realm since it is the public sphere *of* civil society.

16. For an analogous justification of basic human rights from the standpoint of liberal political philosophy, see John Rawls, *The Law of Peoples* (Cambridge, Mass.: Harvard University Press, 1999).

17. G. W. F. Hegel, *Grundlinien der Philosophie des Rechts*, ed. Eva Moldenhauer and Karl Markus Michel (Frankfurt am Main: Suhrkamp, 1970), §330, p. 497; translation from Hegel, *Elements of the Philosophy of Right*, ed. Allen W. Wood, trans. H. B. Nisbet (Cambridge: Cambridge University Press, 1991), p. 366. Hereafter *PR*, cited parenthetically in the text, with page references first from the German, then from the translation, modified where appropriate.

18. Louis Henkin, "Constitutionalism and Human Rights," in *Constitutionalism and Right: The Influence of the United States Constitution Abroad*, ed. Louis Henkin and Albert J. Rosenthal (New York: Columbia University Press, 1990), p. 388.

19. See also Étienne Balibar, "'Rights of Man' and 'Rights of Citizen': The Modern Dialectic of Equality and Freedom" and "What Is a Politics of the Rights of Man?" in *Masses, Classes, and Ideas: Studies on Politics and Philosophy before and after Marx* (New York: Routledge, 1994), pp. 39–59 and

205–225, respectively, for a similar argument about the risky, open-ended, and nonnatural nature of human rights based on a reading of the 1789 Declaration of the Rights of Man and of the Citizen.

20. Immanuel Kant, *Grundlegung zur Metaphysik der Sitten,* in *Werkausgabe,* vol. 7, ed. Wilhelm Weischedel (Frankfurt am Main: Suhrkamp, 1996), pp. 59–60, Ak. 4:428–429; translation from Kant, *Groundwork of the Metaphysics of Morals,* in *Practical Philosophy,* trans. and ed. Mary J. Gregor (Cambridge: Cambridge University Press, 1996), p. 79.

21. Kant, *Grundlegung zur Metaphysik der Sitten,* p. 68, Ak. 4:435; Kant, *Groundwork of the Metaphysics of Morals,* p. 84.

22. Wong Kan Seng, "The Real World of Human Rights," in Tang, *Human Rights and International Relations,* p. 245.

23. Bangkok Declaration, March 29, 1993, reprinted in Tang, *Human Rights and International Relations,* p. 204.

24. Bangkok Declaration, p. 205.

25. *PR,* §331, pp. 498–499/366–367.

26. *PR,* §337R, pp. 501–502/370.

27. *PR,* §333R, p. 500/368.

28. Bangkok NGO Declaration and Response to the Bangkok Declaration, March 29 and April 3, 1993, reprinted in Tang, *Human Rights and International Relations,* p. 209.

29. See Julie Peters and Andrea Wolper, eds., *Women's Rights, Human Rights: International Feminist Perspectives* (New York: Routledge, 1995).

30. See Arati Rao, "The Politics of Gender and Culture in International Human Rights Discourse," ibid., pp. 167–175.

31. See Rhoda E. Howard, "Women's Rights and the Right to Development," ibid., pp. 301–313.

32. Tang, *Human Rights and International Relations,* p. 209.

33. For instance, in his analytical account of an alternative (Asian) normative theory of human rights which respects cultural diversity, Joseph Chan makes repeated appeals to the good faith of rational collective actors at various levels. See Joseph Chan, "The Asian Challenge to Universal Human Rights: A Philosophical Appraisal," in Tang, *Human Rights and International Relations,* pp. 25–38.

34. See Dieter Henrich, "The Contexts of Autonomy: Some Presuppositions of the Comprehensibility of Human Rights," in *Aesthetic Judgment and the Moral Image of the World* (Palo Alto: Stanford University Press, 1992), p. 84: "If one advocates rights generally, it must be because of their universal validity. But then, it must be possible to clarify rights within the context of other cultures and traditions—which again implies that we acknowledge their incompatibility with some forms of life and self-image. Never-

theless, it would have to be shown that real possibilities of life are opened up within their context—and not just those from which the political institutions of the West arose."

35. This causal dependence exists even though human rights considerations are not technically part of trade negotiations, as in the case of China's preferential trade status or its admission into the World Trade Organization. See David E. Sanger, "U.S. Again Tries a Trade Issue as a Carrot and Stick for Beijing," *New York Times,* December 15, 1995, p. A7 (quoting an unnamed Clinton administration official): "'But we are now sending them the message that while human rights is not explicitly part of the negotiations, it is part of the atmosphere, and they are ignoring that at their peril.'"

36. Carlos M. Correa, *Intellectual Property Rights, the WTO, and Developing Countries: The TRIPS Agreement and Policy Options* (Penang, Malaysia: Third World Network, 2000), p. 5.

37. See Chakravarthi Raghavan, *Recolonization: GATT, the Uruguay Round, and the Third World* (Penang: Third World Network, 1990), pp. 38–40. This discussion is a summary of the argument of Raghavan's book.

38. Vandana Shiva, "Biodiversity: A Third World Perspective," in *Monocultures of the Mind: Biodiversity, Biotechnology, and the Third World* (Penang: Third World Network, 1993), p. 80.

39. Vandana Shiva, "Biotechnology and the Environment," ibid., pp. 122–123.

40. See Reginald Chua, "Take Proven Path to Growth, SM Urges Manila," *Straits Times,* November 18, 1992, p. 2. In the next chapter we will see how the entry of Singaporean capital into the Philippines forms a crucial subtext in the uproar over the violation of the human rights of foreign female domestic workers ignited by the hanging of Flor Contemplacion.

41. I have discussed the limits of the normative concept of the public sphere in Chapter 2 of this book and in "Violent Light: The Idea of Publicness in Modern Philosophy and in Global Neocolonialism," *Social Text* 43 (Fall 1995): 163–190.

42. For "global civil society" and the limitations of the concept, see Martin Shaw, "Civil Society and Global Politics: Beyond a Social Movements Approach," *Millennium: Journal of International Studies* 23, no. 3 (1994): 647–667.

43. Cf. M. J. Peterson, "Transnational Activity, International Society, and World Politics," *Millennium: Journal of International Studies* 21, no. 3 (1992): 386: "Societal actors need states. Though political philosophers and visionaries have looked for alternate institutions, a state or something like it appears necessary to provide minimal security, guarantee property rights and help enforce contracts—all three of which are necessary to the good functioning of civil society and the activities of its members."

44. Shaw, "Civil Society and Global Politics," p. 655.

45. To give two examples, Vandana Shiva points out that "sustainable development" and "the Green Revolution" have been co-opted by TNCs and the World Bank in their drive toward biodiversity-destroying agricultural modernization. In his discussion of the precariousness of people's diplomacy in the Philippines, Francisco Nemenzo points to the paradox whereby the appeals of people's diplomacy to world public opinion to place pressure on the government to respect human rights are less effective as a result of the benign image of the Ramos/Aquino regime in the international media and the decline in U.S. interest in the Philippines because of the loss of American military bases. See Francisco Nemenzo, "People's Diplomacy and Human Rights: The Philippines Experience," in Tang, *Human Rights and International Relations,* pp. 112–124.

46. Rao, "The Politics of Gender," p. 171.

47. Ibid., emphasis added.

48. Benedict Anderson, introduction to *Southeast Asian Tribal Groups and Ethnic Minorities: Cultural Survival Report* 22 (1987): 11.

49. Jacques Derrida, "Declarations of Independence," *New Political Science* 15 (Summer 1986): 9–10.

50. *Rural Development and Human Rights in South East Asia* (Penang: International Commission of Jurists and Consumer Association of Penang, 1982), pp. 173–174.

51. Nicholas J. Wheeler, "Pluralist or Solidarist Conceptions of International Society: Bull and Vincent on Humanitarian Intervention," *Millennium: Journal of International Studies* 21, no. 3 (1992): 476.

52. *PR,* §340, p. 503/371.

53. As the Budapest School philosopher György Márkus points out, this is an aestheticizing conception of normativity that reconciles the historicity of origin and universal validity of norms through an analogy with the historical embeddedness and atemporal significance of classical works of art. See György Márkus, "Political Philosophy as Phenomenology: On the Method of the Hegelian 'Philosophy of Right,'" *Thesis Eleven* 48 (February 1997): 1–19.

54. *PR,* §340, p. 503/371.

55. *PR,* §347, pp. 505–506/374.

56. See Fredric Jameson, "Cognitive Mapping," in *Marxism and the Interpretation of Culture,* ed. Cary Nelson and Lawrence Grossberg (Urbana: University of Illinois Press, 1988), pp. 347–360; and more generally Jameson, *Postmodernism, or the Cultural Logic of Late Capitalism* (Durham: Duke University Press, 1991).

57. Derrida has developed this infinite idea of justice into an account of a

New International based on the notion of a global democracy to come. See Jacques Derrida, *Specters of Marx: The State of the Debt, the Work of Mourning, and the New International,* trans. Peggy Kamuf (New York: Routledge, 1994). His New International is rather feeble because it is not institutionally grounded. In contradistinction, I am using Derrida's notion of justice-in-violation to flesh out an account of the normativity of existing human rights practical discourse.

58. Jacques Derrida, "Force of Law: 'The Mystical Foundation of Authority,'" *Cardozo Law Review* 11 (1990): 965. Hereafter FL, cited parenthetically in the text.

59. Jacques Derrida, *Given Time,* vol. 1, *Counterfeit Money,* trans. Peggy Kamuf (Chicago: University of Chicago Press, 1992), p. 30.

60. For the methodological presupposition of the general text, see Jacques Derrida, "Politics and Friendship," in *The Althusserian Legacy,* ed. E. Ann Kaplan and Michael Sprinker (New York: Verso, 1993), p. 223: "*Différance,* the necessary reference to the other, the impossibility for a presence to gather itself in a self-identity or substantiality, compels one to inscribe the reality effect in a general textuality or differential process which, again, is not limited to language."

6. "Bringing into the Home a Stranger Far More Foreign"

1. Saskia Sassen, *Globalization and Its Discontents* (New York: New Press, 1998), pp. xx, 95–100.

2. Michael Hardt and Antonio Negri, *Empire* (Cambridge, Mass.: Harvard University Press, 2000), p. 397.

3. Ibid., p. 400.

4. Concentrating on labor migration between different Southeast Asian countries takes us away from the pervasive prejudice that only countries of the North Atlantic are major agents of economic growth and foreign investment. This has the added advantage of showing us that Asian countries can be engaged in growth and also develop at the expense of and by exploiting migrant labor from other Asian countries. It also takes us beyond the mesmerizing model of migration to the centers of the North Atlantic, which are governed by established discourses of multiculturalism.

5. See Nicole Constable, *Maid to Order in Hong Kong: Stories of Filipina Workers* (Ithaca: Cornell University Press, 1997); and Rhacel Salazar Parreñas, *Servants of Globalization: Women, Migration, and Domestic Work* (Palo Alto: Stanford University Press, 2001).

6. Loo Bee Geok, "Preface: They Too Are Human Beings," in *I Am a Filipino Maid* (Singapore: Path Seekers, 1989), p. 6.

7. Christine Chin, *In Service and Servitude: Foreign Female Domestic Workers and the Malaysian "Modernity" Project* (New York: Columbia University Press, 1998), pp. 205–206.

8. In this and the next chapter I have given fictitious names to the FDWs (foreign domestic workers), employers, and employment agents. The names of diplomats and representatives of church groups have not been changed.

9. See, for instance, "PM Goh's Vision of a New Era for Singapore: Civil Society Needed to Mobilise People's Talents" (Prime Minister Goh Chok Tong's parliamentary speech on Singapore 21), *Straits Times*, June 7, 1997; "Singapore of the Future" (extract from Deputy Prime Minister Lee Hsien Loong's book *Singapore: Re-engineering Success*), *Straits Times*, November 8, 1998; and "The Art of Politics in Singapore" (interview with Trade and Industry Minister George Yeo), *Straits Times*, November 26, 2001.

10. See Richard Florida, *The Rise of the Creative Class: And How It's Transforming Work, Leisure, Community, and Everyday Life* (New York: Basic Books, 2002); and Wayne Arnold, "Quietly, Singapore Lifts Its Ban on Hiring Gays," *International Herald Tribune*, July 4, 2003.

11. C. W. Stahl, "South-North Migration in the Asia-Pacific Region," *International Migration* 29, no. 2 (June 1991): 178.

12. See Folker Fröbel, Jürgen Heinrichs, and Otto Kreye, *The New International Division of Labour* (Cambridge: Cambridge University Press, 1980); Scott Lash and John Urry, *The End of Organised Capitalism* (Cambridge: Polity, 1987); and David Harvey, *The Condition of Postmodernity: An Enquiry into the Origins of Cultural Change* (Cambridge, Mass.: Blackwell, 1990).

13. For a succinct account of this shift from import-substitution industrialization to export-oriented industrialization in Southeast Asia, see Richard Robison, Richard Higgott, and Kevin Hewison, "Crisis in Economic Strategy in the 1980s: The Factors at Work," in *Southeast Asia in the 1980s: The Politics of Economic Crisis,* ed. Robison, Higgott, and Hewison (Sydney: Allen and Unwin, 1987), pp. 1–15. The quotation is from p. 5.

14. For accounts of the relationship between foreign investment in the electronics industry and development in Southeast Asia, see J. W. Henderson, "The New International Division of Labor and American Semiconductor Production in Southeast Asia," in *Multinational Corporations and the Third World,* ed. C. J. Dixon, David Drakakis-Smith, and H. D. Watts (Boulder, Colo.: Westview, 1986), pp. 91–117; and Jeffrey Henderson, "Electronics Industries and the Developing World: Uneven Contributions and Uncertain Prospects," in *Capitalism and Development,* ed. Leslie Sklair (London: Routledge, 1994), pp. 258–288.

15. In Singapore, foreign investment in gross fixed assets in the manufacturing sector rose from S$52.672 billion in 1998 to S$78.386 billion in 2001. Foreign investment in financial and insurance services rose from S$53.000 billion to S$79.919 billion in the same period. Singapore Department of Statistics, *http://www.singstat.gov.sg/keystats/surveys/fei2001.pdf.* The value of direct industrial exports, which was merely S$1.523 billion in 1970, grew to S$213.883 billion by 2003. See *http://www.singstat.gov.sg/keystats/ economy.html#trade.* It should be noted, however, that unlike other countries undergoing development, Singapore does not have a large peasant and agricultural labor population.

16. Henderson, "The New International Division of Labor," pp. 100–102.

17. The desired forms of manufacture include specialty chemicals and pharmaceuticals, precision engineering equipment, and optical instruments and equipment. See Garry Rodan, "The Rise and Fall of Singapore's Second Industrial Revolution," in *Southeast Asia in the 1980s: The Politics of Economic Crisis,* ed. Richard Robison et al. (Sydney: Allen and Unwin, 1987), p. 158. On the importance of the strong Singaporean state and its neutralization of unionized labor, see Garry Rodan, "Industrialisation and the Singapore State in the Context of the New International Division of Labour," in Robison, Higgott, and Hewison, *Southeast Asia,* pp. 172–94; and Jeffrey Henderson, "Changing International Division of Labour in the Electronics Industry," in *Regionalization and Labour Market Interdependence in East and Southeast Asia,* ed. Duncan Campbell, Aurelio Parisotto, and Anil Verma (New York: St. Martin's Press, 1997), pp. 109–110.

18. Rodan, "The Rise and Fall of Singapore's Second Industrial Revolution," p. 163.

19. "The Art of Politics in Singapore" (interview with Trade and Industry Minister George Yeo), *Straits Times,* November 26, 2001.

20. EOI failed in the Philippines because the semiconductors and parts of electronic goods that it produced for export were low-value-added items. Hence, the foreign exchange gained was less than what was lost when the finished products they were part of were imported back to the Philippines. Moreover, there was no transfer of technology or reinvestment of capital since the Philippines state gave special privileges to multinational corporations. See Joaquin L. Gonzalez III, *Philippine Labour Migration: Critical Dimensions of Public Policy* (Singapore: Institute of Southeast Asian Studies, 1998), pp. 60–61.

21. *Yearbook of World Electronics Data, 1992,* vols. 1, 2, and 3 (Oxford: Elsevier Advanced Technology, 1992), cited in Henderson, "Electronics Industries and the Developing World," p. 260. All amounts are in U.S. currency.

22. By comparison, the per capita income in the United States was $25,880.

Statistics are from the World Bank (1996), cited in Tubagus Ferid-hanusetyawan, Charles Stahl, and Phillip Toner, "APEC Labor Markets: Structural Change and the Asian Financial Crisis," *Journal of Contemporary Asia* 31, no. 4 (October 2001): 491–532.

23. Stella Go, "Towards the Twenty-first Century: Whither Philippines Labor Migration?" paper presented at the First National Convention, Philippine Migration Research Network, Quezon City, Philippines, February 6, 1997, p. 14.

24. World Bank, *World Development Report, 1991* (Oxford: Oxford University Press, 1991), p. 93.

25. World Bank, *World Development Report, 1995* (Oxford: Oxford University Press, 1995), pp. 64–66.

26. The secretary of labor declared: "We no longer apologize for the outflow of Filipino labor abroad under such labels as the brain drain. We have decided it in such a manner that it will redound to the national interest. We are scouting aggressively for job markets for excess Filipino skills in many countries of the world." Blas Ople, "Trends and Principles in the Labor Code," address before the National Tripartite Conference on the Labor Code, Development Academy of the Philippines, October 23, 1975, cited in Dan Gatmaytan, "Death and the Maid: Work, Violence, and the Filipina in the International Labor Market," *Harvard Women's Law Journal* 20 (Spring 1997): 237. For a comprehensive discussion of the economic benefits of labor export, see Gonzalez, *Philippine Labour Migration,* chap. 3.

27. From Charles Stahl, "Trade in Labour Services and Migrant Worker Protection with Special Reference to East Asia," *International Migration* 37, no. 3 (1999): 564, table 1.

28. Philippine Overseas Employment Administration, *http://www.poea.gov.ph/html/statistics.html,* National Statistics Office, Republic of the Philippines, *http://www.census.gov.ph/,* and Department of Labor and Employment, Republic of the Philippines, *http://www.dole.gov.ph.*

29. Central Bank of the Philippines, *http://www.bsp.gov.ph/statistics/spei/tab11.htm, http://www.bsp.gov.ph/statistics/spei/tab29.htm,* and *http://www.bsp.gov.ph/statistics/spei/tab1.htm.*

30. These figures come from Gonzalez, *Philippine Labour Migration,* p. 75.

31. Many of these women who join the labor force are motivated either by the ideology of "family repayment" or by what it means to be a good daughter, wife, or mother. For a discussion of rural-to-urban female labor migration in the Philippines, see Sylvia Chant and Cathy McIlwaine, *Women of a Lesser Cost: Female Labour, Foreign Exchange, and Philippine Development* (Manila: Ateneo de Manila University Press, 1995).

32. See Jayati Ghosh, "Gender, Trade, and the WTO: Issues and Evidence from

Developing Asia," in *Trade Liberalisation: Challenges and Opportunities for Women in Southeast Asia,* ed. Vivienne Wee (New York: Unifem and Engender, 1998), esp. pp. 48–52.

33. Ibid., pp. 57–58.

34. See Gonzalez, *Philippine Labour Migration,* pp. 40–43.

35. See Ninotchka Rosca, "Mrs. Contemplacion's Sisters: The Philippines' Shameful Export," *The Nation,* April 17, 1995, pp. 522–527.

36. Lin Lean Lim and Nana Oishi, "International Labor Migration of Asian Women: Distinctive Characteristics and Policy Concerns," in *Asian Women in Migration,* ed. Graziano Battistella and Anthony Paganoni (Quezon City: Scalabrini Migration Center, 1996), p. 26.

37. Immanuel Kant, *Grundlegung zur Metaphysik der Sitten,* in *Werkausgabe,* vol. 7, ed. Wilhelm Weischedel (Frankfurt am Main: Suhrkamp, 1996), pp. 59–60, Ak. 4:428–429; translation from Kant, *Groundwork of the Metaphysics of Morals,* in *Practical Philosophy,* trans. and ed. Mary J. Gregor (Cambridge: Cambridge University Press, 1996), p. 79.

38. Rights thus belong to the sphere of legality and not morality proper. Kant distinguished mere legality from ethics and duties of right from those of virtue. Immanuel Kant, *Die Metaphysik der Sitten,* in *Werkausgabe,* vol. 8, ed. Wilhelm Weischedel (Frankfurt am Main: Suhrkamp, 1996), pp. 323–326, Ak. 6:218–221; translation from Kant, *The Metaphysics of Morals,* in *Practical Philosophy,* pp. 383–385. Hereafter *MS,* with citations first from the German edition, then from the translation.

39. *MS,* p. 345, Ak. 6:237/393.

40. *MS,* p. 345, Ak. 6:237–238/393–394.

41. Art. 25, sec. 1, of the UN Convention stipulates that migrant workers have the right not to be treated less favorably than national workers in respect of conditions and terms of employment "according to national law and practice." The two ILO Conventions are no. 97, Migration for Employment (1949), and no. 143, Migrant Workers (1975). For a fuller discussion of the differences between the ILO and UN Conventions and the processes that led up to the UN Convention, see Roger Bohning, "The ILO and the New UN Convention on Migrant Workers: The Past and Future," *International Migration Review* 25, no. 4 (Winter 1991): 698–709; and Juhani Lonnroth, "The International Convention on the Rights of All Migrant Workers and Members of Their Families in the Context of International Migration Policies: An Analysis of Ten Years of Negotiation," *International Migration Review* 25, no. 4 (Winter 1991): 710–736.

42. Art. 2, sec. 1, of the UN Convention states that "the term 'migrant worker' refers to a person who is to be engaged, is engaged or has been engaged in a remunerated activity in a State of which he or she is not a national."

43. See Shirley Hune, "Migrant Women in the Context of the International Convention on the Rights of All Migrant Workers and Members of Their Families," *International Migration Review* 25, no. 4 (Winter 1991): 812–813. For a discussion of the implications of these instruments for migrant women in Asia, see Lim and Oishi, "International Labor Migration of Asian Women," pp. 46–48; and Pamela Goldberg, "International Protections for Migrant Women as a Human Rights Issue," in Battistella and Paganoni, *Asian Women in Migration,* pp. 170–182.

44. Art. 6, sec. 1, of ILO Convention no. 97 has the same effect: "Each Member for which this Convention is in force undertakes to apply, without discrimination in respect of nationality, race, religion or sex, to immigrants lawfully within its territory, treatment no less favourable than that which it applies to its own nationals in respect of the following matters: (a) in so far as such matters are regulated by law or regulations, or are subject to the control of administrative authorities."

45. See Geertje Lycklama à Nijeholt, "The Changing International Division of Labour and Domestic Workers: A Macro Overview (Regional)," in *The Trade in Domestic Workers: Causes, Mechanisms, and Consequences of International Migration,* ed. Noeleen Heyzer, Geertje Lycklama à Nijeholt, and Nedra Weerakoon (London: Zed Books, 1994), pp. 24–25; see also Alcestis Abrera-Mangahas, "International Labour Standards for Migrant Workers," and Patricia Weinert, "Future Interventions and Actions: An International Organization's Perspective," both in the same volume, pp. 163–167 and 191–192, respectively.

46. A convention does not enter into force until it has been ratified or acceded to by at least twenty states. Being a signatory is not the same as having ratified it. Although it was adopted by the General Assembly on December 18, 1990, the UN Convention only came into force on July 1, 2003. As of June 10, 2003, the Convention had been ratified by twenty-two states, namely, Azerbaijan, Belize, Bolivia, Bosnia and Herzegovina, Cape Verde, Colombia, Ecuador, Egypt, El Salvador, Ghana, Guatemala, Guinea, Mali, Mexico, Morocco, the Philippines, Senegal, Seychelles, Sri Lanka, Tajikistan, Uganda, and Uruguay. Eleven states—Bangladesh, Burkina Faso, Chile, Comoros, Guinea-Bissau, Paraguay, São Tomé and Principe, Sierra Leone, the Sudan, Togo, and Turkey—have signed the Convention. Note that none of the major labor-receiving countries have signed or ratified the Convention. India and Indonesia are major labor-sending states from the South and Southeast Asian region that have not ratified it. ILO Conventions nos. 97 and. 143 have been ratified by forty-five and nineteen countries, respectively. With the exception of Sabah, a component substate of Malaysia, none of the major Asian labor-sending countries

or the major labor-receiving countries in the Middle East and Asia ratified the ILO conventions.

47. Third-generation rights, which are collective economic rights, are summed up under the right to development. I discussed their roots in the previous chapter. Such rights assume that the wretchedness of the South is caused by its economic subjugation by the North and the inequitable global distribution of wealth, which makes it a responsibility of the North to aid in the rapid development of the South. The Declaration of the Right to Development was adopted by the UN General Assembly on December 4, 1986 (res. 41/128). Art. 3, sec. 1, provides that "States have the primary responsibility for the creation of national and international conditions favourable to the realization of the right to development." Art. 3, sec. 3, adds: "States have the duty to co-operate with each other in ensuring development and eliminating obstacles to development. States should realize their rights and fulfill their duties in such a manner as to promote a new international economic order based on sovereign equality, interdependence, mutual interest and cooperation among all States, as well as to encourage the observance and realization of human rights." Art. 4, sec. 2, stresses the importance of national co-operation in promoting rapid development: "Sustained action is required to promote more rapid development of developing countries. As a complement to the efforts of developing countries, effective international cooperation is essential in providing these countries with appropriate means and facilities to foster their comprehensive development."

48. James Hsiung, "Human Rights and International Relations: Morality, Law, and Politics," in *Human Rights of Migrant Workers: Agenda for NGOs,* ed. Graziano Battistella (Quezon City: Scalabrini Migration Center, 1993), p. 186.

49. Ibid.

50. By 2006 the Philippines had reached bilateral labor agreements with nine countries. Unsurprisingly, none of them are major labor-receiving countries.

51. Lim and Oishi, "International Labor Migration of Asian Women," p. 46.

52. For a comprehensive discussion that slightly predates the push to become an information and high technology–based economy, see Pang Eng Fong, "Absorbing Temporary Foreign Workers: The Experience of Singapore," *Asian and Pacific Migration Journal* 1, nos. 3–4 (1992): 495–509.

53. The Web site for Contact Singapore is *http://www.contactsingapore.org.sg.*

54. "Singapore of the Future," extract from Deputy Prime Minister Lee Hsien Loong's book *Singapore: Re-engineering Success, Straits Times,* November 8, 1998.

55. See Brenda S. A. Yeoh and T. C. Chang, "Globalising Singapore: Debat-

ing Transnational Flows in the City," *Urban Studies 38, no. 7 (2001): 1025–44.*

56. For a fuller account from a resolutely bourgeois perspective, see Jean Lee, Kathleen Campbell, and Audrey Chia, *The Three Paradoxes: Working Women in Singapore* (Singapore: AWARE, 1999).

57. The female labor force participation rate grew from 37.9 percent in 1977 to 53.9 percent in 2003, and the number of married women workers rose from 129,300 to 337,600 between 1980 and 1994 (representing an increase in the labor participation rate of married women from 29.3 percent to 45.2 percent). The first pair of figures comes from the Ministry of Manpower, Singapore, *Labour Force Survey* (2003). The second set of figures is cited in Brenda S. A. Yeoh, Shirlena Huang, and Joaquin Gonzalez III, "Migrant Female Domestic Workers: Debating the Economic, Social, and Political Impacts in Singapore," *International Migration Review* 33, no. 1 (Spring 1999): 120. The figures for foreign maids are from "Maid-Sharing Creates Too Many Problems," letter from Ministry of Manpower, *Straits Times,* December 1, 2001. Around 100,000 households out of 900,000 to 1 million households employ a foreign maid (communication from Ministry of Manpower).

58. My reconstruction of Foucault's account of bio-power draws primarily on Michel Foucault, *The History of Sexuality,* vol. 1, *An Introduction,* trans. Robert Hurley (New York: Vintage, 1980), pp. 138–145.

59. Although Foucault clearly states that techniques of government were formed later than those of discipline, he is not precise about when the shift from discipline to government took place other than noting that it occurs in the second half of the eighteenth century with the formulation of the concept of population. Foucault stresses that it is not a matter of replacing a society of discipline with one of government but one of a shift in dominance. See Michel Foucault, "Governmentality," in *Power,* vol. 3 of *Essential Works of Foucault, 1954–1984,* ed. James Faubion (New York: New Press, 2000), pp. 218–219.

60. Cf. Michel Foucault, "The Punitive Society," in *Ethics, Subjectivity, and Truth,* vol. 1 of *Essential Works of Foucault, 1954–1984,* ed. Paul Rabinow (New York: New Press, 1997): "The problem is then to attach workers firmly to the production apparatus, to settle them or move them where it needs them to be, to subject them to its rhythm, to impose the constancy or regularity on them that it requires—in short, to constitute them as a labor force" (p. 34). See also Foucault, "Truth and Juridical Forms,' in *Power,* pp. 78–82.

61. Foucault, *The History of Sexuality,* 1:139.

62. See Michel Foucault, "Security, Territory, and Population," in *Ethics, Sub-*

jectivity, and Truth, pp. 68–71; and Foucault, "The Politics of Health in the Eighteenth Century," in *Power,* pp. 95–96.

63. Foucault, *The History of Sexuality,* 1:139. While Foucault is not always consistent in his terminology, biopolitics appears to be one of the poles of bio-power.

64. Ibid., p. 141.

65. This argument that labor, or more precisely man as a laboring being, does not have the primary status Marx attributed to it but is a product-effect of power fuels Foucault's critique of Marx's base-superstructure model.

66. See Foucault, "Truth and Juridical Forms," pp. 80–82.

67. Foucault, "Governmentality," p. 217.

68. "Maid Dependency Here to Stay, Study Finds," *Straits Times,* February 3, 1996.

69. Gayle Rubin, "The Traffic in Women: Notes on the 'Political Economy' of Sex," in *Toward an Anthropology of Women,* ed. Rayna R. Reiter (New York: Monthly Review Press, 1975), p. 164.

70. Noeleen Heyzer and Vivienne Wee, "Domestic Workers in Transient Overseas Employment: Who Benefits, Who Profits," in Heyzer, Lycklama à Nijeholt, and Weerakoon, *The Trade in Domestic Workers,* p. 63.

71. "PM Goh's vision of a new era for Singapore: Civil Society Needed to Mobilise People's Talents," Prime Minister Goh Chok Tong's parliamentary speech on Singapore 21, *Straits Times,* June 7, 1997.

72. The number of reports of maid abuse rose from 105 in 1994 to 192 in 1997, with 157 of those cases having evidentiary substantiation. To its credit, the Singapore parliament has changed its penal code to impose tougher punishments for abusive employers. The maximum jail term for causing pain through dangerous means has been increased from five to seven years, and that for causing grievous bodily harm has been increased from seven to ten years. See "Tougher Penalties for Maid Abuse," *Straits Times,* April 21, 1998. Between 1997 and 2000, the number of abusive employers banned from hiring maids rose from four to thirty-nine. See "More Banned from Hiring Maids after Abuse," *Straits Times,* December 10, 2001. Harsh punishment would also be meted out to employers who subject maids to mental abuse. See "Courts Get Tough on Mental Abuse," *Straits Times,* March 4, 2002.

73. C. P. Kei, *To Have and to Hold* (Singapore: Armour Publishing, 1993).

74. Ibid., pp. vi, 76, 78.

75. *Employing Foreign Domestic Workers: A Guide for Employers* (Singapore: Ministry of Manpower, n.d.), p. 9.

76. See Heyzer and Wee, "Domestic Workers in Transient Overseas Employment," pp. 62–63.

77. Ibid., p. 45. See also p. 37.
78. Interview with official at Ministry of Manpower, January 9, 2002: "I think their contributions are economic and social. Economic, because these people—FDWs—have actually given our females the opportunity to go out and work and contribute to the economy. 'Social' because they help manage the households too. Some of them end up teaching the children. Some of our domestic workers are fairly well educated, so they end up also playing tutor to the young kids. Quite a lot of them are also active in voluntary work, church activities."
79. Ibid., emphasis added.
80. "'Social Costs' of More Maids Explained," response by Ministry of Manpower, *Straits Times*, September 15, 2000.
81. "Govt Revises Levy for All Foreign Workers," *Straits Times*, November 5, 1997. The FDW levy was first introduced in 1982 and was set at S$120. It has increased steadily and is now reviewed annually.
82. Interview, January 9, 2002.
83. *Straits Times*, March 6, 1992.
84. One employer complained in a letter to the national newspaper that "the recent government proposal to raise the maid levy is another instance where we can see how detached the Government is from the struggles and issues that are dear to the heart of the working class." *Straits Times*, November 21, 1997.
85. Tay Lin Siau, "Review Maid Levy to Lower Abuse," *Straits Times*, December 11, 2001.
86. Security Bond, Immigration Regulation 21, Immigration Act (chap. 133).
87. "'Social Costs' of More Maids Explained," *Straits Times*, September 15, 2000.
88. Daniel Hong, Modern Employment Agency, interview, January 7, 2002.
89. M. K. Lim, Morningfair Agency, interview, January 4, 2002.
90. Interview, December 29, 2001.
91. Mrs. Hong, Modern Employment Agency, interview, January 7, 2002.
92. See Krist Boo, "Taking Maid to Club? Check First," *Straits Times*, July 27, 2000; and "Are Singaporeans Behaving Like the White Raj?" *Straits Times*, August 2, 2000.
93. Letters to the *Straits Times* often discuss the lack of respect shown by children to maids. See, for instance, "Teach Kids to Respect Maids," July 31, 2002.
94. The Malay version of these two rules reads: "Anda tidak boleh tunjukkan wajah yang masam pada majikan [Don't show a sour face to your employer]. Jangan cemberut [Don't be sullen]"; "Anda harus taat dan patuh pada saran majikan sesuai dengan undang-undangnya [You must be obedi-

ent and submit to suggestions from your employer that are appropriate to her orders]"; and "Anda tidak boleh membantah saran/perintah majikan [You cannot oppose/protest against your employer's suggestions/commands]." The English version is sanitized: "You must not show black face to your employer and employer's family," "You must follow your employer's order," and "You must not answer back to your employer."

95. In addition to *To Have and to Hold,* see also Elisabeth Tan and David Suhardy, *Guidebook for Domestic Helpers and Employers,* 2nd ed. (Singapore: First Second Publishing, 1999); and *Maids Handbook: Essential Guide to Hiring and Keeping a Foreign Domestic Helper* (Singapore: Raffles, 2000). Margaret Short Sierakowski, *The Guide to Employing and Managing a Live-in Maid* (Singapore: Landmark Books, 2001), expresses the more liberal attitudes of an expatriate employer.

96. Kei, *To Have and to Hold,* p. 84.

97. Ibid., p. 86.

98. Ibid.

99. *Maids Handbook,* pp. 39–40.

100. Ibid., p. 30.

101. Interview with Felice Banyaga, December 23, 2001.

102. Interview with Joanna Elias, December 30, 2001.

103. Interview, January 9, 2002.

104. "'No' to Standard Maid Contract," *Straits Times,* May 18, 1998.

105. "Just a Piece of Paper?" *Straits Times,* May 3, 1998.

106. See Jürgen Habermas, *The Structural Transformation of the Public Sphere,* trans. Thomas Burger (Cambridge, Mass.: MIT Press, 1989), p. 48: "Although the needs of bourgeois society were not exactly kind to the family's self-image as a sphere of humanity-generating closeness, the ideas of freedom, love, and cultivation of the person that grew out of the experiences of the conjugal family's private sphere were surely more than just ideology."

107. Hing Ai Yun, "Foreign Maids and the Reproduction of Labor in Singapore," *Philippine Sociological Review* 44, nos. 1–4 (1996): 52.

108. "Foreign Maid Levy Needed to Check Demand," letter from the permanent secretary, Ministry of Manpower, *Straits Times,* March 13, 2001.

109. "Employers Obliged to Be Humane to Maids, Says Lee Boon Yang," *Straits Times,* February 22, 1998.

110. Ibid.

111. *Employing Foreign Domestic Workers,* p. 6.

112. See Gatmaytan, "Death and the Maid," pp. 238–239.

113. Cited in Gonzalez, *Philippine Labour Migration,* p. 123.

114. For a more elaborate discussion of the inadequacies of protective measures of the Philippine state prior to March 1995, see Joaquin L. Gonzalez III, "Domestic and International Policies Affecting the Protection of Philippine Migrant Labor: An Overview and Assessment," *Philippine Sociological Review* 44, nos. 1–4 (1996): 164–166.

115. Arnel F. de Guzman, "Protection of the Rights of Migrant Workers in the Philippines," in Battistella, *Human Rights of Migrant Workers*, p. 109.

116. See William Safire, "The Hanging of Flor," *New York Times*, April 24, 1995, p. A17.

117. See Benedict Anderson, "Cacique Democracy in the Philippines," in *The Spectre of Comparisons: Nationalism, Southeast Asia, and the World* (London: Verso, 1998), pp. 204–216; and Walden Bello, "Pacific Panopticon," *New Left Review* 16 (July–August 2002): 71–72.

118. *Report of The Fourth World Conference on Women*, Beijing, September 4–15, 1995, A/CONF.177/20, October 17, 1995.

119. Dianne Otto, "Holding up Half the Sky, but for Whose Benefit? A Critical Analysis of the Fourth World Conference on Women," *Australian Feminist Law Journal* 6 (March 1996): 27. Otto notes that "the emphasis of other strategic objectives is on equipping women to be able to better compete, equally with men, in the global capitalist economy by such measures as making credit more available, directing finance to intermediary institutions that target women's economic activities and encouraging women's entrepreneurial ventures. But is the solution really for every poor woman to become a freelance entrepreneur?" (p. 21)

120. Carmela Torres, "Asian Women in Migration in the Light of the Beijing Conference," in Battistella and Paganoni, *Asian Women in Migration*, p. 188.

121. Jeffrey Henderson points to the formation of regional divisions of labor by foreign direct investment and even dependent production systems organized around commodity chains (subcontracting) in the electronics industries. He further argues that although it is possible for a few societies to move from the periphery to the semi-periphery in the world economy, with the exception of Japan, the semi-periphery remains as such and can never move to the first league. Henderson, "Electronics Industries and the Developing World," pp. 282–284.

122. See Jonathan Karp, "Migrant Workers: A New Kind of Hero," *Far Eastern Economic Review*, March 30, 1995, p. 45. For further discussion of OWWA's programs in Singapore, see Gonzalez, *Philippine Labour Migration*, pp. 112–115.

123. Karp, "Migrant Workers," p. 43.

124. Ibid., p. 45.

7. Humanity within the Field of Instrumentality

1. "Take Proven Path to Growth, SM Urges Manila," *Straits Times,* November 18, 1992, p. 2.
2. By the end of 1994, Singapore's investments had increased to US$69 million (compared to US$42 million the previous year), making it the sixth-largest foreign investor. *Straits Times,* February 15, 1995, p. 1.
3. "Let Us Build on Ties, President Wee Tells Ramos," *Straits Times,* February 12, 1993, p. 25.
4. *Straits Times,* March 13, 1995, p. 15.
5. Ibid., March 17, 1995, p. 17.
6. Ibid., March 21, 1995, p. 13.
7. See *Sunday Chronicle,* March 26, 1995, p. 1; *Manila Chronicle,* May 2, 1995, pp. 1, 7; and Melba Paddilla Maggay, "Flor Contemplacion: Requiem for the People," *Sunday Inquirer Magazine,* May 28, 1995, pp. 3–5, 20.
8. Iskho Lopez, "The Martyr That Is the Philippines," *Sunday Chronicle,* March 26, 1995, p. 6. For analogies between Ninoy and Flor, see Maggay, "Flor Contemplacion," pp. 3–4; and Fermin Adriano, "Flor's Memory Will Haunt the Government," *Manila Chronicle,* March 22, 1995, p. 5.
9. *Straits Times,* March 20, 1995, p. 3.
10. Ibid., March 29, 1995, p. 15.
11. Ibid., April 9, 1995, p. 3.
12. "A Nation of Hangmen," *Manila Chronicle,* March 18, 1995, p. 4.
13. Adriano, "Flor's Memory Will Haunt the Government," p. 5.
14. "Contemplacion a Nat'l Martyr," *Manila Chronicle,* March 17, 1995, p. 4.
15. Bernadette C. Jamir, "Postscript to Flor," *Sunday Chronicle,* March 26, 1995, p. 4.
16. Migrant Workers and Overseas Filipinos Act of 1995 (Republic Act 8042), reprinted in Joaquin L. Gonzalez III, *Philippine Labour Migration: Critical Dimensions of Public Policy* (Singapore: Institute of Southeast Asian Studies, 1998), p. 154. For further discussion of the act and its limitations, see pp. 126–130.
17. *Straits Times,* July 16, 1995, p. 2.
18. "A Big 'Thank You' for Maids," *Straits Times,* December 20, 1999.
19. Such costs include a placement fee, the repatriation bond, Medicare, and an insurance policy.
20. It is not uncommon for maids to have most of their salary for the first six months deducted by their agents. Disadvantageous employment contracts often do not include provisions for leave or days of rest and do not adhere to minimum salary levels.
21. See Nirmal Ghosh, "Manila Briefs 160 Singaporean Recruiters on New

Guidelines on Maids," *Straits Times,* August 9, 1996; and Julie Kee, "Tourist-Maids: Agents and Embassy Don't See Eye-to-Eye," *Straits Times,* February 23, 1997. Under the new guidelines, agents have to deposit a $5,000 security bond at the Philippine embassy in Singapore, which binds them to bringing in maids only through fully documented channels.

22. See Robert Go, "'Temporary Ban' on Indonesian Maids Again," *Straits Times,* July 19, 2001.

23. Mr. Srisena, interview, January 8, 2002.

24. Merriam Cuasay, interview, January 10, 2002.

25. Ibid.

26. Mr. Srisena, interview, January 8, 2002.

27. Ibid.

28. For a fuller discussion of the apolitical character of the social activities of church groups, especially their shirking of advocacy work, see B. S. A. Yeoh and Shirlena Huang, "Spaces at the Margins: Domestic Workers and the Development of Civil Society in Singapore," *Environment and Planning* 31 (1999): 1159–62.

29. Reverend Father Angel Luciano, a Catholic priest who had been at the Church of St. Michael in Singapore since 1999, observed that "after the Flor Contemplacion incident, the Singaporean government was alerted to the need for pastoral care of migrant workers. So the Philippine government applied to Singapore to loosen its rules on ministers." Interview, December 28, 2001.

30. Interview with Ministry of Manpower official, January 9, 2002.

31. See the concluding article in Archdiocesan Commission for the Pastoral Care of Migrants and Itinerant People (Singapore), *Jubilee: People of God on the Move* (2000). The magazine was presented to Pope John Paul II at the celebration of the Jubilee in Rome.

32. Excerpted in Commission for Migrants and Itinerant People (Singapore), *Migration 2002* (2002): 15.

33. CMI pamphlet (n.d.).

34. Archdiocesan Commission, *Jubilee,* p. 12.

35. Ibid., p. 21.

36. The King James version reads: "For I was an hungred, and ye gave me meat: I was thirsty, and ye gave me drink: I was a stranger, and ye took me in."

37. Bridget Lew, interview, January 4, 2002.

38. Archdiocesan Commission, *Jubilee,* p. 3.

39. Ibid., p. 9.

40. Father Angel C. Luciano, chaplain, Church of St. Michael, Singapore, interview, December 28, 2001.

41. Pastor Dong Luciano, Bartley Christian Church, Singapore, interview, December 27, 2001; and Bartley Christian Church pamphlet (2002).
42. Interview, December 28, 2001; and letter to employer, *Pinoy Bulletin* (December 2001): 7.
43. Interview, January 4, 2002, emphasis added.
44. Joyce Carino, pastoral administrative officer, St. Andrew's Cathedral, Singapore, interview, January 4, 2002.
45. Julie David Lopez, in Archdiocesan Commission, *Jubilee,* p. 33.
46. Marissa Pardone, interview, December 23, 2001.
47. Sermon by Pastor Marbs, Touch Community, December 30, 2001. The King James version reads: "And Mary said, Behold the handmaid of the Lord; be it unto me according to thy word."
48. Joanna Elias, cell-group meeting, January 6, 2002.
49. See Kelly Fu and Constance Singam, "The Culture of Exploitation and Abuse," unpublished ms., January 5, 2003.
50. Constance Singam, "Worker Treatment Reflects on Singapore," letter to the editor, *Straits Times,* October 3, 2003.
51. Interview, January 7, 2004. Cf. Braema Mathi, letter to the editor, *Straits Times,* November 7, 2003.
52. See *http://www.aware.org.sg/twc2/objectives.shtml.*
53. See *http://www.aware.org.sg/twc2/wrc.shtml.*
54. "Maids Deserve Respect, Dignity," *Straits Times,* March 10, 2003.
55. Imran Andrew Price and Lim Chi-Sharn for TWC2, "Reliance on Maids: Let's Have Affordable Alternatives," letter, *Straits Times,* October 3, 2003.
56. "Worker Treatment Reflects on Singapore," letter, *Straits Times,* October 3, 2003.
57. Interview, August 12, 2002. I have changed the name of the manager and the firm.
58. Tan Tarn How and Theresa Tan, "New Foreign Maids to Be Told Their Rights," *Straits Times,* January 4, 2004; "MoM Sets Up Department to Look at Issues of Foreign Workers," *Channel News Asia,* October 18, 2003.
59. Ng Shing Yi, "No More Maid Display," *Today,* October 14, 2003.
60. "PM Goh's Vision of a New Era for Singapore," *Straits Times,* June 7, 1997.
61. See Lee Hsien Loong's address at the Harvard Club's thirty-fifth anniversary dinner, reprinted in *Straits Times,* January 7, 2004, pp. 24–25.
62. See Kwok Kian-Woon and Chua Beng Huat, "Sense of 'We' Growing Here," *Straits Times,* November 28, 1999; Kevin Tan, Valentine Winslow, and Lam Peng Er, "Show of Good Faith Needed for Civil Society," *Straits Times,* January 28, 2000; Tan Tarn How, Sue-Ann Chia, and Rebecca Lee, "Of OB Markers and Growing Open Spaces," *Straits Times,* January 10, 2004.
63. See Michel Foucault, "The Birth of Biopolitics," in *Ethics: Subjectivity and Truth,* vol. 1 of *Essential Works of Foucault, 1954–1984,* ed. Paul Rabinow

(New York: New Press, 1997), p. 75: "The idea of society enables a technology of government to be developed based on the principle that it itself is already 'too much,' 'in excess'. . . . Instead of making the distinction between state and civil society into a historical universal that allows us to examine all the concrete systems, we can try to see it as a form of schematization characteristic of a particular technology of government."

64. Zuraidah Ibrahim, "Who's Looking Out for Maids Here?" *Straits Times,* July 27, 2002.

65. Janadas Devan, "Have COEs for Maids," *Straits Times,* September 26, 2003.

66. Tan Tarn How, "Rest Day for Maids: 'Make It a Must,'" *Straits Times,* June 24, 2003.

67. Conrad Raj, "Let's Give Our Maids More," *Streats,* March 10, 2003.

68. Ibid.

69. Dana Lam, "Maid to Order, Made to Suffer," *Today,* November 25, 2003.

70. Sharon Loh, "Clean Up Maid Market," *Straits Times,* October 25, 2003.

71. Max Horkheimer, *Eclipse of Reason* (1947; reprint, New York: Continuum, 2004), pp. 3–4.

72. Herbert Marcuse, "The Struggle against Liberalism in the Totalitarian View of the State," in *Negations: Essays in Critical Theory,* trans. Jeremy Shapiro (Boston: Beacon, 1968), p. 15; translation of Marcuse, "Der Kampf gegen den Liberalismus in der totalitären Staatsauffassung," in *Kultur und Gesellschaft,* vol. 1 (Frankfurt am Main: Suhrkamp, 1965), p. 29: "Such functionalization of reason or of man as a rational organism annihilates [*vernichtet*] the force and effectiveness of reason at its roots, for it leads to a reinterpretation of the irrational pregivens as *normative* ones, which place reason under the heteronomy of the irrational."

73. Max Horkheimer, "The End of Reason," in *The Essential Frankfurt School Reader,* ed. Andrew Arato and Eike Gebhardt (New York: Continuum, 1982), p. 31. Cf. Horkheimer, "Vernunft und Selbsterhaltung," in *Gesammelte Schriften,* vol. 5, ed. Gunzelin Schmid Noerr (Frankfurt am Main: Fischer, 1987), p. 327.

74. Herbert Marcuse, "Some Social Implications of Modern Technology," in *Technology, War, and Fascism: Collected Papers of Herbert Marcuse,* vol. 1, ed. Douglas Kellner (New York: Routledge, 1998), p. 44.

75. Horkheimer, *Eclipse of Reason,* p. v.

76. Max Horkheimer, "The Concept of Man," in *Critique of Instrumental Reason,* trans. Matthew J. O'Connell et al. (New York: Continuum, 1994), p. 12.

77. Marcuse, "Some Social Implications of Modern Technology," p. 46.

78. Horkheimer, *Eclipse of Reason,* p. 64, emphasis added.

79. Jacques Derrida, *Margins of Philosophy,* trans. Alan Bass (Chicago: University of Chicago Press, 1982), p. 17.

Index

315